Women Writing Violence

Women Writing Violence

The Novel and Radical Feminist Imaginaries

Shreerekha Subramanian

SAGE www.sagepublications.com
Los Angeles • London • New Delhi • Singapore • Washington DC

First published in 2013 by

 SAGE Publications India Pvt Ltd
B1/I-1 Mohan Cooperative Industrial Area
Mathura Road, New Delhi 110 044, India
www.sagepub.in

SAGE Publications Inc
2455 Teller Road
Thousand Oaks, California 91320, USA

SAGE Publications Ltd
1 Oliver's Yard, 55 City Road
London EC1Y 1SP, United Kingdom

SAGE Publications Asia-Pacific Pte Ltd
33 Pekin Street
#02-01 Far East Square
Singapore 048763

Published by Vivek Mehra for SAGE Publications India Pvt Ltd, Phototypeset in 10.5/12.5 pt Adobe Garamond Pro by Diligent Typesetter, Delhi and printed at De-Unique, New Delhi.

Library of Congress Cataloging-in-Publication Data

Subramanian, Shreerekha.
    Women writing violence: the novel and radical feminist imaginaries/Shreerekha Subramanian.
        p. cm.
    Includes bibliographical references and index.
    1. Fiction—Women authors—History and criticism. 2. Violence in literature. 3. Women in literature. 4. Feminism and literature. 5. Fiction—20th century—History and criticism. I. Title.
PN3401.S83   809.3'0082—dc23   2012   2012040735

ISBN: 978-81-321-0908-2 (HB)

The SAGE Team: Neelakshi Chakraborty, Dhurjjati Sarma and Nand Kumar Jha

To the late Smt. Karunavathi Amma,
my maternal grandmother, and all the women who survive,
remember, and bear witness.

Thank you for choosing a SAGE product! If you have any comment,
observation or feedback, I would like to personally hear from you.
Please write to me at contactceo@sagepub.in

—Vivek Mehra, Managing Director and CEO,
SAGE Publications India Pvt Ltd, New Delhi

Bulk Sales

SAGE India offers special discounts for purchase of books in bulk.
We also make available special imprints and excerpts from our
books on demand.

For orders and enquiries, write to us at

Marketing Department
SAGE Publications India Pvt Ltd
B1/I-1, Mohan Cooperative Industrial Area
Mathura Road, Post Bag 7
New Delhi 110044, India
E-mail us at marketing@sagepub.in

Get to know more about SAGE, be invited to SAGE events, get on
our mailing list. Write today to marketing@sagepub.in

This book is also available as an e-book.

Contents

Acknowledgment

This book began as a meditation on loss. In the shadow of large-scale events of violence and carnage, I was interested in the agency wrested from those who lost their lives and the agency of those who remained to bear witness. In the tradition of the women's novels of the late twentieth century—feminist novels of the global south in particular—I was interested in how the literary imaginary accorded agency, resisted and coalesced into community that somehow escaped the confines of patriarchal surveillance. Much of my work was done in the isolation of libraries. This project was made possible by communities I imagined through solidarity experienced in solitude. It stems from textual distance; homage paid to books and their authors, and to the knowledge they shared with me.

For initiating serious reflection on the relationship between violence and the written text, many thanks to all my teachers in the Program in Comparative Literature at Rutgers University. For understanding the immateriality of my project and for invaluable insights on how to frame my arguments, I thank Professor Abena Busia. The professors who shepherded me through my project at Rutgers University—Cesar Braga-Pinto, Ben Sifuentes-Jauregui, Sonali Perera, Alessandro Vettori, Ousseina Alidou, Janet Walker, and Renee Larrier. I also thank all my peers at Rutgers University, especially, Julie Rajan and Ateyee Phukan, for the innumerable ways in which they have contributed to and enhanced my critical thinking.

My literary journey began in an imaginary dialog between A. K. Ramanujan and Kamala Das, and it was the reading of the work of Edward Said that rescued me from the formalism of my early training in English literature. The prolific American who embodies the elegance of rage, James Baldwin, infected me early. Safiye Henderson-Holmes, poet, teacher, and mentor, taught me about fearlessness and beauty before she left this planet to find her own. The Creative Writing faculty, especially

Michael Burkard, Arthur Flowers, who were an integral part of my studies at Syracuse University, compelled me to take seriously the practice of critical readings of the word. Hats off to Sugatha Kumari, the feminist activist, who allowed me free access to Abhayashram, a home for the indigent and mentally ill, for one summer in the 1990s which gave me glimpses into alternative grassroots community in the making.

All things begin and end for me with Toni Morrison. I first delved into her work atop a ship on the Bering Sea, when employed as a fishing processor. After cleaning salmon for eighteen hours a day at the age of nineteen, reading her work was the greatest of all rewards. The ship came to a halt but I never stopped reading Morrison. To her I owe my feminist awakening.

I owe tremendous thanks to my home institution, University of Houston-Clear Lake, for vital support offered in the completion of this project over the years. I was the first recipient of Marilyn Mieszkuc Professorship in Women's Studies, 2008. I was also honored to receive three annual Faculty Research Support Funds as well as many Faculty Development Support Funds that enabled me to attend conferences and learn from current scholars in the field. I wish to thank our Office of Sponsored Programs at UHCL for their support in key stages of this book's completion. Without the diligent and meticulous work of my research assistants over the years—Andrew Robinson, Bridget Fernandes, and Meryl Bazaman—this work would have taken much longer to reach fruition. I wish to note the profound joy of being at a university whose students inspire in organic ways my own research—in their presence, sincerity, and commitment toward their academic pursuits. I wish to acknowledge both my students in the free world and my students in prison who often display such rigor and judiciousness that they articulate the purpose of humanities in the liberal arts institution. In that spirit, I wish to thank all my students at Ramsey Unit for keeping me alert to the urgency of the literary project.

Thanks to the anonymous reviewer at SAGE who gave me generous feedback and prompted me to rekindle my relationship with this project that has now spanned over a decade. Thanks also to the editorial team at SAGE who did the hard work in bringing forth the completed text, especially Sugata Ghosh, Rekha Natarajan, Gayeti Singh, and Neelakshi Chakraborty.

An abbreviated version of Chapter 1, "Specters of Public Massacre: Violence and the Collective in Toni Morrison's *Paradise*," appeared in

2006 in the anthology, *James Baldwin and Toni Morrison: Comparative Critical and Theoretical Essays*, edited by Lovalerie King and Lynn Orilla Scott (New York: Palgrave MacMillan). An earlier version of Chapter 2, "Blood, Memory, and Nation: Massacre and Mourning in Edwidge Danticat's *The Farming of Bones*," appeared in 2005 in the anthology edited by Alexandra Isfahani-Hammond, *The Masters and the Slaves: Plantation Relations and Mestizaje in American Imaginaries* (New York: Palgrave MacMillan). I am indebted to both the editors for their honest critiques and generous editorial labors which led to sharper interrogations on my part, and fueled this book in many ways.

I need to mention the intellectual progress I have made by attending and presenting the project in its many stages at numerous conferences, most key gatherings that have charged my work being "Celebrating the African American Novel" conference at Pennsylvania State University, annual conferences of American Comparative Literature Association (ACLA), and National Women's Studies Association (NWSA). I thank my feminist sisters beyond the immediate vicinity of my world at UHCL, Lovalerie King, Fawzia Afzal-Khan, Alka Kurian, Vidya Kalaramadam, Shobha Rajgopal, Pramila Venkateswaran, and Basuli Deb, and hope that it remains ever growing and always in solidarity. For the sisters who sustain me at home in UHCL—Christine Kovic, Maria Curtis, Gaye Cummins, Heather Kanenberg, Deepa Reddy, Jane Chin Davidson, Elizabeth Klett, Neneh Kowai-Bell, Kim Case, and last but not the least, feminist allies, Mike McMullen and Arch Erich. Thanks also for the encouragement provided by Bruce Palmer, Deborah Griffin, Craig White, John Gorman, and Samuel Gladden. A very heartfelt thanks to Neumann Library at UHCL, in particular Karen Wielhorski, William Boatman, Susan Steele, and Neeta Jambhekar. A New York – style "how yadoin" to a fellow transplant, Lori Paolilla, who has more than the requisite *esprit de corps*. Special thanks to Christine Kovic and Francisco Arguelles for the intellectual and spiritual nurture they offer so easily as daily habit.

My deepest thanks will always be to my maternal grandmother, Srimati Karunavathy Amma, who taught me defiance and compassion, a feminism spawned long before intellectual consciousness. Thanks to my long-standing friendship that in my hyperbole often starts before our birth, Anupuma Tuli. You are my eternal sister. Linda Marie Perla— your radiance is ever-present and elusive in these pages; your loss is too fresh and deep and I miss you. Thanks to my aunt, Mrs. Saraswathy

Prabhakaran, for her innumerable gifts, most of all, for gathering us into her fold. Thanks too, Mr. Bhaskara and Mrs. Prasanna Kumar, my Kochachan and Kunjamma, for solidity and good humor always. To Shyam and Gwen, Unni Chettan and Nisha Chechi, Paru, Asha, Anand, Ramesh, Sanjay and Bindu, my sincere gratitude and love for all your support. My mother and father, Santha and Gopi Pillai, have always nourished and sustained my life's work. The structure of my dreams comes out of their infinite love. The magnificence of their love humbles me each day. So does my in-laws Mr. and Mrs. Shankar's, whose patience, sagacity, largesse, and vision live in every page of this book. They have also blessed me with a family that knows the language of borderless love, and their home is a place I wish I could inhabit much more corporeally rather than across this oceanic distance. I wish to pay homage to the members of *Santhi*—Thatha Anna, Manni, Lakshmi Periamma, Ram Mama, Radha Mami, Prasad Mama, and Usha Mami, and most importantly, the stars, Danya and Remya. To my partner and beloved in all things, Santosh, and my two sweets who light up my days and nights, who are the first sound and last word—Sarvesh and Sumana.

Introduction

Questions of Community in the Contemporary Literary Context

"Community" is a fraught and contested term, a polysemic signifier that works in diverse ways depending on the context of its utterance or enunciation. In a globalizing world, community crosses oceans and territorial boundaries with an obstinate resolve, with a sly impunity that threatens stable hegemonies like nation and state. In colloquial Anglo-American usage, the word "communal" might invoke a sense of sharing rooted in the idea of communing or communion. A rather different set of sentiments may be evoked in India by the same word, given the long shadow cast by a "secular" nationalism anxiously preoccupied with politicizing and historicizing "nation" as a superior and impartial logic of societal organization in comparison to the always-partisan "community." What I do in this book is to bring these disparate understandings into conversation, through an engagement with diverse relationships to community in feminist novels that imagine altogether new visions of community without jettisoning the problematic nature of existence within them.

In both the Western and non-Western spaces, this project addresses the inherent patriarchal order of the nation-state which points to an attendant violence in the project of nation making. In many ways, the project seeks to unhinge community from its historical materialist roots in the nation and national capital. Instead, this project addresses alternative imagined communities comprising people at the margins of violent hegemonic orders. Any community that exists within and on the level of the larger patriarchal order pays its dues and can only speak the singular language available to all who coexist within the world order, the language of power and if such compliance does not surface, penalties are sure to follow.

Instead, what I unpack is the emergence of an alternative community, undecipherable under normative codes, that is only possible within the novel. This project aims to pursue the possibilities of liminal conjectures: Is community without violence at its origin possible? Is an anti-heteronormative, anti-colonial, and anti-imperial community that follows its own laws of nonviolence ontologically possible? It is only in the literary imaginary that such a focus is possible, an imaginary that is at once idea and practice. What I seek is not only the liminal and heterodox, but a community that is inspired from the women who have suffered its greatest losses, from the people who have paid with their lives, in fact, an imagined community that cuts across the worlds of the living and the dead. While the medium of film can suggest such complexity and such a zone, it is, I believe, only in the novel as a genre where the texture of liminality can be fully explored. Ultimately, while the project examines the language of violence with which the praxis of community is intimately related, it is also hopeful in terms of bringing forth the voices of the dispossessed as an act of resistance, as a way of forming community that lies outside the more commonly understood parlance of community. Where I begin, with an ephemeral character in Toni Morrison's narrative, it is not only to search out the ramifications of her ghostly beginnings, but also a textual community of women as they emerge in the interstices of this project when novels from the Americas and South Asia begin to speak to one another.

"What the hell happened to Maggie?"[1] Toni Morrison writes, as she concludes her only short story, "Recitatif." The entire story follows the lives of two girls who meet in an orphanage as eight-year olds and then meet again after seven or eight years. The story progresses through their conversations, tensions, and silences. As the title suggests, the story, in its insistent repetition, frees itself from a strict form of narration in that it refuses to yield to popular forms of identity-marking descriptions; it lets us know that the characters Roberta and Twyla are of different races, suggesting black and white in the American context, although we are never told who is who. The story has come to stand as Morrison's shorthand for the meaning of race and race relations, that is, race as a phenotypically sculpted hollow vessel that stymies narratives, rather than propels them forward with plot and momentum.

In her text, *Playing in the Dark*, Morrison delves into the ironies of this narrative: "The only short story I have ever written, 'Recitatif,' was an experiment in the removal of all racial codes from a narrative about two characters of different races for whom racial identity is crucial."[2] Authorized by Morrison herself, the few studies dedicated in full or in part to this story have immersed themselves in introspections based on critical race, feminist, reader-response, and psychoanalytical theories,[3] and have been quite valuable. Maggie, "old and sandy-colored," with "her legs like parentheses,"[4] is a figure given to extremes. While some read in her a lack, an ambiguity of racialized identity, others might see plenitude, an excess symbolizing the longing and despair felt toward the mothers within this story. What needs to be addressed in a study of this story, apart from the significations performed by the category of race, are questions of community.

Twyla and Roberta, in their friendship that enjoins and scatters their stories, wrestle with communication and, in effect, community. Their friendship shapes, binds, and finally brings them a peace that arrives at the heels of memory laid to rest, and this memory has to do with the figure of Maggie. The story is partial atonement for failure of community, its rejection of her humanity in the cruelty of childhood. Twyla and Roberta battle at various points to communicate, even commune. But the event of their communing is at odds, finally dissolving what was merely divisive at the outset. In their childhood, their friendship comprises an excess of the racial differences that defines them up to a point. Once they separate, the difference is reflected as an active presence in each conversation between Twyla and Roberta, until finally Maggie, who is a common memory of their past, becomes the symbolic ruse for their difference. Neither can settle on her racial category and each is tormented by this gap in their communal knowledge.

Abena P. A. Busia, in an analysis of Morrison's shorter works, works out the deliberate craft of racial coding in this story. Busia connects Morrison's "radical act" of refusing to classify her characters by race to *Paradise* and extrapolates its function, "...by resisting the common assumptions designated by skin color and by withdrawing all obvious and loaded racialized physical descriptions, she liberates herself to explore what other racial, class and cultural codes are available for character representation."[5] These other codes are the subtext of torment that seizes and transforms the girls' earlier ruminations. Roberta and Twyla evolve from "who is she," an ontological location of the self, to "what happened to her," a collective determination of her actual condition, something that could only be arrived at through the existence of community between the two in their present and their past, woven into a figure that points to an aporia in their childhood, Maggie.

Morrison's "Recitatif" leads to my own project wherein I wish to both locate community within the literary context, particularly the novel, and also meditate on the hermeneutic quickness with which it disappears as a trope. It is the community that slips out of vision, community so fragile and ephemeral that it hardly presents itself as a trope. Such a study rests on the mystery inherent in the story, the perennial "whodunnit" of nineteenth century detective fiction replaced with "what happened to Maggie," as in what happened to the figures who might commune or those who might be refused community, and who recede from the pale of the narrative. What is such a community? What are its characteristics? What stuff is it made of? What importance is it to the contemporary novel?

My questions about community can be best explained through a medieval Kannada poem translated into English by A. K. Ramanujan, linguist, folklorist, scholar of Dravidian languages, and poet. Ramanujan brings us medieval *vacana*s sung on the streets of ancient kingdom of Mysore by men and women who emerged out of Virasaivism, a devotional movement centered on the God, Siva. This radical stream of Bhakti poems critique the conservative notions of religious and clerical hierarchies. The poets, known to streak naked in their fervor and disregard for the normative, found their iconic poet figure in the man known to us as Basavanna, and it is one of his *vacana*s called "The Temple and the Body" that is emblematic of this entire movement.

> The rich
> Will make temples for Siva.
> What shall I,
> A poor man,
> Do?
>
> My legs are pillars,
> The body the shrine,
> The head a cupola
> Of gold.
>
> Listen, O lord of the meeting rivers,
> Things standing shall fall,
> But the moving ever shall stay.[6]

In the given passage, Ramanujan's interpretation of the *vacana* sheds light on the connections I will make with my own project. In the poem, the devotee raises all the binaries of the Virasaivite movement such as rich/poor, temple/body, make/do, and in offering his body to the lord—unlike the rich who can only make temples—he simultaneously not only writes out of the hierarchical apparatus of Hindu casteism, but also writes himself a new hierarchy wherein he is the eternal and staunchest devotee of Siva. Basavanna, in addressing Siva, his favorite god, Kudalasangamadeva, raises the final binary between that of things standing against things moving. Man-made artifacts that stand, like the temple, are bound to fall while the devotee, ever moving and immortal, withstands the test of time. Things standing, *sthavara*, statist, stagnant, signify the standard of community that I question in this project. Things moving, *jangama*, are the communities in constant movement, redefining themselves; hard to detect and, hardly discernible, they form alternate ontologies of resistance and revision as the imagined communities read in these novels. Basavanna's poetics, alongside Gayatri Spivak's reading of doubled otherness in postcolonial literatures, Lata Mani's historiographical gleaning of female agency in eyewitness accounts of Sati in nineteenth-century British India, and Rajeswari Sunder Rajan's analysis of the state's complicity in elaborating law to female citizens at its margins inform the framework of reading community in the novels interpreted in this book.

The Nothingness of Community

The night is my nudity
the stars are my teeth
I throw myself among the dead
dressed in white sunlight

—Bataille[7]

The primary focus of this book is violence and the novel. It concentrates mainly on women writers and their novels through the lens of community. At the heart of the discussion on the reader's inaccessibility of the characters' racial identity-markers and the inscrutability of Maggie lay the fundamental questions of community. Roberta and Twyla skirt the edges of community beginning with their arrival at an orphanage with mothers still living. Concepts of communing are underdeveloped, teeming with the precariousness of being within the written narrative. It appears as trace, hardly discernible. Morrison's story, as a result, attempts to detail its presence but instead records its rupture. Repeatedly, as in recitation, or a trauma, the characters meet, converse, and disperse, their intermittent union always already fractured. Maggie, a real part of their past, prefigures her inaccessibility, her body bent away and disappearing even in the moments of contact.

The telling of women's narratives born at the margins lingers on linguistic caprice, an uncertainty that heightens the attention given to the unknowability of such communities. Morrison's story circles around and ends with the violence committed upon the body of Maggie, an ever-receding presence not fully encapsulated within discourse, that is, the oral exchanges of the two friends and the written form of the story. Bataille's work has been located as "unwork" by Barthes, Blanchot, and Derrida, and characterized as "*desoeuvre*, in the sense that its negativity is unemployed. Fred Botting and Scot Wilson explain Bataille's community as being in the service of nothing and no one, inoperative in respect of specified and useful goals."[8] The sum total of his essays— "Christ," "Torment," "Death," "Sacrifice," or "Madame Edwarda"— reveals the headlessness of a community whose very structures produce a malevolence of meaning. Bataille's sketches hint at agony at the center of community, and his characterization of violence, crime, and aggression within the foundation of community serve as signposts in this discussion. In defining community arising out of a wound to God and humankind, Bataille offers:

> Communication cannot proceed from one full and intact individual to another. It requires individuals whose separate existence in themselves is risked, placed at the limit of death and nothingness; the moral summit is the moment of risk taking, it is a being suspended in the beyond of oneself, at the limit of nothingness.[9]

For Roberta and Twyla, their meetings stem out of a lack and a risk, a suspension of their individual selves over the nothingness from which springs the possibility of community.

Community in Morrison's later novel, *Paradise* (1998), poised on the margins, deceptive and tragic, arises out of the nothingness prefigured in its genesis. While the question Twyla asks Roberta during one of their meetings, "How long?"[10] calls for an account of their temporal and spatial differences, the absolute loss of Maggie and the collective unknowability in which the story articulates its anguish marks their mutual culpability in the gap between communication and community.

I speak of alternative communities that are less culpable and more communicative—communities on the move that are hardly discernible and exist under the radar of normative cultures within the literary landscape. Within novelistic discourse, one sees such communities that are different because instead of originary violence and wound, they arrive under the markers of consolation, balm, and succor. Such communities that exist on tangential coordinates without committing the guilt of godly and human wounds to memory are what distinguish the particular American and South Asian novels selected. The writers, almost all of whom are women, intuitively work this community into their fictive matrix. Morrison's *Paradise* sketches out an archetypal community of an ephemeral basis, constructed by and about women, who intend to turn their truncated and pockmarked pasts into a new and readable present. Instead of possession, which is the common way of accessing the psyche and affection of those close to us, the women in Connie Sosa's (central character in Morrison's *Paradise*) convent seek to redefine themselves out of their losses so that they no longer feel struck, shrunk, or deformed. Connie Sosa's community, teetering on a radical ontotheology because of its difference from normative practices of community, is punished. Connie's practices, frowned upon by the townspeople of Haven, is ritualized *chorā*, a habit of self-seeking the indeterminate and indefinite knowledge that lies within the self and the world, a habit that is ultimately deemed too strange and sacrilegious to persist even at the outskirts of a good town. The question again rises: What is such a community? What stuff is it made of? What importance is it to the contemporary novel?

Morrison's landscape built upon a "good clean darkness"[11] is founded upon the distinct knowledge of African American epistemology of loss, survival, and trauma. In fact, the body of her work rests on suturing African American sense-making into a coherent historiography of profound effects in novels such as *Song of Solomon* and *Beloved* where death is remade. We see in Morrison what is present as a resounding thematic in the African American literary landscape—the presence of the ancestors, once slaves, whose spirits walk free for posterity. The spirits speak to Milkman Dead and make him whole. Beloved is present, living in 129 with her mother and sister long after the event of her infanticide.

Death is the beginning of another way of being. Such knowledge is of serious import in my configurations of community because this alternate community, I suggest, always already existed in the African American, Caribbean, and West African cosmogony long before the novel came around to textualize the collective psyche.[12] .

Abena P. A. Busia performs a literary and historiographical act in talking us through the resignification of death in Paule Marshall's *Praisesong for the Widow* (1983), Toni Morrison's *Song of Solomon* (1977), David Bradley's *The Chaneysville Incident* (1981), and Julie Dash's film, *Daughters of the Dust* (1991) in Busia's paper, "Those Ibos! Jus' Upped and Walked Away: The Story of the Slaves at Ibo Landing as Transcendental Ritual." It is useful to attend to Busia's conclusion in her configuration of the defiance of the death act present within these works:

> There are many forms of resistance and revolt, what the story of the slaves at Ibo Landing suggests is a refusal to accept an epistemology that accepts control of the body as an acknowledgment of authority including control of the spirit. What is claimed is not an act of despair, but an act of collective self-assertion. However, this act is only meaningful if you accept the larger context the slaves are claiming, that the world is a continuum of the living, the ancestors and the yet to be born, that those ancestors can guide us, and in extremis, claim us, and that what happens to the body does not limit what happens to the spirit, and that the collective spirit is eternally strong.[13]

Busia attends to the remapping of power and dynamism upon the space reserved for morbidity and finality within the Western canon, death. She raises continuity as a feature of death when she draws our attention to John Washington's epiphanous digressions that stitch together his hunt for his ancestor, the protagonist of David Bradley's novel, who reminds us that death is referenced by black persons as "passing away" or "going home to his village" or "going home to Guinea," but never with the simple finality suggested in the semantic of "dying."

David Bradley's novel is the metaphoric hunt of a historian who seeks to find answers to his father's mysterious "suicide" at the very site where his grandfather and a cavalcade of twelve runaway slaves had their graves. Within the American context, the absence of archives which narrate the voices of the enslaved is a lacunae and a haunting melancholy that is finally addressed by the literary imaginary. What the character, Washington, comes to understands is that for his father,

Moses Washington, death was not about dying. It was his way of continuing the hunt by inhabiting the mind of the game and going where the game goes, in this case, to his long-dead ancestor, C. K. Washington. We, the readers, are led to those final moments at Chaneysville just before Harriette Brewer takes out her knife, Azacca, the old man, tells the story about the Great Sky God who wishes to let men know "that The Stillness That Comes To All, that they called Death, was not an ending of things, but a passing on of spirit, a change of shape, and nothing more; that when the Stillness came upon those they loved, they should not fear or grieve, but rejoice, because the loved one had merely left the body that bound him to the ground and become a spirit who could fly wherever he willed."[14] For those who have known the institution of slavery so intimately then, the "will" is more significant than life itself.

Azacca's tale is succor and inspiration for the tough act to follow for his band en route to freedom. Instead of some fictive promised land up north, they aspire for the liberation promised at the threshold of death. However, Bradley does not leave it there, at this African American epistemology that is authentic and profound. He brings it right to the door of European rationalist hegemony that governs the contemporary present, presenting in his novel a critique of the Enlightenment project itself. Not only does the father, Moses, follow C. K. to continue his narrative after death, but John, the protagonist, the calm, brilliant historian with many laurels, believes and understands what has generally been inaccessible to those housed in the symbolic home of Enlightenment, the academy. John engaged as lover and teacher of a white woman who is on a quest to hear the truth, places this alternate epistemology not in some secret enclave but in his discourse with Judith, a meeting space of reason and vision. Bradley produces the dialectic by situating in John the alternative community of dead who keep running (Basavanna's "things moving"), their panting still audible to John; these alternative communities emerge in intimate places, always moving, already and eternally present all at once.

Marlon T. Riggs, the documentary and filmmaker who committed the unforgettable to memory in his art by recording his own excruciating final days of dying with AIDS in the documentary, *Black Is, Black Ain't*, dwelt presciently on the subject of selfhood, friendship, and community, all in the light of color and African American history. Much is to be learned regarding community, its poisons and antidotes from his oeuvre that covered the spectrum from the history of black art to the black presence in theater and film to black gay life. For one, his is a community that exists underneath the radar of normative heterosexual white American communities and because they are alternate and held suspect in most places, he engages in systems of community that touch upon the isolation and individuation found in Morrison's novel. The viewer follows Riggs as he jauntily walks down sun-drenched streets of San Francisco, lonely, yet in intimate communion with his viewers; Riggs records all that passes in front of him, through him, to the extent that in *Black Is, Black Ain't*, we see him literally disappear under the bright white hospital sheets, syringes, and tubes. Riggs, in taking us to the moments of his death, always talking, albeit feeble, is sonorous, confident, and undaunted. His transition hints at less visible communities that are only apparent to the tutored eye.[15] The subtext of this dramatic documentary suggests the passing nature of death, a "transcendental"[16] transition so that Riggs remains with us, and his spirit continues to narrate where his body leaves the screen.

Maurice Blanchot, reflecting on friendship when he thinks back to his own with Georges Bataille, spells out a different form of friendship, one based on a différance that does not attempt the binaries or hierarchies that rise implicitly alongside bonds of affection. Roberta and Twyla seek a definite possession of each other, and their past, all of which never materializes and thus they commune on notes of devolution, conversations in abeyance. Blanchot's characterizations of différance as acceptance of the unknown, anti-dependence, strangeness of the familiar are promising tenets of the community that is sought within novelistic discourse in this study. Here, relations are based on discretion, and knowledge arises out of the silence of dialogic exchanges. Instead of attending to the "I," Blanchot invites a meditation on *chorā*, the indeterminate "who" that circumscribes knowledge:

> And when we ask ourselves the question "Who was the subject of this experience?" this question is perhaps already an answer if, even to him who led it, the experience asserted itself in this interrogative form, by substituting the openness of a "Who?" without answer for the close and singular "I"; not that this means that he had simply to ask himself "What is this I that I am?" but much more radically to recover himself without reprieve, no longer as "I" but as a "Who?" the unknown and slippery being of an indefinite "Who?"[17]

Paradise suggests itself as novelistic discourse suspended on the "who," a project of radical recovery initiated by Connie but once initiated by her, it mutates out of Blanchot's design into an imagined community that is non-modular, elusive, and recondite.

Effects of Modernity and Postcoloniality

Community has been prefigured as an imbrication of the individual in the collective, via compering or communication present in all variations, except perhaps a fascist machine that systematically erodes the core of communitarianism. What I suggest is that the earlier derivations of community are impacted in profound ways by the remapping of community within the melancholic multiracial collectives that emerge out of the postcolonial event of modernity, an event that necessitates alternative roadmaps to the insistent work of community-making. Much of Jean-Luc Nancy's projections, formulated through the lattices traced through Bataille and Blanchot, inform these current notions. His plot in the *Inoperative Community* points to a triple mourning at the heart of community—death of the other, birth of the self, and death of the self. The work intersects the schema of sharing of an identity, reflections that seep into the imprint of the lovers' kiss on paper. Since his work dwells on the relationship between community and literary works, he argues toward the immanence of resistance within the transcendent work of community. This, I view as the resistance of women's writings in particular as evident within communities born out of the contemporary novel. Here, I differ from Nancy when he writes: "The emergence and our increasing consciousness of decolonized communities has not profoundly modified this state of affairs, nor has today's growth of unprecedented forms of being-in-common—through channels of information as well as through what is called the 'multiracial society'—triggered any genuine renewal of the question of community."[18] Nancy's prognostications bear witness to conflagrations that arise consistently at the end of communities.

However, the mysticism that Nancy dismisses to the past is all too alive in the jumbled melee that augurs the postcolonial present, an event where elements of a native past, a colonizing present, a postcolonial modernizing future, all interact to form a voluble maelstrom. In the context of this project, the African American and Haitian narratives present an active dialectic between the mythic African and voodoo traditions alive within these communities in tandem with the violent and alienating apparatus of modernity. Despite Nancy's open-ended gesture to think beyond existent models, his illuminations leave *in the dark* how postcolonial literary landscapes radically renew questions of community.

Toward the end of *Paradise*, Morrison concludes with a section called "Sightings" to which I devote the culminating section of Chapter 1. The women, suspended between life and death, since we are not assured who is dead and who is alive, travel, work, and are seen together. Yet the reader is not fully sure of what is seen. Much like "Recitatif," *Paradise* is resistant to easy adaptions into film, into what can be rendered visual. When these women lived in the convent and fully arrived into the community etched out by Connie, they wrote in chalk their dreams, and shaped their identities on the floor, dancing around it, it is easy to mistake them for some aberrant cult as the townsmen do. The women, while communing and later, while laboring at good works to construct some form of a paradise, are described at times as naked. They write upon their bodies, akin to Bataille's stylistics in the excruciating honesty of his prose as he makes his way to Madame Edwarda's quarters, pants in hand: "In my hand I held my straight-risen sex."[19] Morrison draws the rooms in which her women characters exercise the sublime freedom of discoursing with the self, denuding themselves of all-imposed surfaces, and, ultimately, marching on familiar streets in forms not fully comprehensible. Nancy's invention, "excribe," serves the purpose of linking the act of community to the act of writing: "The nakedness of writing *is* the nakedness of existence. Writing is naked because it 'excribes'; existence is naked because it is 'excribed'."[20] Nancy relates this act of excribing to jouissance, and I posit that extreme melancholy and euphoria lead us to the discursive coherence of the postcolonial and heretofore peripheral narratives in which questions of community are configured anew.

The newness of the communities within these writings is that it is not only about the other, but an "other" that is no longer present in the fullest sense of the word. The absence of the other is absolute: the other has been exiled and has left the location or has been killed. Within this context of modernizing state machinery as it unfolds within the novels, the individual seeks community with the other which is in another realm, perhaps geographically or literally, thrust from this world to some other liminal space, a *chorā* which sets the founding stone for communing only and through distance. How Nancy sees the presence of being as possible only through the presence of others is critical in imagining this community with absence, an imagined community with the dead. Nancy terms this the coming into freedom:

> This is the coming to presence of our freedom, the common experience of the exposure in which the community is founded, but founded only through and for an infinite resistance to every appropriation of the essence, collective or individual, of its sharing, or of its foundation.[21]

Nancy's community suggests an idealization evident in the metaphysics of presence within Morrison's *Paradise*. In my estimate, Morrison concludes her novel with the questions of community that she raises in the short story, "Recitatif," and, in effect, serves up characters who realize their own identities by communing and experiencing the births and deaths of their friends, and also their pasts and futures that had previously haunted and kept them on the run.

Connie, the melancholic alcoholic who had nearly given up on humanity, emerges from the basement, a world below, to commune with the women and finally establish a paradise on earth, devises a refuge that threatens the fabric of larger communities. She lives in a deserted convent on the margins of Haven, a town that is built on maxims of exclusion, accepting through the lineage from Big Papa's journey of men and women who were born out of that exodus and who are dark enough to be considered righteous in the biblically based tradition of their forefathers. Connie's community is absent of such preconditions; it accepts any and everyone who walks in the door seeking shelter or belonging so that it heralds Giorgio Agamben's "negative community," a community that exists "by the simple absence of conditions … by belonging itself."[22] However, as Agamben extrapolates, such communities that evolve without setting conditions are deemed most threatening and generally suffer violent erasure by the state. Perhaps with this realistic backdrop, it is quite ordinary that Morrison chooses to begin her novel with the violent erasure of such a community. "They shoot the white girl first,"[23] introduces us to this community at the moment of its demise, but then the novel forces us, by refusing to precisely identify the woman, to confront the identity of the "who," literally and metaphorically as a hermeneutic tool. Both verb and object of the sentence are shaded over in ambiguity for Morrison sutures "shot" (a continuation after death) and "white woman" (who is never precisely named) into "Sightings." The entire novel arises as an explanation of this sentence, and yet Morrison's brilliance lies in never explaining it so fully that all ambiguity can be laid to rest.

Instead of arriving at a cogent "I," we leave this novelistic discourse implicating the community into the literality of the question. We have to disband the enduring Manicheanism of I/we and locate a new set of parameters for community within the contemporary novelistic discourse. This discourse is affected both by the gendered pen and the postcolonial historicity. If, for a moment, we direct our attention to the anticolonialist, nationalist struggles of the South Asian subcontinent in the first half of the twentieth century—dismissed by Nancy—then they reveal a rather remarkable intimacy between the function of community and the rise of a right-wing religious sentiment, linking it to Bataille's expressions of distrust in "headed" community. Christophe Jaffrelot demonstrates this link in *The Hindu Nationalist Movement and Indian Politics* when he quotes at length, a man known as a "freedom fighter," within modern India, Lala Lajpat Rai. In the excerpt that follows, Rai is addressing the first Punjab Hindu conference held at Lahore in 1909, the year when British government introduced a restricted franchise in British India, awarding separate electorates to Hindus and Muslims:

> It may be that the Hindus by themselves cannot form themselves into a nation in the modern sense of the term, but that is only a play on words. Modern nations are political units. A political unit ordinarily includes all the peoples who live under one common political system and form a State ... That is the sense is which the expression is used in connection with the body called the "Indian National Congress" ... But that is not the only sense in which it is or can be used. In fact, the German word "Nation" did not necessarily signify a political nation or a State. In that language it connoted what is generally conveyed by the English expression "people" implying a community possessing a certain civilization and culture. Using it in that sense, there can be no doubt that Hindus are a "nation" in themselves, because they represent a type of civilization all their own.[24]

Lajpat Rai's logos, in arguing for an ethnically and religiously concocted nationalism, also problematizes the arc of "community" as it travels through the Hindu lexicon of Indian popular politics to find its place on the crest of a rising fundamentalist movement that peaks in the 1990s. This movement, toxically marked by the razing of the Babri Masjid in Ayodhya in 1992, a watershed moment in the Indian body politic, advances little beyond these irreconcilable differences in the 2010 Supreme Court decision to divide the city along religious lines. Community remains a contested and difficult terrain, a territory that promises peace only after further cartographic divisions are etched into a landscape that reflects the German sense of nation as one people rather than the early twentieth century Congress vision of nation as many people knit together into the one community of nation. Thus nation takes its place in popular lexicon as the defining historical and semantic movement associated with "community," a word that I seek to shift and open up within this project.

Passion of the Event/The Passionate Word

Novelistic discourse arises from multiple places, each of which is influenced by various languages, traditions, and peoples who mingle and seep into the written page. The novels under study from the Americas and South Asia present an integration of worlds at large. While the novels from the West balance native, Haitian, French, English, Spanish, and West African speech patterns into the English narrative, the Hindi novels mostly from India reflect the polyglossia of a subcontinent at ease with the numerous languages filtering in and out of their character's tongues. We read in Hindi the effect of its relation with itself and kin languages such as Urdu, Punjabi, Bengali, as well as the differences of class, gender, status, etc., as interpreted through the languages. The strength of novelistic discourse is then a depiction of the diversity of the social fabric within the given communities, as evidenced in the subtleties of linguistic differences. Since the novels that were written by women and which are part of this study tend to depict lives lived at the margins of hegemonic cultures, the dialectic of differences lives in an area of intersections. Bakhtin writes in *Discourse in the Novel*,

> The more intensive, differentiated and highly developed the social life of a speaking collective, the greater is the importance attaching, among other possible subjects of talk, to another's words, another's utterance,

since another's word will be the subject of passionate communication, an object of interpretation, discussion, evaluation, rebuttal, support, further development and so on.[25]

I argue that the distinctions of community-formation, as seen especially in *Paradise* lend itself to a nonunderstanding between its participants. This pattern emerges over the course of its novelistic momentum as it becomes clear that the townsmen of Haven and the women of the convent literally speak different languages. This distinction is of central import in imagining alternative communities, conditions of communicability floating into community-building that pertains directly to the surface of languages included within the narratives. Roberta and Twyla's words are examples of "passionate communication," leaving behind words that are memorized, repeated, thought, interpreted, developed to such an extent that they have a parallel life alongside the characters who meet again after a period in which both the words and the women have been transformed. Morrison resists marking the characters under the sign of race, infects her heteroglossic narrative with a richness that cannot be fully ascribed to any one character. While we can attribute a separateness to each character, they are double-voiced, their conversations literally an emplotment of narrative. It is useful to note Bakhtin's larger point about languages and limits here:

> Double-voicedness in the novel, as distinct from double-voicedness in rhetorical or other forms, always tends toward a double-*languagedness* as its own outside limit. Therefore novelistic double-voicedness cannot be unfolded into logical contradictions or into purely dramatic contrasts. It is this quality that determines the distinctiveness of novelistic dialogues, which push to the limit the mutual nonunderstanding represented by people *who speak in different languages.*[26]

This "mutual nonunderstanding" performs the double function of extinguishing and generating meaning, the lens through which community is refracted.

Regarding the pattern of community found within the novel, the question merits asking: Whose community? Who benefits? Who is a member? Who, ultimately, has access? In her text, *On the Political: Thinking in Action*, Chantal Mouffe is the exemplar of the Saidian intellectual who takes the entire "free world" to task for being a ruse to advance cold capitalistic free market economies and self-advancement. She writes, "The new rights of cosmopolitan citizens are therefore a chimera: they are moral claims, not democratic rights that could be exercised."[27] Mary Dietz does the same in a more streamlined way; she points out the flaws in the liberal humanist vision of citizenship and goes on to outline feminist critiques of this dominant vision, in particular, the Marxist feminists and the maternalists. Finally, it is Dietz's own position of "democratic citizenship" that is the solution, wherein she outlines the formation of a new political community, which encapsulates all the best of feminism, liberalism, and citizenship. However, even in the most well-meaning critique of the status quo, the generality of the rhetoric fails to address the specificity of class, race, and gender, and its valence to the fundamentals of community. When Dietz talks about discarding the positional and single-party rhetoric in favor of an all-encompassing "political vision" in order to access the full profundity of citizenship, she is still only addressing the privileged few who can afford the visions with which they can transform ideas into value, not the larger masses of women who have little or no luxury "to claim a truly liberatory politics of their own."[28] A scholar who truly brings the project of feminist intellectual activism in a transnational way to both her texts and practice, is Chandra Talpade Mohanty.[29] Her corpus of intellectual production is significant in informing the way that this project too cuts across disciplines, battling cultural habits and collective amnesia to work toward a cohesive solidarity that is both literary and worldly.

Place of Women in Spaces of Violence

It is essential to cathect the political with the literary in terms of the disenfranchised—that is, the women who inhabit the literary borderlands within the episteme of the novelistic oeuvre. Even though "Recitatif" questions the place-holder of race in discussions about race, it raises key issues about the very dialogs that take place on the borderlands, the exchanges between women populating the margins who speak on their marginalized pasts. "Recitatif" is refracted through *Paradise* in that Roberta and Twyla's discourse is magnified in intensity and scope at the gathering of disparate women at the convent. Gayatri Spivak invites this wariness in her essay on literature in her backward-looking text, *A Critique of Postcolonial Reason: Toward a History of the Vanishing Present*, "The price of learning such a tropological deconstruction of masculism, however, was the performance of a blindness to the *other woman* in the text."[30] Spivak decodes the trouble with deconstruction as often a double-production of a lie, and her caution lends itself to stretching the meaning and turning in unfamiliar directions to contextualizing these discussions. In many ways, these discussions simultaneously contest patriarchal and statist systems, as well as second—and even third—wave feminists who might often bypass or read their positionality in an overdetermined way. These discussions heighten the contradictions present in the unconscious reinforcement between patriarchal systems of domination and resistance to these systems that implicitly reify the hegemonic structures. However, such a perspective requires stitching together the cultural theory to positions more grounded in the economy of the laboring classes, a scenario that does not escape Morrison because she posits that where the worlds of the women in the convent meets the larger world of the townspeople is the language of commodity exchange, or the market. They bake bread and prepare pickles, and jam that cannot be substituted or replicated by Haven. Also, they barter their way into a form of subsistence-level livelihood—dependent, but at the same time not complicit, in the way that the women within Haven are to the patriarchal systems that govern all their lives. Samir Amin's polemical text, *Eurocentrism*, is a valuable reminder of resistance to the prevailing structure of market-driven capitalism, "… internal factors take on a decisive role in societal evolution only when a peripheralized society can free itself through delinking from the domination of international value."[31] Amin's "delinking" and Spivak's "blindness of deconstructionism" invite a form of feminist practice that is charged with the type of "critical alertness" demanded by Said or Baldwin, and informed by feminist postcolonial scholars who attend to the "secondariness" of a set of layered identifications: race, gender, empire, etc.

Here one ought to pay heed to the significant discursive maps provided by feminist scholarship of Lata Mani and Rajeswari Sunder Rajan. Their work attends to gaps in the ways we have been tutored to review our pasts and present. In particular, I am interested in Mani's feminist and anticolonialist historiography that reviews the practice of sati in nineteenth-century Bengal in her text, *Contentious Traditions: The Debate on Sati in Colonial India* and Rajan's positing of the relationship between the woman and the state in her text, *The Scandal of the State: Women, Law, and Citizenship in Postcolonial India*. Lata Mani's historical analysis on the practice of sati informs my project of identifying imagined communities materializing out of the very specter of absence. In the eyewitness accounts of the practice of sati, Mani teases out the subtext of the roving gaze under the impositions of ritual, as recorded by British or native presence at the scene. This gaze, in telling of the level of success or failure of the brutality, tragedy, and mystery surrounding the widows, fails to tell of any agency or choice on part of the women involved. As Mani writes,

> ... within the discourse on *sati*, women are represented in two mutually exclusive ways: as heroines able to withstand the raging blaze of the funeral pyre or else as pathetic victims coerced against their will into the flames. These poles preclude the possibility of a female subjectivity that is shifting, contradictory, inconsistent. This reductive and binary view of agency is unable to capture the dynamic and complex relation of women to social and familial expectations. In particular, the constrained notion of agency that underwrites the representation of women as victims discursively positions women as objects to be saved—never as subjects who act, even if within overdetermined and restricted conditions.[32]

Mani, in contesting the general docile passivity of the female subjects, also charts a pattern of subjecthood for not only the female agents of history, but also for the female characters of literature who are banished to an exile by the process of unnaming. This project, in reading "imagined communities" through the novels written by female novelists, addresses the double act of assertion by those banished from the realms of autonomy.

Rajeswari Sunder Rajan adds to the critical apparatus of reidentifying female subjecthood as she studies a range of events from cases of divorce, rape, prostitution, infanticide, and a host of other questions of women's relationship to the state. Hailing from the left, Sunder Rajan, a radical feminist with poststructuralist inclinations, identifies the general unease between the state, communities, and the female self. Hoping to add to the ways of looking and tackling this triangulation, she points to the need for consideration when opting to resist with a capital "R," because such practices can silence the very violence they hope to unhinge. She writes:

> Almost any system we deplore and hope to reform or eliminate—slavery, child labor, the class system, marriage, for example—is, after all, susceptible to similar rewriting in terms of practices of subversion, survival,

wresting spaces of resistance and even enjoyment on the part of the oppressed subject. But such rewriting must not be achieved at the cost of
turning into a defense or a demand for the perpetuation of the systems.
While we must acknowledge and accord due respect to the subjectivities and capacities of those otherwise regarded solely as victims, and also
perhaps grant the functionalism of these systems, these must not hide
the perspective of structural domination and oppression that sustains
them.[33]

In effect, Sunder Rajan's work is, at heart, a structuralist critique
of poststructuralist left-wing protest of normative generalizations and
groupings. Her critique routes back to the complaint at the ideological
center of these discussions—the injustice of ideologies and the injustice
of systems of disempowerment, or more precisely, in the context of my
project, how questions of community adhere to normative discourse,
thereby undermining the radical dismantling of the master's house using
a composite of his tools and self-made ones.

Stitched together, Lata Mani's search for female subjectivity and
Rajeswari Sunder Rajan's wariness of ideologies of resistance raise
healthy questions regarding the blueprint of community. In Mani's
study, often the community bearing witness equals the community
writing over the female individual self. Sunder Rajan advises caution
when reading narratives espousing resistance when such rhetoric blinds
itself to the implicit nature of systemic domination that undergirds the
very notion of community. *Paradise* lays bare these theoretical nuances.
Haven, a community that is founded because it felt under siege by the
state, resists and reproduces an alternate existence. However, its narrative of resistance undergoes a cathectic shift once it disallows any other
forms of resistance that arise autochthonously within its purview. For
the townspeople, men and women alike, the function of bearing witness is a complicated one. In the violent and cataclysmic end to several
female selves who resided at the edges of their township, no one is clear
as to what came to pass. Morrison's novel is an effective response to the
absence Lata Mani detects within the historical archive. Morrison has a
certain historiographic panache in her novelistic discourse wherein she
is insistent on spelling out the female subjectivity, the centripetal force
of the final and elusive section of *Paradise*. In what follows, two forms of
interventions show how these theories help in literary analysis, and, second, the role of trauma theory as indispensable to the project at hand.

First, to point to the necessity of melancholic studies to the project, I point to two texts, one as an example of absence and the other of presence. Peter Homans in his edited anthology of essays, *Symbolic Loss: The Ambiguity of Mourning and Memory at Century's End*, records the decline of mourning in the West, which allows mourning to only emerge as an individual or familial loss, and thus reduces mourning to symbolic loss. The text meticulously charts the evolution of theories of melancholia from Freud to Fussell, and in advocating an understanding that emerges out of such affect, studies Wolf Lepenies to Jay Winters, but dwells mainly on the West, evincing a tautological failure. Paul A. Anderson's essay is the only voice in the anthology that emerges from the dialogically rich location of being from the non-hegemonic West, namely the sorrow songs of Harlem Renaissance. However it remains insufficient as the sole arbiter in giving the reader the dialectic between W. E. B. DuBois and Zora Neale Hurston, the latter raising the ire of black nationalists and intelligentsia by single-handedly doing the work of "mournful recuperation and ancestral commemoration."[34] Thus, the anthology bares the yawning gap in melancholic theories that need to address the regions and literatures of the world that fall outside the epistemic identity of the West. William Watkin, on the other hand, in his text informed by 9/11, *On Mourning: Theories of Loss in Modern Literature*, calibrates Freud to poststructuralist and postmodern theories of mourning and informs his literary readings to arrive at the relationship between mourning and ethics. He covers vast territory from Derrida to Deleuze, Julia Kristeva to John Bowlby, who are different from Freud and Kristeva in his emphasis on loss of the environment, all of which he layers into his readings of the novels of Ian McEwan, Douglas Copeland, and Dave Eggers. Again, despite Watkin's presence of mind with which he theorizes and definitively concludes, "reading literature of loss should be the activity of considering the proximity to otherness encountered in an environment,"[35] his gaze rests within the familiar epistemic map of dominant discourse, that is, writings by writers of the West. In what ways can this dynamic be enlivened by an inclusion of literatures and writers categorized as the other?

Trauma theory sheds critical light upon this project on violence. In *Testimony: Crises of Witnessing in Literature, Psychoanalysis, and History*, Shoshana Felman's chapters on Albert Camus's *The Plague* and *The Fall*, offer a discursive lead on the relationship between narrative and history. In light of Camus's active resistance during the Second World War and his elliptical narrative frame for the novel, *The Plague*, which was written in the immediate aftermath of war, Felman reads a certain urgency to events of history, their tendency to vanish within history, and appearance as "unqualified testimonies" in literature, only after a debt of silence is paid. Felman establishes a fine balance between the task of the writer who has to make sense of cataclysms of history and a history that can be the actual plague, erasing its own subjects and note-takers alike.

The dialectic between the writer, the cataclysm, and acts of historiographical narration or intervention are of radical import to the novels in this project that examine the terrain of the twentieth century in transnationally conscious terms. Though Felman's vocabulary does not pointedly spell it out, community reconfigured—much as in the praxis fueled by Agamben or Blanchot—is at stake within her emphasis on the labor of testimony. She formulates a crossing of sorts, of walls, of conventions, of reason, of life forces being let down in the absolute telling as she writes,

> But the purpose of testimony is, precisely, to cross these lines in an opposite direction to the way the condemnation cancels them out: to come out on the other side—of death, of life, of the limits of belonging, of history as total condemnation. To come out on the other side of language: "the concentration camp language," writes Elie Wiesel, "negated all other language and took its place. Rather than link, it became wall. Can the reader be brought to the other side?"[36]

Morrison's "Sightings" can be precisely located as this "other side," as literature that goes through the wall of history.

In her story, however, Morrison does not go to the other side, but very meaningfully withholds certain categorical information from her reader, thereby forcing the reader to place the characters in a separate space, a fuzzy exteriority that prohibits them from placing a blanket racial identifier upon the character. One can argue that as early as "Recitatif," Morrison plays with prefiguring other sides to the generic narration that abounds in an excess of detail that can somehow simply make the story vanish; this is a concern raised by Felman regarding the "event" in history. Roberta and Twyla meet again and again, revisiting their days spent together at the orphanage or revisiting their trauma. According to Cathy

Caruth, repetition is at the very heart of trauma, an event that returns with blunt regularity because of the very impossibility of digesting it fully or grasping its coherence. The very inaccessibility of trauma makes it the site frequented by those who suffer; for example, in the context of the exodus of the Jews, history itself is a narrative of trauma, the literal and metaphoric impossibility of fully understanding the first murder on which the entire narrative is founded. Caruth writes,

> For history to be a history of trauma means that it is referential precisely to the extent that it is not fully perceived as it occurs; or to put it somewhat differently, that a history can be grasped only in the very inaccessibility of its occurrence.[37]

In a sense, Caruth's psychoanalysis solves the conundrum that plagues Roberta and Twyla who are haunted by the impossibility of placing the racial signifier upon Maggie, and conversely that of the readers, who are haunted by the indeterminability of these two characters. Maybe the final laugh Roberta and Twyla share is on us, their witnesses who can never fully participate in the inaccessible event that narratives of violence inevitably are.

Such inaccessibility as the propelling force of a narrative is at the heart of Chapter 1, "Specters of Public Massacre: Violence and the Collective in Toni Morrison's *Paradise*." Set in the American South and Southwest, this chapter establishes the discursive lead into the project, both as a pathfinder and frame setter of the dialogic of novelistic discourse. The novel can be seen as an elaborate exercise in constructing an alternate community of women who are born out of the turbulence of the civil rights movement and women's liberation, communing at a one-time convent, governed by little else than a thin exchange of bread and pickles with the nearest town of Haven. In the vein of Nancy, Blanchot, and Agamben, Morrison's novel is an extended muse on the exclusions and contrariness prevalent in the very founding principles of community. This chapter works out the polemics of community in the analysis of the final section of the novel called "The Sightings." It serves a proleptic precursor to an idealized community of women constituted of corporeal, metaphysical, and transformative components in the purposefully female labor of making a paradise. The only relief for the trope of community is then in its transmutation onto another plane entirely, but one that remains populated and governed by women who operate under the aegis of labor, not the other commonly held signifiers of community, survival, and profit.

Race, the silent arbiter matters of history and social justice, is of import in the Chapter 2, "Imagining Community in Edwidge Danticat's *The Farming of Bones.*" This chapter, like the opening chapter, places importance on the final event of this novel. The chapter follows the central character, Amabelle Desir's survival of the massacre of Haitians committed in 1937 upon the orders of Rafael Trujillo, the Dominican President of thirty years. This novel is Danticat's fictional account of a character through her years spent remembering Haiti, her return to the plantation in her final days, and her willful end upon the river of crossings, the River Massacre named after the event. As in the opening chapter, Amabelle's journey is followed to decode the meanings laden in her final moments spent as she star-gazes upon the river before being taken in by its undertow. In this novel, community is configured by those who lose their very existence, and others who survive this period of horror, with a will to exist and the desire to testify. Amabelle's color is like driftwood ashes in the rain, as described by her lover Sebastien Onius, who suffers his end in the massacre that discriminates in favor of those of lighter hues. For those who lose their lives and others who are left, diasporic and longing for the severed portions of their lives, community is reconfigured along radical ontologies that trespass boundaries between the living and the dead. Chapter 2 places significance on the imagination of those systematically marginalized and erased from history, the subalterns of the contemporary novel.

Chapter 3 conforms to the pattern of pondering the significance of endings, but in doing so breaks the pattern. Questions of community wrestle for ascendance throughout the novel in this chapter entitled, "Partition and the Woman's Body in Bapsi Sidhwa's *Cracking India.*" Sidhwa's portrayal of an idealized community based on differences, fragile and ruptured, brings to the surface the anxious revelation that the colonialist gaze is not the lone hegemonic oppressor. Violence erupts at the birth of the nation-state, at that putatively glorious moment of nation-making memorialized in elementary school text books. The postcolonial nation-state is spelled out violently on the woman's body. This chapter sediments the project's larger critique of institutionalized patriarchy as the ultimate language of violence, a medium of exploitation borne by the female characters. This is evidenced in figure of Ayah upon whose body the shifting mutations of community are literally inscribed.

Bapsi Sidhwa's narrative opens the concomitant discussion on the South Asian subcontinent. Chapter 4 involves a study of novels written primarily in South Asian languages, and read in Hindi. Chapter 4 examines South Asian novels in Hindi: Tahmina Durrani's *Kufr*, Mridula Garg's *Kathgulab*, and Mahasweta Devi's *Hazaar Chaurasi Ki Maa* (Mother of 1084, in English translation) that arrive at notions of female self-empowerment worked out on a public sphere. This chapter addresses de-emphasis on authorship. To Barthes who births the reader only at the death of the author, the binary is systematically eroded by novelistic narratives that refuse to be bound by such Manicheanism. For the women writers who are the names behind these novels, writing is not a destruction of voice, subject, or identity. Neither is the author's name weighty in a traditionalist manner because these women arrive as flag-bearers of new traditions; nor is her name vaporous in the sense of becoming a mere subject. Author-function is part and parcel of the meaning that accumulates in the gravity of these narratives that step into their own shadow dances of "community." Tapping into the interstitial spaces offered by rupture, these readings posit new ways of raising and sometimes answering questions of community as they arise in select works from the Americas and South Asia, devising bridges and skyways that recharge the old dialectic of discourse, repetition, and memory that is always already evident as a metonym in "Recitatif."

The final chapter furthers the focus on writings from India. In Chapter 5, "The Cracking of India in Amrita Pritam's *Pinjar* and Mohandas Nemishrai's *Aaj Bazaar Band Hai*," ideas about community are contextualized alongside the question of women's agency. These novels are narratives that capitalize around women's kidnappings and women's bodies. The texts target the sexual economy alongside the larger narrative of a national economy as it is born and comes into consciousness. The conclusion, "Notes from the Trenches of Patriarchy," attempts to conceptualize this entire project of bringing Toni Morrison in conversation with South Asian feminist writing through the politics of radical feminist epistemologies. Writing in the differing national (*desh*) and diasporic (*videsh*) spaces, from Tahmina Durrani to Mridula Garg, women novelists creatively resist the law of the father by contradicting and eliding the symbolic order. To quote Cixous, they steal language; however, they do so not only to produce *écriture féminine* but to unwrite patriarchal inscriptions on the woman's body. This final chapter engages in a form of deterritorialization inspired by Edouard Glissant's future of community where poetics is a form of desire and relations is novelistic expression. Further, I draw from Deleuze's rhizomatic multiplicity of the "book," a place of discursive liberation, healing, and bridge-building apart from Hegelianism, hierarchy, and Manicheanism. Thus, this book concludes by moving beyond the tired representations of "borders" as landscapes teeming with armed soldiers to a reframing, through women's writing, of the nations as metonyms where India, Pakistan, and Bangladesh can be reimagined through modalities of past antiquity, present struggle, and future dream. Such agglutination, then, is the novelistic step away from the politics of partition, national identities formed of trauma and thus, a step forward into the poetics of reconciliation.

While these stories have little presence to a world audience and representation in global print capital, it is all the more reason to revivify the discussions around how, despite the inscriptions of patriarchy on the literary imaginary, these stories empower and access community in feminisms of the global south that need to be addressed and understood. Since this project wrestles with notions of violence and the novel, to an extent, it is informed by the pressing reality of 9/11 in the United States and 26/11 in India, only two in a very long list of terrorist events of the twenty-first century. Questions of community arise around the spectacular performance of rage. In what ways do people mourn? How do communities form around this mourning? Is there a possible way in which those who live and those who do not speak to one another? And is there a way to exercise agency in a condition that is a rebuttal of individual and collective choice? For those of us attuned to the stories outside the context of the United States, especially South Asia, it also becomes important to remember how such loss is commonplace for many people and communities around the world. It is necessary then to somehow capture within one's own work the place of the world, that is, relate the text to the world and vice versa. Edward Said's call in the immediate aftermath of the United States' first war with Iraq alerts us to the role of the intellectual as one that requires a certain amount of cerebral soldiering:

> There is no question in my mind that the intellectual belongs on the same side with the weak and the unrepresented.... At bottom, the intellectual, in my sense of the word, is neither a pacifier nor a consensus-builder, but someone whose whole being is staked on a critical sense, a sense of being unwilling to accept easy formulas, or ready-made clichés,

or the smooth, ever-so-accommodating confirmations of what the powerful or conventional have to say, and what they do. Not just passively unwillingly, but actively willing to say so in public.[38]

This public speech, this act of alertness, is certainly present in good deal of intellectual work that has been produced in this post-9/11 world of outrage and solidarity with the subalterns.

Isabel Allende, writing about the political impetus of her writing and her world of writers, explains the troubles she encountered in her second novel, *Of Love and Shadow* (1988) when imagining the *desaparecidos* (the disappeared).

> They didn't like the fact that in the novel, solidarity and hope prevail over death and torture. If the main characters, Irene and Francisco, had died in a torture chamber, or at least if the violent experiences they endured had drowned them in despair and destroyed forever their capacity to love and to dream, these critics might have been more tolerant. Evidently it's hard to accept in literature that love can be stronger than hatred, although it frequently is in life.[39]

Allende's impulse is, like that of many novelists working out the effects of cataclysmic violence of their pasts and present, to write to resurrect. This project, in addressing novels that write into the wound of collective loss, is an argument against finalities, an argument for the right to exist even into death, women writing violence as measure of a feminist forging in worlds drenched in darkness.

1

Specters of Public Massacre: Violence and the Collective in Toni Morrison's *Paradise*

Community lies at the heart of Toni Morrison's novel, *Paradise* (1998). Toni Morrison weaves together African American history with the biblical exodus of the Hebrews to the Promised Land to create the question mark that begins this novel: Why does community based on commonly understood principles of love, familiality, trust, and shelter finally extinguishes its own? Put more precisely, how does community turn itself from a place of shelter to a place of punishment? In the novel then, community transforms from a space of life to one of death, and thereby, I pose, community is finite, containing in its genesis seeds of its own destruction.

In Jean-Luc Nancy's theses—community arises in the absence or vacuum of God, forming in the hollow space left by divinity, raises its head in *Paradise*. Community arises in the "disappearance of the gods"[1] and this establishment writing itself over the gods urges an interjection in Haven. As long as the exodus is moving, as in Basavanna's "things moving," they remain enspirited. Their God travels with them and inscribes his orders upon the collective oven. As soon as they turn immobile, i.e., Basavanna's "things standing," they are bereft of the divine presence and turn stagnant. Communion recedes from community, and in standing, Haven becomes the very places from which they ran. Such a community identifies more with hunters than healers. *Paradise* opens at the moment of this transformation with an act of violence.

Paradise tells the story of a band of African Americans trekking across the United States in late nineteenth century[2] to form an ideal community of autonomous farmers in Oklahoma. Having faced rejection along the way, Big Papa, the leader of the group, establishes their community at the site where they install their communal oven, a town called Haven which is later renamed Ruby. Descendants of Big Papa form this community of patriarchs, their blue black color a badge of authenticity and membership, under the current aegis of Steward and Deacon Morgan. This double-headed leadership is in opposition to Bataille's figurations of the ideal community as a body that is headless, acephalic. It also doubles the punishment for disobedience by prefiguring its own demise.

Outside Ruby lays a convent in ruins which is occupied by a band of women who find it by happenstance and decide to stay there for shelter. Neither severed from Ruby, nor obedient to the laws of the patriarchs, the women listen to a leader of their own choosing, Connie. The events of the plot bring the town of Ruby in an anxious fervor over this peculiar community living at their margins. The men of Ruby act to eliminate what seemingly threatens their idyll, an ill, according to them, that arises from the convent like a virus. The novel opens on this moment when the men are shooting the women in the convent. The novel closes on the same women who continue after death. They are engaged in the female labor-making of paradise. Basavanna's "things moving" infects the final sightings when the dead return to the living and seek redress. While the opening and closing are temporally continuous, they present an ontological rupture. The very women who are shot in the opening scene are present, traveling, talking, and addressing people in different cities in the closing sections, thereby reinvigorating death with new meaning.

On Community

Multiple communities, at various stages of empowerment, exist in this novel. Even this patriarchal community is a marginal one in context of the nation at large, since it is a historical attempt by an African American group of East-coast farmers who seek their fortune in a better state. The women's community at issue on the edges of this foundational community, thus, suffers from a form of double exclusion. It exists on the margins of both the nation-state and the patriarchal community which is its immediate neighbor.

In the context of American history, exclusion is implicit in the thematic of community. The founding community of United States rests on the exclusion of the existing population of native Americans and the enslaved population of African Americans. Toni Morrison writes into this wound of exclusion that forms the flesh of community. Excluded by the flawed practice of democracy promised by the constitution, at least from the perspective of those left out of the narrative, the band of African American families follow Big Papa and suffer a bigger slight at the hands of their own. En route to finding their haven, they are exiled from a similar community of African Americans, distinguished from the former only by their lighter skin. Wound upon wound writes itself into the bible of community the Ruby forefathers call their collective history, the narrative eulogized in every sermon by the pastors, deacons, and the Morgan brothers. Finally, it is this wound that erupts and causes the vengeful surveillance of those who are prohibited from joining the sanctioned community of Haven.

Cathy Caruth helps in decoding the events of the novel in her reading of Freud's account of the exodus in *Moses and Monotheism*.[3] The Hebrew exodus is the historical and sacred referent to the characters beginning with Big Papa who is self-consciously likened to Moses.[4] Morrison's landscape is layered with rejections: the larger corpus of the state which forgets its own people by recording once "enslaved" as now "subordinate" or "marginal" and the communities composed of light skinned African Americans who decline hospitality to their kin by historical circumstance. The consequences of such rejections cause death, despair, and a fractured sense of historical identity. No matter if the rejections cause physical or psychic damage, violence is encoded in the blueprint of this community. The trauma, as Caruth points, returns and haunts this very recurrence sutured into the rest of Haven's narrative.

Morrison, as in many of her previous novels, works at constructing a specifically female language that allows for the expression of a female creativity. In *Paradise* particularly, she is concerned with how does one give textual narrativity to an all-female community, in the line of its feminist foremothers like Charlotte Perkins Gilman's *Herland* (1979 [1915]),[5] Sojourner Truth's *Ain't I a Woman?* (1863),[6] or even, the Bengali Muslim educator and activist, Rokeya Shakawat Hossain in her story, "Sultana's Dream" (written in 1905),[7] but again imbued with differences: race, class, history, etc. Underlying all of this is the basic principle: How does one write women into history? Excluded from master narratives and even counter-narratives, such as that of the fathers of Ruby, the convent becomes an experimental space. This space with shifting names, addresses, and identities becomes the site of telling such an anti-history or a gynocentric history.

How does one envision the space of the convent? Posted at the out-skirts of Ruby, and existing in a tacit underground barter economy of homemade breads and pickles with the townspeople, especially the townswomen, the convent can be understood as that which Shirley and Edwin Ardener have called the "wild zone."[8] Specifically female in its occupants, habits, desires, and despair, the convent is a space almost unnoticed by the men until the women enter the larger space of Ruby's community, especially a gathering of its entire people for a festive wedding party. It is beyond Ruby's purview, unquestioned by any of the men who wield power; the convent is problematic and ungovernable. The Ardeners characterize the "wild zone" as a site con-stituted by females, supportive of their creativity, a space outside the purview of patriarchy. The convent is a "wild zone," the men are not even aware of its existence for a long period, and when they do be-come aware, they are excluded from knowledge of what occurs within. Though the women at the convent are deeply aware of Ruby—their joys and especially their sorrows, the men of Ruby do not comprehend its grammar.

Finally, when the women at the convent reach stasis, Basavanna's "things standing," and establish their livelihood, habits, and rituals, they are under threat. Stasis is the precondition for detection and visibility. The women are allowed to be as long as they do not matter, as long as they do not create or stir or make themselves known. Once they enter the stage of self-assertion and thereby, self-knowledge, they are punished for transgression of the normative patterns of the larger community. Much like the metaphysics of body and space in her earlier novels, *Beloved* (1987)[9] and *Jazz* (1992),[10] Morrison makes the presence of the women known in acts of paradise-making. Here, Juliet Mitchell's psy-choanalytical and powerful question holds valence: "What are we in the process of becoming?"[11] Mitchell charts the project of women novelists along a binary of accepting and writing within the social structures of patriarchal law or writing into a difference where the subject is always in process of becoming something else. The great mystery of the text is finally, at the end of community, after its dissolution. What have the women of the community become? And what new meaning does this imagined community write into the literary text?

Imagining Community with the Dead

What is the condition of those brought to death through injustice and violence? That is, what can be said about those who are dead before their time? Their sudden death begins to matter, as Reverend Misner asserts in his sentimental eulogy, "What is sown is not alive until it dies"[12] and this fence-sitting performed so deftly by the renegades in the convent, is of interest here. The dead in this novel break all accepted traditions. It is not the living who commune but the dead who travel and converse with the living. The dead remove finality from the death and do so through the labor of making paradise, a female labor which inverts the hierarchical order because they descend to make a paradise down on earth. Reverend Misner speaks out of an African American cosmogony that never simply ends life in death. Within this tradition, the dead wander, return to advice, and populate the same spaces as their living brethren. Morrison's novel works out its acephalic community at the novel's end: the text charts disembodied women in acts of paradise-making, a form of community for, by, and of the dead. Community-making in this paradigm is also an act of power-making, wresting power from a space of double exclusion into an actual space of exercising agency within the text. This radical repossession of space by the female characters resonates in the work of Chela Sandoval when she confronts Jameson, Derrida, and Barthes in her critique of poststructuralist/postmodernist ethos in *Methodology of the Oppressed* (2000).[13] She locates sites of greater volatility than Derrida's "difference," attending to the sites of radical liberation intended in Anzaldua's "la conciencia de la mestiza" or Patricia Hill Collins' "outsider-within" and concludes with a reformulation of the Derridean "middle voice" instead of a philosophical calibration of différance; it is the argument of the marginalized who turn discourse on its head; Sandoval's theoretical underpinnings furnish the lattice upon which many such other worlds can be constructed.

This life in death, and earlier, death in life, the ambiguity between the two, the constant haggling and balance between these two extremities is performed in sobriety and normality by the women at the convent. Perhaps they preserve weak links with the living but their structural fault, the flaw for which the larger society vilifies them and calls them aberrant is their strong link with the dead. These are women who imagine a community[14] with the dead, such as Mavis who cares for and celebrates the birthdays of her dead twins and brings them with her to the convent. They imagine community with urgency and desire that stuns the righteous caught in structures that blind them. The imagined community that spills out of cars and buses at novel's end exists in these very interstices refusing to accept normative epistemologies on the way to live and die.

Scholars have theorized variously about the three novels considered to follow the unity of a trilogy colored by confusion between excess of both love and hate. For proportions of this excess, I borrow from Marc C. Conner's astute deductions with which he links all three novels as an excess of love marked at the same time by hate.[15] Conner adduces in *Paradise* an excess of love of God, who, according to Nancy, is no longer present. Community is a troubled enterprise only to be saved by the wandering itinerants who revive Basavanna's "things moving" and bring communion back into community.

Which Way Is Heaven from Here?

Paradise travels to the depth of our material distance from any such geography stipulated by the title. *Paradise* is the third in the trilogy preceded by *Beloved* and *Jazz*. Morrison works her literary oeuvre into the era of civil rights and black empowerment of the latter half of the twentieth century albeit apart from metropolitan centers, in a country all its own that configures its own laws, covenants, and ambition. Set apart from the fires raging in Washington, D. C. or Montgomery; Alabama or Newark; New Jersey, Morrison charts the embers falling in a faraway black star buried deep in the Oklahoma desert town named after a dead black woman. Ruby dies because she is refused to be treated by doctors at the nearest white hospitals in Demby ninety miles away. Morrison's intellectual project articulates the link made by the late Edward Said between text and empire.[16] She narrates out of the broad sweep of post-Civil War migration up north and out west that occurred all the way through late nineteenth century and early twentieth century. While these migrations represent the black search for land away from the immediate structures of oppression prevailing in the south, the new settlements nurture a Saidian intimacy between the text and power so that an oppressive hegemony takes root within the community of Haven as soon as it considers itself to be a righteous settlement of good people.

In her own essays in which she reads the silent and urgent presence of blackness in canonic American literature from Poe to Welty, Morrison writes about how attempts at paradise fail. Her key example is the new-world attempt at erasing the errors of the world they leave behind, only to recreate an equally flawed version, an idea taken further by this 1998 novel that stresses this inevitable recurrence. The peoples who leave for the new world seek a refuge from the penalty for difference and yet, many people already inhabiting or brought against their will in the new world are made to pay far greater price for their differences. Race is the empty metaphor that provides information but scant knowledge in Morrison's own summations.[17] From the racial marker, one can gather details but scarcely do these details add up to anything coherent or correct regarding the individual except a body with which many measure their own self-worth.

Ruby's history is layered repeatedly by rejections of the white nation and then their black brethren of lighter skin and greater wealth who refuse them haven. En route, the exodus of Ruby's forefathers encounter towns populated by lighter skin-toned African Americans who deny them the chance to live beside them on account of their much darker hue. The original families trek further out west led by the Moses-like figure of Big Papa who finds the town they name aptly for themselves, Haven. Years later, a second rejection, and a second birthing from the same oven transported miles further west, produces Ruby.[18]

At once the narrative of the genesis of a patriarchal alternate community within the heartland of a white patriarchal nation wrangling with its own identity in *fin-de-siècle* United States, *Paradise* accounts the parallel genesis of a matrifocal community at its margins. Evocative of the third of Dante's famous trilogy, *Paradiso*, Missy Dehn Kubitschek offers a chart of the differences between the two works as a pointed mapping of the distinct ambition of the latter. She writes:

> Dante's paradise transcends earth, whereas Morrison's shows earth and the spiritual world as inextricably mixed. Morrison's earlier novels have shown the persistence of spirits after human characters die, but *Paradise* shows these spirits as far more active in human life—a traditional African view. For the first time in a Morrison novel, spirits continue to grow and age after their human deaths. Further, certain human beings may be incarnations of eternal, divine energies. Whereas the Divine Comedy poetically expresses Catholic cosmology, *Paradise* conveys an Africanist, feminist religious sensibility.[19]

Along the exodus of 8-Rock[20] families from the East-coast into the Oklahoma blue, we witness journeys that call less attention to themselves; the convent experiences generations of distinct populations. Nuns, Arapaho Indian girls,[21] a saved Latin from unnamed South American wastelands, and singular specimen of female detritus flock to the embezzler's mansion, known popularly as the convent. Kristin Hunt meditates on the haunting presence of the Arapaho Indian presence in the novel:

> The Arapaho are shadowy elements throughout the novel. They are never represented as physically present but are spiritually omnipresent. As the novel progresses, the Arapaho serve as a reminder of an irrecoverable, aboriginal past. The land of Haven once belonged to the Arapaho, and the Convent outside of the town of Ruby once served as a school for Arapaho girls but has long been abandoned. One gets the sense that the Arapaho culture has been lost, conquered, and replaced by the black townships and others. However, Morrison constantly reminds the reader that the ways of the Arapaho live on as part of the environment.[22]

Anna, the town historian, is the only one to sense this loss long before the denouement. Ruby suffers from having lost touch with its native and African pasts and this is particularly relevant to the resignification of death offered by the moving spirits of the women because the town residents have forgotten this legacy. The only one who remembers it is Misner. In the collective amnesia, people forget the ancestral knowledge production which taught that death is not the final word on any matter. The patriarchs, escaping the cloying and dehumanizing hegemonic structure of the larger nation-state that enslaved its people, manages to reproduce and become the very machine it set out to exorcize from its existence.

Courage, Humor, Cunning, and Fortitude

The female community, haphazard, unplanned but genuinely supportive of all the flotsam and jetsam that descends into its ore, without intending for transcendence births a paradise upon earth. The answer to the opening question, Haven, only one letter removed from its divine counterpart, does not mirror its ethereal cousin in its first incarnation as Haven or second one as Ruby. Somewhere in the murky geography within the convent, a place hard to pin down on maps, within language, or rational epistemology lies the answer to this quest for directions. As we map this narrative of a black utopia within the white heartland of America, it bears to pay attention to Theodor W. Adorno's collection of essays in *Prisms*, when he talks about the émigrés in early America, De Tocqueville, and Huxley's *Brave New World* (1932) and community as a failure of former idealizations:

> "Community, Identity, and Stability" replaces the motto of the French Revolution. Community defines a collectivity in which each individual is unconditionally subordinated to the functioning of the whole (the question of the point of this whole is no longer permitted or even possible in the New World). Identity means the elimination of individual differences, standardization even down to biological constitution; stability, the end of all social dynamics. The artfully balanced situation is an extrapolation from certain indications of a reduction in the economic "play of forces" in late capitalism—the perversion of the millennium. The panacea that guarantees social stasis is "conditioning."[23]

Huxley leaves little hope for utopias; Adorno's refusal of such order as structurally flawed and bereft of meaning leads to greater room for the "conditioning" which Morrison's women at the convent escape to create a "paradise down below" somewhere before the end of the narrative. Paradise is a community that exists without the force of conditioning.

Walter Benjamin's fourth "Thesis on the Philosophy of History" is coded, cautionary and useful for locating meanings in Morrison's text:

> The class struggle, which is always present to a historian influenced by Marx, is a fight for the crude and material things without which no refined and spiritual things could exist. Nevertheless, it is not in the form of the spoils which fall to the victor that the latter make their presence felt in the class struggle. They manifest themselves in this struggle as courage, humor, cunning, and fortitude. They have retroactive force and will constantly call in question every victory, past and present, of the rulers. As flowers turn toward the sun, by dint of a secret heliotropism the past strives to turn toward the sun which is rising in the sky of history. A historical materialist must be aware of this most inconspicuous of all transformations.[24]

The "courage, humor, cunning, and fortitude" of the latter will be essential rubrics with which to understand the women in the convent, especially toward the end of the novel. The woman, signifying the past of Ruby, never becomes the "spoils" of the victors or their assailants. Instead they make their presence known "by dint of a secret heliotropism" or "paradise making" revealed in the final pages of the text. As Benjamin cautions the historical materialist to be aware of this "inconspicuous of all transformations," it is a transformation that Morrison charts from the convent's dead women to the ambiguous beings of power that insist upon their own presence at the end.

Reverend Richard Misner, a central character around whom the narrative turns, is born, christened, revealed, and integral to all the sections of this chapter, sanctified by the author and in place of her in the text, says in the funerary elegy for Save-Marie, the youngest of Jeff and Sweetie's children and the first to die in the town of immortals, "To know that 'what is sown is not alive until it dies.'"[25] Misner echoes in his sentimental mysticism for a dead baby the Benjaminesque "retroactive force" of the past which works its way into the force of the subaltern.[26] The dead, in refusing to die, "call in question every victory, past and present, of the rulers." When the women return, they are seen visiting the sites of their old traumas, correcting the narrative; they travel in style. Sometimes armed with weapons, other times with a joke, always together, they are Benjamin's rubrics of humor and fortitude brought to life. The novel spatializes this "most inconspicuous of all transformations" in the sightings that are seen by the privileged few who are relevant. In contrast to the patriarchal communion that seeks the convert, the women are an enigma causing struggle and mystery, resonant with the female labor of paradise-making.

How do notions of violence cast root? In what forms do they absorb water and grow into ideologies of power? Are they also secretly heliotropic, like Benjamin's "past" and reach toward the sun of center–peripheries so that they can ripen in the center and decimate the periphery most effectively? While those sponsoring systemic violence exemplified by the massacre are remembered interestingly enough by annals of history, I follow the populations, the subalterns erased in such ruptures, the subjects under erasure within the master narratives. Here, Morrison's own notions of history become necessarily imbricated with her literary project. Katrine Dalsgard outlines Morrison's deconstructive post-structuralist sense of history as never being outside itself, always implicated in its own project of hegemonies at war, more Barthes and Foucault than black feminist nationalists like E. Francis White. History, as a polyphony of multivalent voices always surging for dominance on several axis of meaning, resonates with Bhabha's notions of nationhood.[27] It is not a straight line from the powerful to the powerless, from the state to the stateless but a grammar of differences that bridges the narratives of those in United States to those in Ruby, and those in Ruby to the women in the convent. This teleology of violence yields to a community of resistance, the space identified initially within the convent and later, as paradise.

Inferno as Prelude to Paradise

Friction exists in both the communities identified so far; the one marked 'center' or Ruby, recognizing the relativity of all such nomenclature for the center here, is marginal to the larger nation. What needs to be noted here is that such spatial dichotomy results in a cost borne by those at the margins. At the periphery of Ruby's patriarchy is the "wild zone," the convent. K.D., the Morgan nephew and prince-in-line of patriarchal authority, assesses upon entering that space with a mission to obliterate, "Bodacious black Eves unredeemed by Mary, they are like panicked does leaping toward a sun that has finished burning off the mist and now pours its holy oil over the hides of game. God at their side, the men take aim. For Ruby."[28] The venom of the center towards its periphery overshadows the smaller tensions rocking its boat in eddies of despair long before they target or decide that their rage has a direction, and that should be directed to the margin.[29] Within itself, Ruby faces a host of problems that flank patriarchy in its rigid need to maintain order, decorum, and tradition set in place by founding fathers, and of those, Ruby has an assortment of no less than fifteen.[30]

The twins, Steward and Deacon Morgan, consider themselves heir to the patriarchal empire set in motion by Big Papa's exodus to the west. Able to read one another's thoughts, experiences and without need of immediate conversation, so alike that it is uncomfortable for townspeople at times, the twins are different too. Their greatest difference is in the pitch of their stridency with which they carry their father's histories on their backs. Brothers themselves, they marry sisters, Dovey and Soane, continuing the endogamous tradition of a town that grows to value foremost its own purity. They come in the line of 8-Rock blood of blue black people scorned by the larger nation-state, worshipped within their own newly configured prescriptions, problematic nevertheless at both ends. Both devotion and derision frame the inferno in Ruby, a prelude to paradise.

Apart from the power struggle between blood, there is also spiritual declension between the reverends, the religious gatekeepers who arbitrate on history and hatred while the younger ones, like Misner, defiant of the implacable clutches of deadly traditions in rigor mortis, beckon the new. The elders guard the fort against the passion of youth. The struggle over the missing words in the motto carved upon the oven between the two generations is never resolved, simply ended at Steward's unmistakable threat of violence, "If you, any one of you, ignore, change, take away, or add to the words in the mouth of that Oven, I will blow your head off just like you was a hood-eye snake."[31] Whether it is the youth, the women, or any group too disenfranchised to ever dissent, any speech act is akin to revolt. The heat of the inferno dictates to the residents of Ruby: free speech is the devil dancing on the tongue. The only heretic and apostate blasphemers within Ruby are identified as the women living in the desacralized space of the convent.

Also, there are outsiders within the insiders, or those who have been inside for a long time but still never fully belong. The following catalogue also doubles as the rupture within community, the fault lines along which the failure of community is prewritten. Billy Delia is too light to be truly 8-Rock; Anna Flood is the unusual agent of her own economic destiny and thoughts; Pat chronicles lives led in Ruby, and carries the guilt of having sacrificed her daughter Billie Delia to the ravages of a close-minded community; Lone DuPres is adopted and adept in midwifery but no longer needed in a time that shrugs her domestic charity and opts for the modern convenience of hospitals. Each woman is a metonym for the problem intrinsic to centers.

Morrison critiques the knowledge production of "things standing." Indeed, the elderly and wise, those who transmit and enlighten, do so incorrectly in the stagnant world of Ruby. Nathan, the oldest gent, childless and wifeless, stands like the prophet in King David's court, the first teller of parables, codes which if interpreted correctly augur good things to come. Morrison provides here a latter-day Nathan too old and unwieldy to interpret the profound nature of his own dream, and in his misinterpretation, lay the beginning of the end. His dream is like a fabulous art by Joseph Cornell of the never-ending mise-en-scène of boxes within boxes. He is prophet within a prophet; he dreams a Cheyenne Indian warns him that the bean crop is not good, that the water is foul and the flowers of the wrong color.

Though Nathan sees the blood-red for a split moment, he concludes, "It shows the strength of our crop if we understand it. But it can break us if we don't. And bloody us too. May God bless the pure and holy and may nothing keep us apart from each other nor from the One who does the blessing."[32] Instead of warning his own flock about the disease within, he returns to the established norm of self-adulation and an insistence on purity, in direct opposition to the ill foreseen within the dream. The illness is within and it can erupt in violence, as seen by the blood red flowers. Nathan pats the congregation and layers upon their righteous souls another stroke of endogamy rather than decipher what he himself sees as urgent, the need to comprehend properly. The wise habitually misread the text; this abuse of knowledge is also part of Ruby's descent.

This is not to say that the alternate community formed under a maternal auspice is free of friction. Mavis and Gigi continually fight, often physically till one or the other caves in with fatigue. Connie, the Grand Mater, often too inebriated to emerge in the kitchen with the rest, riling against the "disorder, deception, and drift" defining her indefinite freeloaders, she bristles against their collective condition of depravity.

> When she was sipping Saint-Émilion or the smoky Jarnac, she could tolerate them, but more and more she wanted to snap their necks. Anything to stop the badly cooked indigestible food, the greedy hammering music, the fights, the raucous empty laughter, the claims. But especially the drift.[33]

Connie, suffering under the long-lasting disability of a physical love gone awry, doubles her melancholy by the more recent loss of her first love, Sister Mary Magna. She is alone, intoxicated, and disconnected from the great God she had learned to love in her first home, the Catholic Church. She is disconsolate and shaken, despite her continual generosity, by the band of loud rabble she has managed to collect under her expansive roof.

Yes, friction is present at the alternate abode; however, it is not a friction of wrestling powers, philosophies, generations, genders, or misunderstandings. Instead it is an overall exhaustion with the structures in place, structures that keep Consolata Sosa in perpetual exile through her entire wounded existence. These structures bring a tormented mother, Mavis, haunted by the horrors visited upon her by family life by an abusive husband and her dead twins. These structures also bring a brokenhearted Gigi in search of the eternal lovers or entwined trees. Pallas escapes from a Succubus-like mother, and Seneca, repeatedly abandoned by her mother escapes the prison of home for the convent.

All the residents suffer from claustrophobia of closed systems that allow them little room to exercise their own will, little room to alter the course and devise new ways of being. They come from broken communities, from broken places with broken bodies and hearts. They are not sure how to be around one another when there is no perpetrator involved, no one present to deliver the blow to the temple. Unplanned, they happen upon the haven not named with any clarity, decide to linger and make of it the only genuine family they have known. Much like women in other times and places who suffered seclusion in its various forms, each woman finds her way out of her particular seclusion to the convent. The convent is a space of inclusion, paradise at its outset.

Friction leads to rupture, a rupture that can lead to resolution or dissolution. The patriarchs of Ruby, the husbands, fathers, and grandfathers, galvanized under the steady gaze of the overseeing twins, believe all troubles in Ruby are born from the uncontrolled evil present in the convent. They assess that their troubles are merely what began as an illegitimate dissemination spreading from the convent, or the margin to its center. Girls talk back to their mothers because of the wanton women living without men in the convent. Men beat their lovers because of wantonness set loose out there. Babies are born sickly and the young talk of rewriting the archive of their ancestors because of evil that began in the non-Christian convent, no longer a house for any god.

Men, emerging in the Manichean dualism as actors rather than bearers, do act. They resolve this contagion of the "wild zone" by meeting, conspiring, and acting as men are supposed to do to resolve a problem. This one act leads to dissolution. Anna Flood, upon returning from the conference and planning to celebrate her engagement to Reverend Misner, finds herself "sorting out what looked like the total collapse of a town."[34] The men, after eating meat and lacing coffee with liquor, armed with ropes and guns, attack the convent at dawn, preparing to shoot the blaspheming women. And so, Morrison opens the novel the way she does. The men shoot the women.

Friction within Ruby is resolved by a total dissolution of known structures. The men engage in the familiar habit of violence by inscribing it upon the women's bodies, a way to write over the *écriture féminine*. Here, the recurrence of trauma beckons violence, the physical manifestation of originary violence. The community recovers but they bear the burden of a reality steeped in horror; they no longer remain the prelapsarian community of immortals. Fallen, they have to scramble together new covenants with which to rescue themselves. They are no longer the gems who imagined their holy communion with a town they named Ruby. No one fully grasps the horror of their witness but they all tell versions of it with such variation that Misner is not able to draw data worthy of a sermon. Many could not even agree on whether a shooting took place or if the women drove off or changed form. The central act of the novel framing it as the beginning and ending—the massacre at the convent—is beyond telling. Cathy Caruth crystallizes the impossibility of recovering the narrative of violence since trauma inscribes at its inception, anti-narration.

> For history to be a history of trauma means that it is referential precisely to the extent that it is not fully perceived as it occurs; or to put it somewhat differently, that a history can be grasped only in the very inaccessibility of its occurrence.[35]

When the women hit bottom long before any thoughts of the end of the world, they resolve the friction inside and betwixt them as communities of women might have through the ages. They do this not through war, or might, or erasures, but by writing out their fears. Connie rises from the crypt of her wine-stocked cellar, engages them all together in a hair-shearing ritual, makes them draw themselves upon the floor and then teaches them to dream aloud. Slowly, they learn to wrench themselves apart from their nightmares, sever their shell-shocked pasts from their biology, and inhabit the geography of the convent fully. The night preceding the massacre, they welcome the rain, let it dance on their bald heads, and dance. Liberated, the characters commune with one another and form a support not ventured within the auspices of state constitutions or pioneer, brave new worlds like Haven and Ruby. Having tumbled onto one another from nowhere places while going nowhere, with no clear plans, no agendas crafted and no ambition in sight, the characters sublimate friction into resolution as close to heaven from here as possible. The novel narrates from the unique point of view of women characters perched in paradise.

Founding Fathers of Ruby

To date, Morrison represents an oeuvre of such significance that an exhaustive and well-written encyclopedia exists solely devoted to her works. She writes, as Elizabeth Ann Beaulieu points, about bruised and battered black women marginalized within the margins.[36] Morrison, also deeply interested in the forgotten facet of African American history and their trek westward into deserted deserts of Oklahoma, Kansas, and such states, reads newspapers from the turn of the century when many fledgling black towns invited new residents, but accepted only those with capital.[37] Both the twins hear the same stories, store it as the largest occupant in their minds, and yet, ultimately they digest differently.

They listened to, imagined and remembered every single thing because each detail was a jolt of pleasure, erotic as a dream, out-thrilling and more purposeful than even the war they had fought in.[38]

Their "mutual resentment which surfaced in small ways"[39] ends exploding in the climactic moment during the violence at the convent when Deacon lifts arms to stop the carnage and Steward shoots Connie in the forehead. In Steward, memory manifests ultimately as an excess of violence while in Deacon, it initially manifests as an excess of love. Deacon, having transgressed against the institutions of history, patriarchy, matrimony, and the unsaid laws of Ruby, by engaging in a passionate affair with a younger Consolata, seems to inhabit a more troubled space. His conscience exercises greater autonomy than is permitted within the strictures laid upon the oven. He is not the one to threaten to shoot the youngster who might see a different motto than "beware" on the oven. He has been in the space where amidst the entwined trees on rocks and leaves, he just was. He has inhabited the space of "be." He is willing to read the same past he shares with Steward differently. Realizing that meaning is slippery, history resistant to discourse, when finally he understands Steward is the stronger man, Deek knows he does not want to possess such strength. He walks across town barefoot and confesses their tale of violence to Richard Misner while knowing that it is only a very diffident beginning. At the end of everything, in the aftermath of the bloodbath at the convent, Deek is interested in how the future might be written with remorse, rather than rage. In those moments, a story of brotherly love gone awry appears in contrary light and he accepts it. Big Papa, or Zechariah, a.k.a. Coffee, the setter in stone of the words on the oven, left behind a brother named Tea who chooses to dance for taunting whites while Coffee chooses to take a bullet in the foot. Always having been troubled by Big Papa's decision to leave behind his twin brother, Deek realizes after the massacre that the shame of Tea's actions was in him, a shame so deep and horrifying that he chooses to split rather than remain brothers. Deek understands this history in his own impulse to sever the twinhood he shares with Steward. Deek, too, lives in a community imagined with the fathers who travel across the country, but his is an a posteriori conversation that is organic, sliding, and ready to adapt itself to the crisis at hand.[40] Memory lingers in different shapes in the two identical bodies of Steward and Deek, bodies so identical that when Connie rides in Steward's truck mistaking him for her ex-lover, she identifies the difference long before the conflagration at the convent by the antithetical aura of a man she does not know. Headed by dualism, the town of Ruby maintains a Manichean core.

From Matriarchal Labor to Patriarchal Symbol: The Oven

The oven is the symbolic heart of this community's body.[41] It, too, is wrested of meaning and becomes a marker of massacre instead of lushness and life. A deeply feminine symbol, metonym for the domestic sphere orchestrated by women, it is instituted by the founding fathers of Haven at its town's center so that it can operate as a collective kitchen. It boasts openly that the black women of Haven and later, Ruby never cooked in other people's kitchens, meaning white masters or wealthy employers. Instituted by the women to bake bread for all of Haven until modernity and in the case of Ruby, the convent bread, an alternate feminine site of labor replaces the utility of the communal oven. As the oven transform from its original purposes over time, so does the discourse that peoples its geography. Earlier, women gathered, baking bread together and channeling the long course of their trek to this ground of stability where their men could break bread in peace, removed from the ills structuring the larger world.

One imagines a community bustling with the women, men, their ancestors, ghosts of those who died on the way, and the significant characters of history who only exist in the mouths of their progeny. No longer used by women, it is reinvested by the very patriarchy that originated it, moved it piece by piece from Haven to Ruby, and reassembled it carefully with the motto in place. It is the location of the male culture that forbids the youth from expressing their positions, voicing dissent, or rereading the partly visible inscription upon the oven walls, the site where Royal and his peers attempt to empower their place in the history and political life of the larger nation, the place where they are denied their basic right to speak. The oven is literally where patriarchy is inscribed upon the body of the woman, and the site from where its judgments ensue. Toward the climactic moment in the text as the momentum toward the massacre builds, the oven is the very location where Lone DuPres overhears the male conspiracy to attack, shoot, and destroy the female residents of the convent.

This gendered psychic affect of oppression bears kinship to subaltern scholarship that charts the relationship between colonialism, nationalism, and the women. Partha Chatterjee[42] writes much about this triangulation of power where the nationalists, in order to develop their own identity as separate from their colonialist oppressors, dictate upon the woman's body the burdens of bearing the new nation. The women, by staying shuttered in the domestic sphere, and representing the new nation as different from the hegemonic systems which speaks of a feminist liberation, serve to define the new state at the cost of their own exclusion. Here women represent the mores and traditions of Ruby. Thus, by removing themselves from any active role in the public sphere, to the extent of even removing their female community founded at the oven, patriarchal prescriptions are written similarly upon their bodies as on the body of the oven. Ruby, a haven found by both men and women only seems to mention the founding fathers in public performances of their particular history. Once the oven diminishes as the space where the public and private sphere collapse and the woman can be seen, or possibly heard, the women recede from the frontlines of Ruby along with the oven as if they too do not exist.

Once a space of animus, the oven becomes the site of animosity. When patriarchal orders of power and destruction occupy the original site of feminine inspiration, the community, imagined and alive crumbles. The oven, once a site of nurturing community turns into the symbol of massacre.

In the midst of the debate about the motto held at the calvary, Misner intrudes on a key moment when asked to silence the brazen youth, he replies, "Why would I want to? We're here not just to talk but to listen too."[43] Misner sets the stage for community as he envisions it, an open circuit of affect and discourse never practiced before in Ruby. Misner warrants change, in that he wants to alter the reigning order within Ruby which dictates only the 8-Rocks remember, and remember correctly. Only their history matters and dictates the future, and the elders lay the law on how the young will live their lives. His willingness to listen marks a radical departure from the wall between generations that disallows dialog. By inhabiting the position of double-consciousness in a historically African American way, reigning in a place of power and allying with the dispossessed such as the youth, Misner cultivates disorder within the ordered echelons of Ruby. But, in placing Misner in the midst of the African American diaspora, Morrison presents a double critique; while the novel enfolds along the parallel life of white racism and its repercussions on their black brethren, Morrison does not let the black denizens of Ruby go uncharged for excesses of power themselves. Peter Widdowson, in charting the detailed real history alongside the chronology created in non-linear subtlety by Morrison, adduces this tantamount fact in the middle of his own essay. He writes:

> Thus, Morrison on the one hand offers a specifically *black* history, pointing to the culpability for it of white America's "failures" to apportion basic civil rights equally, whilst simultaneously celebrating that history's achievements and identifying its own failings. But, on the other, she seems to be offering a general history of America from the re-angled perspective of black experience; as she notes in *Playing in the Dark:* "Africanism is inextricable from the definition of Americanness—from its origins on through its integrated or disintegrating twentieth-century self" (Morrison 1992: 65). The history of black America over two hundred years, in other words, is the history of America over that period—and especially of the "failure" of its founding principles. Neither is this just a history of the way white America has treated black Americans: at a more allegorical level, it is indeed a history of the whole American experience.[44]

The youth, whose voice is presumably presented during the calvary meeting by the Beauchamp brothers, Royal and Destry, represent an effort to empower the present, translate the powerful legacy of their past into brilliant light for the future. They want to erase fear and wrath from their collective psychology, symbolized by the word, "beware" in the motto, and read it as they imagine their forefathers treasured for them, "be." The ontological verb carries within its linguistic capacity, room for self-empowerment, agency, and the ability to see God within the self, rather than an outside force of instruction and retribution. Like the elders, they are guilty in a gendered way; "but they didn't want to discuss; they wanted to instruct." Unlike the elders, they want to resist the law that threatens to swallow them whole, the Law of the Father.[45]

The conversation is symbolic at the outset because it haggles on the placement of a motto written generations ago upon an anachronism, the collective oven. According to Rob Davidson, the novel itself is an allegorical reworking of America, its novelistic time set in 1976, the bicentennial celebration of United States of America, and both, examples of failure considering the goals of inclusion and community set at the outset. Davidson asserts that within all documents of civilization are the coded documents of barbarism. Regarding the quality of history and the difference between the young and the old as deciphered from the dialectic established at the oven, he writes,

> The scene exposes competing concepts of communal historiography. The older generation is firmly committed to its extant narrative. As they understand it, the story includes every fact about how the 8-Rocks got to Haven and the meaning of that ordeal. They are loathe to change it. Misner and the younger generation want to rewrite the extant narrative. For them, history is open and dynamic.[46]

In Davidson's paradigm, there is a striking similarity between the Ruby bildungsroman, as the life story of a community, and the traditional American immigrant saga of arrival, with the elders wanting to maintain their memory, ordeal, and customs in a static ritual, against the younger ones who wish for grace and fluid interchange between several cultures. Ruby patriarchs adopt the classic American pilgrim allegory, in its stead forgetting the heritage of African American saga of exclusion from the norm, and an acceptance greater than any other community. In their corruption, the elders write their demise in their own greatness, bearing a fatal resonance to the patricide of Oedipus. The youth want their share in writing the future of the community. The elders, in ignoring this participation of the populace thriving within their own community, sow the seeds of discord amidst their own. Community is always already in a state of fallen grace.

In pledging to stay in this community, and vowing that there is "no better place to be than among these outrageously beautiful, flawed and proud people,"[47] I believe for Misner the community, though spiritually profound in his declaration that nothing is alive until it dies, is really an allusion to the imagined community I will touch upon later. He lives within the material world, and this point is underlined by his material union with Anna Flood. He cares for the material world's upkeep, maintenance, and betterment. Justine Tally, in her analysis of these two characters, dwells on their unearthly experience in the convent after the massacre. Anna sees a closed door and Richard an open window, evidence of the symbology of the other as always already present within the lives of these two characters who represent the future of Ruby.[48]

While the dead enter Misner's geography through that closed door he sees at the convent, they provide radical political authority to the youth. Not directly implicated or affected by the massacre, or violence so direct that it erases completely, they suffer the consequence of violence implicit in the linguistic structure of their community. The dead are relevant, and imagining them is critical, but it is not as populated and voluble a space as will be apparent in the following section which turns its attention to the women at the convent.

Community at the Convent

Death is alive for the women at the convent. It is a part of existence, not the end of it. Neither is the convent what its name implies, nor are its women nuns. Though started as a missionary school by nuns for Indian girls, the last nun dies like a Grand Mater under the care of Consolata Sosa. The last Indian refugee is a distant memory as the first drifter drifts in like dry leaves of autumn, Mavis. Following Mavis, the large mansion, once a deceptor's dream, becomes the haven for the lost and the weary, directed or finding on their own the single place that would house their vagabond selves. They occupy the "out there"—a "wild zone," "unmonitored and seething; became a void where random and organized evil erupted when and where it chose—behind any standing tree, behind the door of any house, humble or grand."[49] The "out there" is formed as a result of a second exodus undertaken by the pioneers who move their original Haven to Ruby, and the outside is necessary to this band of insiders who prosper on their community that invites no one and thrives on solitude.

Once the oven within Ruby relinquishes its role as the bread-maker of the community, the women gain stability and find a route to their material survival. For their exquisite breads, pickles, and sauces, they enter a secret economy to survive replacing their function as the outcaste kitchen to become, in fact, the de facto hearth of Ruby's home. Roberta Rubenstein observes in her discourse on domesticity the centrality of food to this narrative of failed transcendence.[50] To add to Rubenstein's observation that all the female characters are associated with food, the women of the convent, though they occupy the "wild zone" also double as the "domestic," albeit their association with food, nurture, and appetites remains under the official radar of the town's patriarchs. Food is a secret language that belongs to the female characters alone and bridges the women in the town proper to the women who live "out there." All at once haven and kitchen and womb[51] outside the sanctioned authority of the patriarchs or 8-Rocks of Ruby, they exist only in the various townspeople's separate interactions with it but remain outside in that they are ungoverned, managed neither by the patriarchs of the state or the town.

However the townspeople of every generation are implicated in this trade of desire, food, and home that the convent symbolizes over time. It almost becomes the Haven that Ruby was in the process of attempting to be, but under the surveillance of "beware," it falls short of its goals. Ruby falls short of completely erasing the other it deems to be out of control, foul, and corroding the moral fiber of its own pure fabric, and this sentiment is expressed in the way Nada Elia connects Mary Louise Pratt's theory of "contact zone" to the discourse of difference within the text. She writes:

> I also argue that the two poles respectively represent the Western and Africana polarities, and the different sets of values that go with these epistemologies: materialism, individualism, and linearity in the Western sphere, spirituality, communality and cyclicality in the Africana sphere. As in Pratt's coinage, "contact zone," where unequal systems come together,

the interaction of these epistemologies parallels that of dominant/ subordinate discourses, in that the first also seeks to impose its values on the subordinate, unaware that in doing so, it necessarily renders the subordinate polyvocal: it is impossible to ever completely erase alternative or unofficial knowledge, only temporarily suppress it.[52]

The convent is the contact zone and even after the massacre of its residents, resistance emerges and polyvocality persists. Despite their presence at the margins and further marginalization by the violent erasure, however, these women are never fully erased from the memory or psyche of the denizens of Ruby.

Kubitschek's earlier point about the failure of the written and the oral within the image offered in this novel echoes again in a point made by Justine Tally about writing on the body. Once a symbol of pain, "the body becomes the tableau for the inscription of trauma,"[53] as in the case of Seneca bloodying her wrists and Pallas kicking dirt on to her name she scrawls in the dirt. The woman's body becomes a site of affirmation in the convent, with the women accepting one another, calling each other by name, and under Connie's guidance, writing their fears upon the edifice of their very lives, their bodies. What is important to the town is not what is important to the women. They live, literally and metaphysically, in a world all their own, liberated by the borderless seams of their own chalky mapmaking.[54]

Ghost Children

Mavis comes home to the convent, after having driven for days as a fugitive from the law, her family, and her living children. At the convent, there is no radio and no newspaper. Thus the outside world is not only abstract, but absent. So are the murders she is running from, the murder of her twin babies, Merle and Pearl, whom she left in a hot car without a window open in order to buy some canned meat. In the middle of an incomplete dinner she is preparing, she does this in the fear of a husband who helped her find her way to the hospital ten times because of the brutality of his "love." Abused and overwhelmed, her crime is explained to the media in terms of her "stupidity," never as part of a narrative of abuse. Gender remains the qualifier ignored on all sides of the discussion except the categorization of her as a "dumb woman."

Punished and broken, unwilling to help Connie shell the pecans, she hears the twins amidst a number of other ghost children who populate the mansion. Thinking she is hallucinating, she closes her eyes and opens them only to find the presence stronger and salient. In the ethereal upper room where the Grand Mater lies, there is a peculiar light without any electricity and the irascible old woman talks about children crowding her door in the empty mansion. The imagined beings are a regular and constant presence at the convent. Before even being formally welcomed by Connie or the dying Grand Mater, Mavis already becomes a part of an imagined community with the dead at the convent.

Mavis leaves many times only to come back and lives there till the day of the massacre in 1976, growing older with her children, stitching dresses for them, weaving love alongside her guilt, and watching them grow in a world where the border between the world of the living and the dead is porous. Merle and Pearl and their residence in the convent draws Mavis back over and over again, more of a home than the one from which she runs: children whom she fears, a husband who beats her blue. "In fact she had an outer-rim sensation that the kitchen was crowded with children—laughing? Singing?—two of whom were Merle and Pearl."[55] The imagined community with the dead is not only available, but progresses in time, sustaining Mavis and resuscitating her back to life. The dead bring her back into the land of the living.

Stonecold Lovers

Rock hard, self-sufficient, unnervingly beautiful, sexy and lonely, Grace, under the alias Gigi is the stone woman. She seeks a large stone sculpture of two figures making love in the desert taking up the sky, "Moving, moving, all the time moving."[56] Somewhere outside Wish, Arizona, she hopes her boyfriend Mikey, the convict, will show up as he had conjured up these elusive lovers she cannot seem to find in any western town. When the trail runs cold, she finds the convent, arriving in the heart of Ruby dressed to the nines. She inflames the men, irritates the women, and ends up in the convent being an even greater annoyance to Mavis, who is not used to such effrontery and decadence.

K.D., the loose stone in the edifice of Ruby's bulwark, rolls toward her and she kicks him around for fun, holds him close, warms him, and then throws him back to the wind from where he came. Deathly afraid of the dead, and all it implies for the end of her ebullience, as shown by her arrival on the eve of Grand Mater's death, her hesitation from the hearse, and fear of sleeping anywhere where the body had been, Gigi is not as practical and wary of the supernatural as her fears imply. Her desire points to the surreal in her wish to find a place where sculptures move, stone sighs, and a couple without life remains moving for eternity.

Gigi, lost and unmoored, deserting a granddaddy out east and a lover in prison, or possibly having been deserted, seeks to find in her loud talking, devil may care, eyebrow raising attitude to life, a certain quest to find herself apart from the debris of a life steeped in loneliness and rejection. Asked to leave the wedding for being brazen, dressed for the dance club rather than a church wedding, Gigi continues her never-ending fight with Mavis. They even stop the car to fight on the road side, the two of them pulling out hair and clothing to vent their grievances. She almost finds the eternal couple, or a comparable delight, two trees intertwined by a brook.

Gigi stays around for years at a home without any hierarchy, without men, or familiar routes of escape. It is a place marked by death at the beginning. Strange events transpire during her duration there. Women live in communion with the dead, and Gigi endures on, undaunted and absolutely at home till the very end. Apart from the ruling rubric of her sensual odyssey which sets her apart, Gigi without really being aware, becomes an active resident and prime navigator of the imagined community with the dead.

The Woman Who Was Five

Seneca, abandoned at the age of five in an apartment in government housing project, hitches rides hidden behind trucks all over the country. She forgets in her nationwide sojourns for whom she continues her search but everywhere, she is unable to endure the sight of a crying black woman. Seneca's affect, a melancholic connection to the souls of black women, makes her the prototypical resident of the convent community.

At the age of five, she spends five long days alone in an apartment doing all the things she thinks will bring her caretaker back. Five days into this horror, she finds the same woman, crying, almost turned a different color, with a caseworker who handles her life and distributes her to various anonymous institutions from then on. The saddest part of the saddest episode of her life is the blurred nature of her melancholy; she has never been told and is not fully sure if the woman who abandoned her was her mother or an older sister. To Seneca, family is splintered at the blurred genesis of her existence. The convent community plays the foil for a lifetime of accumulated losses. Severed from the familial community at the age of five, Seneca houses in her skeletal arms thousands of bereaved, becoming a one-woman community at every truck-stop. She carries her own truckload of ghosts in a house already full of ghosts; to her, imagining community with the dead is an old habit that finds its proper home at the convent.

Last to Come, First to Die

Pallas arrives decked in plastic and reeking of wealth and vomit. Billie Delia delivers her to the convent where women in trouble can land without questions being asked and food being given. The nature of her trouble remains ambiguous as Kubitschek writes, "Unprotected and alone, she undergoes some kind of violation near a pond. Pallas is haunted by nightmare images from her real experience—a crazy woman saying 'Here's pussy. Want some pussy, pussy' and memories of the pond."[57] Upon arriving, Seneca guides her to Connie and Pallas sits on the matriarch's lap and pours out her answer to Connie's, "Who hurt you, little one?"[58] To the youngest and newest arrival at the convent, even with the alcohol and morbidity of her own past, Connie comes into full form as Grand Mater, the mother to all lost souls. Mourning the death of Sister Mary, she occupies the vacated throne by inaugurating community with every stray arrival, her munificence bridging her to her acolytes.

Violence trails each woman. The details of Pallas's violation gain physicality through her expanding belly. She tells about her journey across unknown terrain in a truck full of Indians and finding herself in Billie Delia Cato's hospital ward. Intent on calling her irate father, she ends up as the youngest resident, wide-eyed and unsure, but at peace in a house she hopes will be as "peaceful" as Mavis declares it to be. She had fallen in love with a sculptor-janitor who worked in her high school and she ran away from her father with him to find her artist-mother in New York. The mother, upon being found, delves into learning the contours of Carlos more intimately than the daughter had intended in her journey out east. Discovering the truth of her condition as a double outcaste, at home on neither coast, Pallas finds herself at sea in the heartland. Pallas Truelove finds love in the eerie and surreal unexpected house of women she never could have located on a map from either coast. The question of race remains unresolved. Who exactly is the white woman who is shot in the opening? Many scholars contend it is Pallas. I insist on ambiguity; either Pallas or Seneca could be white. In a refusal to identify along racial lines exists the method to really understand how bodies are read in non-normative fashion within the convent walls. Morrison is playing here with notions of race, and how writers have placed negative values on its darker characters while allowing the white characters to signify normativity. McKay Jenkins pays attention to Morrison's analysis of this dichotomy in her formidable text, *Playing in the Dark*, while writing his essay on Lillian Smith in a particularly significant anthology, since it was edited, in part, by a teacher of mine who did not live to see its publication, Safiya Henderson-Holmes, along with Ellen J. Gouldner. Interestingly enough, this anthology, *Racing and (E)racing Language: Living with the Color of our Words* began its inspiration from Toni Morrison's call for more dialogs on race within the American nation-state. Within Morrison's umbra, observes McKay, there is a two-way price paid for dehumanizing metaphors. Both blacks and whites are emptied of meaning within this landscape of hollowed affect, and both races become tinged with excess.[59] These self-limiting ontologies offer the blacks an excess of sexuality and the whites, an excess of isolation and repression.

The convent, marked racially as an "othered" space where at least one of its residents is white, though inconsequentially so, the blackness of its space casts within its pale the metaphor of an excessive and aberrant "sexuality" normatively coded as black. Jenkins' observation about the "disembodied ghosts" ever present in Morrison's landscapes, the white women and children are abundant to the point of an anonymous over-population within this apocalyptic novel. Whatever her race might be, her history of exile, suffering, and violation make Pallas at one with the community established "out there" in the convent's walls.

Excess of Love

Consolata Sosa is the boatswain on River Styx, the most candid camer-
awoman of happenings beyond the realm of the normal. Always having
been in the middle of things, neither here nor there, Connie, picked up
in anonymous slums in South America by Sister Mary Magna who falls
in love with her green eyes, is neither black nor white, the two races that
register in 1970s American ethos. But her home is also in the middle of
things, a convent in the heart of Oklahoma that is Catholic in Protestant
territory, and slowly stops being Catholic or a convent once its charges
dwindle into absence. Born into a new life as Connie, cared for by Mary
Magna, she becomes the caretaker soon enough and looks after her life-
giver. Their roles switch and Connie makes the mansion viable in more
ways than merely economic. Instead of merely meditating on the bread
of life, namely the Catholic Church, she bakes bread to barter.

She bakes bread for the town but is never part of the official kitchens of Ruby, nor considered a legitimate female entity by its powers.
She loves with profound ardor once, her brief and anguished affair with
Deacon Morgan, but is left desolate. Left in the heat of love, she recoils
back in a middle space between her great love for God and an earthly
love for Mary Magna. She is neither guardian nor mother to the women
who arrive at her doorstep, heartbroken, broken bodied, full of questions but she occupies a central position in the middle of their lives.
Neither witch nor saint, what the people of Ruby or her cohabitants
might consider her, she assumes charge of her scattered congregation
and leads them from darkness into light, from the land of the living for
forays into the other world, shepherding them between worlds into the
middle space that has always housed her. If paradise is located here and
now, somewhere in the arid landscape of the American hinterland, then
Connie possesses the imaginary map to its locus.

Tired of the "disorder, deception, and drift" of her boarders, Connie
rises to take charge and lead them into the world of their own, a world
that is available to them and at once, imprisons them. She unlocks the
cages and leads them in, through chalk drawings of the body and more
elaborate etching of all their fears and demons. Already skilled in Lone
DuPres's work as midwife and recommended and tutored by the same
guru, skilled in rescuing those who teeter on the brink of death by pouring her life force, or light into them and bringing them back, Connie

is trained in inhabiting middle spaces. She learns its power to heal the hurt. Long before making paradise with the women, Connie's work involves in engaging with community at its most vulnerable: birthing the babies and rescuing the dying.

The town father, Deacon Morgan, a man who can afford no trespass beyond the norm, falls for Connie in 1954 in the early years of Ruby. She, in turn, falls in absolute love with him. When he leaves her, he is horrified and troubled by his condition and her great lust which makes her bite his lips in passion and then lick the blood, an action he is never able to obliterate from his mind. The very same image aids in the project of vanquishing such a brood of women from the convent during the massacre. Deek's wife, Soane, becomes fast friends with the same woman who takes her husband away from her, albeit for brief spells throughout her waking life. Connie rescues their son, Scout after a roadside accident and infuses her light into his dead body, kindling in Soane not only forgiveness, but a gratitude so enormous that one lifetime of empathy does not completely satisfy what she feels for Connie, even though her sons return in body bags from the war in Vietnam later. Connie was able to give Soane what the state took away later, her son's life. Even from the center of Ruby, Soane becomes a permanent member of the convent's community.

When Connie, deeply in love with the living man, Deacon, makes love under the intertwining fig trees, that first symbol of innocence and shame, Deek says, "I've never seen anything like you. How could anything be put together like you? Do you know how beautiful you are?"[60] Later spent and desolate, alone, broken, lost in liquor and memory, Connie rises to find a space marked "beautiful" and leads her raggedy band of nomads with her. Beauty, not on the body or skin-deep, neither inside or outside, but an actual space which reveals the self to the self and renders one less repugnant each day on this earthly odyssey. She configures the biology of beauty by dissociating each of the women from their elaborate map of pain, isolation, and violence. Beauty, instead, arises from wells deep within each woman. These women's bodies were marked under the patriarchal gaze of the state and kinship structures as suspicious, criminal, and unworthy. With Connie's practice of an excess of love, the women learn to commune and redefine notions of beauty and self-worth. Bald and inspired, the women dance under the moonlight like witches, and all of their power poses clear threat to normative structures of power and patriarchy set in the town of fathers, Ruby. Outside the law of the father, they dare to rename themselves in a community of their own imagination. For this, they are shot.

Connie, the queen of the middle space, rendered dead by what is living, manages to learn the art of turning death into life and life into a heaven on earth. Like the female author, her progenitor Morrison who considers the imaginary a key function of her art, or bell hooks, slightly different in her utilizing the function of her art as therapeutic, Connie and these writers reconfigure the political alongside the symbolic.[61] Her difference is precisely the secret of her success, the reason paradise is possible from the convent, but not from Ruby. Richard Schur, while locating the novel within the purview of contemporary critical race theory and Morrison's own project to remove the racialized gaze from the narrative, and place racial ambiguity upon some of the itinerants at the convent, points that Connie's success comes in her hybridity, or difference that is a welcoming embrace to the wanderers. Connecting it to Homi Bhabha's discourse on "hybridity" or "thirdness," Schur writes:

> It is Consolata who offers the path toward decolonization. Unlike the eight-rock who claim racial purity, Consolata constitutes the path of negotiation and hybridity.... The attack on the convent coincides with the women's effort to decolonize their minds. This decolonization begins with a pronouncement from Connie: "I call myself Consolata Sosa...." In this passage, Connie renames herself Consolata, which constitutes an effort to make herself anew and cast off the colonialist gaze that has marked her body and mind.[62]

The end of her affair, the consolation given to Consolata moves into the moment when a sun ray blinds her and gifts her by endowing her with the brilliance of a second sight, a sixth sense, a subliminal energy which lets her see more, beyond the ordinary, even beyond the living. The darkness fails her when she bites her lover and treads into dangerous depth of intoxication but at the same time, it is darkness that suits her best in the condition of blindingly new vision, the darkness that helps her see with precision everything that the rest cannot see, "She might not have agreed so quickly, but as Mary Magna led her out of the chapel into the schoolroom, a sunshot seared her right eye, announcing the beginning of her bat vision, and she began to see best in the dark. Consolata had been spoken to."[63] Connie is a visionary; her blindness and second sight enable her to see what others cannot and ignore the ordinary details available to all. Her community is the result of this splendid vision, and it then becomes necessary for the patriarchs to erase this alternative vision for community space as envisioned in the convent "out there."

Before the first uninvited occupant, Mavis, Connie already is a specimen of solitude and fortitude, having lost language, embarrassment, and vision. "Every now and then she found herself speaking and thinking in that in-between place, the valley between the regulation of the first language and the vocabulary of the second."[64] Always in between places, faces, and stories, Connie is able to enter people, narrative, and geography with an access that makes her indubitably and disarmingly the arresting soul of lost spaces, the interlocutor of the unseen. Connie is Morrison's blind old woman who lives in the parable she tells her Swedish audience at Stockholm upon receiving the Nobel Prize for literature in 1993, the seeress like Cassandra no one believes, especially the young who want to test her, and then learn from her. Blind, marginalized, living on the crossroads of legitimacy,[65] Connie like the heroine of the parable retains a power and precision of vision that allows her to see the power of language. She knows the power is in their hands, the broken and marked hands of the women surrounding her. She locates agency within the people who populate her convent when she awakens to redeem the weak and begin her work with pregnant Pallas's gloom.

Linda Krumholz surmises a delicate connection between Connie's "stepping-in," the women painting on the floor, and the reader entering this narrative, a reader-response theory that engages the text and the axis upon which its characters stand all at once.[66] In a radical act of community that envelops even the reader, the text extends its "out there" to the reader out there who is peeping into this ethereal world of both the bodied and the disembodied.

Nurturing the babies and the brazen, the ruined and the dead, she rises from her alcoholic stupor and engages the living around her to accept themselves. She commands them:

> I call myself Consolata Sosa. If you want to be here you do what I say. Eat how I say. Sleep when I say. And I will teach you what you are hungry for … if you have a place that you should be in and somebody who loves you waiting there, then go. If not stay here and follow me. Someone could want to meet you.[67]

Connie's insistence on hierarchy stands apart from the patriarchal need to subjugate, regulate, or dictate the movements of the masses; instead she wants to unleash what is hidden and silenced. She wants to support the women in finding their secret selves, cauterizing the wounds, and battering the damage that enfeebles their lives. Her hierarchy, insistent like the anarchy of Dionysus, is an invitation to revel, cajole, and submit to the pleasures in a dance away from the normative or valorized. Contrasting the Apollonian order of Haven, the convent is the Dionysian space of anarchic revelry. The "someone" who might want to meet these vagabond spirits is possibly the already dead, and Connie unleashes irregular forces of liberation to replace the oppression that marks the lives of her freeloaders.

Imagining a community outside the borders of Ruby, or for that matter, the wild space of the convent, even outside the purview of any seen authorities, Connie, with her enlightened green gaze and luminous skin, enlivens the dead and invigorates the living by teaching them to tread the middle space. The women step into an empowerment offered outside the aegis of patriarchal inscriptions. "Out there," Connie forges a community that lays the blue print for imagining community with the dead.

Heaven on Earth, Hallowed at Last

During the event of violence, a massacre to be exact, since men point and shoot guns at unarmed and surprised women, the narrative remains ambiguous about what exactly happens. Who is shot? Who dies? Who remains alive? How do they escape?[68] Morrison develops the sort of narrative that is impossible to encapsulate within the straightforward frame of the journalistic encounter with the incident. In the gray of early morning light, the shooters are not clear on who all falls, except for the white woman and Connie whom Steward shoots in the middle of her forehead. In the aftermath of the massacre, the story refuses to stabilize and changes within the vagaries of storytelling, depending on the speaker, context, and audience.

The massacre brings death into the community of immortals in Ruby, making the death of Save-Marie the first event mapping the postlapsarian world of Ruby. Morrison maps traditional African American theology into Ruby's genesis and we are led to believe that the pure line of 8-Rocks do not die. Encapsulated in the protagonist, John Washington's historical ruminations in David Bradley's novel,[69] we are told, "For before the white men came to Guinea to strip-mine field hands for the greater glory of God, King and the Royal Africa Company, black people did not die."[70] Death, in this context, is never the final act for the dead mingle with the living, never so alien as to be mourned and severed from their kin. Lone's word, "livid" and fleshy in the extreme, stands at a lonely extreme, ready to be disbelieved as the ravings of a radical old woman no one needs anymore.

The Edenic community is fractured; the "othered" one rises to live anew. Even though in life they were oppressed, once extracorporeal, they return as spirits fully engaged in the female labor of paradise-making. Once again, the imagined community that communes undetected by the surveillance systems of the powerful is Basavanna's "things moving." They float above and beyond regulatory systems, disembodied and beyond punishment for transgression. The liminal zone of the dead functions as the site of profound transgression.

Women Rising

Post-massacre, the novel evidences sightings of each of the women who were killed at the convent. Scholars point to these last visitations as the presence of Africanist traditions within the narrative that configures the return of life ended violently as a spirit, or *revenant*.[71] However, Morrison's text differs from the traditional discourse maintained in Afro-Caribbean thought; instead of the spirits returning to advice and guide those who are living, here the women return to redress old wounds. They correct and complete the site of their individual traumas and do so giving a glimpse into an alternate community of the dead who wander, speak, and exert agency to such a degree that the existential question arises: Who are they? Of what matter are they made? These are the women engaged in a specifically female labor of paradise-making. Each sighting remains teeming with ambiguity, and one cannot surmise with certitude if the women are alive, spirits, or memories of the tormented souls they left behind. Philip Page, in his effort to place the function of free interpretation upon the reader akin to Connie's "stepping in" comes closest to the amplitude of this final geography.[72] Page's point about "passing beyond the merely rational" helps us access the less visible community that marks an ungovernable site of resistance. What I offer is a suggestion to avoid formalist details and instead *imagine* this community of the dead which cannot be contained within pragmatic epistemologies of the material world.

Next to the water, where Grace's father the lifer is working on the road, she sits on a picnic blanket, dressed in soldierly outfit, camouflage, heavy boots, black t-shirt. Later her father thinks that she is "packing." Her image signifies a transformed Gigi, part soldier, part seductress. She likes to bathe nude in open stretches of water, carries guns, and sounds more like a warrior woman than a woman lost. To her excited father's questions about a place he can send her his two-stamps worth of love, she replies, "I don't have an address yet,"[73] leaving mysterious the ground beneath her feet, her exact location on terra firma. Gigi, warrior turned goddess, looks to the water where "her companion was just coming ashore."[74] Gigi's turning is evidence at a collective effort, a force singular yet unified, and tells the presence of other women, her convent cohabitants trekking everywhere with her, swimming underwater as she meets her last necessary link.

In a similar vein, when Pallas is sighted, the event is inflected with greater ethereal quality. Her mother, the woman who betrays Pallas with her lover, witnesses her beside the house, rummaging under the guest bed for an expensive pair of her own shoes. Pallas means to walk a long way wherever she is going and she means to go far away from the source of her pain. The mother is not able to make sounds, just illegible grunts, indistinct or recognizable to her daughter who does not stop to listen. She carries a baby and a sword, the baby strapped to her chest, and the sword held aloft in her hand, both symbolizing the warrior and woman at once. Similar to Merle and Perle who grow older in the mansion, Pallas has miraculously given birth after being shot and the baby is a creature born in the hereafter. Here again the mother witnesses companions, not clearly male or female, but waiting in a car which "they drove off into a violet so ultra it broke her heart."[75] Gigi's companion arises out of water akin to the birth of a goddess, signifying a community in a state of apotheosis rather than the solitary sighting of these figures.

Mavis meets the daughter, Sal or Sally Albright whose extraordinarily forceful pinches catapult her into a life of anonymity. Mavis is nonchalant, eager to eat, and ready to disappear. Mavis is physical in her appetites, sprite-like in affect. Sally, contrite and troubled, begs her mother to stay, come back again, and talk to the brother who is sinking. "Sally felt as though her mother was sliding away, acting like their seeing each other wasn't important,"[76] and though the "sliding" is cushioned in Sally's inference, the verb itself signifies more about the condition of existence which Mavis exudes, a middle space that makes even her presence a disappearing act.

Sliding suggests instability of meaning, so that Sally is left gleaning through a meeting that ends before it begins, and a past that disrupts her every waking moment. Like Pallas, Mavis is also bald striking her gold-dyed daughter as a bold and fashionable presence in the diner with other egg, bacon, and grit eaters. Mavis, the vegetarian, continues down the road shown by Connie and confesses to a mysterious pain in her side, the bullet wound that leaves her sore, but not dead. Mavis, the possible student and next-in-line to Connie's genius of stepping-in gives her daughter the gift of light in a moment so quick it is easily forgotten if it were not for that remarkable specter of light that surrounded the dark room of Mary Magna. Sal absorbs the light that fills her along with the mouthful of food she tastes from her mother's plate. Skilled or partly divine, Mavis, always generous and gifted like Connie, gives without telling. "Sally felt the nicest thing then. Something long and deep and slow and bright."[77] Mavis also disappears into crowd, but the "crowd" is significant because it contains the presence of sisters of the soul who accompany one another through these last farewells.

Finally we are presented, in a flashback in the woman's memory so the historical time remains unnamable, the specter of the mother who abandons her daughter to drugs and other people, Jean. In her many searches for her daughter whom she rightly sees at the back of trucks, she sees Seneca. Like the crucified Christ, Seneca is bleeding at the arms, but not alone in the parking lot of a stadium, with a girlfriend, who is wiping up the blood and patching up her broken pieces. There is poetic justice; Seneca refuses to recognize her cousin/mother who is forgiven at the same time, "That's okay. Everybody makes mistakes,"[78] as if forgiving her mother-in-disguise for abandoning her all those years ago, for daring to find her in this grim place of modern architecture, a place of darkness after all the games have ended, after life itself has receded. Jean finds in the car with her husband that she was the one who was wrong about her address; in fact, the bleeding girl had been right. The projects were located on Beacon, meaning a ray of light from which she arrived to lift the gloom from Jean's haunted conscience.

The women are fighting, walking, and going places. They eat, drink, and appear all at once to complete the narratives that excluded them on earth. Bald, armed, and golden, they fight and nurture one another, carrying babies or sopping up blood but always in the middle of things, doing, and being. Hierarchy is absent in this community's compass. The sightings point to an idealized women's community, immaterial in that it exists completely outside the name of the father, and is able to do everything in a collective of harmony and compassion.

Morrison represents powerful female characters who are not only anti-imperial, anti-patriarchal, but also, anti-material. She is impossible to locate, airy like a sprite, and present with others of like-spiritedness so that she is ready to fight. Each woman is never fully alone and always already present where she is. Living in some middle space between life and death, possibly alive or dead, they stay with one another, giving evidence of an imagined community no longer with the dead. In a Lacanian sense, they have traveled back through the Imaginary and the Symbolic to the Real, a space before language, ordering, and hierarchy, a place that is not reachable or understandable to the individuals who live their ordered existence upon earth.

Paradise is located in the Real. In a community of women who can fight the world, go where they place, trespass nowhere since they cannot be seen by the patriarchal authority, as with Gigi and the state guard that does not notice her presence in the gang of working prisoners, they stay bound together for eternity giving solace and contentment to one another. Once they treaded lightly on chalk imagining a community and now, they are the imagined community. They make a home in a middle space where they are at all places at once. Even in death, the women access agency in their persistent relationship with "be," redefining their sense of self-worth and right to exist within the syntagma of everyday living. By doing so in a community of women laboring to "do," unlike Basavanna's rich men who "make" temples, they mediate the nether space inaccessible through language but nevertheless textually situated within the novel.

Black Goddess Down Below

The women form the closest to an earthly paradise, involving "endless work they were created to do down here in Paradise,"[79] implying that it is not a condition of eternal permanence entombed within any religious, spiritual, or nationalistic discourse, nor fully part of Puritan, Catholic, Protestant, or Pagan metaphysics. Instead it is a place below, rather than the traditional height upon which such luminosity is imagined. Unlike the patriarchs of the larger nation-state or the ones of Ruby who fall prey to the same ills visited upon nation makers, these women move beyond the Manichean terms of binary good and evil. Ana Fraile Marcos posits *Paradise* as a critique of the American idea of nation-state arising from its historically puritan ethos,[80] allowing for the free interchange of race, gender, class, role, and authority. Marcos writes, pointing to the convent as Bhabha's third space of enunciation about its residents, "Their evolution testifies to the possibility of achieving the dream of an earthly paradise only by acknowledging difference and the integration of opposites."[81]

Bridging the distance between the Virgin Mary and the fallen Eve, Connie brings them to an order which involves a serene ideology of amalgamation between the two. By rejecting the separate, hierarchal organization of identity that excludes admission, Connie, by opening her home to any and all who wander in, and having lifted herself out of her own melancholy to do the noble deed of helping Pallas love her unborn child, Connie becomes like Christ. She is a leader, teacher, healer, and soothsayer outside any institutions.[82] Their sanctum sanctorum is the company they provide each other in which they dream aloud, inhabit one another's nightmares and divest themselves of the pasts that corrode and undermine their will to live, rejoice, dance under the falling rain. Here the text finally begins to answer to the haunting question posed at the beginning: How can a community form without the trope of self-destruction? The women form such a community that bestows upon its members the fundamental rights to agency, dignity, and vitality.

I return here to the moments when Connie carries them initially into liberation through her speech, and paints for them the world we see closest to paradise before the violent end of their corporality:

> She told them of a place where white sidewalks met the sea and fish the color of plums swam alongside children. She spoke of fruit that tasted the

way sapphires look and boys using rubies for dice. Of scented cathedrals made of gold where gods and goddesses sat in the pews with the congregation. Of carnations tall as trees. Dwarfs with diamonds for teeth. Snakes aroused by poetry and bells. Then she told them of a woman named Piedade, who sang but never said a word.[83]

Piedade is present, wrapping the world in her muse without uttering a word, an impossible presence that defies logic but symbolizes the integration of separateness espoused by dominant traditions of theology.

Piedade, a play on the Pietà, the figure of a mourning Mary with the Jesus on her lap, resonates with other such mythic play in the text. Pallas is black Athena, springing out of her father's solitude, who later strides with a sword and a child into eternity. Seneca calls to mind the stoic Roman philosopher who wrote the trilogy of treatises called *Consolationes*, returning to the figure of Consolate, the nucleus of this narrative. I refer to Ron David's explanations on the author that shed light on mythic and historical ground covered within the Morrison imaginary.[84] To David, the text points to women's mythology and feminine divinities all come to "be" in the final segments. Connie leads her flock closer to the paradise as realized in the presence of Piedade so it is doubly necessary for Morrison to end her text on a vision of Connie with her tea-brown hair resting on Piedad's "black as firewood" lap. Paradise, not out there or up there, not revealed in a book deified by an institution, a Piedade impossible to locate in any tract on religious authority but present marginally and always important, black, singing, full of "solace" in a landscape that recalls the polluted beaches of a world ruined by modernity, avarice, and progress. In this image of consolation configured between the goddess and Connie, even the memory is of what never was, an ideal community which allows for an open home, barring exclusion, "the ease of coming back to love begun."

"Morrison's *Paradise* explores coalition processes that are more accommodative, caring, and loving, rather than exploitative, and that are aimed principally at survival and at moving toward a new, alternative form of non-hierarchical justice, rather than at maximizing power and winning," writes Magali Michael. The "crew and passengers, lost and saved, atremble, for they have been disconsolate for some time," arrive on ships, the significance that there is no distinction or gradations made between the saved and the damned, for they all arrive together and "rest before shouldering the endless work they were created to do down here in Paradise."[85] It should not be lost on the reader that Morrison infects the melancholic image of the middle passage—sad people disembarking from ships—with the power of making paradise. Paradise is not a space for the select few who understand the biblical language; its liberatory work is done by the masses that were once oppressed, enslaved, denounced, and rejected. Together they toil to "do" the headless community. Piedade's earthly paradise is one in which labor the women who once inhabited her ideals in a convent, embracing both the body and spirit, unlike the embezzler or the nuns who were its occupants before. Piedade's paradise extends its membership to Mavis with her twins, a newly armed Gigi, Seneca with her blood map on wrists, Pallas with a bouncing baby born after she dies of a bullet, and Connie, shot in the forehead, singing, resting, dreaming, and desiring to make the earthly paradise continue its long trudge home.

The women transgress the norms of Ruby's culture by imagining a community aloof from the patriarchal legitimacy that excludes them. The massacre does not stop them from the act of imagination. They continue imagining community with the dead so that after being shot, violated and bloodied, they travel across the nation in a greater state of liberation. The community that begins in the hidden rooms of the convent guided by Connie continues in spaces where each woman ascends into the power endowed by mourning, sacrifice, and self-denigration, which had provided thematic unity to their narratives upon earth. Betwixt their labors, they rest on one another, recalling the Pietà except that each one of them is Mother Mary and each one is a daughter of God also. Such a vision of divinity is jarring to conventional theological discourse.

Generally leisure is reserved for the gods, and labor for humanity. The gods command while mortals serve. Heaven requires ascent and hell means a spiraling descent. In the final segment of the text, community is signified in contrast to all that has been conventional within the doctrine of the church and the laity. These women labor, love, and follow the visceral physicality of their earthly lives descending to do more in a paradise below. Such a circular return to the very space that violently assaulted their corporeal bodies is the same space imbued with divinity; Morrison's text suggests no real difference between the spaces traditionally separated by the tripartite structure common to nearly all world cultures: heaven, earth, and hell.

The community once imagined collectively at the convent is a narrative without interruption; the women return in more powerful forms to do more powerful labor. The former act of imagining community with the dead also means that one has to imagine community with the living, and both acts of imagination require a vitality that is configured by the liberation offered within the enlightenment particular to the women who arrive battered at the convent. The text points to the power of the broken, the ones wrested of voice. Lit by a peculiar light, such as the one lighting Mary Magna on her deathbed, Morrison's novel transmits a kinetic energy that connects the rest of the novels in this book.

2

Imagining Community in Edwidge Danticat's *The Farming of Bones*

In *The Farming of Bones* (1998), Edwidge Danticat writes about the tragic episode in Haitian history when thousands were massacred in 1937 by the Dominican president at the time, Rafael Trujillo. Edwidge Danticat, a Haitian-American writer whose literary works abound with themes of arrivals, memories, losses, acculturations and other crises in the context of Haitian communal experience in the United States, dwells on this historical chapter which left its mark on twentieth century Haitian history as well as Haitian and Dominican relations. In this novel, Danticat writes about this historical event by telling about the lives of a young pair of lovers, Amabelle Désir and Sebastien Onius, Haitians who work at the plantation of a Dominican family. The novel tells the stories of the Haitians and other laboring people who die in the massacre of 1937 and, in turn, we are made to witness the survival and melancholy of those who live, such as Amabelle. Amabelle crosses River Massacre that separates the two nations on the island of Hispaniola and retreats to Haiti and finds a sense of community amidst those who grieve and those who survive. As an old woman, Amabelle revisits her old plantation and its mistress after the death of Trujillo in 1960. Then instead of returning to her home in Haiti, Amabelle gives up her life on River Massacre, the place of crossings in this novel.

Through Amabelle, we begin to trace a living community with the dead. In the first section that follows, I start with what led Danticat into this subject and provide a brief historical and political context of this event and other phenomenon that contribute to the ontological tensions of these two nations inhabiting one island. In the second section of the chapter, I outline Amabelle's invocation of Sebastien Onius; also, Amabelle's repeated memories of her parents, drowning. In the third section I discuss, Amabelle's precarious link with the living—Señora Valencia, Juana, Luis, Papi, Kongo, and even Yves, her life-long mate; also, Amabelle's comfort in the arms of women who know death well— Man Rapadou, Man Denise, and even her own mother, Irelle Pradelle. In the fourth section, the chapter touches on Amabelle's fearlessness of the mad professor at River Massacre before she lies down on the river on the anniversary of the cutting of 1937, a gesture of good-bye and hello, Amabelle floats in comfort as if back in the womb. This leads to the fifth and final section where I extrapolate an imagined community with the dead within the text. The chapter remains marked by Amabelle's own watery death. In this final episode, her reassurance to the young driver of the jeep that she is not dead is only realized when she willingly forfeits life for what promises to be not simply death but a dawn. She carries herself into "...Sebastien's cave, my father's laughter, my mother's eternity."[1]

Reading What Is Not There

Danticat spins a historical fiction, a love story between two Haitian workers, Amabelle Désir and Sebastien Onius caught on the wrong side of the island in the cutting winds of 1937, related through the voice of young Amabelle. Authorial inspiration resides at the site of death itself, a space that swallows memory.

> It wasn't until Danticat stood on the banks of the River Massacre itself, where the killings had taken place, that she fully realized that she wanted to make a novel out of the story. (The river is named after another 19th century genocidal episode that had occurred on its banks.) "It was really strange to stand there—it was low tide, and people were bathing, and washing their clothes in the water," recalls Danticat. "There were no markers. I felt like I was standing on top of a huge mass grave, and just couldn't see the bodies. That's the first time I remember thinking, 'Nature has no memory'—a line that later made its way into the book—'and that's why we have to have memory.'"[2]

Danticat's own immersion in the imagined lives of her characters evokes Walter Benjamin's triadic bleeding between storyteller and history, memory, and audience. Danticat, oddly in tradition with Benjamin's storyteller, Nikolai Leskov, authentically manages to speak to not only the pool of Haitian audience within its nation and scattered elsewhere, but citizens and non-citizens of different nation-states, arising from the dialogic condition of the literary community generated by the writer.[3] Danticat upon the river, strikingly resonant of the last scene where we see Amabelle pondering the deceptive calm of the river, brings to us a beginning of story imbued with the spirit of Benjamin's authentic storyteller. Her narrative fosters an intimacy with death, making Danticat's story authentic in Leskov's manner of inviting mortality into the aegis of the story. Returning to Danticat, standing atop the river which has no markers for all those people who lie buried in its water, the question arises—how to categorize and remember these people, how to best address them?

In meditating upon the lives of the dispossessed, Danticat's central concern is reflected in the intellectual project forwarded by Ranjana Khanna's *Asylum and Its Indignities*. In her talk on this book, Khanna presents the limitations of our vocabulary when dealing with those categorized as "refugees," theorized as the wretched of the earth or subalterns or those who are discussed within the discourse of dignity. She suggests an alternative word, "disposable," because its many meanings such as "availability" or "excess" or "throwaway" bleed together when utilized in the context of "disposable people."[4] Danticat's narrative addresses the plight, voice, and assertions of a people who, in Khanna's estimate, are "disposable" to the world community at large.

Twentieth century is a century of massacre. Carolyn Forché's anthology of twentieth century poetry, *Against Forgetting* (1993) is an effort to record the event of horror through poets who directly suffered the violence of their times. Troubled by the traditional divide between the personal and the political, Forché carves out the space of the "social" where these poems fall, a space where both the personal and the political are urgently transfigured rooted in the despair of death and witness. While the poets speak of the injustices suffered when faced with despotic forces, Ariel Dorfman writes of insufficiency of words to tell the stories of such extreme violence. He writes, "Let them speak for themselves." Forché notes, in turn, "Witness, in this light, is problematic: even if one has witnessed atrocity, one cannot necessarily speak *about* it, let alone *for* it."[5] As Forché goes on to underscore the significance of religion in understanding tropes of witness, Danticat's narrativizing hints at the project of wrestling with the absent. Danticat's novel seeks to understand the present and past in the context of crossings: Danticat standing atop the river looking to the Haitian past for a more accurate lesson on history, but also the living who look to the dead for a form of community. Thus, instead of speaking *about* or *for* those who suffered in 1937, Danticat enlivens a discourse of community that brings us on to the discussion of the consequence of massacres.

Massacres signify a violent absence, an erasure of those who were present but were wrested of their agency, rights, and their very lives. In what way can the dead be remembered because the massacre when instituted by the state suggests that these were lives that were not important enough to be accorded the status of "life." When the modern nation that is supposed to protect the rights of its citizen turns on the very same body, in what way might the rejected exert any force back on the body politic? And what if this process of rejection exists on a supra-level, where the existence of one nation is such an anathema to its neighbors that the world stage pretends amnesia to the nation's losses. While Haiti's closest neighbors might have wished to outlaw its very existence as an autonomous nation, the European hegemons, vis-à-vis the colonialist bloc, assumed a putative superiority which deemed the nation not deserving of a global stage or audience. This brings us to the question of Haiti, its deafening and awe-inspiring blackness,[6] and a massacre that clouds its historical imagination for the entire century that just passed. Joan Dayan and Susan Buck-Morss' works are powerful interventions in understanding the historical anxiety caused by the absence of Haiti as a subject in the academy. Excavating the detritus of history, I am curious as to what is left, the materials with which a ravaged people navigate their current course.[7]

> In 1937, without a qualm, *El Jefe* had ordered the slaughter of some twenty thousand black Haitians. Killing, he had decided, was the easiest, cheapest and most efficient method of removing the blacks who squatted on Dominican territory or toiled as sugar cutters in its large plantations. A Negrophobe, Trujillo disguised the fact that he had Negro blood in his own veins. Even the dusky tinge to his complexion was lightened with makeup. He ignored the fact that most Dominicans were, like himself, of mixed blood or Negro, and declared his nation officially white.[8]

Bernard Diederich writes about the leader known more familiarly as the "Goat," a text Edwidge Danticat reads before beginning her walk into the history that informs, *The Farming of Bones*. President Rafael Trujillo, Hitlerian in vision and brutality, unable to see his own body in relation to the history, writes upon the back of his people, declares his nation, Dominican Republic, to be white. In order to keep it so, he decides to reduce the blight of blackness by eliminating as many blacks as possible, mostly Haitian workers in Dominican Republic and darker Dominicans whose phenotype excludes them from the new racialized nationalistic vision.

Historians remain uncertain about the numbers slaughtered, driven mad, the disappeared, and the drowned and ascribe it between 5,000 to 30,000; the numbers swim in the murky forced erasure of a period which Trujillo justified as necessary but necessarily kept vague. Haiti, having won its independence in 1804, the earliest herald of postcoloniality, became the first sovereign black nation in the western hemisphere. In its freedom, it augurs the nemesis of all ruling European nations and classes, especially its sister nation on the island of Hispaniola, Dominican Republic. Ernesto Sagás writes on the repellent ideology of antihaitianismo in his groundbreaking text, *Race and Politics in the Dominican Republic* (2000), where he outlines the history of hate between these juxtaposed nations, particularly bringing to light Haiti's position as the other not only within the European mind but the Caribbean and Central Amercian dialectic as well.

> As the product of a bloody slave insurrection and racial strife, the independence of Haiti in 1804 represented a terrifying prospect for white nations: the massacre of most whites, the destruction of European civilization, and their replacement by a black republic led by the ex-slaves themselves. Even the newly independent Latin American nations turned their backs on Haiti and excluded it from hemispheric deliberations, such as the 1826 Congress of Panama. In spite of its human achievements, in the minds of white elites the Haitian Revolution became synonymous with chaos, violence, and black savagery. If the Haitian Revolution provoked feelings of rejection by elites in the rest of the hemisphere, for the Dominican elites, neighboring Haiti was their gravest concern. Antihaitianismo ideology thus provided Dominicans with a convenient shield of cultural superiority vis-à-vis an ostracized nation. As contradictory as it may seem, and as a result of antihaitianismo ideology, even the lowest, poorest, and darkest Dominicans are prone to claim cultural—and even racial—superiority over the Haitian people.[9]

Haunting questions arise out of such historic seismic quakes—questions such as how do a people remember their ancestors and valuable stories in a world which disremembers their history and claims that it never happened or whatever happened is not worth remembering.[10] For those who have their lives, loves, and the very nation wrenched from them, in what possible way do they exercise their humanity and world citizenship? In a nation such as Haiti whose blackness casts the pall of invisibility upon the body politic and causes the demagogues, hegemons, and their own hemispheric Latin cousins to shroud their stories, emerges the true narrative of Haitian survival. Such a condition fosters the emergence of a community with the dead.

What drives the narrative forward and keeps Amabelle moving is her desire to meet the dead. Her most solemn link is with the dead: her dead parents, Antoine Désir and Irelle Pradelle, and her dead love, Sebastien Onius. It is in this imagined community with the dead that the survivor of the massacre finds her humanity, her link to a fleshy past, the story of her origins, and her desire to write the rest. For such, dying becomes the easier half of life. For the witnesses to massacre of such chilling proportion, remembering is a political exercise and not letting go of the dead a further act of love. In the time period under study, the Haitians are the laboring classes of Dominican Republic and reap little profit from their labors as explained in Deborah Cohn's work.[11] However in the aftermath of massacre, remembering is the labor that bears the fruit of community.

Finally, having lived fully in a world peopled by the dead, dying transmutes into a rebirth. This connection, seemingly absurd in discursive orders founded on rational epistemologies, is possible only in the aftermath of such a massacre. A massacre seizes not only the very life of its people but also their songs, their past, their very being. An exercise in liberty then becomes a fraternity with the dead, equality between those who live a death in life and those who attain life in death.

The narrative of Haiti's liberation followed by a succession of demagogues and parallel spate of relentless national instability, the yoke of French empire loosened only to be tightened in the twentieth century under the American empire, Haiti remains to this day in fratricidal relationship with the other nation on the same island. Trujillo's cruelty toward the Haitian population, the Dominican writing of acceptable history, the social machine that repairs its way away from its Haitian counterparts, a memory that refuses to capitulate under the limiting demands of universal history, and capitalism all play their parts as if elaborated and rehearsed upon the Deleuze and Guattari paradigm of the socius.[12] In this animated space of the socius, Danticat presents a dialogic[13] and dual reality. Her language reveals the profound awareness of the differences between French and Kréyol while being recorded in the English by a Haitian–American writer deeply conscious of writing in the French–Caribbean tradition of Jacques Romain, Joseph Zobel, Maryse Condé, Patrick Chamoiseau, and Marie Chauvet.

This chapter rests in the dialectic between Edouard Glissant's notion of forced poetics and Walter Benjamin's notes on history and redemption. Ernesto Sagas' historical work provides context for the events that transpire in this novel. While points made by Freud, Derrida, Cixous, and Anderson will be extrapolated, and at times, contested, Fanon, Dayan, Glissant, Bhabha, and the Latin subalternists inform this chapter. Lois Parkinson Zamora's vision of usable past, a history kindled alive by story, formulated further into the discourse of postslavery literatures by George Handley lays the groundwork for the essay. Since this project regards the subject of silencing the past, wresting agency unto those already dead, essentially reading what is not there, a poem, interlocution into all absences, comes to mind: Michael Burkard's "The Boy Who Had No Shadow." The river, a place of crossings, longings, and loss, a place where young Amabelle ends her narrative translates from the location of endings to one of beginnings within *The Farming of Bones*. The context of the poem leads us to the subject of silencing, othering, and the double-sided coin of cruelty and fear with a precision leading us directly to the sociohistorical condition of massacre.

One thing led to another:
if I have no shadow
I will eventually be followed
by those who do have shadows.
Sooner or later they will greet me
at the river and, judging me
as peculiar, will shove me into the river
to drown.

And the boy who had no shadow was correct.
But before he was shoved into the river,
days and days before, he was asked innocent
questions by innocent bystanders:
"Does your mother have a shadow?"

"Were you conceived in shadow?"
"Are you perhaps your own version
of your own shadow?"

And they were difficult questions
because he had no answer
or, the boy who had no shadow
had no answer.

So they thought he was up to no good.
The questions became less innocent.
And because, by now, he was also judged
as not belonging to any crucial historical epoch,
he was shoved into the river
and kept beneath the surface by poles.

Not a particularly unique circumstance.
But the reason was unique and they knew that.
So, just to be sure, just to be sure
the boy had no shadow, they kept him down for days.

Lest the shadow which he had not,
which he had been murdered for,
escape in the river and flee.[14]

While the poem resonates with the sociopolitical stages on which the
rhetoric of massacre is inaugurated, in the final moments where the boy
is being kept under water by poles, a Dante-esque reference to the fiends
who do the same to souls in the inferno, "lest the shadow which he had
not ... escape in the river and flee," also suggests the alarm and silence
around the narratives of survival that emerge from the brutal episodes
of history—narratives from the submerged. Like the boy who had no
shadow, people are punished for "unseeable" and "undoable" crimes,
and from this space of punishment, they utter their witness. The space
of punishment transforms within Danticat's novel into a place of power
and collective agency. This book addresses the power, position, and function of the imagined community of the dead. Since even in death, the
dead are not safe,[15] I find it urgent to dissemble the ideological apparatus
that reifies such lacunae. Literature, free of official censorship or state-
sanctioned interventions, stands alone possibly at times as ultraviolet light
upon the palimpsest; it allows us, as in Danticat's literary phoenix written
from the ashes of the 1937 massacre, to read what cannot be seen.

In Skin the Color of Driftwood Ashes in the Rain[16]

In the opening of the novel where we encounter Amabelle Désir and her beloved, Sebastien Onius making love by the light of the castor oil lamp in her small shack, he promises to take her to the cave across the river. It is the place they both left behind, the place that took their parents from them, the place that returns to them in their dream. He retreats to the darkest corner of the room as she strips in order to tutor her in being able to see the unseen. He says, "It is good for you to learn and trust that I am near you even when you can't place the balls of your eyes on me."[17] This statement is doubly evocative because for much of the novel, Sebastien is dead, and even though Amabelle cannot "place the balls of her eyes on him," she has learned to feel his presence.

From here on, we realize that never are the two alone, their rooms and meetings peopled by more than just the living, the ghosts of their memories occupy visceral space. Already Amabelle tells us that her lover guards her from the shadows, and sometimes he becomes the shadows. It is not clear whether the tense refers to the Sebastien who is alive and adoring her or the ghost of Sebastien who lingers around Amabelle kissing her well into his own death. The ambivalent tense simply signifies that he not only guards but guides her toward the shadows that mark her own ending, or birthing, as one wills. Zamora's adduction about postmodernity within magical realism becomes relevant here; her arguments about the ghosts populating such texts are a crucial antidote to the sobering figurations of Enlightenment discourse. When Zamora asserts about ghosts, "They dissent, furthermore, from modernity's (and the novel's) psychological assumptions about autonomous consciousness and self-constituted identity, proposing instead a model of the self that is collective; subjectivity is not singular but several, not only individual and existential but also mythic, cumulative, and participatory,"[18] she articulates the essential features of Danticat's imaginative terrain, marked by the mythic and collective, a mourning that is as realistic as it is magical. The act of mourning is not a solipsistic act burying the individual further into the recesses of hermeticism; instead, it is the passport into the "mythic, cumulative, and participatory" imagined community wherein lives the dynamic exchanges enlivening the dead and inspiring the living.

Amabelle's invocation involves an opening that insists upon naming the cane worker whom she loves. Her lover is a man murdered with his brethren, part of a mass of invisible anonymous blackness, workers whose own masters, like Pico, hardly know their names, even when they are mercenary enough to take a worker's life, as Pico does with Joel. The project of the Latin Subaltern Studies Collective initiated and heralded by Ileana Rodriguez and Maria Milagros Lopez is central in placing this charge upon Amabelle, the charge of returning the master's gaze, especially in context of Milagros's postmarxist ways of dissembling domination. Sebastien and Congo and Joel are subaltern figures, Haitian cane workers on a Dominican hacienda, outside the auspices of state and institutional structures of power. In the Latin Subaltern Studies Collective's effort to locate these figures not "as Calibans but in struggle for meaning," humanity is asserted in the transgression against the state. In these very minute spaces between Amabelle and Sebastien's body in the dark peopled by the ghosts from the other world, the people who crossed the river sometime ago, the master's gaze is stripped of its ominous power. The characters cross borders despite limits placed upon the territory of the dead. Domination is rendered mute in light of such crossings. Instead of reading the powerless within the epistemologies of the master, we read the subaltern in her terms.

> "Ungovernability" is a term I use to introduce transgression; that is, a cultural behavior that does not conform or submit to the norms. Ungovernability constitutes an area that escapes the control of dominant hermeneutics, where subalterns are not lumped together under the generic names of "Negro" or "slave". But dominant cultures frequently appropriate materials from other cultures and transform them symbolically into something else. Reading them against the grain, we can suggest that ridicule, irony, and the sense of the despicable—that is, everything that falls into the asymmetrical and barbaresque, or that is labeled grotesque—is part of what we have called "distancing." In distancing, the enunciating subject as imperial reveals that what he sees in the colonies is, as Bakhtin would have it, carnival, a parody of his own society turned upside down.[19]

The subaltern figures fall within Rodriguez's definition of "ungovernable" or transgressive. In acts of love affirming their humanity, they "distance" themselves from the barbaresque purview of the master, turning the Dominican hacienda upside down in a revelation of subaltern desire, akin to a wild space outside the surveillance of the father or the state, the patriarchal symbolic order. Repeatedly Amabelle tells us, "His name is Sebastien Onius," as if the institutional erasure demands of her a repetition, an incantation, talisman against the shadows and into the shadows. It should not be forgotten that the shadows, glimpses into the world of the dead, resemble the subaltern shade of skin in this context. The shadows mirror the blighted blackness that is the hated color, the punished indictment constituting the antihaitianismo dictating Trujillo's second massacre at River Massacre and these shadows resemble Amabelle's deep black skin. When Sebastien gathers his child-woman lover into his arms, he notices how she radiates light despite "skin that is the color of driftwood ashes in the rain."[20]

In the lovemaking between a domestic worker and a plantation worker whose face bears the multiple scars of hacking cane, humanity is achieved in the immediacy of the story's inception. In the repeated invocation of his name, Sebastien Onius, we know of his existence despite his forced erasure in history; Trujillo had made sure that the official state archives gave hardly any importance or gravity to the events of 1937. In the shadows that play and dance along with the young lovers, we know that the two forge a community with the dead, a link undecipherable and a force indomitable. They are the navigators of this ungovernable space. Though Amabelle's utterance proves against the historiographical grain, it differs from the slippery slope of never-fulfilled desire as explained by Lacan.[21] Amabelle owns and navigates her losses and trains herself into an apprenticeship into a new community of the dead: she outlives the living and prefigures the dead. Her lack transcends the melancholy of loss into a language of crossings and companionship which emboldens her through the years and liberates her on the day of Trujillo's death to publicly dance. Amabelle and the shadows tread together through the imaginary into the symbolic, her naming ordering their universe while making "desire the desire of the other" and thereby, impossible to achieve but satisfied in this alternative ontology of community with the dead. Even though dissatisfaction shadows Amabelle till the end, she realizes an end of desire within the act of ending itself.[22]

When Amabelle lies alone in her room, she remembers Sebastien's advice to lie naked, naked as the day one emerged from the womb, naked and alone. In the sweat that gathers between her back and the floor, she hopes little water will be left in her body with which to cry, mourn the losses she accrues each passing day. In this moment of bereavement that haunts Amabelle throughout the text, she forms a community with the sweat that puddles under the weight of her body, knowing in water lies the answers she seeks. It is no wonder that lying in such manner resembles the final lying on River Massacre where she lies upon the womb of water, innocent as a newborn. The river that runs through the island of Hispaniola forms an important symbol. It is a burial ground where there is no burial or ground. It swallows incomplete narratives, a river that rises at whim and consumes the sojourners like Amabelle's parents. It is the silent repository for all those hacked upon its banks, drowned while crossing like Odette, or countless others, thus making the river, along with water, rain, tears, and blood symbol of liquid crossings to the other side. Some make it to the nation on the other side, others to the other world. The place of transition, significant in West African inflected cosmologies of the Caribbean, is also a place of possibility and community.

It is critical to add here that when alone or together, in the hours marked by Sebastien, Amabelle is a woman who makes central the question of woman's pleasure, *jouissance*.[23] Since the text opens on a scene of the young couple making love, the centrality of this recurrent act should not recede into the horizon of despair. Unlike Cixous' world where women's desire is excess, women's pleasure is at the heart of Sebastien and Amabelle's lovemaking and intermittent conversations in the dark. While the state and the familial figure of patriarchy, Señor Pico, all ignore their very existence, Sebastien pays attention to Amabelle in a way that exceeds the expectations of Cixous' critique of masculinity. The fulfillment, partially cut due to the lack of time or luxury for contemplation, seen in the opening scene haunts Amabelle as she seeks such a union with the absent Sebastien through the rest of the narrative. Once having owned her pleasure, and inhabited the central position of *jouissance*, Amabelle is haunted by the ghosts of both pleasure and pain. After his disappearance in Trujillo's bloodbath, it is only possible for Amabelle to meet Sebastien in the lush world peopled again by memory, dream, and death.

Long before an old Amabelle slips into the currents of River Massacre unclothed, she promises to meet Sebastien in the waterfall. She knows that he is a resident shadow in the waterfall cave, his ghost mingling with the succor of falling water, praying that his last fall included water that broke and softened the blow of death. She dreams her entire life spent in Yves' home under the generous awning of his mother, Man Rapadou that Sebastien lives in the cave behind the water, and she conjures him from the dead, a spirit who returns to comfort her in life, in her death in life.

Despite Amabelle's certitude that that they no longer share a language, that large masses of land and water separate their beings, she resolves to meet him at his waterfall. Water and death are linked as is community with those already dead. It is then doubly significant that the suffering mother of Sebastien and Mimi names her son after a saint who dies twice. St. Sebastien is a saint who returns to his assailants to show the power of love only to be stoned to death a second time, the paucity of life and richness of death assume direct proportion. To think of Sebastien and in turn, Amabelle's grief, we need to attend to the place of crossings in this novel, River Massacre. Derrida's formulations on the significations of "between" help in reading this place of loss and gleaning in the novel.

> If we replace "hymen" by "marriage" or "crime," "identity" or "difference," etc., the effect would be the same, the only loss being a certain economic condensation or accumulation, which has not gone unnoticed. It is the "between," whether it names fusion or separation, that thus carries all the force of the operation. The hymen must be determined by the entre and not the other way around. The hymen in the text (crime, sexual act, incest, suicide, simulacrum) is inscribed at the very tip of this indecision. This tip advances according to the irreducible excess of the syntactic over the semantic. The word "between" has no full meaning of its own = an incomplete signification.[24]

If we deconstruct the text based on a Derridean tearing of the hymen, we can name the hymen "massacre" or "crime" or "difference," suggestions that carry the pathos of the "between." In Derrida's attempt to explicate the incomplete signification of the word "entre" inscribing in it the indecision of the excess of the syntactic over the semantic, we return to River Massacre where Amabelle's family attempts to return to their side of the island in the height of flood season. Antoine Désir and his wife, Irelle Pradelle, the woman without a smile, disappear into the sudden swell of a tide with their arms raised. They leave behind a curious gesture to their muted daughter watching at the shores, waiting their return—a farewell, a victory sign, a defeat, another signal in the secret language of melancholia.

Is their departure a fusion or separation? Amabelle communes with the dead long after they are dead. River Massacre, symbolic of the "entre," marks neither fusion nor separation as the path between life and death, consciousness and dream, child and parent, voiced and voiceless, history and fantasy. Between Amabelle's unsmiling and tight-lipped mother who constantly smiles when she reappears after death and her father, Antoine Désir whose healing work extends into healing his daughter's wound upon their death, the parents rest in the "entre," leaving behind a daughter who can heal, birth, and smile, a daughter who loses her life in the same waters that took theirs.

Mourning for Eternity

Immediately after Amabelle watches her parents drown, shocked and helpless at the riverbank, she walks into the river and attempts to plunge in a similar way so as not to be separated from them. She is saved upon the forced pressure from the river rats, boys who pull her on to land and remind her angrily, "Unless you want to die, you will never see those people again."[25] Nevertheless Amabelle meets her parents in every dream and waking fantasy, where without dying she meets them in a space she has carved for herself in her life, a space marked "death," or Derrida's "entre," a place impossible to navigate in rational discourse or the sanity of Spanish. In Kreyòl, she hears her parents calling out to her. In the dust storms that cloud the valley, Amabelle makes out a mass of human beings. She sees people walking all around her while she is the little girl her parents left, still holding their hands, and upon the clearing of storm, finds herself being led forward with hands extended upward, as if in prayer, as if in union with the ethereal.

When Señora Valencia paints the baby coffin for little Rafi with her brushes and wood varnish, Amabelle envies the dead baby who at least has a final bed. Her parents, swallowed by a wave, jolt eternally on the crests and nadirs of their daughter's watery memory. They, like Joel who dies under the rash wheels of Pico's vehicular arrogance, return in the same condition they arrive, coffinless and naked. Here, it is useful to draw in Hardt and Negri's meditations on a unified paradigm for struggle, the imperial machine, its necessary destruction and postulates about "a movement of the multitude."[26] The multitude, traced back from Althusser through Spinoza to Marx, carries within it the creation and destruction of the Empire it feeds. I propose that the dead, like Amabelle's parents swept into the river, and Joel and Sebastien also constitute the redemptive and prophetic power of this vital multitude. Pico's father's guilt over the murder his son commits adds fuel to this fiery multitude. Kongo, the name of the father, refusing to reveal to anyone his true name, stands as metonym for Africa, and allegory for the nation historically cheated out of his sons by the slave traders of Europe and Africa. Embedded deep within Danticat's text is the mourning of an entire continent for the historical injustice of the enslavement of its sons and daughters.[27]

Having made the long journey home into Haiti, having been publicly flogged and having lost most of her travel companions due to horrors of the historical reality, Amabelle wakes up in a makeshift hospital where her only respite is sleep that feels akin to death. Here, memories of her mother have Irelle Pradelle dressed in glass, smiling, comforting, and assuring her daughter that she will never be alone. They talk, confide, and comfort each other. Jokingly, the ghost calls her daughter an imbecile. The ghost says, "Your mother was never as far from you as you supposed. You were like my shadow. Always fled when I came to you and only followed when I left you alone. You will be well again, ma belle, Amabelle. I know this to be true. And how can you have ever doubted my love? You, my eternity?"[28] "Mother ghosts" as companions to their daughters in their darkest moments appears earlier in the text in the sympathetic figure of Valencia who stands at the crossroads between master–slave. Valencia informs Amabelle on the eve of delivering her twins that her dead mother gave her company through the night and never let her feel the fear of delivery pain.

Without Irelle Pradelle, it is possible Amabelle would have found a simpler harmony with her parents, by joining them in their world. However it is the community with dead kin that inspires Amabelle back into life. It is her mother's assurance that the daughter is never truly alone. In a complicated gesture, the mother calls her daughter, "my eternity," wiping away the linear function of time and letting the agency of time rest in the hands of those who have it wrenched from them. In the end when Amabelle, an old woman, decides to lie on the river's womb to close her eyes, she imagines she will be carried "into Sebastien's cave, my father's laughter, my mother's eternity."[29]

Amabelle decides to take the bold step of literally changing worlds. She calls her mother "eternity" as if it is a possession her mother has, as if time is negotiable and pliable to the demands of a broken heart. Time is an ally in this Haitian landscape where death mingles with life, sometimes to erase it, other times just to shout a greeting. And for the living and dead who believe that they possess eternity, time is a pliable creature. For those willing to invite and imagine a community with the dead, time is yet another companion, necessary for narrative but easy to disregard when one wishes to exercise the political right to exist in the same space as the people she loves.

At the final moment, in the blackness of night when Amabelle can imagine the silent river does not exist, that everyone swallowed in the undertow actually died peaceful deaths, she recalls her mother's exit. She remembers how her drowning parents signal desperately a final message that remained undecipherable till this moment when she realizes that nature has no memory. In her mother's raised arm that could have been asking her daughter to jump in or move farther away lay the lifelong puzzle that remains unanswered even during Amabelle's ascent into her watery grave, or womb as she tells us. In this conundrum of expression that remains the shifting signifier in Amabelle's life, Edouard Glissant's ruminations on poetics stay relevant.

> Forced poetics exist where a need for expression confronts an inability to achieve expression. It can happen that this confrontation is fixed in an opposition between the content to be expressed and the language suggested or imposed.... A forced poetics is created from the awareness of the opposition between a language that one uses and a form of expression that one needs.[30]

Not only is the condition of the Haitian in Dominican Republic forced poetics, especially at the brutal articulation of "perejil" so is the mother's last flailing gesture as she drowns a symbol of ambiguity and erasure throughout Amabelle's lifetime. In the difference between the language that one uses, Creole in this case, or a child's wounded silence, and the form of expression that one needs, Spanish, or the child's ability to decipher what is being said to her, rest the meaningful eddies of history. More than her native Creole, Amabelle needs a more lucid language as a form of expression to fulfill her needs and in the final moments at River Massacre, she finds it in the repose she chooses for herself after a life spent weaving.

Amabelle's connection to the living, the flesh of this world, is frail. To say it simply, the small earlier portion of the text in which she mingles with the living shows her a ghost. But in the rest of the text, her search for the dead prompts her actions. The interactions with the living leave so much death in their wake that it is sensible for Amabelle to find death a force more enduring than any other form of being. It is not the death instinct that degenerates into the pathology Freud elucidates but rather an instinct at being far more fluent at the language after death than the one given in life.

> In other words, our image of happiness is indissolubly bound up with the image of redemption. The same applies to our view of the past, which is the concern of history. The past carries with it a temporal index by which it is referred to redemption. There is a secret agreement between past generations and the present one. Our coming was expected on earth. Like every generation that preceded us, we have been endowed with a weak Messianic power, a power to which the past has a claim. That claim cannot be settled cheaply. Historical materialists are aware of that.[31]

The condition of the dead brings them into their ends, specifically Haitian ends. Even those like Sebastien's father who died in the hurricane or Amabelle's parents who drowned in the flood, their ends mark the desperation of their condition as Haitian laborers who cross borders and illegally enter forbidden territories to survive. Theirs is a negotiation that interpellates their life in an Althusserian paradigm with the vagaries of nature. Were they not Haitian, they would not have been in such a hurry to cross the river. At a moment when even the expert river rats, little boys who ferry wayfarers on their back, refuse to cross the river, Amabelle's parents insist upon crossing because of their fear as marked "other" to stay in Dajabon, the first Dominican town across the border. Their daughter waiting her father's return at the banks, waiting for him to carry her across to the safer shores, waits forever with two shining pots, empty vessels that spill over her lifetime with ghosts who populate her dreams.

Amabelle's condition speaks to Benjamin's notions of history. Her happiness is indissolubly bound up with the image of redemption, of the river retreating to reveal her parents, the bullet returning to a place of stasis before consuming Sebastien and his sister, Mimi's life. The past has a hold on Amabelle; it speaks to her directly and dictates her living desires. It is a strong claim, a claim that cannot be settled cheaply. Amabelle, endowed with messianic power after having witnessed the deaths of those closest to her heart, with this power endures her passage with the living. Here, it adds affective power to read George Handley's project of linking family history with postslavery narrative, "a thematic and structural sine qua non"[32] because the erasure emerges within the repressed lineage despite the Haitian plantocracy and pro-Trujillo nationalists in power at the moment within the narrative.

It is the same power that brings Amabelle back to take a final look at the living with whom she shared her childhood, Señora Valencia and her kingdom across the border in Dominican Republic, and then to the river itself, the river where all lives cross into the next.

> Mourning is regularly the reaction to the loss of a loved person, or to the loss of some abstraction which has taken the place of one, such as one's country, liberty, an ideal, and so on. In some people the same influences produce melancholia instead of mourning and we consequently suspect them of a pathological disposition.... The melancholic displays something else besides which is lacking in mourning—an extraordinary diminution in his self-regard, an impoverishment of his ego on a grand scale. In mourning it is the world which has become poor and empty; in melancholia it is the ego itself.[33]

In an essay delving into the particular nature of mourning and its ceaseless counterpart, melancholia, Freud's famous words, the twentieth century marker of all things lost, needs mention. Those in power and those without any, mourn. Fathers mourn the untimely death of their sons; lovers like Félice mourn the passing of Joel; Señora Valencia weeps for her child, Rafael, named after the generallismo; and Juana and Luis, the childless domestic-worker couple also mourns after the passing of their mistress' child. In distinguishing Freud's definition of mourning against the pathological condition of melancholia, I read "melancholia" as the racialized figures of otherness attempting to survive an island of whiteness.

Here, Ranjana Khanna's project in her text, *Dark Continents: Psychoanalysis and Colonialism* (2003), is quite useful. Khanna utilizes the terms "melancholy" and "mourning" to understand the status quo in practices of psychoanalysis and colonialism, and in a Saidian fashion, comes to find profound connections between the two institutions. She writes, "What Echo was to Narcissus, melancholia is to mourning. And if Freud would eventually transfer the critical agency found in melancholia into the normalizing function of the superego, I would salvage it, putting the melancholic's manic critical agency into the unworking of conformity, and into the critique of the status quo."[34] Amabelle's profound link with the world of the dead is not a pathological or diseased condition; instead, it is normative, necessary, and empowering. Khanna's project helps in reading Amabelle's "critical agency" in bringing about the "unworking of conformity," and "critique of the status quo." It brings relief and hope, Benjamin's indissoluble happiness in the face of a cruel history. It brings a political power, in the rightful exercise of choosing to not let go of what was wrenched from the self. In this dire alchemy of class and race hierarchies, the place of the domestic worker, her existence as a complete being, her generous gift of love for which no payments are deemed necessary, is obliterated from the narrative of the master's loss and mourning. Amabelle learns this lesson well. George Handley's reading of Derek Walcott's poetics sheds needed relief: "...slavery is never really behind us, not only because similar conditions may exist in the present, but because it provides the strangely fertile soil from which a wide array of unpredictable, beautiful cultural forms emerge."[35] Though Amabelle births the babies, saves her mistress/childhood companion/ supposed friend's life, she unhesitatingly packs to leave the moment she realizes the cutting of Haitians has begun in their area. She leaves without a look back, worrying only of her journey to the border, and the more pressing need to gather Sebastien and Mimi into her fold.

As Señor Pico teaches his wife to shoot a rifle, a protection mechanism to defend herself in these changing times of war when he will not be around to be her guardian, she nearly shoots a scampering Amabelle. Amabelle is not surprised. Of Señor Pico and the nation that emerges out of the brand of patriotism he espouses under President Trujillo, Sagás writes:

> The Dominican Republic is a good case study of the deliberate manipulation of racial prejudice and nationalism by elites bent on promoting their own definition of nationhood and on maintaining their hold on political and economic power ... antihaitianismo has its origins in the racial prejudices of Spanish colonial society in Santo Domingo. Even before there was a Haiti, the roots of antihaitianismo ideology had been planted by the Spanish.[36]

In such ethos, there is little room in Señor Pico to feel any regret or anxiety around the imminent death of one of his Haitian domestic workers. After all, his work at the border is the project of materializing the disappearance of the very people who help clean, cook, garden, and care for his home and family. Naturally in this landscape, Amabelle's depressive condition is psychically bound in the political reality of the nation space she inhabits, a detachment as necessary for her survival as her instinct to dodge the flying piece of metal. The melancholic's condition with the powers to making the dead return leaves little room for petty revolutions, complaints against the inhumanity of their masters. Of this incident, a shuddering Amabelle says, "The señora's strong. She's a good markswoman."[37] Despite the fact that the only family Amabelle knows is the one her mistress provides her, and that she has spent more of her waking life under their awning than with her parents, her link to their world is tenuous. She occupies the space of her body and performs as the body does, with all its dexterity, grace, and skill. She heals when the time arises; she is the mid-wife when the doctor is not around; she gets nearly run over by armored tanks or escapes a whizzing bullet—all because her body does exist in the temporal space of Alegría, yet her soul, her spirit, her desire, her dreams flit far away to a place on the riverside called "redemption" where time is made irrelevant.

Even with Yves, Sebastien's friend, who not only becomes her companion on the dangerous trek to the border and across into Haiti, but her provider who extends his home to her for the rest of her life, she remains distant. Fanon's prophetic words assume relevance in the relationship forged between these two fugitives who remain shrouded in a silence only the two of them can share. Fanon writes, "A national culture under colonial domination is a contested culture whose destruction is sought in systematic fashion. It very quickly becomes a culture condemned to secrecy."[38] Condemned to secrecy, Amabelle experiences liberation from domination upon the death of Trujillo in 1960 when she finally breaks her silence, revisits her past, and enters into conversation. However Amabelle and Yves' secrecy is not one of silence alone; for Amabelle, her secrecy is one of the foremothers of birthing the imagined community with the dead.

As for the two survivors, they suffer deeply, in part due to bearing witness to the brutal vanquishing of several of their companions who had joined them in the journey across the border into Haiti. It was to squelch the wife's instinctive scream at her husband's shooting that Amabelle holds Odette's head under water, long enough that in the moment of terror that follows, Amabelle does not realize she has killed the woman. When Tibon is dragged through the streets and murdered, his mouth stuffed with parsley, Yves and Amabelle do their best to be invisible, not shed a tear, not express any connection to the dying man so that they can live. Yet they are beaten publicly and left for dead when Odette and Wilner rescue them and take them to the river that becomes the burial ground of their saviors.

Through Tibon's murder, Wilner's shooting, and Odette's drowning, Yves and Amabelle find that the more they witness death, the more they want to live. Bound by the horror of witnessing the vagaries of their history firsthand, the massacre of their beloved and distant kin, remaining guilty of survival, wherein one's survival depends on the annihilation of other lives. For this, Amabelle, caretaker of the dead, calculator of memories, keeper of mausoleums in the head, never forgives herself.

Yves is witness to the carting away of Sebastien and Mimi; knowing they go into their deaths, he hides. Yves and Amabelle make love once and never return to each other's bodies the same way. Their one act of love was to simply answer the question if after all the barbarity, any pleasure was possible. For twenty-four years, they share the same courtyard without exchanging many words, their link an oath of secrecy, a great betrayal.

For Amabelle, living is the sin. Living, that takes its daily toll in the form of the silence between her and Yves, the sole survivors of their treacherous journey, leaves the two unable to just love each other and write a new story. Instead the choice Amabelle makes toward the end signifies that her long wait had been for the death of the Goat, President Trujillo, upon whose death she, now Man Amabelle, a grand old dame in their parts, does the kalanda evoking hoots of appreciative laughter from the youth. Only then does she decide to return and meet the denizens of Alegría, her old home, one final time. Long before the twilight of her life when Amabelle rests in Sebastien's arms in Alegría, he explains to her that all of them are *vwayajè*, wayfarers and that is why they had to travel so far to meet each other.[39] Wayfarers also connote divine beings like Legba, God of the Crossroads, or energy that can transmit either way, creatures who can both populate the world of the living and the dead contiguously. Amabelle, Sebastien's wayfarer, belongs nowhere like a nomad and is at home everywhere, even in the realm of the dead long before she commits herself to the womb of the river.

The Messiah comes not only as the redeemer; he comes as the subduer of Antichrist. Only that historian will have the gift of fanning the spark of hope in the past who is firmly convinced that even the dead will not be safe from the enemy if he wins. And this enemy has not ceased to be victorious.[40]

Benjamin's notions of history are relevant in his caution to the historical materialist. He places upon the capitalist machine the burden of scripture and warns that without the subjugation of the Antichrist even the dead will not be safe. While Freud sees implicit in the art of memory the act of reconstruction, within Danticat's text, memory is an act of construction, bridges that take one from here to the beyond in legitimate human discourse. In Amabelle's world, the dead reside in solidarity with her living self. She keeps them safe by not crossing the border and returning to the nation that expelled all the darker races in the year of massacres. Endowed with minor messianic powers, there are only two living beings Amabelle manages to forge a deep link with. They are Man Rapadou, Yves' mother who welcomes the tired and beaten Amabelle into her expansive fold, and Man Denise, Sebastien and Mimi's mother whose only question for Amabelle is if her children wear the bracelets she made for them, coffee beans painted yellow gold.

Both women are mothers who have known death well; it is inevitable that the connection that compels Amabelle toward them both is melancholic, the necessary antidote to Benjamin's Antichrist.

Man Rapadou welcomes the strange woman Yves brings almost as her own daughter, without making demands, without asking her to love her lonely son in return, and feeds the bruised heartsick Amabelle pumpkin soup. Instead of insisting on Amabelle marrying her son, the old woman loves Amabelle unconditionally and shares with her the secret of her own husband's betrayal of the nation.

Evocative of Judith slaying Holofernes in the Hebrew Bible, Man Rapadou prepares his favorite foods, poisoned, and feeds him his last meal. She shares her dreams of falling before letting go, and shares her thoughts on death. Man Rapadou says how death should come gently, like a man's hand approaching a woman's body. She also shares with Amabelle how she had wished for things to be otherwise. It is the final melancholic revelation that she wished death had come sooner, "I wish the sun had set on my days when I was still a young, happy woman whose man was by her side, with joy in his eyes and honor in his heart."[41] The odd mixture of life lessons here is that while death becomes the punishment for transgression against one's own people, Man Rapadou also sees it as a welcome respite, a place to sojourn when one is in bloom on this side of the chasm. In fact, the distance seems neither interminable nor forbidding. Death becomes the symbol of the man she never had, a suitor who comes too late, a tryst that is sensual, continuing, sublime, and mortal all at once. To both women, death promises the community denied to them in life.

Amabelle never finds in Man Denise, her lover's mother, the same openhearted camaraderie she finds in Man Rapadou. Yet unconsciously she moves and hovers around Man Denise long after their joint sojourns all those days with the thousands of others seeking futilely to document their grief with the Justice of the Peace. She stays in Man Denise's house joining the crowd of soothsayers and venders who stay to give the silent and grieving mother some company while seeking shelter for the night. The mother speaks to her deep into the night despite her initial command to leave her alone, and tells Amabelle about their life, their separations, her hopes that her children would return to her from the country of the dead. Death is a nubile and voluptuous place, a signifier of constant journey and reportage, unlike the nation next door from where even fewer children return. Amabelle, long a resident of both countries, Haiti and Dominican Republic, the dead and the living, understands this wish well despite the accounts Man Denise provides of hearing from many that her children were lined up and shot in the back of their heads. Yet she refuses to let Amabelle reach out and touch the three yellow-gold coffee beans that are part of the bracelets she made for her children. She tells Amabelle about why she names her son after a saint who dies twice. She tells her why it is wrong for children to die far from the bones of their own, why it is bad timing for children to go before they even understand the meaning of death and yet, she asks Amabelle to leave. But Man Denise, similar to Amabelle, wants to be left alone to "dream up my children."[42] In other words, their image of happiness is indissolubly bound up with the image of redemption. Theirs is a condition of mourning without end, mourning for eternity.

Both women journey to meet the dead who should not be yet dead, the living caught off-guard in sudden death. Yet between the two, Amabelle is only able to allude to the fierce energy that brings her to stalking the older woman, watching her from afar for days before approaching her for a first hello. It is Man Denise who spends her days dreaming up the dead giving Amabelle a sense of collective anguish, a shape of an entire people tied by mourning, a shadowy map of a people emboldened

by melancholia, and a race at home in this world and the next with
equanimity.

> The tradition of the oppressed teaches us that the "state of emergency"
> in which we live is not the exception but the rule. We must attain to a
> conception of history that is in keeping with this insight. Then we shall
> clearly realize that it is our task to bring about a real state of emergency,
> and this will improve our position in the struggle against Fascism. One
> reason why Fascism has a chance is that in the name of progress its op-
> ponents treat it as a historical norm. The current amazement that the
> things we are experiencing are "still" possible in the twentieth century is
> not philosophical. This amazement is not the beginning of knowledge—
> unless it is the knowledge that the view of history which gives rise to it
> is untenable.[43]

Walter Benjamin reminds us that only in equipping ourselves with
the knowledge of the atrocities of the twentieth century as a rule can
we begin to imagine the radical struggle against the fascist agendas, evidenced in this novel in Trujillo's campaign to cleanse the body politic
of Dominican Republic of its blackness. If we continue to think of the
violence of the state as an exception, we fail to revise the epistemic fabric
of the history which pushes forward its momentum of injustices. Man
Denise represents the alternative in seeing the status quo for what it is
allowing her to radically reimagine her contemporaneity. Amabelle is
transfixed and initiated into the imaginings of the older woman through
the common language of grief.

Damp Kisses upon the Waterfront

Benjamin's caution to the liberal intellectuals augurs well but Amabelle,
caught in the daily eddies of a life marked by "states of emergency" im-
proves her position by doing what is markedly the most concrete step
in her fluid oscillation between the two worlds. She returns to River
Massacre upon the anniversary of the Kout Kouto, or the stabbing as
remembered in Kreyòl, strips off her clothes, and lies on the calm waves
of the water to begin her final journey. It is at the border, the marker
of the possible union or rupture between the two nation-states Amabelle inhabits the most profound meaning, metaphor, and action of the

text.[44] Her happiness, bound in the image of redemption, leads her to a reunion with the ghosts who people her entire life.

In another dream encounter with her love, she promises him, "Two mountains can never meet, but perhaps you and I can meet again. I am coming to your waterfall."[45] This lyricism follows upon the heels of an apology for not having died sooner, a cowardice that possibly allows her to enter both worlds at once. Susan Strehle reads Danticat's novel as a traditional romance until this genre dissolves into a new space that falls outside the prescriptive norms of both traditional history and romance. However the radical rupture from the romance genre occurs, in my estimate, much earlier than its devolution in its collision with history.[46] The opening itself, which Strehle identifies as romantic in pointing out the steel-hard body of Sebastien to whom we are introduced locked with Amabelle's smaller one, I see a celebration of not only black love, but the black body, a body that has been generally denigrated, deracinated, or forgotten within hegemonic accounts. It is with urgency beyond mere romance that Danticat places Sebastien's scarred body in Amabelle's arms, his name on her lips through the entire text. Divinity has to be contended with at this juncture, when Amabelle floating upon the nether space of loss and crossings, remembers her entire life, and creates narrative like some distant god at the beginning of time spinning out the universe in words.

Pinel, Tuke, Freud, Lacan, Foucault, Gilbert, and Gubar map discursive order upon the condition of madness. Nevertheless, madness continues through societal exclusion, portrayed in the figure of the Pwofesè who inhabits the banks of River Massacre. Strehle's summations of the professor's condition is a useful insight in which it inscribes upon this character the clinical history of perspective and proves to be ultimately a reductive and incomplete reading.

> Her man turns out to be the crazy "professor," an old man whose sanity has been blasted by the slaughter. This last, ironic patriarch calls forth visions of what Sebastien might be, had he survived, what Halle became, in Morrison's *Beloved*: the measure of a permanent, irredeemable shattering of identity and the proof that some cataclysms cannot be survived.[47]

Neither is the madman patriarchal, nor blasted. He is, like Amabelle, a guardian of liminal spaces, non-violent to the extreme in that his greatest act of madness is placing kisses on the lips of passers-by. Had

Sebastien lived, he would not be the old man, but the alternative, Father Roumain who was saved by the poultice of love in the arms of a healing woman. Had they survived and found each other, as in the beginning of the novel, where the lovers managed to erase the treachery and brutality of their subaltern existence when with each other, they might have continued the same miraculous performance of love into the sunset of their lives.

As the women on the banks inform her laughingly, the professor's kiss brings good luck. Madness is inverted in this world into a symbol of good fortune just as dead are not the other to living or solitude the end of civilization. Madness is prefigured in the earlier bout of madness suffered by Father Romain who is tortured by the army and suffocated into a claustrophobic dizziness of speech. As the Name of the Father inscribes itself on the mind of this Father, he discards his holy robes for more material ones and fluidly returns to the careful speech of the sane, "It took a love closer to the earth, closer to my own body, to stop my tears. Perhaps I have lost, but I have also gained an even greater understanding of things both godly and earthly."[48]

The mad professor, Pwofesè, who lives on the banks of the river, demented by same horrors, plants a damp kiss on her lips. As she bends to wash it away in the river, the women advise her against it because the kiss of a madman brings luck. She does not tell the women that she has been granted all the luck she needs already; nevertheless, her journey across the border into Alegría goes without detection or punishment. She returns safe to the river at dawn, ready to fulfill her promise to Sebastien, ready to die on her own terms. In this sense, death is no longer a tool of the master, a punitive measure of evisceration. Instead, it is a choice made by those still living to travel the place of crossings and commune perfectly with the dead.

The Pwofesè, "a tall, bowlegged man with a tangled gray beard, wearing three layers of clothing padded with straw, walked up behind me. His clothes and hands were covered with dirt, but his face was clean, smelling of vanilla and coconut. His eyes seemed a bright cerise, lush and dense like velvet,"[49] replies to the women's question about where he is going with a metaphoric, "Grass won't grow where I stand. I'm walking to the dawn."[50] This is the same dawn in which Danticat ends her text, or Amabelle ends her journey, lying on the river's surface returning to her parents and Sebastien, the dawn that is the symbolic representative of the meeting space between the now and after, the living and the dead, a place of light and darkness. It is not simply the dawn of a new day, but a dawn with the special light of these multiple worlds linked together. Similarly, the Pwofesè is not simply the mad man on the riverbanks but a liminal figure of the crossroads, a wayfarer like Amabelle and Sebastien, a wayfarer between the worlds of the living and the dead.[51] He, like Amabelle, walks both worlds.

On the river, she journeys to the place where it begins to fall, Man Rapadou's falling, Man Denise's dream of her children, Amabelle's sugar woman and her mother's smile made of glass where her lover stands still in half-lit glow under the waterfall. Even when she meets Valencia and finally sees the waterfall where she first made love with Sebastien, through it all, the fragility of her connection to the land of the living becomes stark. Nothing is where she remembers it to be; no one is who she remembers them to be; in the moments that her affect for Valencia sublimates like a meager ration, she herself dissolves from corporeal to ethereal. Even the driver who takes her to the edge feels that she is hardly there at all. She thinks, "All the time I had known her, we had always been dangling between being strangers and being friends. Now we were neither strangers nor friends. We were like two strangers passing each other on the street, exchanging a lengthy meaningless greeting. And at last I wanted it to end."[52] It is necessary here to provide concrete historical evidence, or its lack thereof, so as to make clear the project of erasure under effect by the national authorities, an effect absorbed by Dominican citizens like Valencia who never learn any story completely. For Valencia, it is enough that Amabelle supposedly had been killed. Clarity beyond that is never provided. Nor is it sought. On this, Sagás writes:

> To justify the 1937 massacre, Trujillo's ideologues created the myth of peace and national security. Accordingly, only Trujillo's use of extreme measures saved the Dominican Republic from "the Haitian danger." If the border was still intact, it was only thanks to Trujillo. Furthermore, official references to the 1937 massacre were absent. No documentation with direct references to the massacre—before, during, or after it—has been found in Dominican archives. It was as if it never happened. And for many Dominicans, misinformed by Trujillo's propaganda machine, it never did.[53]

After Amabelle witnesses the perfect mirror of the stream, the only scene of value in her mind, a collection of water memories, the puddle of sweat, the rising river, and here the stream, Amabelle bids farewell to Señora Valencia, asking her to go in peace. Their friendship, fragile and politically freighted, now more than before, is absent. On the way home, she sleeps deeply, not interested in recording the land of the living. Without fear, she gazes upon water so still it almost looks like it is not there. She does not blanche at the sudden appearance of the crazy professor making his way into the night. She simply wishes for the river to relinquish his sanity back to him. In these moments when Amabelle gazes upon the river, Benedict Anderson's affective connection between nationalism and death is relevant, especially since Amabelle stands on a grave which cannot be seen. Consequently she has to imagine what is not there.

> Yet void as these tombs are of identifiable mortal remains of immortal souls, they are nonetheless saturated with ghostly national imaginings ... if the nationalist imagining is so concerned, this suggests a strong affinity with religious imaginings. As this affinity is by no means fortuitous, it may be useful to begin a consideration of the cultural roots of nationalism with death, as the last of a whole gamut of fatalities.[54]

In Anderson's evocation of "ghostly national imaginings," there is a link made to what Freud articulates as the "death instinct" and in Amabelle, all these are interpellated at the moment of deepest meaning. As Anderson begins to situate nationalism at its beginnings in death, an idea to which he does not dwell for the more rational and material world of an imagined community amidst the living, I posit that the dead are integral subjects in the imagination of the nation. However this point differs from Anderson's because the dead of this novel are the dead who are "disposable," in Khanna's terms, and are not given the status accorded to the soldiers whose remains are missing in war.

Yet, this community of the dead exerts a force significant enough to become a part of the national imagination of the body politic. In the context of Danticat's novel, the Haitians are a complex people who quest after the record[55] while balancing a dialectic with the dead. The spirits discourse with the bureaucrats in an awkward shadow boxing match and without the bureaucrats becoming aware, write themselves into the master narrative even though the names of their dead and the record of their torture remains invisible.

Here I leave behind the Andersonian dead signified by the tombs of unknown soldiers, but rather move toward the more populated death zones of the subaltern dead, killed outside war or volition, outside any terms or contracts of citizenship, killed by the state outright for unarticulated reasons to maintain the state as it is. The voices of these "invisible" and "unsung" dead also formulate part of the imagined community that inhabits the zone of the nation-state. Yanick Lahens's conjectures about "the Antillean memory as being painfully bruised" and the observation that Haitian culture and literary construct is "a permanent oscillation between anchorage and flight"[56] helps move us closer to the exact location of this space, a liminal alterity that marks the very essence of Haitian literature. We locate this place early in the text, as early as when the two young lovers are together and share their fears, and Amabelle knows that "Sebastien is haunted by the crooning of pigeons."[57] To him, pigeons are metonyms for the dead, crooning their sadness by burying their beaks in their breasts, their song a contagion of melancholy that crosses over from the animal to the human, from the sky to the earth, and from the dead to the living.

Meanwhile Amabelle lies on the water looking for the dawn, a speck of light that will unite her with those she loves, "paddling like a newborn in a washbasin."[58] Some days before Amabelle makes sense out of the foamy seas and loamy land on the river bed, even before she visits Father Roumain or begins her journey back to Alegría, Amabelle recounts her life and passions, and catalogues in the signature manner of an old woman, her words suggestive of grief, guilt, and awareness of the prejudices of history.

> It is perhaps the great discomfort of those trying to silence the world to discover that we have voices sealed inside our heads, voices that with each passing day, grow even louder than the clamor of the world outside.
> The slaughter is the only thing that is mine enough to pass on. All I want to do is find a place to lay it down now and again, a safe nest where it will neither be scattered by the winds, nor remain forever buried beneath the sod.
> I just need to lay it down sometimes. Even in the rare silence of the night, with no faces around.[59]

In this section of self-conscious survey of her past ruins, Amabelle, while expostulating on the dead season, borders, veils of water, the word, and the dead, gleans great meaning in the imperial projects and her own agency within this landscape of massacre. The ambiguous nature of her self-assessment adds to the richness of this brief manifesto on empower-ment. What is signified by "the voices sealed inside our heads" resonates like a palimpsest, layers buried under layers of meanings. Possibly this clamor alludes to the voices Amabelle finally listens in her rest upon the river, the voice that allows her to understand that the Pwofesè is also in search of dawn, and the voice that will take her to the site of her losses. Finally these voices signify the community with the dead in the clear-est instance available in this text that situates itself as an archive against the master archive, the archive within the body[60] that rises to meet the population within and outside it. Testimony becomes an effort at collec-tive memory; Amabelle's testimony, in particular, becomes evidence of things only seen by those who experience the loss from massacre.

In her search for all the love she lost, this is the moment of profound meaning. Like the nation symbolized by the madman who also searches for a dawn out of the dark veil of history, she goes into death looking for dawn. Here, we return to Zamora fishing for a usable past through the lens of poets like Charles Simic and writers like Jorge Luis Borges in order to come upon "the historicity of all narrative"[61] and are able to visualize the history pooling around Amabelle's slowly-dissolving body. Amabelle's narrative, her quest for discourse with the dead, a dialectic of loss is a legitimate counterpart to the hegemonic notion of history.

Communing with the Dead

The imagined community exists in this politically charged movement that the Haitian citizen performs after surviving a massacre of biblical propor-tion. Amabelle Désir's link to the dead keeps her living. Danticat evokes the slaying of 40,000 Ephraimites at the hands of their victors, Jephthah on the Jordan, directly excerpted from the Judges at the opening of her novel. Massacres and tragedies of all variations, as Benjamin reminds us, is the condition of history. Our religious and historical imagination remains rooted in such loss. Resurrection, within the Judeo-Christian tradition, arises in a time of great suffering and cruelty, symbolized perhaps most effectively by Jesus. Within the Haitian tradition, where voudoun plays an integral role in cultural and spiritual imagination of the collective, a religion that only recently received state credence as legitimate, and is a syncretic merging of Yoruba, Catholicism, and other native belief systems, posits that the afterlife is in fluid continuity with the life we know.

The dead are not really dead and they travel without trespass. I wish to emphasize three points of iteration: first, resurrection, alluding to a rising from the dead, hinting at a possible community that is always in a state of absent presence, is an ancient idea and marks the intersection between religion and history; two, Haitian religion, in particular, fluent in the metaphysics of Yoruba, Catholicism, Taino spirituality amidst many other traditions, holds on dearly to the idea of resurrection because of the suffering inscribed upon the master narrative of its history from the time of Henri Christophe to the contemporary; three, I wish to locate this imagined community not in a religious space, but an alternate space between religion and history, a place of collective loss and melancholia that bridges the bridge of textual possibilities, the literary. The literary contains the knowledge of this loss and forms the bridge to its alterity where reside a loud and cacophonous mass of communities in negotiation with their own erasure.

In her earlier story in the collection titled *Krik? Krak!*, "Nineteen Thirty-Seven" she offers the blueprint of the novel two years later. In the short story, we meet a woman named Josephine grieving for her mother locked in a Haitian prison long after 1937 because she is suspected of witchcraft. Her mother dies in prison due to severe beating by the guards after a long period of malnutrition and suffering. Josephine arrives with an older woman, Jacqueline who was part of the group of mothers and daughters who would travel to the edge of River Massacre every year on November first to commemorate their losses, remember their mothers who were killed and thrown into the river from the other side, and the very place which gave birth to Josephine. Unlike *The Farming of Bones*, in which the central character hardly knows her mother in life and never bears children herself, retaining the functionary of mourning absolute, in the story, we see a community of women mourning for the irreparable loss and damage of that massacre instituted by the Dominican state on the eve of November 1, 1937. What unites the two works, and where I see the blueprint prefigured in the earlier work, is the concrete presence of a community of mourning, women who recognize each other not based on sight but collective experience of weeping at the riverbanks and recognize each other based on the code of question and answers that only they would know.

"You hear my mother who speaks through me. She is the shadow that follows my shadow. The flame at the tip of my candle. The ripple in the stream where I wash my face. Yes. I will eat my tongue if ever I whisper that name, the name of that place across the river that took my mother from me."

I knew then that she had been with us, for she knew all the answers to the questions I asked.[62]

These woman, wrestled out of agency by the Dominican and Haitian state, wrest agency in the refusal to name the place across the river, the place that marks the horror of their greatest combined losses. The Manman's ability in this story to make the stone Madonna cry becomes metonymic for the condition of these women as people outside state, their relationship to the religious institutions both European and African represent an ability to mourn symbolized by the weeping Madonna. Thus, their flight, what the state charges as their blasphemy, becomes an act of liberation, marking their mourning as excess of their positions as women, domestic workers, itinerants, and subalterns and thus, they are punished for excess by imprisonment and death. This flight after death is seen earlier when the daughter finally understands that her mother flew across River Massacre with the child in her belly, flying her way into life.

It is a fundamental bifurcation presented in this metaphorically charged story that the state does not sanction or support the liberation of these women or the excesses implied by their condition of melancholia. For the women, the state itself becomes an intrusive power, whether it is the Dominican state interested in ethnic cleansing or the state labeled as their own, Haiti, where women can be punished for witchcraft and criminalized for crimes impossible to prove in a court of law. In reading this fracture between the state and this imagined community with the dead formed by the subaltern female figure, it is revealed that the imagined community exists in the interstices between the dominant notions of power, and lies aloof from state, religion, and hegemonic notions of paying homage to only those whom death entitles to be recorded in the state archives.

It is necessary to suture this knowledge with collective melancholia that keeps the survivors living and the dead alive. I bring to the frontlines the notion of those left out of national and global citizenship. The very beings without any public access to privilege, caught as Spivak articulates in the condition of diasporas old and new, are the ones with the messianic power to make the dead live.[63] In their community lies the ultimate power to undercut the authority of the state in order to invoke powers both ancient and far more enormous than the nation-states that define their existence upon modern and manichean racialized ideologies. The slip of a girl who turns into a shard of a woman, Amabelle Désir, a vessel of memory and desire, contains in her the power to transmute rules of the nation and the universe in order to fashion her losses the way she wants. The plea is to remember against labeling such a character, metonym for an entire nation, as powerless or a mere performer in the master–slave dialectic. Amabelle's trespass is symbol of her innate ability to exist, exercise political right, spiritual power, and mourn beyond redemption and her humanity despite all her loss that overwhelms the fissures in the master narrative.

To end, I turn to Homi Bhabha and Joan Dayan's in-between spaces wherein they locate culture and Haiti respectively. In light of contemporary projects to locate the histories within a history that consumes and subsumes its own as well as others, Bhabha brings forth the necessity of interstices, the in-between spaces, and stresses the legitimacy of the border, the nowhere land between places. While reading Morrison's *Beloved*, he interprets what she means when she concludes with the injunction that this is not a story to pass on; instead, he observes, it is a story engraved "in the deepest resources of our amnesia, of our unconsciousness."[64] The imagined community with the dead that I am positing, embedded as an integral stage space within the Danticat novel, then becomes a project to raise and re-interpret the discourse from the imaginary into the symbolic, an effort at ordering what remains hidden beneath history, hegemony, and empire. As Bhabha sees within Sethe's act of infanticide an effort by the oppressed to own the property of their body (refer to the ideas of imagined community in Chapter 1 on Morrison's *Paradise*), the condition of this community becomes indubitable within the dialectic of the marginal. "It is not there," I say, "it is there there in Amabelle's here," forms a fulcrum of plot momentum within the text.

Joan Dayan locates the irrefutable presence of metaphysics in the material when articulating the complicated notion of history in the context of Haiti. The subversion of the master–slave dialectic on the tumultuous soils of the first black nation in the western hemisphere demands a new form of history and its notion of gods, spirits, amidst others. As Dayan layers story upon story to complete the story of the end of Dessalines, the first President of Haiti, like a cubist refraction, she points to the need for inversions as an inherent act of resistance, "The dispossession accomplished by slavery became the model for possession in vodou, for making a man not into a thing but into a spirit."[65] Dayan's estimate makes the connection valid between dispossession, resistance, and the world of the spirits.

In Haiti where the world of the spirits has historically placed itself within the material realm due to the historical contingency of repeated instability in light of attempts at self-definition against a world alarmed by such acts, an imagined community with the dead is not only plausible but reasonable and pragmatic. The thing lost that the melancholic swallows exerts itself outwards on the body of the oppressor. In the context of Danticat's novel, the "disposable" people write themselves back into the master narrative of the state. These are not collective acts of melancholy—instead, they are melancholic acts on part of the masses to inscribe their voices upon the body politic, write themselves unto the lacunae-ridden text of history.

3

Partition and the Woman's Body in Bapsi Sidhwa's *Cracking India*

Cracking India is a guilt narrative. Told within the confessionary mode of an author continents and decades removed from the site of violence, it charts narrative out of the repository of sparse memories of a childhood spent in the ruins of British India as the nation-states of India and Pakistan came into fratricidal being. Bapsi Sidhwa, the Pakistani Canadian author, remembers of her childhood spent in Lahore, the undressed upper body, tussled hair, and dismembered torso of a man spilling out of a gunny sack on a road side, and out of it, she creates the guilt narrative of a Parsi child.

The central character in Sidhwa's novel, Lenny, narrates this episode of history through the unflinching gaze of the child. Situated as the arbitrator or uninvolved observer of the systemic violence of nation making, Lenny belongs to the minority Zoroastrian community, neither Hindu, Muslim, nor Sikh but a wealthy Parsi family who suffers the trauma in the most vicarious of terms, through the loss of friends, neighbors, and domestic workers. Narrated with the detail and honesty of a child's voice, the text is permeated with the Bakhtinian features intrinsic to novel-making, laughter, and polyglossia[1] in the conversations that form the impetus in narrative momentum. Ian Watt's *The Rise of the Novel* (2001[1957]) informs how much of Lenny's keen gaze is imbued with aspects of "formal realism."[2] Lenny's situatedness in the contexts of history is as critical as the fictions of her mind.

Lenny turns the "compressed world" of this novel's opening sentence into a microcosm of larger systemic violence, a street that marks the rupture of the beginning of a postcolonial world. We travel and emerge with her, matured like her from a dewy-eyed seven year old to a chastened nine year old. Recreated by a middle-aged woman who leaves us at the border, we exit at an ending in which the main characters dissolve "across the Wagah border" and all we are left with is the unspeakable guilt of a child. The child betrays a figure who metonymically stands as the nation—her Ayah, domestic worker, formerly Santha, then Mumtaz. Lenny, specially privileged by her household due to a crippled leg from the aftereffects of Polio, who cherishing herself for this bountiful separation from all other children, is looked after from morning to night by her Ayah, named only once in passing but referred through the narrative by her function, namely that of a domestic worker.

Lenny, sheltered from the maelstrom of freedom struggles brewing across the landscape for multiple reasons, sees the world and experiences lessons through the figure of Ayah. Ayah is a young woman beautiful in body and spirit who generates a gaggle of men of all persuasions and occupations, flocking around her in a halcyonic bliss hoping to be meted a favor or glance from her. Lenny, a center of the center of sorts, meets the man who wins the courting game, Masseur with his gentle fingers; and the Ice-candy-man, ready to sell any commodity that fetches its due price but a man who fails at winning Ayah's heart. All the other stories and characters—Lenny's younger brother and older cousin, aunts and uncles, neighbors who flee and domestic workers who stay, Papoo the untouchable married at eleven—disappear as the narrative gathers force and Lenny arrives at the narrative moment where the forces of alarm and disquiet, the rabble of the streets, Muslim since this is the land given to Pakistan by the British cartographer, arrive at her doors. The multitudes demand any Hindus who might be hiding or in disguise in this Parsi household. Upon everyone's declaration that Ayah has fled the scene, it is Lenny whose eyes lock into none other than the man still sour from the loss of his obsession, Ice-candy-man. To him, Lenny confesses that Ayah is somewhere inside and then, immediately realizes that he is not separate from the pillaging masses, but their conduit into her house. To him again, Lenny attempts to revise her statement as he sits down to light his bidi and lets his comrades do the kidnapping. It is all to no avail. Despite Ayah's recovery months later, in a brutally altered state of being and dress, and despite the flamboyance of a love story that continues in the wake of systemic violence, we are left with Lenny's voice that seeks Ayah decades after her disappearance into the Wagah border. The mature Lenny seeks not only an unshakable truth about the whereabouts of the woman she loved more than her mother or a lover or possibly both, she seeks release from that narrative in which she loses and betrays her closest consort.

Ayah is raped in the purgatory marked as the historical event that turns the colonial British state into postcolonial nation-states with its own borders, structures of order and power hierarchies. While identified by modernity and its ensuing historians as a moment of liberation and epistemic break from colonial structures of oppression, the ontological condition of the newly demarcated territories also spelt bodies in trouble: bodies committing crimes upon other bodies, and bodies forced to move, escape, or relocate under extreme duress. The historian, Frederick Cooper offers necessary criticism of the singular lens which comes to define the reflection on such a period of turmoil; his caution regarding studies about such periods also pertain to the studies imagined about such periods, such as Bapsi Sidhwa's novel. He writes:

> Finally, empires established circuits along which personnel, commodities, and ideas moved, but were also vulnerable to redirection by traders and subordinate officials. Empires were crosscut by circuits that they could not necessarily control—the ethnic diaspora of Chinese traders in Southeast Asia, for example, or the diasporas created by imperialism and enslavement, such as the linkages established by African Americans across the Atlantic world. Benedict Anderson has used the idea of a circuit to explain the origins of creole nationalisms, but that was only one form of political imagination that grew up within and across colonial systems. The metanarrative of a long-term shift from empire to nation risks masking these diverse forms of political imagination in a singular teleology.[3]

Just as later in his study, he points to the teeming number of modernities wrestling against one another to assert a singular meaning, there are a number of histories, many buried underneath the top soil of overarching stories of postcolonial liberation, such as the creation of India and Pakistan being easily dwarfed by what happened in Haiti nearly 250 years before modern nation making touched the South Asian sphere. Ayah's rape and silence thereafter are part of the multiple teleologies to which Cooper calls our attention.

Ayah does not speak. The violence practiced upon her body eludes the story. Ayah, as the subaltern female figure of Sidhwa's narrative, leads us directly to Spivak's pathbreaking question, that has now been studied and commemorated, "Can the Subaltern Speak?"[4] However ours is not the obsessive quest for the ever-receding figure of alterity within the academy, but a careful understanding of the character as presented, and in this character's shadow, a comprehension of the positioning of the imagined community therein. Instead of seeking the figure upon whom is the authorial stamp of subalternity—the Ayah, I focus upon Lenny, a figure of alterity beyond subalternity out of whom the imagined community exists. In this self-ascribed marginal text, the story attempts to tell the narrative of a nation-state in the making through a peripheral voice—a child, a female one at that, disabled, and one who comes from neither of the dominant religions, a Parsee. I wish to wrestle with notions of self-constructed alterity against a privilege of being the outsider in a time of civil war and fratricide, an *outsider-within*, an elite wealthy community that escapes the pain of nation making by deliberately remaining at the sidelines and watching history unfold upon itself, as powerful as any fictional narrative, but removed from the realm of the real.

Much in the manner of Rabindranath Tagore's Bimala who is metaphorically both mother-goddess and mother of the nation, both home and the world, women who continue from the colonial into the postcolonial eras becomes the symbol of the newly-formed nations, and thus, both a sign of excess and erasure of meaning. While their gendered choices remain limited, they come to represent the power and aspirations of the entire nation. This paradoxical condition brings them to the border, or more precisely, a place beyond or between nations. Robert Young, in his exposition on postcolonialism as a discipline, writes about the condition of the woman:

> The ideal of the nation is often imaged as a woman, and the ideology of nationalism often invests the nation's core identity upon an idealized, patriarchal image of ideal womanhood. When this happens, women, as Virginia Woolf put it, effectively have no nation.[5]

Bapsi Sidhwa deliberately engages with the border—the political border as it is redrawn in the blood and tears of its inhabitants arbitrarily moved from one side to the other, as well as borders that decry the cost of difference: class, caste, color, religion, and gender amidst of a host of complexities that surface in the narrative. By deliberating on difference from within and laboring on indubitably "border work," Sidhwa shows the border as the stage upon which the nationalistic articulation of desire is enacted, the laboratory in which the powers experiment with newly-shaped identities. In the place beyond or between nations, the place where women's bodies do the border work is also the place where one can locate imagined communities with the dead. The propositions within Sidhwa's project resonate with the intellectual theses put forth by Abdirahman Hussein as central to the life work of the late Edward W. Said.

> ...the idea of boundary is not merely an end in itself, but is further deployed as an instrument of ideology critique. It is therefore particularly apposite to note that, in my view, the notion of the in-between zone, as it is rendered in Said's writing, is far more than a studied ambivalence—a kind of equipoised (and ultimately aesthetic) contemplation of difference; nor is it an indication of ambiguity in the semantic or formalist senses; nor finally is it a state of neutrality and passivity, a symptom of confusion and lack of rigor, or a species of nomadic restlessness embarked upon for its own sake. Rather, it must be conceived both as an active field of engagement—hence an experiential gestalt or space—and as a multi-vectored process, that is, an awareness of transformation in a temporal dimension.[6]

Hussein's position on Said attends to the active engagement needed in understanding the ephemeral communities populating the border, the women's bodies who do the border work. After Santha is carted off by the mob of men, and she is reduced in the reader's eye to the metonymic violation of all women in men's wars, Santha hardly speaks, and when she does, it is to show her dissatisfaction with the spaces of her latest confinement. Elaine Scarry's close reading of Marx, Genesis, documents of prisoner torture amidst other pieces of evidence is urgent in informing the relationship between the body and pain,[7] or more concisely, the impossibility of conveying in language the affect of the tortured body. Santha's kidnapping and subsequent rapes that last uncertainly over a period of several months, and then the descent to the quarters of Lahore's red light district, charts a disintegration of her world as identified and mapped by Scarry over two decades ago.

Much like Lenny's world is "compressed" because of the limited mobility of the privileged and crippled child, Ayah's world, like the prisoner or torture victim, is compressed. Toward the end of the narrative, it is from this double imprisonment, akin to the "doubled silence" of the female Victorian heroines like Jane Eyre, she escapes. One can, of course, not mention Jane without confronting the cost paid by her dark double, Bertha. Read as class by Terry Eagleton, psychological "dark double" by Gilbert and Gubar, and Spivak adds to the analytical corpus by contesting Kant to shed light on the violation of Bertha.[8] In sum, it is important to notice the difference and separations that exist between the Jane–Bertha dialectic of colonizer and colonized against Lenny–Santha dialectic of master–domestic worker/patron–lover/parent–child/goddess–devotee that exist in the latter novel. Just as Santha is never the shadowy othered figure caged throughout the narrative beyond any visual observation, a body that is never allowed to be described, and is only described in its descent from the high turrets of the house as it flies down burning, Lenny is by no means Jane.

Santha is referred through her function, a domestic worker, an Ayah. Reduced symbolically to what she represents in the eyes of her young protégé, Ayah shifts to her given Hindu name, Santha in the company of her equals in class, either the domestic workers in the Parsi household or her admiring bog. Later in the novel, she is turned into Mumtaz, a name given to her by her assailant, husband, and traitor, Ice-candy-man referring poetically, and at that point, sadistically to the great love of Emperor Shah Jahan, Mumtaz Mahal, for whom he constructs the monument, Taj Mahal.

A complicated web of women's voices mingle in this narrative to also form their own community, imagined within the text and peopled even beyond the surface of the immediate story. The three appellations itself commingle to form a community of the disenfranchised and the transfigured. Sidhwa engages in a prototype of subversion defined by Graham Huggan as "staged marginality."[9] The difference is inherent in subordinate exclusion serving the secret function of resistance and revolution from within, the domestic workers being very much a part of the territory inside and outside the household. Though Sidhwa veers away from the tourist spectacle rife in Rushdie and Naipaul's landscape as seen by Huggan, Ayah and her entourage in the garden are themselves one of the multiple versions of "staged marginality" rife in Sidhwa's novelistic discourse.

Within the house, i.e., the homes of the same class and family to which Lenny is related reside a number of women whose connection to institutions of power is tenuous, yet who wield power in order to be able to institute changes, women such as Lenny's mother, Godmother, and even Slave Sister to some extent. Outside the constructs of this house, another community of women live in its awning, or benevolent despotism, the domestic workers, the poor, and the dislocated—Papoo and her abusive mother, Muccho, Imam Chacha's extended family of mostly women from the countryside, and Hamida and the innumerable masses of anonymous women in the shelter for spoilt women next door. Even though none of these women sit easily with one another, and there are recorded instances of differences, such as Muccho's abuse of Papoo and Hamida's escape from the shelter to find a shelter which actually assures its namesake, these women within and without the house, as I examine, form an alternate community granting a privileged shelter from the system of patriarchal oppression inscribed within the public sphere of nation making.

Lenny's cry after her betrayal, when she hopes to attract the attention of Ice-candy-man and revise her earlier statement about Ayah's location, is the symbolic cry to patriarchy. It is a sound before and beyond language that never reaches consequence or audience except an older Lenny decades later who reimagines the story for her literate English novel-reading audience. In case of the women, I argue for a community tied together by the impossibility of shared discourse, a community that cannot realize its pain in language, and thus exists configured from its own negation. Thus, this novel will be intersected from three different spaces, geography of dislocation being a fundamental tenet in the examination of the notion of community: first, the community of men who admire Santha and surround her in an idealized simulation of the nation-to-be; second, the various communities of women that implicitly and explicitly exist at different moments through the narrative; and finally, the imagined community which is derivative and antecedent of all the other spaces in the novel.

Jannah or Paradise Surrounding Peace: Santha's Entourage

Paradise is a place below from the beginning of Sidhwa's novel, a geography that echoes the manner in which Morrison ends her novel where the labor of paradise occurs down below. While the elites live in their removed world of British-styled tea parties and the politicos of the day dictate national movements locked in secret chambers from metropolitan centers, the laboring class of knife-sellers, gardeners, masseurs, and Ice-candy-men form a haphazard union around their common love for the beautiful Santha. Her name meaning "peace," echoed at the beginning and ending of Hindu prayers, is made famous as the ironic invocation of the same at the ending of T. S. Eliot's high modernist poem, "The Wasteland." Santha's admirers gather around her like devotees around the goddess, a deification of sorts where Lenny begins her narrative. Ayah's voluptuous curves and munificent gaze command Hindu, Muslim, Sikh, Parsee, and British acolytes to her pedestal of the perfectly curved body.

> The covetous glances Ayah draws educate me. Up and down, they look at her. Stub-handed twisted beggars and dusty old beggars on crutches drop their poses and stare at her with hard, alert eyes. Holy men, masked in piety, shove aside their pretenses to ogle her with lust. Hawkers, cart-drivers, cooks, coolies and cyclists turn their heads as she passes, pushing my pram with the unconcern of the Hindu goddess she worships.[10]

Much in the stream of her more famous literary predecessor, Bimala of Rabindranath Tagore's *Home and the World* (1915), who at the onset of Bengali nationalist movement symbolizes both Mother India and Mother Goddess, Santha is the center of meaning in a religious and nationalist sense. Santha is at once the goddess and the nation, her body transfigured from beauty to divinity.

This entourage of admirers generally gathers in the Queen's Park, in the umbra of the Victorian English Crown, another matriarchal figure who looms large across the novel. Later in the novel, after the British leave and British India is carved into the twin states of India and Pakistan, and also, a distant kin, East Pakistan, the queen is severed from her pedestal. This occurrence is simultaneous in the ruination of the men's club, its deteriorating components, and finally Ayah's brutal removal from her elevated status amidst her acolytes. At the early stage of the ideal gathering, differences subside around the nucleus of their gathering so that the Hindu gardener, Sikh zookeeper, Muslim Masseur, Ice-candy-man, knife-sharpener, wrestler, butcher, etc., coexist with the Hindu Ayah in their midst who is the caretaker of the "lame limpet," a Parsee child. Through this pluralistic panoply of characters, larger historical events and presences are filtered, pointing to a distant darkening horizon. The English remain at this juncture, despite the year being 1947, the blustering red-faced lecherous old man who reprimands

Lenny for not walking while ogling Ayah at the beginning of the novel. Even Gandhi is a farcical figure, surrounded by young women to whom he administers enemas himself, ghastly pale, and obsessive about bodily functions rather than national awakenings in his one entry directly into Lenny's world.

However foreshadowing being the key piece of Sidhwa's narrative technique, Lenny lowers her gaze when directly facing Bapu, just as the narrative finally bows down before the weight of historical events. Similarly, though the park is the location of *jannah* or heaven in Arabic, it remains a site of infection, the precise location where cultures mingle and self-preservation weakens, signified in Lenny's mother's guilt over allowing her child access to the park where she probably contracted her crippling disease, Polio. Later the park precisely becomes the mimetic location reflecting divisions born of the new nation-states as the communities divide and begin to disappear altogether, or sit separately as prescribed under the new political ethos.

Though none of the men in the narrative surrounding Santha make history in any direct sense, within the novel, they are the hegemons, through whom events on the national stage are deciphered. The knife-sharpener tells Santha about strange stabbings in the night; Ice-candy-man bicycles in and informs the group about the infamous train from Gurdaspur that arrives filled only with dead bodies and a gunny sack full of breasts. Less harrowing but nevertheless recording the rising heat of national tumult, the entourage discusses speeches of Gandhi, Nehru, Jinnah, and Bose in order to disseminate amidst one another the imminent making of the imagined national community. All these remain but filters inessential to the gathering because Ayah's one sharp dismissal ends all discourse, "If all you talk of is nothing but this Hindu–Muslim business, I'll stop coming to the park."[11] Of course, it has to be noted that her dismissal comes in the wake of rising animosity between the men as they bait one another over the method and manner in which particular leaders ally themselves in the nationalist movement of liberation, not simply when the conversation turns political and revelatory. Ayah attempts in the subtle way of women in power have informally negotiated reversals in their immediate coterie.

Their's is the perfect world—competing against one another to tell the funniest jokes and make Ayah laugh so much that she might unravel, waiting for that sudden movement with which her sari palloo slips from her shoulders and the tellers of jokes can glimpse at the round orbs of their heaven, the *jannah* of Santha's bosom. A gendered illusion of paradise in which men of all these different communities collect to remove themselves from the more historical fratricide marking this period, they narrate to one another alternative tales of languor, pleasure, and ribaldry by which they mock the very differences that separate their usual selves. Reminiscent of more famous frame narratives in which people gather to tell one another fabulous stories of mirth and sensuousness in order to escape the spectacle of death looming large, such as *The Thousand and One Nights, Decameron,* or *Panchatantra*, these are all narratives removed from the teller of tales by several degrees, so that it is through Lenny's childhood self as recalled by a middle-aged woman decades later that we receive the story.

Lenny, along with the men, love Ayah with the intensity needed to make a paradise on earth. Through her entire journey of the compressed world, she accompanies Ayah everywhere, even her secret amorous trysts with the one man to whom she gives her heart and body, the gentle Masseur. Thus, Lenny participates in all the lovemaking, watching from within while Ice-candy-man watches from the threshold. Early in the novel when Lenny narrates the solitary meetings between Ayah and Masseur, she observes how the young man continues the ministrations he begins upon Lenny's withered legs to his beloved's body in private; Lenny, perhaps unconsciously or actually through her own imaginative will, transforms the lover's meetings into an ecstatic occasion for herself too. She writes, "I recall the choking hell of milky vapors and discover that heaven has a dark fragrance." This fragrance contained the whiff of more noxious odors that turn Ice-candy-man into a monstrous and cataclysmic figure, torn by jealousy and violence all at once.

The "complex rites"[12] by which Ayah's admirers coexist cease to function in the post-partition apartheid of minorities in which all, including Masseur and Ayah pay for the sin of selection. Already married to a woman condemned to live in the village separate from Ice-candy-man, he expresses his jealousy to Ayah when Lenny wonders if his wife would want to run away from him, and he replies, "She won't. They have no tailors in the village. No masseurs either ... with their cunning fingers taking liberties!"[13] The first and only open reprimand made to Ayah, he warns of impending doom with the certitude he knows that the woman he considers to be his cannot be taken away from him. Despite Masseur's best efforts to bring harmony to the growing friction in their gatherings in a time when their groups remains the only pluralistic one in the garden, Ice-candy-man banishes all efforts with his divisive declarations and doubts in the probable leader of a liberated India, Nehru. To Lenny, he is symbolic of the serpent in the Garden of Eden, or Judas amidst the twelve disciples of Jesus Christ. Lenny notices then his "poisonous insights" and counts to see that "we are thirteen," and realizes, "I am not too young to know it is an uneasy number."[14] Ice-candy-man is of dubious lineage, a fact revealed only toward the end of the novel, raised in the Kotha with a mother who is a prostitute and a father who could be any in the teeming nation wrestling against its colonial masters for its own identity. An outsider and insider at the same time, his eyes betraying him to be one from somewhere further north like Afghanistan or Iran, or born of a British father, his role in oppressing Santha retains little difference in the master–slave dialectic. John Thieme offers this complex politico–historical analysis while looking at the "problematic parentage" rife in postcolonial literatures that "write back" to the British Empire. Thieme writes,

> Problematic parentage becomes a major trope in postcolonial con-texts, where the genealogical bloodlines of transmission are frequently delegitimized by multiple ancestral legacies, usually but not always initiated by imperialism. Orphans and bastards abound in postcolonial texts and the engagement with issues of parentage is often as intense as in, say, a Fielding novel where the social order can be reaffirmed by the revelation that the picaresque hero of uncertain birth is really a gentleman. The difference is, of course, that postcolonial texts seldom, if ever, offer such comfortable resolutions. Illegitimacy preponderates, a metonym for both social plurality and the severing of the bloodlines from the supposed colonial father.[15]

Unlike Rabindranath Tagore's Gora, born of British parents and raised by a Bengali family, or the English Englightenment characters whose dubious parentage only later reveals their upper crust origins, Ice-candy-man, like many of his kin in postcolonial literatures, arises out of murkier clay than posited; his father is nameless, so the Name of the Father is an even more acute incongruity. The specter of violence could point in multiple directions, the colonialist, colonized, or a host of other hybridities with equal culpability. Or, a form of empty tablet of the self on which he alone, the son inscribes his own story. Easy answers are not offered here. This most charged character in this novel is marked by hazy origins, much like the heroes of Judeo-Christian mythology or their latter-day counterparts, men from the postcolonial peripheries. The quotient of carnage is politics; the entourage in the garden allies itself along communal lines with a changed Ice-candy-man declaring openly his participation in the riots, and orders the remaining Hindus to either convert or flee. A frightened Ayah gains solace in the arms of her lover, the only voice of secular perspicacity in the fires raging across Lahore, the Masseur. It is apparent that the Ayah, as she is sobbing to Masseur's proposal to marry her, says, "I'm already yours,"[16] echoing its more unspeakable undercurrent, "I'm already lost."

When Lenny finally stops to devote an entire chapter, albeit a short one, Chapter 20, to the figures of this time, Nehru and Jinnah, both fathers of the two new nation-states, this active act of historiography arrests the literary narrative, stops the simulation to enter the real, and infects the inner circle of Santha with the impending nationalistic violence of India and Pakistan. By this point, the garden is already in a state of disheveled ruin, and though tense, remains the last of such pluralistic beacons of hope. However the closer the national narrative approaches the stories circulating in Santha's umbra, the more paradise wavers. Finally, when a chapter strictly attempts to account the master narrative of history, the distance dissolves. The inner circle and outer circle of the novel are one and the same. *Jannah* comes to its inevitable end. The camaraderie of Santha's suitors comes to an end; and Santha herself pays. She discharges the woman's function as goddess and nation both of whom suffer and create worlds out of their own decimation.

In these historiographical biographies of the two patriarchs, a more feminine figure emerges, all but forgotten and insignificant to the master narrative, Jinnah's wife, a Parsee beauty who dies "at twenty-nine. Her heart was broken."[17] Lenny equates this character with her mother for courage and Ayah for generosity. A parallel female figure upon whose loss national narratives continue uninterrupted, Jinnah's wife echoes in future anteriority Ayah's suffering. As *jannah* disappears, other imagined communities begin to wrestle for separate control of newly-formed spheres.

In a grotesque simulation, the ideal community around Ayah dissolves along political and religious fractions. Both winds of love and war fracture the community. The wealthier groups gather under Godmother's aegis, when she entertains her smooth-talking brother-in-law, Dr. Mody, and it begins to reflect the condition of masculine community, a continuing absorption with the female body without any actual concern for the condition of these same bodies. Such a disjunction is evident in the benefit gala for the doctor at the historical moment of waves of relocation, Hindus from Lahore who leave for the other side of border and Muslims from Amritsar and neighboring towns resigning themselves in opposing journeys. At the onset of the largest human relocation known in modern history, Dr. Mody's dehumanized observations equate beauty with pain, and the eyes of the women become functional entities in place of the women themselves.

Reading from below, I find an authority in the gaze of the broken or damaged. Repeatedly it is noted in literature stemming from the partition (Saadat Hasan Manto, Bhisham Sahni, Amrita Pritam, Yashpal) that the eyes of the "conquered" offer an alternate account of history. Eyes remain imprinted on the mind long after the instance of seeing, both the person seeing and the person seen recall the instance of deadlocked "gaze" which in this instance of narrativity, inarguably becomes the originary point of the story's force. Long before the hapless Lenny turns in her Ayah to the pillaging mob of men gathered at her doors, she overhears the bawdy conversation between adults, much of such conversations peppering and informing Sidhwa's narrative as she attempts to guard at once notions of childhood and storytelling.

In a gathering of medical students for the benefit of her visiting brother-in-law, Dr. Manek Mody, Godmother, her younger sister dubbed Slave Sister, and her silent husband, Oldhusband, talk about Ayah's beautiful eyes, the eyes of the kidnapped Punjabi girls, and Lenny's cross-eyed perspective much to the narrator's chagrin. As Dr. Mody ogles after Ayah's lustrous eyes and she bats her eye lashes to their full effect, Dr. Mody laments the growing absence of a number of beautiful eyes in their midst, the green and hazel eyes of the abductees. Disrupting the ribaldry surrounding Ayah and the absent women, Ayah here standing as metonym, her eyes symbolizing all the ones captured already in the battles of men, Oldhusband pounces out with significant invective: "What's all this business about eyes! Eyes! Eyes!" he explodes. "You can't poke the damn thing into their eyes!"[18] Here, once again eyes retain their function as witness to massacre because in the authority of the aging patriarch, numbed and befuddled at his own silence in a house dominated by women, he deploys the ultimate weapon: he reminds his feminine audience that the site of violation is located elsewhere and that women pay the price of nationhood and exile through the currency of their bodies. By bringing the banter from the liminal to the physical space, Oldhusband underlines Sidhwa's purpose of foreshadowing the future looming in their living room. At the same time, he also articulates that what is left as quotient by the victor, deemed unimportant in this death dance of power played upon the woman's body, her eyes stay locked, haunting like the absent women, or mocking like Ayah's gaze upon the doctor's revulsion of the flies about whom she says, "Let it be: it will hardly eat anything,"[19] While the female body becomes metonym of massacre, the eyes serve as metonym of massacre recorded.

Further on, after the grotesque discovery of Masseur's dead body, butchered and stuffed in a gunny bag, soon after, we arrive at Lenny's betrayal of Ayah to the teeming masses of men who want to devour and consume her alive, "the other of the other" Sidhwa arrives at the purpose of her narrative which is to show that "women suffer the most from political upheavals ... and vengeance is taken on a woman's body in her part of the world."[20] Ayah's body as it is lifted over Lenny's head on to the crowd of men, seemingly, she is being stretched, pulled, and divided, mirroring the condition of the land, her body emblematizing the historical epoch of partition and fratricide. As the nation is torn apart at the seams, so are Ayah's clothes torn to reveal the secrets of the woman's body under the violent public gaze. Here, Lenny recalls:

> The last thing I noticed was Ayah, her mouth slack and piteously gaping, her disheveled hair flying into her kidnapper's faces, staring at us as if she wanted to leave behind her wide-open and terrified eyes.[21]

There are a number of ways to read this memory, this need putatively on Ayah's part to leave her eyes behind, or Lenny's in remembering this need. Eyes stand both as sign of guilt and witness. In Ayah wanting to leave behind the eyes, a double absence is imagined. First, the text represents the inarticulability of extreme horror by placing rape outside the text's narrativity, Ayah's mouth remains "slack and piteously gaping" unable to form words except the incoherent "O" of fear. Second, in its imaginary, Ayah also would rather leave her eyes behind, so that not only does Lenny, or the text, and by implication, us, the audience not experience the horror of such violence, but she herself be spared the extremities of this suffering. Yet, her eyes do not close; they remain "wide-open" recording, remembering, and indicting those left behind.

Following in the Indo-Persian poetic tradition of the ghazal, eyes figure as the windows into the soul, so when Lenny finally meets her absent nanny after a furtive and fierce search on part of the women in her family, Ayah, dressed as a "dancing girl" of the red-light district of Lahore, Hira Mandi keeps her eyes appropriately lowered. Shuttered from communication, Lenny finds no route in to perform the ecstasy of her fantasy reunions. Only when Ayah raises her eyes, Lenny, after fully recording the horror articulated therein, jumps into the familiar lap and nestles in the unfamiliar scents of attar and henna. Santha is precariously perched on the edge of a velvet seat in her high heels and outrageous silks, her apparel and décor marking the daily carnival of the diamond market where women are the precious stones, bought and sold by the hour. Here, Lenny sees and relates what Santha has undergone:

> Where have the radiance and animation gone? Can the soul be extracted from its living body? Her vacant eyes are bigger than ever: wide-opened with what they've seen and felt: wider even than the frightening saucers and dinner plates that describe the watchful orbs of the three dogs who guard the wicked Tinder Box witches' treasures in underground chambers. Colder than the ice that lurks behind the hazel in Ice-candy-man's beguiling eyes.[22]

Lenny sees what Santha has seen, not from eye-witness account of first person narration, but the "seeing" gaze of Santha. The eyes of the violated remain open for the record, upraised and accusatory and asking for redemption. They push against their own "vacant" melancholy by expressing the rage and desire of the decimated. They are fierce; Lenny notices, "Even Godmother can't bear the look in her eyes." While Godmother instructs on fate and forgiveness in attempts to console the younger woman who wants to be carted off across the border to her family in Amritsar, the eyes fill the gaps generated by the specter of violence. Bejeweled, glittering, the body stands as a site of carnival where structures of patriarchy collude to subvert the same system, utilizing the body of the woman as a tool of masculine resistance.

Cracking India is a tale of guilt: Lenny's guilt at her great betrayal of the mother figure in her life, her Ayah, who also becomes the easy allegory for "Mother India" as she is brutalized, mutilated, raped, and rendered damaged in the act of division of warring communities.

Ambreen Hai, in her article, "Border Work, Border Trouble: Postcolonial Feminism and the Ayah in Bapsi Sidhwa's *Cracking India*,"[23] disputes the scholars before her who valorize this text as the great voice of border discourse, unmanned and liberating, such as Jill Didur[24] and Harveen Sachdeva Mann.[25] Hai contests the pure celebration of Sidhwa's text, now taught widely in the American Academy as the legitimate voice of the subaltern, the distressed other not heard in the master narrative. She indicts Sidhwa as part of the culpable problematic which inscribes Ayah's namelessness and silence into the novel. In the silence of the victim and the silence of the narrative about this suffering, the novel "represents, is not representative" of the subaltern voice, and the actual acts of violence covered in the Victorian prudery of Sidhwa's own Parsee prurience, casts the pall of "narratavial unspeakability" into the story. Here, Hai quotes Gayatri Spivak to point out her issue with the allegory of Santha as the nation: "When the woman's body is used only as a metaphor (or anything else), feminists correctly object to the effacement of the materiality of that body."

Though I agree with Hai on the complicity of the text to its own part in the carving of Ayah's body, I find Lenny's desire for her nanny far less deceitful than Hai purports it to be. In the garden, all young men of various skills and professions compete with Lenny for room on Ayah's much-desired and voluptuous body. Even if Sidhwa might be unaware of a lesbian love coloring her nostalgia for Santha, she unabashedly documents the pleasure of observing the aesthetic genius of Ayah's body, the lugubrious glances of British, Hindu, Muslim, and Parsee alike when watching this very same body, and Lenny's own manipulation to command Ayah's attentions. Lenny, ever present as the crippled child in Ayah's care, is witness to Ayah's amorous dalliances and participates by triangulating the play of desire between Ayah and Masseur, or the Pathan, or Ice-candy-man, the Muslim popsicle vender who assumes professions to suit his proclivity for capitalistic enterprise.

In the final and only scene of intimacy between Ayah and her great love, the Masseur, Lenny is present and vying for room. Amidst the growing tensions of an impending partition, Ayah confesses her fears and wonders if she should leave for Amritsar where she has relatives. As Masseur assures her with lover's promises and a marriage, Lenny inserts her alarm at the thought of Ayah's absence. Upon Ayah's succor that Lenny will always have someone to take care of her, Lenny says, "I don't want another Ayah … I will never let another Ayah touch me!"[26] If one was to miss Lenny's desire for Ayah as ethereal alone, the next and final line of chapter nineteen dispels any ambivalence: "I start sobbing. I kiss Ayah wherever Masseur is not touching her in the dark."[27]

The woman's body, reduced to the token status of a tool in men's articulation of identity and assertion, is eviscerated of self-given meaning. Instead of becoming the nexus for a diverse community that represents the prelapsarian ideal, the body is body alone, decorated and marched in public, or in a place like Hira Mandi that collapses the distance between public and private sphere, is at once, here and nowhere. She wants to flee from here to there, where also she is not sure of welcome or refuge, and the eyes stand as symbols of the grotesque. Dilated beyond recognition or solace, the former nanny, giver of refuge repeats her request for refuge from the "sweets" man who commodified and consumed her at will. Santha's eyes in this instance have a dual metonymic function: they mark both the dead and the exiled from this massacre of history called the partition of British India. Dead while living and exiled from the familiar in terms of home, labor, and love, Santha's eyes provide the "unsayable" alternate history, the "unsayable" like the "dead" writing history with their absence.

Considering the preponderance of eyes in the novel, it is not surprising that the novel ends with a final act of resistance offered by the eyes. Before Santha disappears across the border, followed closely by Ice-candy-man, she sees him wasting away on the roadside, pining for her attentions and instead of offering any response, outrage or indictment, "behaves as if he is invisible."[28] In the condition of a historical episode like the partition which to this day has not been easily categorized due to the structured and unstructured forces that brought it to its form of absolute violence and relocation of citizenry, resistance also becomes doubly difficult to articulate. One has to find, within the literary imaginary, these places of secrets and silence, layered with the discourse of absence, and further, comprehend that its mourning contains within itself gestures of defiance.

Fall from Paradise: Women's Communities

I recall another childhood nightmare from the past. Children lie in a warehouse. Mother and Ayah move about solicitously. The atmosphere is businesslike and relaxed. Godmother sits by my bed smiling indulgently as men in uniforms quietly slice off a child's arm here, a leg there. She strokes my head as they dismember me. I feel no pain. Only an abysmal sense of loss—and a chilling horror that no one is concerned about what's happening.[29]

Sidhwa pays particular attention to the severe price paid by women in classic patriarchy, as is her stated goal by writing a novel in which a woman, in the figure of the Ayah, pays the greatest price for men's wars and nationalistic endeavors. While doing so, she also foregrounds numerous methods through which she charts the gruesome specter of the dehumanization of women: the figures of the battered women who begin pouring into the shelter next door, Imam Chacha's relatives from Pir Pindo, especially all the women and young girls, and closer to home, the damage inflicted upon Papoo. Women, as a whole, systemically and historically pay a heavy price for their gendered condition of secondary citizenship throughout Sidhwa's landscape. As a whole, the women are a disenfranchised class. Only in secret ways which goes unnoticed by the systems of order at large do women inhabit a sisterhood, nearly non-existent during times of peace and subversive during war. Only in the brutal dehumanization after death are they allowed to exist openly as a collective, a sort of aberration of a community, or its own negation. Thus, in this section, I articulate a gendered disenfranchisement, while showing occasional efforts at sisterhood that succeed in the culminating event of death. This section will end with the end of hope for Ice-candy-man in the train from Gurdaspur that brings in it only dead bodies, including all of his relatives.

The women even in the more powerful circles of wealth and status arrive at meaning only in their relationship to a man. Even Lenny's mother, the epitome of beauty and a detached nonchalance with regards to power, has to play the coquette to attain money for daily expenses. When her husband takes his postprandial nap, she massages his feet. Godmother and her younger sister, whom Lenny has given the appellate, Slave Sister, exist in self-prescribed imprisonment, a house of women rendered inconsequential within the norm and continues its cacophonous bickering as an emblem of unrest between women. Godmother torments Slave Sister as an asinine and impertinent shadow. Slave Sister mumbles, retorts or rages back, unable to even donate blood at her own will, their own names, their names Roda and Mini forgotten in the melee of their vitriolic abode. Not even allowed to donate her blood like the others, including Rodabai, we never hear

Mini's side of the narrative, her voice dulled into an indecipherable and unimportant drone.

Even Lenny is not safe from the condition of being the second sex. She finds herself fending off the unwanted attentions of her older cousin who gropes her despite all prohibitions and succeeds on one occasion to touch her private parts. Lenny, clearly a mimic of Ayah, who learns lessons and sees the world through her maid/domestic worker's almond-shaped eyes, also begins to experience a similar fate. While Ayah fended off the attention of a host of admirers, Lenny finds herself thwarting the desire of her solitary cousin who approaches her with the rabid obsession of Ice-candy-man. In a culminating moment of lessons learned, Cousin, in order to teach Lenny about Hira Mandi where the women are the diamonds and men buy these diamonds, shows Lenny how a man uses a woman. "Ever ready to illuminate, teach and show me things, Cousin squeezes my breasts and lifts my dress and grabs my elasticized cotton knickers. But having only the two hands to do all this with he can't pull them down because galvanized to action I grab and jab him with my elbows and knees, and turning and twisting, with my toes and heels."[30] Cousin does succeed in his mission of continuing to fondle Lenny while she exasperatedly asks him, "Who told you all this?"[31] As the child's body turns into a woman, she finds through immediate contact and verbatim information about her position of being the second sex.

In the immediate circle of domestic workers, Muccho is the untouchable woman who abuses her daughter, Papoo out of a seeming fear of her defiance and corruptibility. She repeatedly beats her unconscious so that early in the novel, Ayah, with the help of Lenny's mother, packs Papoo off to the hospital to heal before the next volley. The untouchables, treated as outcastes and existing at the edges and interstices of national–religious communities, do not look toward the formation of a Hindu India as a possible avenue of betterment of their lot.[32] Many convert to Buddhism or Christianity, Papoo's father Moti choosing the latter and turning into David Masih. Still they continue their status as the butt of all humor so much so that when the mob enters the household, they joke that with David's newfound status, he can sail off to England and marry a white woman, Christianity being of course conflated with the religion of the colonialist and the white man at once. To a population that is deemed to be pariahs, not allowed to stand on the lowest rung of the ladder, conversion causes little actual change in a man's life except a chance to evade death at the hands of an enraged mob. Muccho sells her pre-pubescent eleven year old daughter, trained in all the domestic chores with a fire of rebellion still sparkling in her eyes to a dwarf old enough to be her grandfather. Drugged and decorated by her own mother, Papoo's oppression marks the internalized perpetuation of hegemonic domination with no relief in sight at the onset of modernity. Though the new state governments have instituted laws since independence to uplift this most downtrodden of communities, often times reality points to an ostracization that continues to this day.

The male gardener, a Hindu with a caste mark of the bodhi atop his bald head, Hari is tormented through the narrative for his difference. Frequently, all the domestic workers, young boys, and even the unflappable Imam Din gang up on the hapless fellow threatening to undress his single wrap, dhoti to embarrass him in public in front of all the women and children. Finally, when the barbarism of war affects the horseplay to such an extent that even Lenny jumps in, smelling blood, the group manages to undress and complete this spectacle of emasculation. The evening when Lenny realizes that her shadow besmirches the Brahmin Pundit, "One man's religion is another man's poison,"[33] the hordes zero in on Hari and denude him of his loincloth. Lenny remembers, "Like a withered tree frozen in a winter landscape Hari stands isolated in the bleak center of our violence: prickly with goose bumps, sooty genitals on display."[34] Laughter and a cruel parody mark such details in the novel where a body in pain causes the crowd to erupt into hilarity. Alamgir Hashmi, while reflecting on the Pakistani postcoloniality, considers this to be a signature Sidhwa moment. Hashmi writes,

> Two of Bapsi Sidhwa's three novels, *The Crow Eaters* (1978) and *Ice-Candy-Man* (1988), have introduced a farcical strain on another plane of performance into the Pakistani novel in English, a strain in which "sacred facts" appear laughable, and family and communal reserves and loyalties are put to a severe comic or eccentric test, even if it is only to explain, rationalize or accept those very facts.[35]

Hari, his name carrying the mythological weight of God Krishna, who brings to an abrupt halt Draupadi's undressing by giving her endless yards of a sari that tires the muscular Duhssana into capitulation, is not able to live up to his given name. Hari's molestation is the product of a patriarchal homosocial environment in which men make it an athletic feat to humiliate the weakest in their vicinity, and by doing so, effeminize him, pecking the unwanted male into the subordinate status of the second sex.

As the post-partition violence degenerates from ribaldry into mob frenzy, the men at Lenny's door, before kidnapping Ayah, denude Hari. The crowd wants to see if he is truly circumcised as he claims, the irony of his new name, Himmat meaning courage, failing him yet again at this dire moment. Caste system is itself, historically speaking, an aberration of Hindu dharma, a rigidification of acāra against the Vedic prescriptions for just law and merciful behavior. As each of the Hindu ages mark a decline in the human condition, the last age before doom, Kaliyuga, the current age is marked by the ossification of a system of occupational stratification into caste system, so that a sizeable population of Asia, 260 million to date,[36] remain absolutely disenfranchised. In India itself, 100,000 crimes are reported against the community of untouchables, now known more favorably as "Dalits" and this is only due to underreporting, the actual number being much higher than this gargantuan numeral. Of course, one has to also bear in mind at this juncture the difficulty of fully recording, accounting, and participating in a global conversation on Dalit Rights, an issue whose complexity is richly detailed by Deepa Reddy who offers anthropological insight into the difficulty of discursively equating caste with ethnicity.[37] Hogan, in re-reading Bhikhu Parekh's *Colonialism, Tradition, and Reform: An Analysis of Gandhi's Political Discourse*, writes lucidly about this latter day development:

> Colonialism creates an irreconcilable conflict between *yugadharma* and *manavdharma*. Indeed, it exacerbates the conflict between *manavdharma* and *acara*, by rigidifying *varnadharma* (caste dharma) and the dharma of wives. For example, as noted in the preceding chapter, the practice of Sati, previously in decline, spread and intensified under British rule. The conflicts are not easy to resolve. In short, colonialism—that great intensification of adharma in kaliyuga—has made all real options adharmic.[38]

Ranna's story completes the blank spots of the disappearing women Dr. Mody laments. He carries the burden of having watched his naked sisters run madly across the courtyard while he was in hiding with other men. As he made his way from Pir Pindo to Lahore, he passed ruined villages and dead corpses, the women in complete states of undress, and occasionally if alive, pleading to their assailants for merciful obliteration.

He heard a woman cry, "Do anything you want with me, but don't torment me ... For God's sake, don't torture me!" Later in the tale, when Lenny confronts the sad replacement for Ayah, a Muslim woman named Hamida, Hamida confesses that Lenny's mother also knows that she came from the camp for "Fallen Women." The camp, simulation of the woman's community, is shaped by the silence of its "inmates," the general sounds being one of sudden moans or wailing in the middle of the night. Instead of a collective strengthening, Lenny observes a morbid marooned condition making the supposed respite a place of stigma, a place from which its populace seeks to withdraw, such as Hamida who crosses over to the other side of the wall. Here, Kelly Oliver's psychoanalytic study on the troubling condition and consequences of self-hatred, which is institutional and hegemonic in her paradigm, is worth reading, especially the chapter where she looks carefully at the gendered secondariness of women's ontology. Oliver writes,

> The melancholic, suffering from social melancholy, experiences the shame assigned to her by culture as her own inferiority or defective being. In addition to feeling guilty, she is made to feel flawed in her very sense of self. The self-beratement caused by shame can be more painful than that caused by guilt because it attacks the core of identity and self-esteem. While we can make amends or reparations for wrongs done, we cannot make amends or reparations for wrong being. We can apologize or ask forgiveness for bad acts, but what does it mean to apologize or ask forgiveness for being bad?[39]

Lenny sympathizes so profoundly that when she cries for Hamida's condition, her sorrow is the sorrow of an adult. Lenny matures in Hamida's pain. Although Lenny is feminist enough to quake against the injustice perpetrated upon all the women of partition, she, in turn, is unable to forgive her own error, "wrong being" from which she attempts recovery by retelling the entire nightmare from which she is not able to wake forty years later. Thus, Oliver's "colonization of psychic space" is also the fuel for this novelistic discourse.

Though Hamida is not able to clarify Lenny's doubts about this fallen status, Godmother, the purveyor of sense and logic, explains that Hamida was kidnapped and kept in Amritsar, and now back in Lahore, she will not be accepted by her family. "Some folk feel that way—they can't stand their women being touched by other men."[40] While Godmother's tone is strangely accepting of this injustice, Lenny digests it by naturalizing it; if touched by human hands, sparrows peck their own chicks to death. Sidhwa places at the forefront of her narrative various forms of the woman in pain; in direct relation to the Civil War that brings into being the two nations, women pay the price by carrying the pain of both body and soul. Women's incoherent cries of pain, beyond language and expression, rupture Ranna's story. Sidhwa provides us a closer look by pushing Hamida out of the shelter directly into the narrative gaze of Lenny who hears her sobbing at night, missing her children and family, and accepting her lot as fate. Hamida tells Lenny the story about the king's son destined to die by a tiger who dies of fright by looking at the painting of a tiger. She accepts reality as fate. This story also points to the power of simulation; in turn, the readers of Lenny's narrative are able to feel the affect of women in pain—body and soul, and bear the burden of this disenfranchisement despite being leagues removed from the site of patriarchal carnage.

Eluding the surveillance of the masculine gaze, women exist who attempt to forge a sisterhood to alleviate suffering. Such is the umbra cast by Lenny's mother and her Godmother. While Lenny suspects her mother of arson, her mother has secretly been accumulating petrol and providing it to her neighbors and others who have been fleeing to India—the Hindus and Sikhs of Lahore. She also whisks women to safety, women outside the patriarchal norm having been violated, and brings many to the shelter next to her own home. Moreover, she does not hesitate to bring one among the many in the shelter to her own home as an Ayah for her children. Since each act of sisterhood is secretive, to the innocent like Lenny, who are not told anything, imagine that their mother and aunt are busy burning the city. When finally Lenny confronts her mother, she hears the truth, "I wish I'd told you ... We were only smuggling the rationed petrol to help our Hindu and Sikh friends run away ... and also for convoys to send kidnapped women, like your ayah, to their families across the border,"[41] already revealed to Lenny by Godmother. Mother's acts of subversion cast a pall of gloom rather than illuminating an underground network of solace amidst the women of means to the women without any.

Godmother, fiercely bellicose to her own sister, takes upon herself the charge of freeing Ayah and allowing her to go in whichever direction she pleases. Godmother finds out Ayah's whereabouts, visits her in Hira Mandi with Lenny as her accompaniment, and has her transported to the shelter before shepherding her across the border to Indian Punjab. It has to be noted that even in this autonomous vein, Godmother instills in Ayah the values normative to her sex, asking her if she had rather not continue the life she has with her rapist and traitor, Ice-candy-man. Even a figure as staunchly self-determined and dynamic as Godmother dictates to Ayah the motto of the patriarchal institution which flourishes only upon the assent and subservience of the oppressed gender, "What's happened has happened. But you are married to him now. You must make the best of things. He truly cares for you."[42] Ayah falls at Godmother's feet and begs to be anywhere but there, in those rooms with the velvet curtains and satin skirts and rhinestone studded dais where women's bodies are bartered every night. Here, Elaine Scarry's express attention paid to the torture chambers is useful. Scarry writes:

> In torture, the world is reduced to a single room or a set of rooms. Called "guest rooms" in Greece and "safe houses" in Philippines, the torture rooms are often given names that acknowledge and call attention to the generous, civilizing impulse normally present in the human shelter. They call attention to this impulse only as prelude to announcing its annihilation. The torture room is not just the setting in which the torture occurs; it is not just the space that happens to house the various instruments used for beating and burning and producing electric shock. It is itself literally converted into another weapon, into an agent of pain.[43]

The torture room, like the victim's disintegrating world, becomes a weapon that furthers her pain. Here, the torture room is also present in the guise of civility and decorum, the plump luxury of the decadent courtesan's chamber where rich men buy their favorite women for an evening's entertainment. Santha, not surprisingly, wishes to leave these rooms she views as sites of torture and prison memory. Once Ayah desists and sticks to her disinclination to stay mired in the status quo, Godmother moves with a pace incongruous with her slow amble, and lifts Ayah from the imprisonment of Hira Mandi to some anonymous future specter that remains ambiguous, but streaked with the possibility of a future away from the mercenary love of Ice-candy-man.

He, the perpetrator of much of the violence in this novel—one man symbolizing through his solitary being all the crimes of partition, is chastened when Godmother lifts her hands from his head and refuses to bless his marriage. Later he is beaten by a crowd as he follows Ayah to the Recovered Women's Shelter. Much to the reader's satisfaction,

Ice-candy-man's punishment is doled out to him before our very eyes, and suffers his sins on the novelistic stage. "He is a deflated poet, a collapsed peddler—and while Ayah is haunted by her past, Ice-candy-man is haunted by his future: and his macabre future already appears to be stamped on his face."[44] Neither Godmother nor Lenny's mother need the other women. Community is the attempt of women of luxury and means to reach out to the less fortunate, a philanthropic effort thwarted, at times, by the ignorance of the very classes they set out to save. Community then defines itself as an act of largesse transmitted from one to another, and not autonomous selves making a collective all together.

Furtive efforts at sisterhood are made; some significant acts are done. Yet these remain furtive, excluded from the larger patriarchal narrative, unable to make any radical alterations to the narrative of violence. Secret at best, they remain unknown even to the kith and kin of the ones involved. The stories of resistance remain a ghost story yet to be unraveled. Like Spivak's own ancestor, Bhubaneswari Bhaduri provides a narrative of resistance to imperialism, yet remains divested from the authentic mark of veracity, Mother and Godmother remain alien characters, even distant from the main events within the novel, hardly present through most of it, and at many momentous turns, absent. An ending that remains tortured by uncertainty, and rife with future tensions, Lenny concludes, "I am told that Ayah, at last, has gone to her family in Amritsar.... And Ice-candy-man, too, disappears across the Wagah border into India."[45] Godmother is not successful in helping to heal Ayah; neither is she successful in keeping her safe from her perennial stalker, Ice-candy-man. The story continues beyond the reach of a sisterhood fractured at its most germinal stages. To return to Lenny's childhood nightmare quoted at the beginning of this section, it is crucial to note that present in this dreamscape are the pivotal characters who could or seemingly engage in women's communities, the mother, Godmother, and Ayah, and yet, no one notes or cares the horror happening within the purview of their munificent gaze. Lenny, the recipient of mass brutality, lies prone in "horror" and "loss" that no one cares to observe, protest, or change these events. Much of the efforts at women's communities rest in this presence and absence, the women located exactly where horrible events are transpiring but also, unable to exercise any power of action.

Somewhere after Lahore begins burning and before Ice-candy-man assumes a deadly swagger and openly encourages the Hindus and Sikhs to leave, the train from Gurdaspur arrives in Lahore. He bicycles in like a menacing wind and tells his dwindling group, "A train from Gurdaspur has just come in. Everyone in it is dead. Butchered. They are all Muslim. There are no young women among the dead! Only two gunny-bags full of women's breasts! I was expecting relatives ... For three days ... for twelve hours each day ... I waited for that train!"[46]

In complete opposition of the spirit of woman's community which heads this section, I believe that such a collective is allowed only after death in the most debased and grotesque manner possible; the breasts in the gunny sack is the only place where a collectivity is allowed. Women's community is prohibited, not permissible within the echelons of patriarchal power. Subversive at best, nonexistent in general. The breasts, as metonyms for women and womanhood, severed from the source of life, bloodied, brutalized, and collected like non-entities from the anonymity of raped bodies is the ultimate act of patriarchal oppression—insistence on the formation of the new state, its refusal to admit a community deemed as the other, and a coded message.

Ice-candy-man's observation that the dead bodies do not contain young women suggest that the young women lie unburied, dead, or nearly dead but continually tortured and refused the bliss of a quiet shelter at least after death. Like a telegraph or radio signal, the breasts in the train carry a message—your women are not part of our newfound community. Your women are only good as bodies, and we have used these bodies. These bodies will not reproduce. The men on one side talk to the men on the other side. Milk is replaced by blood, so that the message is conveyed with utmost clarity: not only will we not allow your community to grow on our side of the border, but we had rather your community not grow at all. And in this sadistic condition of anonymous lifeless disembodied erasure, the women are finally allowed to gather in one space within the confines of the patriarchal structure.

Touching in the Dark: Imagined Communities

Disenfranchisement is the precondition for the emergence of imagined communities. Lenny, a Parsee child whose community defines their presence through their absence, as unthreatening as sugar in a full glass of milk, and careful about never exercising real power, is a girl child at the margins because of her secondary status in a beleaguered community. Her's is a community of less than two hundred Parsees whose inclination to commune comes not from the need to cohere or exert power in their adopted homelands but to simply be allowed to exist. This state leads to impossibility of coexisting in a community in any legitimate sense. Lenny is born into a time of war, fratricide, communalism, and disruption. Of her childhood, she writes, "I was born with an awareness of the war: and I recall the dim, faraway fear of bombs that tinged with bitterness my mother's milk."[47] Deeply sensitive to the emotional vagrancy present in others, and machinations deeper inside, she is born ready to commune with those in her vicinity and within the larger locus of British India that soon divides into two states. Attuned to the madness inherent to a time of patriarchal reordering of the empire into postcolonial states by the stroke of cartographic pens, she relates to us at an episodic pace the quality of nightmares that haunt her subconscious, leading us from the realm of the symbolic to the imaginary where the pain of others seeps into her being: "That night I have the first nightmare that connects me to the pain of others."[48]

Pain is the essential component of forming a community, one's own pain and the pain of others. If a bridge is somehow formed between the two, and since it does not subsist strictly in conversations within a room or common space but in nether regions of the heart, here begins the locus for the imagined community. This imagined community exists in four parts: between Lenny and the children dispersed through the novel; between Lenny and all the people who die during the relocation and riots of partition, especially the dead and battered women afflicted from this period; between Lenny and her disappeared Ayah and dead Masseur; and finally, between an older Lenny who is remembering the child narrating.

Lenny's direct conversations in the novel are with her brother, Adi and her cohort, Cousin. However a whole gamut of other children's voices and stories echo through the narrative. Much of her subconscious battles specters of mass violence against children, she is one amidst thousands suffering similar fates. In the earliest one, she is lying prostrate in a sterile environment with endless beds of other children, everyone being dismembered without a single adult wincing at their collective fates. The dismemberment, like much of her imaginary, wrestles with the madness of national spaces being clinically divided, referring to the renamed title of Sidhwa's novel, cracking India. The dream of dismemberment haunts this narrative and returns in altered forms as the political scene turns more gruesome and deadly. As the entourage turns unfriendly and Lenny notices them to be thirteen, connecting with the guilelessness of childhood an earlier thirteen which betrayed its own, she returns to the dream:

> I am back in the factory filled with children lying on their backs on beds. Godmother sits by me, looking composed, as competent soldiers move about hammering nails into our hands and feet. The room fills with the hopeless moans of crucified children—and with their collective sighs as they breathe in and out, in and out, with an eerie horrifying insistence.[49]

In the world of the here and now, Lenny is as separated from Papoo, Ranna, Khatija, and Parveen as high walls and gravel roads allow. But in her dreams, she is in a collective, suffering together. Lenny forms an imagined community with all the children of her story. And in forging such a link, she also attributes agency, valor, and power to a group generally deprived of voice within patriarchal structures while critiquing the ignominy of adults who force children to pay the ultimate price for their squabbles over rhetorical blowtorches like land and freedom.

The very children removed from Lenny in terms of religion, caste, and class are the ones with whom she forges community. Papoo, an untouchable treated accordingly by her own mother, Muccho, claims the greatest sympathy from Lenny who has to be assured by Ayah that when unconscious from another bout of mother love, she will be all right. Lenny does not give us a child broken by parental and societal abuse heaped plenty upon her but a plucky girl who is "sprightly, defiant, devilish, and as delightful as ever."[50] Even the evening Lenny hears about Papoo's arranged marriage at the age of eleven, she describes her to be, "cheeky as ever with her mother. And forever smiling her handsome roguish smile at us."[51] In fact, the only time one does not see Papoo sparkle and fight back is when she is drugged and given in marriage to a dwarf old enough to be her grandfather. Asleep, she does not exert her usual power but remains ensconced firmly in the imagined community where Lenny reads resistance, not defeat.

Ranna, Imam Din's great-grandson from Pir Pindo, with a bellybutton that extends like a finger, who imitates Lenny's stunted walk and likes her, is in turn given room in her narrative to tell his story.

When the Sikhs oust the Muslims from their ancestral village, Ranna alone makes it to his uncle's village and from there, to a refugee procession that snakes its way to Lahore. Intermingled in his story are his older sisters of eleven or twelve for whom Lenny has a soft corner, Parveen and Khatija, already trained in the quiet ways of womanhood, alarmed at Lenny for her short dresses and shorter hair. Ranna, as much a part of Lenny's voice as her own, thinks he saw the last of Khatija while hiding under the bodies. "Once he thought he saw his eleven-year-old sister, Khatija, run stark naked into their courtyard: her long hair disheveled, her boyish body bruised, her lips cut and swollen and a bloody scab where her front teeth were missing."[52] The torment suffered by Ranna and his sisters, probably dead before that day ended, occupies profound space in Lenny's imaginary, wounding her long before the actual ravages begin. In an earlier trip when she visits Pir Pindo with Imam Chacha and attends the town meeting about the changing political climate, she leaves the village "with a heavy heart and a guilty conscience,"[53] aware with clairvoyance death looming large in their midst, and also knowing guiltily that she was absolved of all such occurrences. This proclivity for recognizing truth leads to the great moment of betrayal when Lenny, unaware with the others that Ice-candy-man has turned foe, tells Ayah's whereabouts to the bloodthirsty mob, and leads to a period of adults glowering at her in incredulity at her truth-telling powers, is the very penchant that bares the field for other form of communities to exist.

Lenny is born ahead of her nation. When it is finally born, it happens to be the same date as her birth. Her immediate circle is too busy paying attention to the grief flung in the wake of a new state to celebrate her eighth birthday with the fanfare she decries. Sharing the birthday of her nation, Lenny also forges an imagined community with all who died and suffered the atrocities of partition on both the Indian and Pakistani sides. Many of Lenny's literary predecessors wonder about the impossibility of carving up land like a piece of cake, standing in the very same spot that can be called a new name the next day. Take, for example, the writer, Saadat Hasan Manto's mad male character, Toba Tek Singh, who ends up assuming the most sane and most peaceful stance, refusing to budge from the no-man's land between the two newly formed states. In the end, he gives up his life standing in that position. Unable to work out to her satisfaction the logic of "batwara" or partition, Lenny wonders, "And the vision of a torn Punjab. Will the earth bleed? And what about the sundered rivers? Won't their waters drain into the jagged cracks? Not satisfied by breaking India, they now want to tear the Punjab."[54]

Unlike her more famous predecessor, another midnight's child, Salman Rushdie's Saleem Sinai, who meets all the other hundreds of children born at the stroke of midnight in telegenic conferences in his head, Lenny connects in invisible ways through the language of pain. Beyond verbal representation, the pain of populations broken by this epistemic breaking of spaces, Lenny engages with them in a community that refuses to loosen its yoke long after Ayah disappears across the border and all we are left is Lenny's guilty conscience. Moving onward with the sensitivity of a synesthetic nose, Lenny smells the vitriol disturbing the tranquil air of the Queen's garden. At the count of thirteen, she writes, "I try not to inhale, but I must; the charged air about our table distills poisonous insights. Blue envy: green avidity: the gray and black stirrings of predators and the incipient distillation of fear in their prey. A slimy gray-green balloon forms beyond my shut lids. There is something so dangerous about the tangible colors the passions around me have assumed that I blink open my eyes and sit up."[55] The physical and psychic wounds of partition are insisted through Sidhwa's narrative as being beyond expression. When incidents defy rhetorical encapsulation, sounds, smells, and stares replace words. From Ice-candy-man's terrace, a terrified Lenny watches a Sikh mob wave a child who is speared through her shoulder blades; beyond sound or recognition, she stares up at Lenny. Much like Ayah's stare at the threshold of Lenny's home, the stare speaks the volumes that necessitate the imagined community between Lenny and all the dead from this fratricidal episode. In the women's shelter next door, she hears women wailing all night, much like her own new Ayah, Hamida's sobs. Pain of partition, in which bodies are carved with the same precision and unflappability as property, progresses to a state beyond language and fosters the imagined community contained within Lenny's narrative.

While the community with the wounded exists in an implicit manner, Lenny is deeply attached to the community formed with both Ayah and her lover, the Masseur. Attached to Ayah like a third arm, she is part of all her experiences, from the entourage in the garden to her secret rendezvous with Masseur. Hardly a duo, with Lenny a symbol in their heated equations, the trio adorn the scenic hideaways where Ayah treks to meet her paramour, followed in tandem by Ice-candy-man. Removed by decades from the scenes of loss and rupture, an older Lenny continues to exist in an imagined community with the pair of lovers and their stalker. "Ayah comes. And with her, like a lame limpet, come I."[56] A "lame limpet" is quite clearly a precisely used terminology to define all of Lenny's existence in relation to her Ayah, far more than a polished alliteration. Clinging persistently like a mollusk on some sea rock or animal, Lenny molds herself to Ayah's body, attempting throughout her childhood to see the world through Ayah's lovely eyes, and separating only when Lenny herself becomes the cause of this rude severing. A limpet, in its tertiary meaning, also suggests the type of weapon which when touching the helm of a ship, explodes. In Ayah's life, Lenny serves that function as well.

Upon more careful reading of the climactic portion of Sidhwa's novelistic enterprise, it is apparent that Lenny also destroys the ship that is Ayah in the terms of her dearest attachment. What is necessary to note is that such a weapon by its very action also suggests a self-destruction, and Lenny, regretful from the moment of betrayal long after into her waning years as she recollects the story, remains partially destroyed, like a shard remembering its own wholeness. Stunted in her childhood with polio and depending on Ayah for mobility and support, Lenny continues her stunted condition in adulthood, a deformed malaise that haunts her spirit and inspires a narrative around her own betrayal of Ayah. If there is any ambiguity about the doubled triangulations present in the love between Ayah and Masseur, as imposed by the third hidden presence of Ice-candy-man, then it is underlined in the final scene to which we return again between Ayah and Masseur when the young man consoles his beloved and urges her to marry him and ward off the political trouble on the horizon ahead. At this, Lenny crumbles at the fear that Ayah will leave her for Masseur and stages a tantrum. "I start sobbing. I kiss Ayah wherever Masseur is not touching her in the dark."[57] Lenny loves Ayah; of this, there is no doubt. Later in retrospect, she forms an imagined community with not only her beloved Ayah but her lover as well.

The two great tragedies within this novel are Ayah's loss of Masseur and Ayah's loss of herself. Hidden underneath these two is another tragedy: the tragedy of Ice-candy-man, who pursues the haunted Ayah, "hand in hand, two hungry wombs … Impotent mothers under the skin."[58] And underneath everything, the long-remembering Lenny's loss of her other self. Lenny lays aside the corporeal boundaries and enters the sentient being in each of these characters and forms with them an imagined community that transcends the limitations of space and time. Alighting upon the assault on Masseur, she finds his mutilated body spilling out of a half-open gunnysack at the roadside. While others watch with detached consternation, she absorbs along with her own horror and loss, the sensuous details that make up his body and all that was vital to life in him. Simultaneously she observes, "He isn't (a person). He has been reduced to a body. A thing. One side of his handsome face already buried in the dusty sidewalk."[59] Signifying in its valences the "ashes to ashes, dust to dust" liturgy said upon the body being buried, she also possibly equates a part of his handsome face with the sidewalk itself, a grotesque metonymic transfer that alters Masseur forever from sentience to materiality or immateriality, either being apt as stages without life. Ayah, with "haunted eyes"[60] from memories of her lover croons his songs and weeps in solitude, though punctuated by Lenny's much-seeing eyes that detect the amorous stalker behind their every step. Peculiar alchemy dots this landscape of melancholy: while the Masseur becomes the ground upon which they walk and Ayah is nothing but eyes. The most vindictive of the lot, Ice-candy-man is gendered female in the extremity of his desire, his hands, like empty wombs, that need to be filled by Ayah; it is as though his hands wish to maternally birth the life they snuffed out in the Name of the Father. Lenny, the sole arbitrator in the web of desire, orchestrates the drama from afar, populating the imagined community with the pathos appropriated in their actual historical moments.

Once again, the violence remains outside the text. What exactly happens to Ayah once kidnapped, the rapes and beatings remain at best suggestions. We see her only before and then, after the brutalization. Lenny, expert at entering and exiting at will in a less obvious way than Salman Rusdhie's most powerful midnight's child, Saleem Sinai, watches Ayah and sees in her open mouth, "the dead child's screamless mouth."[61] While much of the novel involves itself in Lenny aping the Ayah in unconscious ways, living vicariously through her pleasures, here Ayah reflects Lenny's condition in a reversed manner, reduced to a child in fear parallel to the powerful Masseur who turns into a thing. Lenny, the child memoirist, the adult historian, the traitor and the lover, rekindles community when recollecting not only the date of events, but the transformations that articulate vulnerability rather than structures, shapelessness over the order of loss. Here, Bart Moore-Gilbert's exegesis on Spivak is useful to remember: just as Spivak criticizes the canonic Anglo-American feminist text, *Jane Eyre* in that Jane's heroism rests on Bertha's imprisoned body—violated, erased, and burnt by the end of the text,[62] Lenny's memory, munificence, and passion rest on Santha's butchered body that is never allowed to speak.

Burdened by truth after her betrayal, Lenny repeatedly vomits and is unable to look at anyone in the eyes, especially men like Sharbat Khan who say, "Children are the Devil ... They only know the truth."[63] At night, she is unable to sleep.

> The twenty-foot-high ceiling recedes and the pale light that blurs the ventilators creeps in, assuming the angry shapes of swirling phantom babies, of gaping wounds forming deformed crescents—and of Masseur's slender, skillful fingers searching the nightroom for Ayah.
>
> And when I do fall asleep the slogans of the mobs reverberate in my dreams, pierced by women's wails and shrieks—and I awaken screaming for Ayah.[64]

Haunted mercilessly by images of the possible horrors Ayah undergoes, as explicated by her Cousin, Lenny finally confronts her mother and besieges Godmother to visit Ayah in the Diamond Market. When Ayah was physically present in Lenny's life, Lenny's sharpest desire emerged in secret, caressing whatever space offered by Masseur's expert fingers. Without Ayah, Lenny desires her presence in all hours and openly confronts others about this loss. Even though she is amenable to Hamida as a replacement, never does she call her "Ayah" nor does she ever bother to love the woman she permits employment out of guilt. The condition of violence and woman, class and labor could be the subject of a separate chapter, as it applies to the desperate condition of Hamida in this plush household. What is clear is that Lenny, during and after the crisis of this novel, remains embroiled deeply in the imagined community of her Ayah, the men, and the mob. While the screams continue long after the event, the characters continue their mime long into the present from which Lenny recalls the cracking year of 1947.

Lenny's metanarrative, repeatedly interjected by the adult voice which intrusively shares epiphanies of the middle-aged woman upon the voice of the seven year old child, brings to attention the implacable and resolute bond between the two main story tellers, a young Lenny of 1947 and a rueful older woman four decades later.

And as the years advance, my sense of inadequacy and unworth advances. I have to think faster—on my toes as it were ... offering lengthier and lengthier chatter to fill up the infernal time of Father's mute meals. Is that when I learn to tell tales?[65]

While Lenny tells her story as the seven-year-old child too young to know about the inner workings of women as commodities on the Diamond Market or the intricacies of sex, an older Lenny occasionally slips in unnoticed at the end of chapters to ruminate upon the story, her actions in it, and the traitorous condition inherent to the writer. The novel is a lengthy exercise in self-explanation to fill the uncomfortable silence of history's outrages. Another way to pass time in hell, the reason according to many mythologists about why stories originally evolve, and then lead to the sort of frame stories seen in *The Thousand and One Nights*[66] or *The Decameron*[67] where the tellers of tale are literally warding off death with each episode recited. As she learns to fill the silences of her father's "infernal" meals, the adult Lenny posits it as the moment that launches her into the space of story teller and creative historiographer. As she breaks plates and tells the truth about her crimes, she realizes with adult acumen, "I smashed livers, kidneys, hearts, eyes ... The path to virtue is strewn with broken people and shattered china."[68] The adult Lenny commiserates, counsels, and reconfigures the voice of the little Lenny who tells the truth only because she does not know alternate narratives.

A memory and a muse—it calibrates the difference in degree and heat between the mobs of partition that consumed its own against its earlier counterpart in small processions on Warris Road. The narrator herself declares: "Memory demands poetic license,"[69] in creating the illusion that the fires burned Lahore for months. Lenny is not one but several beings in communion with one another, switching roles, speaking in code, and occasionally interpellating her many selves into one to give the semblance of a unified story or one single novel. As the mob drags Ayah away, a moment to which we return repeatedly in this chapter, Lenny leaves herself and watches her own childhood self and articulation from outside: "I am the monkey-man's performing monkey, the trained circus elephant, the snake-man's charmed cobra, an animal with conditioned reflexes that cannot lie ..."[70]

This very inclination to tell the truth marks her passage into an adulthood that operates on the freedom from such a straitjacket; as an author, she learns to imagine her way into and around and away from the narrow road to truth. The final pages are littered with such expositions on womanhood, love, adulthood, and nostalgia articulated with the finesse of an old hand at telling new tales. She wonders about the right target for such grand betrayal. She weeps like adults over Hamida's twisted and bizarre condition of exile. Upon finding Ayah gone across the border at the end, she knows about the disappearance before the fact because of her missing fragrance. In these pages, it is not clear who is the child and who is the woman; where Ayah stops and Lenny begins, where the children cease to be separate individuals and become mass repositories of interrupted memories, where the lovers untangle and reveal the little Lenny weaving in and out of everyone's stories. Imagined community exists in lieu of the completed narratives of each of these characters caught shackled in their dreadful history. While Lenny remains the stable character present in the various imagined communities, it is also clear that she herself is a multiplicity of characters and can, at best, be pictured in motion.

Conclusion

Cracking India is more than a guilt narrative. It presents a tableau of resistance, an imagined community peopled by those who died, suffered, and remembered, but nevertheless, persevered against absolute erasure and loss of identity. The state does not dictate the course of their stories and their suffering becomes the nexus for telling the litany of their names and loves anew. The Ayah is a human figure of resistance. Pursued by patriarchy in all its forms throughout the novel, from British soldiers to statesmen to laborers and idlers alike, she is victimized but not conquered. Even at the end, she escapes the limiting fold of the novel and escapes across the liminal border space. David Punter proposes the existence of such human figures of resistance in postcolonial writing, a figure that rejects the hegemony of the state and continues its state of mobility, rootlessness beyond the text. About his new world order, Punter writes:

> One of the phenomena with which we are presented in postcolonial writing is, then, a whole panoply of maps, a treasure chest of charts, piled in heaps, lapped over one another, imaginary geographies, but ones in

which the root of power that has nourished them is in the slow process of being exposed. Geography, we might say, would be the key to resistance, even though geography is itself not immovable, as we remember when we see the Yangtse dammed, the Indonesian forest in flames. Would it be possible to find a human image that would approximate in some way to this resistance, that would in the terms of Deleuze and Guattari appropriate the position of the absolute nomad, would enact a final rejection of the state apparatus, the war machine and all their cartographic works?[71]

Within the rigid purview of the state, worsened by systemic ills of caste, gender, and religious degradations that are in practice, community, as such, is a pragmatic nonentity, excepting the cry of the bereaved. Men's community centers around the figure of the woman who is dehumanized in an exalted state, both as the mother goddess and mother of the nation, mythic yet rendered mute in a gendered apotheosis of the feminine figure. Women's community exists in an embryonic form; good-will efforts made that remain in an infancy of the sort of community seen in Christa Wolf's rewriting of the Trojan landscape, *Cassandra*. Wolf's river women exist under the radar of the patriarchal figures at battle, Trojan heroes like Hektor against the Achaean Achilleus and Patroklos and Ajax. While the men slay one another on the battlefield and in more domestic or sacred places even, the river women dissolve class-based hierarchies to meet at the river to dance, sing, weave, and celebrate. Between the choices of killing and dying, this woman's community exists in its voluptuous fullness and chooses the third way: living. Such is the stuff of the idealized woman's community—works of re-imagining masculine narratives of battle and glory with feminist affect. *Cracking India* does not permit for the existence of such a community, even when imagined by a Pakistani–Canadian émigré who writes under the impulse to unsheathe the cruelty suffered by women in fratricidal wars.

Jannah and fall from it are elements like mercury; they disappear upon contact. Too volatile to exist by itself, it is always present, but assumes the shape of what surrounds it and can never be destroyed. Community, ever present in its idea and elementality, comes into statehood finally in its imagined form. Santha's haunted eyes that chart a pain beyond language and Lenny's scream immediately after the moment of betrayal, "No! I scream,"[72] mark the fallibility within the structures of language. Santha's eyes inform the absence of violence in the text. The closest we come to understanding the horrors she undergoes is written in her eyes, but left unsaid, *unnarratable* event that is central and also absent in the novel. Lenny's scream, on the other hand, fuels the narrative forward to its rushed disappearance at the end, Ayah across Wagah, a place of mysterious import even at this moment today when the two nation-states separated by it bicker over dead bodies, ideologies, relocated populations, innocent civilians, trade, commerce, and human history. Ignored in the mob's bloodthirsty pursuit into the home that shelters Ayah, Lenny's scream uttered once in the novel forms the invisible tissue of its narratological order.

Imagined community arises out of the double paradox inherent to novelistic discourse: the novel, the most detail oriented genre of literary oeuvre, is also engorged with silences and complicity. Imagined community exists in the language employed to tell this tale: Lenny's community as it is unveiled in her partnership with all the children of midnight, all the victims and survivors of South Asian history's most tragic spectacle of human loss, and the men and women she loved in particular, most significant of them being, her own childhood self. In addition to this allegiance, imagined community exists in all that is not narrated, the moans of the rape victims, the anguished guttural pleas of women who ask to be killed to spare more torture, Khatija's naked and terrified body in the courtyard, or all the nameless women of Lahore who make one more hole in stories too fragile for telling. Lenny's scream and Santha's "wide-open and terrified eyes" are the beginning and end of the sentence which spells out the imagined community of Lahore's partition. It hints at bodies in pain—the tale itself remains to be told.

4

Beyond Cloisters of Domesticity: Tahmina Durrani's *Kufr*, Mridula Garg's *Kathgulab*, and Mahasweta Devi's *Hazaar Chaurasi Ki Maa*

In sharp contrast to contemporary feminist voices in the popular Indian literary imaginary, the Hindi literary canon bears signs of a notable absence. Where is the gendered voice questing for justice? The range of great writers remains determined by the extent to which critics and scholars limit themselves to a close reading of canonical texts. Globalization has slimmed the market for the vernacular novel as writers in languages like Hindi, Gujarati, Marathi, and Malayalam increasingly tend to write for visual media like television or film. The average reader knows many of these writers, such as Kamleshwar and Bhisham Sahni because of their contributions to the movies and televised dramas, rather than their novels. The catalogue of great Hindi writers is limited not only due to the limited circulation of names, but the lack of its diversity. Male writers seemingly dominate the print medium. In fact, even today, in commonly found lists of renowned Hindi writers, Mahadevi Varma is generally the only woman writer to be found among names like Premchand, Maithili Sharan Gupt, Bhisham Sahni, Yashpal, Kamleshwar, Nirala, Agyeya, Dinkar, Mohan Rakesh, Srilal Shukla, and Krishna Sobti.

David Rubin substantiates this argument when he reviews Meenakshi Mukherjee's survey text of the Indian novel, *Realism and Reality: The Novel and Society in India* (1985),[1] in which she reads texts in

Marathi, Hindi, and Bengali (and others in translation). Rubin commends her for moving beyond the early era of novel development with her close readings of *Pather Panchali*,[2] *Samskara*,[3] and *Godan*[4] but criticizes her reading *Umrao Jaan Ada*[5] in English. According to Rubin, Mukherjee fails to read the nuances of Premchand's grand novel and does not see how it fits neatly into the European novelistic tradition. Rubin is nevertheless appreciative for one more serious text in the meager bibliography of English criticism of novels from Indian vernacular languages: "She is an insightful critic and one would like to see her go on to produce a more focused or deeper study of the Bengali or Hindi novel. *Realism and Reality*, despite its limitations, provides a useful addition to the small bibliography in English dealing with Indian vernacular fiction."[6]

In this context, an examination of the state of the art of women writers is doubly urgent. First, it underlines the paucity of such studies. Second, it helps to bring attention to how South Asian women writers are adapting the novel to the social experience of their life-worlds. In my research into the contemporary Hindi novel by women-writers, I also found a dialogue between Hindi and other North Indian languages like Urdu, Punjabi, and Bengali. In this chapter, I examine an Urdu novel translated into Hindi and a novel written in Hindi, to arrive at conclusions regarding notions of community in the feminist novel from South Asia, specifically Pakistan and India. Tahmina Durrani's *Kufr* (Urdu, 2004), Mridula Garg's *Kathgulab* (Hindi, 1996), and Mahasweta Devi's *Hazaar Chaurasi Ki Maa* (Bengali, 1979) are novels that chronicle the condition of struggle lived by women, albeit in communities delineated by the specifics of region, history, and language. All three novels contain many of the elements defined by Malcolm Bradbury and James McFarlane as tenets of European modernism: the desire to break from tradition, a heterodox irreverence and apocalyptic multiplicity in voice, the shadow of history that portrays the present as bleak, in a state of disintegration.[7] Marshall Berman's comments on the dynamism of nineteenth-century modernisms are worth considering here:

> Paradoxically, these first modernists may turn out to understand us—
> the modernization and modernism that constitute our lives—better than
> we understand ourselves … We will feel our community with people all
> over the world who have been struggling with the same dilemmas as our
> own.[8]

Berman's hope for transcendence based on a similitude of dilemmas informs my approach to the works of Durrani, Garg, and Devi, in the connections I make amidst their stories and Morrison's *Paradise*.[9] Durrani, Garg, and Devi are overt in their feminist polemic because the purpose of the novelistic enterprise is to write a stage on which women are empowered to speak. Devi has long been in the lead in establishing a radical feminist stage wherein she works out the relationship of the marginalized and deterritorialized peoples' relationship to the state in her very prolific literary career that parallels the history of the nascent nation-state and predates its inception.

Elaine Showalter's concept of "three stages" is vital to my understanding of the politics of women writing the South Asian novel. Showalter theorizes transitions made by women's writing as a progression from the feminine phase to the self-constituted "female" stage.[10] It is in the female stage that authentic self-exploration and a confident engagement with the world can occur. *Kufr* is written in the voice of a widow who narrates the protracted abuse suffered as part of "conjugal duties," and offers an unrelenting testimony on the hypocrisy of a public man, a pir (spiritual leader) in his private domain. *Kathgulab*, on the other hand, traverses across the spheres and characters, providing a window into the stories of several women of different classes and backgrounds in order to stitch a dynamic web of individuals and community. The narrative of *Kathgulab* also begins with the flight of one of its central characters, Smita who disappears from her home and city after severe physical and sexual abuse within her own filial family. Finally, *Hazaar Chaurasi Ki Maa* traces the awakening of a middle-class mother in a Bengali household, and is an archetypal feminist narrative—the mother in the story who begins as a feminine character recalls her early days as a feminist only to arrive in the scope of the novel's one day of narration into a "female" stage. This moment of arrival contains such an excess of meaning that Devi employs the classic feminist literary technique of staging her character's exit on the scream, indecipherable because the knowledge conferred to the character in this moment of awakening cannot simply be evoked in words. The novels establish a dialectic in that the characters wrestle to self-define against the pressures of patriarchal erasure; they form communities that are also volatile, almost ready to disintegrate at the slightest detection by larger structures of power.

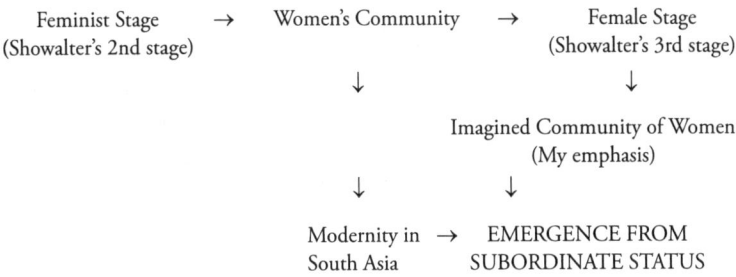

The formula I offer above conceptualizes the movement occurring within these novels. The call for minority rights inherent in the feminist stage harkens to the birth and rise of modernity in South Asia, which can be said to include the effects of industry, colonialism, interaction with the west, and the literary wave known as "modernism," etc. It is crucial not to conflate modernization with westernization as noted by Samuel Huntington when he writes that the projects which are primarily anti-west use techniques of modernity to enact their purposes.[11] This proclamation of the rights of selfhood for women is the symbolic "coming out," exiting the quarantine of the home for the maelstrom of the world, theorized by Partha Chatterjee in his work on nineteenth century Bengal.

> Applying the inner/outer distinction to the matter of concrete day-to-day living separates the social space into *ghar* and *bāhir*, the home and the world. The world is the external, the domain of the material; the home represents one's inner spiritual self, one's true identity. The world is a treacherous terrain of the pursuit of material interests, where practical considerations reign supreme. It is also typically the domain of the male. The home in its essence must remain unaffected by the profane activities of the material world—and woman is its representation. And so one gets an identification of social roles by gender to correspond with the separation of the social space into *ghar* and *bāhir*.[12]

Chatterjee's *ghar/bāhir* binary, while elevating the domestic realm as feminine, spiritual, and emblematic of the goddess culture, leaves out the repercussions on the lives of day-to-day women. The domestic realm, its inner quarters often called the "zenana" where only women stay, is also a place which women are not generally permitted to leave, unless in the company of the patriarch or some other sanctioned male member of the family. While the historian notes purity and promotion for the woman under authority of the father, it has to duly be noted that the era of modernity also ushers the women into domestic seclusion.

Only in solidarity with the women of the world, or better yet, a sense of camaraderie with global women's movements across borders, the woman emerges slowly from her quarters into the street. The emergence from home fluidly moves from self-empowerment into self-definition, or the female stage, which is also the moment of emergence from "subordinate state" as defined by Oliver Mendelsohn and Upendra Baxi (1994).[13] If we bring Mendelsohn and Baxi's definition into our context, women as a community are the social formation subordinated in order to fluently exercise the patriarchal will.

This spatial and social prescription is present in nineteenth-century Europe as well, evident in the rise of the flâneur narrated in the poetics of Baudelaire through the essays of Walter Benjamin, a distinctly male practice recorded in the public sphere. Janet Wolff defines, "The literature of modernity describes the experiences of men," and further, she finds that the same literature "has been impoverished by ignoring the lives of women."[14] These definitions do away with simpler notions of marginality and hint at the very complication that is at the heart of this project, the shifting meanings of community.

It is critical to note that despite a sense of community with women's movements or sisterhood of self-empowerment, women are not allowed corporeal community with one another within the domestic space, which continues the tyranny of the colonizer under the renewed chokehold of the nationalist patriarch. The home, a place of upholding patriarchal institutions, also turns the women within it to functionaries for preserving the systems in place, Deniz Kandiyoti's "classic patriarchy" taken up in the last chapter. Consequently, the only community left for women is an imagined community with the dead, a sphere that can continue to operate undetected and invincible to the patriarch, leaving the material realm for fractured, disturbed, and betrayed communities of the living.

These novelistic readings emphasize my larger point that emerges from this chapter, that every act of self-assertion by the women characters are considered or read in their social milieu as blasphemy, speech acts of sacrilege that threaten the social order. A community of women's bodies, i.e., corporeal and discernible by patriarchal and state tools of surveillance, foments in the feminist stage. However, the sthāvara/ jāngama binary from the introduction suggests that things standing shall fall. The corporeal community is not sanctioned by patriarchy and is thus, not allowed to exist. In the novels, these discernible communities are scrutinized and punished. In turn, what emerges in the texts is a more rootless, mobile, and indiscernible form of community, i.e., community of and with the dead. Since these are "things moving," they endure against the spatial and temporal oppression of patriarchy and forge community beyond cloisters of domesticity.

Tahmina Durrani's *Kufr*

In Tahmina Durrani's 2004 novel, *Kufr*, or *Blasphemy*, translated by Vinita Gupta into Hindi, the sthāvara/jāngama binary is starkly portrayed. Imagined community is ultimately a female entity that cannot be seen. It is a novel that accounts in detail the gruesome levels of torture experienced by a young woman, Heer, who is married at the age of fifteen to a man thrice her age, known for his good deeds and status in the community, Pir Sai. The novel opens with the gathering of mourners at Pir Sai's burial and ends on a much more ambiguous note, on some realm that is between heaven and earth and affords Heer a taste of agency.

For twenty-five years, Heer suffers physical abuse, rape, and harsh labor under Pir's autocracy, a whip wielded upon all the women of his household, relatives, and domestic workers alike. Pir is the physical embodiment of patriarchal authority, and the narrative finds him literally branding the father's name on the women he governs in the *ghar*. The novel charts the chronicle of debauchery Pir Sai engages in while consuming the richest of foods and drinks, a narrative of consumption and virility unchecked. His murder brings to the fore the submerged feelings of hatred felt by other women besides Heer. Durrani resists the categorization of this novel within any one genre.

By its climax, the novel reads in multiple genres and ends, much like Morrison's *Paradise*, in terra infirma giving us a glimpse of heaven and earth and realities that lie beyond Baudrillard's mirrors of production. Symbology is the key in understanding this text that could be read on the singular level of the autobiographical. Pir Sai, a spiritual leader and sage of the community he directs, is a monster. Pir Sai is a monster analogous to Aimé Césaire's depiction of the colonizer as uncivil, brutal, and savage due to the practice of colonialism which is an institution of "violence, race hatred, and moral relativism."[15] He turns the domestic space into a prison for his wife, and all this occurs without unhinging the narrative of his largesse. While Durrani's novel is about the domestic sphere, it hints at the institutionalization of patriarchal powers to such an extent that it begins to reflect a set of systems much like the concrete and lock prison complex.

Arun Kumar praises Durrani for her courage in bringing to light the ills of patriarchal culture in Pakistan, especially in the latter-day rise of Islamic fundamentalism and its effects on further limiting women's role in the public sphere. Even within the domestic realm, it comes to mean that the woman has to accept the atrocities of her husband as God's way, much like Durrani's own experience in life with an abusive husband, and her character, Heer in *Kufr*. Her autobiography, *Mere Aaka*, translated into English as *My Feudal Lord*, charts the course of her own suffering. Kumar's friend gives anecdotal information that in contemporary Pakistani milieu, it has become common on part of husbands to warn their wives not to become another Tahmina. The third wife of the Governor of Punjab, Mustafa Khar, she was known for her great beauty and ability to suffer her husband's severe abuse wordlessly, without flinching. With three wives, Mustafa also took Tahmina's younger sister, Adila as his lover. Kumar writes that extreme cruelty and lust were characteristic family traits of the Khar dynasty. Kumar writes with historical insight about Mustafa's involvement with border politics and Indira Gandhi's government, and the fact that there was no lack of characters like Pir Sant in Pakistan. It was with the daring that fuels her work that Tahmina urged Mustafa to give her the divorce which allowed for the expression of her real self, not Tahmina Khar but Tahmina Durrani. This insistence upon the woman's unique and autonomous identity forms the crux of much of her literary work.[16]

This novel, written in Urdu but read in Hindi, raises an interesting linguistic question. Urdu is written in the Persianized Nastaliq script, and Hindi utilizes the Sanskritik Nagri script. However, the act of translation from Urdu to Hindi, unlike the violence that I perform in my endnotes by turning Urdu into English, is mainly visible in print media and generally more fluid in oratory.[17] To me, then, reading an Urdu novel as part of my project reads against the state-directed differences that have arisen between the two in post-independence India and Pakistan and is, in a way, an overt feminist politic of reading across borders. *Kufr* is a powerful, unsparing, and site-specific critique of patriarchy that I find in contemporary literature by women. The slippage is chronic in Durrani's landscape and begins at the title; it is never clear, even after the conclusion, if the blasphemy of the title points itself to revealing Pir Sai's acts of villainy, or the patriarchal structure at large, or Heer's own participation in the system at will, or finally, to the act of recording conversations with God which finally lead us to a heaven where God is absent. However it is clear that Durrani does intend irony in a bold and feminist acceptance of the role of the apostate by openly pointing to the excesses of patriarchy as the normative condition for humanity. To this, she adds her own novel as a bold entry into the female stage of self-expression where the character forges bonds with an imagined community that lies in a wild zone—outside the purview of patriarchy.

Dard Jhelna, *or the Feminine Art of Suffering Pain*

The "feminine" of the title refers to Showalter's first stage when the women who write are aware of their gender and produce within patriarchal prescriptions a deeply-conscious and self-reflective style that can be deemed feminine. In this gendered vein, Heer's narrative, rendered in first person, indicts patriarchy at large. Pir, at forty-four, after the mysterious deaths of his first two wives, marries Heer, only fifteen at the time. The women's community in this house, all marked by Pir's abuse, serves a man who inherits his authority and sadism as his hereditary right. An ancestor, asked by a British official to give evidence of his power, points to a domestic worker who jumps to his death following his master's command. Heer learns this from the community she forms with the ghost, a woman who haunts the grand mansion of Pir and educates his wife in self-assertion through historical knowledge. The novel, a detailed chart of abuse and an indictment, offers alternatives of unhinging systems from within.

The ritual of mourning is done in accordance with societal norms on how to give respect to the passing of the patriarch. The women, despite the passing of Pir, continue their roles as informants and watch one another for signs of betrayal, and thus, Heer cries the loudest so that her jubilation stays secret. In this theater of death, she chain-smokes in the bathroom relishing the thought that Pir, with his delusions of grandeur, will finally be waited upon by ants and worms. The greatest weight of her life is how she learned to wear fear like a garment, and was fluent in its language, a code of silence.

पीर साईं जा चुका था। लेकिन इस ख़याल का आदी होना मुश्किल था। जब तक वह ज़िन्दा था, उसकी मौजूदगी इतनी ज़बरदस्त थी कि कभी उसकी ग़ैर-मौजूदगी पता ही नहीं चली। घर से उसके चले जाने पर हम हमेशा इतने घबराए रहते थे कि हर लम्हा उसके लौटने की बाबत सोचते बीतता। उसकी गाड़ी पर नज़र पड़ते ही गाँव वाले कूदकर एक तरफ हो जाते और जब तक उसकी गाड़ी की उड़ाई हुई धूल बैठ नहीं जाती, वे अपने सिर हाथों में लिये रहते। घर में औरतें लगातार बेचैनी की हालत में बनी रहतीं - डरी हुई। और मैं ? उसके कदमों को सुनने के लिए मैं अपने भीतर सिमट जाती। जैसे-जैसे वे नज़दीक आते मुझको लगता कि वे मेरे दिल को रौंद रहें हैं ।[18]

[Pir Sai was gone. But it was difficult to get used to this thought. Till the last day of his life, his presence was so forceful that his absence was never felt. When he would leave the house we would remain petrified each moment expecting his return. As soon as the villagers spotted his car, they would jump to one side and keep their heads bowed in their hands and not raise them until the dust from his car settled. The women in the house were in a constant state of anxiety—full of fear. And me? Waiting for his footsteps, I would retreat into myself. The closer he came, the more I felt my heart being crushed.]

Durrani makes a radical case for systemic and social change by recording what can seem to be non-novelistic, non-creative, and non-entertaining, i.e., writing a novel in the image of the memoir. The women, all living by the law of the father in the punitive surveillance of his gaze, betray one another. Heer is watched for twenty-five years by a woman who speaks to only Pir, whom Heer dubs *cheel*, a scavenger of wounds whose only relationship with language is to cause pain.

Any periods of joy felt by Heer in this text are so fleeting that one has to but note the strange use of "time" in this novel. Remarkably different from the Bakhtinian notion given to us as the "chronotope," where a novel stands suspended in a proper location of time and place, and accounts for ways in which real or fictional history shapes its narrative, Durrani's text is curiously absent of any such markers. One is not sure if this novel takes place in the nineteenth or the twentieth century. The British Empire is a thing of the past due to the ghost's stories, but apart from that, it is not clear where and when the story takes place. There are no references to any place in Pakistan, or any specific decade or historical moment. No state laws or events make their way into Heer's deeply secluded zenana. Pir beats Heer with the cold calculation of a sadist the first time the day after their wedding. She violates the first in a series of cardinal rules by greeting her mother and some domestic workers without her veil, or *burqa*. The beating is public and precisely executed. Heer is incapacitated for days. Events of the larger world as evident in print media are largely absent from the text. And yet, "time" as in units that record its passage, is very much present. The day Heer enters Pir's prison, the days and nights of torture, the long days it takes to heal from elongated stretches of physical abuse and rape, the months and years that pass in delivering children, and then, their problematic passage into an adulthood dictated by their perverted father—time becomes another tool of patriarchal torture. What Durrani offers is a feminized account of time within her novelistic discourse of *Kufr*. Time, instead of appearing as records of large-scale events of nation-making in the world, assumes a feminine form by appearing in the hours spent within the patriarchal prison known in common parlance as the home.

Returning to Heer's moment of joy, it is her impression that the man who comes to propose to her when she returns from school is her friend Chandi's brother whom she thinks of as *Ranjha*.[19] Her misinformation is soon revised when she understands that her husband is a twice-married old man. Heer, aware of the differences between her misogynistic mother and her long-dead father, knows her father would have never made a deal of his daughter. Women's autonomy through education, rather than class, is a central trope to this novel. Of the hovels and their smiling occupants, her father had once said, "These folks are liberated from the empty show of wealth and power!"[20] Though the statement refuses to humanize the poor, it critiques the value system of the mother, Pir, and all who function by economic muscle alone. He had once said that, had she been born elsewhere, she would have been famous for her mind, not her beauty.[21] Heer's plight speaks to a feminist reckoning which cuts across borders and really attends to patriarchal oppression within the domestic sphere. Within the domestic space, while Heer assumes privileges not available to the working class members of her household who are answerable to her, Heer also does not have unfettered access to the capital Pir embodies. Class, in this sense, is complicated by the condition of women's oppression. This is a point clarified in Chandra Talpade Mohanty's revisitation of her earlier text, *Under Western Eyes*, "These realist theorizations explicitly link a historical materialist understanding of social location to the theorization of epistemic privilege and the construction of social identity, thus suggesting the complexities of the narratives of marginalized peoples in terms of relationality rather than separation."[22] To put it simply, I am attending to the relationality (points of empathic connection) amidst the female characters in this novel rather than the separations.

The more Heer comes to understand her new status, she learns the feminine art of swallowing her pain, or *dard jhelna*. She is asked to maintain silence as Pir beats her in inventive ways, sometimes sitting on her back and other times squeezing her temples with his knees or breaking her wrists by placing them underneath tables. Survival means induction into the art of silence. Introduction to connubial bliss is a night-long rape, and then, a morning command to bathe because she is "haram" in her deflowered state. Heer's act of remembrance and Durrani's in recording this in writing then becomes an exercise of self-preservation, a way to battle against the disappearing self and save the trace on the slippery stage of paper. Once inaugurated under identity-markers, writing adopts specific author-function of being Muslim, woman, and of Pakistani nationality in our contemporary present. Writing, then, is not the performance of constant acts of disappearance, but for the veiled Heer, namesake for an actual woman, Durrani saves traces of appearance and provides the literary space upon which to perform the speech of a woman who managed to live despite patriarchal tyranny. In a way then, the telling of this tale is the first step in the emergence of a feminist voice, the woman's speech act which is named a *kufr* or blasphemy.

Showalter's second stage, the feminist phase, is manifest in Heer's efforts at community-making, which are in effect, corporeal and discernible. In effect, they are "things standing" doomed to fall. Her new friends are old ghosts—Toti, Kali, and her own daughter, Guppi. To save Guppi from her father's brutality, Heer offers a disabled child servant instead. Thus, women's community, in the shadow of patriarchal violence, stages maternal love as a shade, perverse manifestations of father-right. The narrative logic exorcizes this community and it too disappears with the progression of time.

Main Kaun Thi, *or the Making of the Feminine Self*

Heer facilitates patriarchal excess by participating in feeding Pir's depraved appetites. Though she does this to save her own daughter, Guppi, the community of women bears the cost of her compromise. The sale of Yatimdi, the limping child, to Pir is followed by a long string of little girls who are sacrificed to Pir's cavernous appetite while their mothers remain indebted to Sai's munificence. Even the exercise of maternal love comes upon the exploitation of others; class correlates to kinship so that the figure exploited becomes the exploiter. Despite a narrative of harrowing abuse, easy victimizations are in question because interrogations are implicitly woven into the novel around class.

Chote Sai, her eldest son, falls for Yatimdi and spends a night with her; he is whipped so severely by his father that he loses his hearing and senses. It takes him two months to recover at a hospital and afterwards, the only affection he displays is for his sister, Guppi's newborn. Extinguished of his identity and purposes by his own father, he dies soon afterward, an event which haunts Heer till the end of her narrative. Heer, Chotte Sai, Yatimadi and the all the children march into Pir's chamber in tune with the Law of the Father. Through it all, Pir remains a monstrous caricature, the narrative rendering him devoid of all humanity.

The novel reads as belonging to the genre of horror, thriller, science fiction, pornography, and high brow literary novel. Jean Baudrillard's *Mirror of Production* (1975)[23] helps in reading the novel once the television, vcr, and recording equipment enter the milieu; the novel is divided into Baudrillard's three stages: real, simulation, and simulacra. In transcending the limitations of patriarchal surveillance upon the woman's body, the intra-textual simulacrum engages in doubled discursivity; the suffering female exploited by the male gaze is also the feminist self who transgresses the limitations of selfhood. Pir stoops to new levels of perversion once he brings the instruments of visual entertainment into the quarantined world of his wife and domestic workers, and the immediate utility of having the world enter the living room is that the people in the living room also enter the world. Heer, the veiled wife no one would recognize on the streets of Pir's own village, acts the porn star upon her husband's orders. Heer, given the street alias, *Pyaari*, or love, acts as pornographic star and prostitute for her husband's friends, none of whom recognize her as the wife of the great Pir Sai because within the household, her face is always veiled. Here the veil has the double function of secluding the woman within the domestic while making her body available for public consumption. The secrecy imposed upon the woman's physical identity, another aspect of patriarchal regulation of women's bodies, serves to systemically confine the women at his will.

Simulacra abounds in the chapter entitled, "*Kaise kaise Hero*" (Types of Heroes), the title itself a reference to the film industry and its production of hundreds of films each year that mythologize good-looking young men as heroes, and for Heer, acting against her will as a partner to the variety of men, finds them to defy prototypes of "heroism" on the screen, since all of them reek, have onion and garlic breath, and never seem to wash. Self-medicated with nearly five packs of cigarettes a day and alcohol, Heer plays the prostitute, losing count of her clients all of whom would not be allowed to look at her directly had she appeared veiled as Pir's wife.

Durrani's solitary white character, a female journalist, raises questions about the nature of truth. Her naked legs remind Heer of the legs she sees on the screen; inversely, the news article she produces mimics her distance from reality. Who is Pir Sai? How would his family characterize him as opposed to the objective journalist? The journalist is the one blinded by Pir's glory. And Heer, well-versed in the versatility of a woman who is both the lady and the prostitute, lives a life rife with contesting narratives herself.

Ontological questions on selfhood arise at this juncture: Heer asks herself, "Who am I?" When she stares into the mirror, she realizes that she is finished, without receiving anything in return for the unfair deal of matrimony with a monster. When she contemplates the sterility of her life, she wonders, "मैं कौन थी ?", or who was I. Pir's vitriol infects her own senses. She thinks, "उसने भी मुझे कभी इन्सान नही माना, औरत मानने की बात तो अलग l"[24] (He never thought of me as a human being; forget about being thought of as a woman.) Apart from this being the condition of a melancholic, it is also radical in its comprehension of the place of the woman's body in the market economy of desire. Pir consumes Heer's body in the earlier days of their marriage in every manner possible, and then, he brings in the camera behind which he can watch the performance of the sex act, and immortalize it against its own evanescence. The underground economy of sex charts simultaneously the disintegration of the women's communities that had manifested earlier in the novel.

Death of the Father/Birth of the Female Self

Since the title of the novel points to sacrilege, a person who blasphemes against the law of the Quran, *Kufr*, it suggests the double presence of both

Pir and Heer. Pir, the man of God sins against his own prescriptions, and Heer, undoubtedly, performs the sins dictated by her husband. Much like the Sufis, Cabbalahists, and mystics of many religions, she enters the gap between sin and circumstance when she poses to Allah, "यह किसका पाप है? मेरा? यह किसका जहान है? तेरा?"[25] (Whose sin is this? Mine? Whose world is this? Yours?) When forced to watch and then enact the sexual acts that seem depraved to her, she knows suicide as a way out is closed to her because it ends her self-willed conversations with an Allah she continues to call in her darkest hours. Never able to leave the God who deserted her, she is able to adopt holy discourse to justify twenty-five years of murder in her heart:

पीर साईं धर्मद्रोह का प्रतीक था।
मैं एक सिपाही थी।
यह एक जिहाद था।[26]

[Pir Sai was a symbol of betrayal of Dharma.
I was a soldier.
This was a Jihad.]

Heer's comfort is a sense of community and conversation; if her dialog with the women in her household is stifled, she continues it with god by asking questions, providing arguments, and finding solace within the self. In the way of Amina Wadud, Asma Barlas, and the many powerful feminist voices of faith in Islam today, she has given herself the authority to interpret the scriptures (*tafsir*)[27] and form her own bridge with Allah. This is particularly ironic since Pir remains entitled due to this authoritative relationship with the holy book and God. This is a very particular space wherein the radical feminist imaginary mobilizes the Jihad as a conceptual struggle, negotiating between the imagined symbol and the real substance of struggle. This rescues Jihad from the foreclosures of fatalism and locates it within the dimensions of everyday practices of resistance, as exemplified most recently in the theatrical collaboration of Fawzia Afzal-Khan and Bina Sharif in their one-act play, "Jihad Against Violence."[28] It is even more interesting when we consider that the word "Pir" is associated here with a tyrant and the woman he oppresses is a soldier, aware of the militancy of her struggle. There is also an uncanny pairing here of (betrayal of) Dharma and (faith in) Jihad, which, I suggest, may well be a pairing that could only be mobilized in the work, labor, and imaginaries of global south *écriture feminine*.

The ending of the novel, another step to further the ambiguity of the text, much like Toni Morrison's *Paradise*, shows a glimpse of Heer through a white burqa standing by her own grave. Witness to the ghosts of her father and her son, she thinks she must be in *Jannat*, or heaven. The text poses a distance or slippage between its understanding of God and heaven. Nowhere in its imagination of heaven is God mentioned. Heaven is more about an actualization of desire, rather than location of the divine. In this final phase of the novel, community moves beyond corporeality.

Heer is in proximity to the divine. She speaks to God. Her conversations with God lead to the lost Ranjha, a man who is idealized since God falls from her estimate as the all-powerful entity. For him, Heer starts epistolary discourse: she writes letters to Ranjha and writes letters from him to her. When her sisters and mother find her collection of letters, they assume them to be real. Heer enacts the role she most favors, and imagines a reunion with Ranjha, the man who still loves her. She writes as Ranjha that a union could only be possible if she were to change forms, or find a new identity. Death follows soon after, and Heer, dreaming at the end of her life of another life, finds one such strand in the realm identified ambiguously by Tahmina Durrani as "*Aur Aakhir Mein*" (And in the End) resonant with Morrison's final section of *Paradise* where the women appear in altered forms.

The murder of the patriarch is executed by his most loyal spy, Cheel. Heer had failed to see that the person who harbored the greatest vendetta against Pir was none other than Cheel, the enemy spy. During Cheel's last breath, Heer enters into a kinship forged on glances. On her own deathbed, Heer lists these women in one breath as if they all belong together, "काली और तारा और तोती, यतीमड़ी, चील और मैं।बहनों, बेटियों, बीवियों और माँओं की जैसी औरतें पानी के बुलबुलों में बदल गईं और फट गईं।"[29] (Kaali and Tara and Toti, Yatimdi, Cheel, and I. Women who were like sisters, daughters, wives, and mothers turned into bubbles of water and burst.) The statement can signify the temporality of community but in the context that it comes on the heels of Heer's love letter written to the self, it is also about a change of identity, the birth of the female self when each woman exercises autonomy and experiences liberation from patriarchy, individual and collective at once.

Symbolic of Showalter's third stage, the female here announces truth without fear. Heer leaves the domestic space and rejoices under the stars with Tara, her *azadi* (liberation). To the men in the village, she declares the truth about her identity: Pyaari, the porn star, and Biwi Sai, the wife, are one and the same. With the death of the Father, she emerges from her subordinate status, communing, identifying, and loving at will. She has voice, speaks about her rights, and writes her own story.

Time, in its oddly proportioned role in Durrani's landscape brings us to a year later standing in front of Heer's simple cemetery stone, where a woman idealizes Heer for having dared to reveal the truth about the powerful Pir Sai. Heer is mythic, her acts disseminated and celebrated as the activist work of a single woman against the iniquities of patriarchy. Unlike the younger son who calls her a *randi* (prostitute), Heer undergoes an apotheosis and her life becomes the stuff of legend. Heer's own earlier conversations with God continue as a thematic in feminist discourse with divinity. While Durrani plays with the question of planes of reality (it is left unexplained if it is possible that somehow Heer manages to stage her own end and indeed finds a life of pleasure with Ranjha), it is actually more significant to leave the knot as it is, read the novel as simulacra where reality is impossible to ascertain. Durrani's portrayal of the severity of patriarchy is written over by the assertion of the female self who emerges using wit, desire, and play so that her story wins over the villainy of time. Much like the women in *Paradise* who are seen righting the wrongs and addressing the sites of their wounds, we see Heer, disguised or as a ghost, communing and existing in another realm that is not discernible to the patriarchal apparatus. Here the novel ends on the rootless and ambiguous community of women in perpetual motion, women who cannot be seen. The novel ends on the note that in life and in death, Heer has played a trick on patriarchy. The imagined community with and of the dead is, in essence, manifestation of the female emergence from subordinate status.

Mridula Garg's *Kathgulab*

Mridula Garg's 1996 novel *Kathgulab*, translated by Manisha Chaudhry to *Country of Goodbyes* (2004), furthers the questions of community raised in *Kufr*. Garg was awarded the eminent Vyaas Sanman Award in

2004 for *Kathgulab*, formerly given to Hindi literature heavyweights like Dharamvir Bharati, Kunwar Narayan, Srilal Shukla, Giriraj Kishore, all male writers. Garg is a familiar figure on the Indian literary scene, as a writer who has traveled abroad for literary conferences and also been arrested at home for publishing "obscene works," creating works that tend to rankle conservative nerves. Garg has been imprisoned and reviled for writing about matters that are generally preferred to be glossed over, such as reproductive rights, sexuality, and other such issues considered peripheral to the progress of a nation and in opposition to state-making.

The Hindi novel, *Kathgulab*, furthers notions of community through the interconnected narratives of multiple characters who move toward a form of feminist coalition-building. The novel is narrated in the voice of five characters: Smita, Marianne, Narmada, Aseema, and Vipin. Smita is the traveler who weaves the stories together. Her flight originates in an escape from familial abuse, replicated in an abusive marriage to Jim Jarvis, her psychoanalyst in Boston. She finally finds empowerment and community in a domestic violence shelter where she works, called RAW in Chicago. Her friend at RAW, Marianne, is a white woman who chronicles her story in a Hindi peppered with English. She suffers the dysfunctional materialism of American family life and grows into fame as an author after her tenure in Chicago as a shelter counselor. Her husband, who makes his fame by stealing Marianne's dissertation ideas, is brought down by the poetic justice of a wife who exceeds his initial literary advent.

Once back in India, Smita connects to Narmada, her sister's domestic worker, whose narrative is one of poverty, abuse, and forced marriage to her brother-in-law. Narmada seeks refuge through employment in the house of the radical feminist in the lot, Aseema, the unmarried daughter of a woman, Darjin Bibi (Stitching Lady, playing on the trope of weaving women that populate mythic histories), who leaves her husband due to philosophical differences. Aseema changes her name from Seema (limit) to one without limits and labors with a grass-root organization toward education for village girls. A black belt in Karate, she embodies the enraged feminist. Upon the death of her mother, Aseema takes over the stitching school which also substitutes as a site of attaining self-sufficiency for less-privileged women. Vipin, the only man given room in this novel, shocked by the suffocation implied by normative relationships searches for a way to forge alternative kinship bonds with Aseema, Smita, and finally, settles for the daughter of Nameeta, a medical student, Neeraja. Unable to reproduce, Neeraja leaves to marry a young widower with children. Meanwhile, Vipin journeys to join Aseema and Smita in a small village, Godhra in the state of Gujarat to help them in the project of constructing a school for girls. In his hands he carries the seeds of *kathgulab* (wood-rose), a plant that will grow only with the greatest ministrations. Despite their various states of melancholy, the characters carry a liberation that can spread like fire and enlighten.

The novel's momentum directs us toward non-traditional forms of kinship and community. Instead of its formation based on familial relationships or religious or ethnic notions of belonging, the novel cuts across the boundaries and brings women together on a local and global scale. Women forge kinship with one another and realize that with the greatest effort, new relationships and greater coalitions can begin. The characters, always in transit from larger metropolitan centers to the periphery, and in the esteemed place given to the late Darjin Bibi's vision, form the *jangama* community, that is, community in motion. Rootless, mobile, and possibly transient, the efforts sketched out by the end of the novel bring to light the less discernible form of female community-making on which this project rests. In the rest of the chapter, questions of community will help decipher the various facets of this novel—from the melancholic communities at the outset to individual and collective actions which found the alternate community given to us at its climax.

Melancholic Messianic Communities

Melancholy forms the route to a messianic sense of self-formation, i.e., a validation of the self when the state, dominant history, and modernity denies the individual any such significance. Messianism, in the sense outlined by Walter Benjamin,[30] affords the individual who stands under the arc of history and desires an alternative process of historiography, provides the in-roads toward the construction of community. This melancholy, in case of *Kathgulab*, as in Toni Morrison's *Paradise*, leads to a specifically located women's community, a feminized utopian space of self-exploration and existence.

Gurleen Grewal, when introducing the novels of Toni Morrison in her text, *Circles of Sorrow, Lines of Struggle* (1998), uses the features identified by Deleuze and Guattari in their study of Kafka as archetypal features of minority discourses: "the deterritorialization of language, the connection of the individual to a political immediacy, and the collective assemblage of enunciation." Grewal comments on how Morrison deterritorializes Anglo-American English. Morrison appropriates its canonic images and reframes it as the black experience, mapping black history unto the world. Morrison foregrounds the political and centralizes the collective and charges sounds with an intense dialogic unique to the literature of revolution.[31] Grewal's critique is a useful starting place to also unpack the inclinations present in Garg's 1996 novel. Garg unhinges traditional notions of novel writing and the woman's function as ornament, goddess, or mother in the Hindi canon. She shows women who return and attempt to make changes, women who dare to think beyond the domestic sphere in terms of progress of society-at-large, and women who refuse to reproduce.

The novel is unabashedly political. For all the women who do not comply with the normative order of biological reproduction, the collective is also a place of procreation and continuity, the site where the limitations of biology are countered by the birth of ideas. RAW, the non-profit agency that plays with the name of the Indian intelligence unit, is displaced. The gendered agent, instead of the RAW official, is now reconfigured as agency, a feminist praxis.

Darjin Bibi's home is the site of the informal collective, an echo of *Paradise*, where the matriarch encourages those in her tutelage to learn and grow. Unlike middle-class habits of comfort that rest upon the exploitation of the laboring classes, Darjin Bibi teaches Narmada so that she is ready to lead the establishment when the time comes. By the time Darjin Bibi dies, Narmada is ready to run the stitching school. Darjan Bibi's home is transformed into a site of collective melancholy, resistance, and redefinition. An equality arises out of the barrenness of womb, and this is not the same as the patriarchal derision of women who do not fulfill their womanly function, instead a maternal claim of their absence. Outside of the simple binaries imposed by the patriarchal hegemony, as Hélène Cixous begins to look for her, she writes:

> In the extreme the world of "being" can function to the exclusion of the mother. No need for mother—provided that there is something of the maternal: and it is the father then who acts as—is—the mother. Either

the woman is passive; or she doesn't exist. What is left is unthinkable, unthought of. She does not enter into the oppositions, she is not coupled with the father (who is coupled with the son).[32]

According to Cixous, a woman exists in her absence. A woman as herself, embodying the traditional feminine qualities such as kindness and maternalism, is inherently erased in the phallogocentric order. Aseema's room where the women gather, identify one another, and cry together is an awakening from the words and laws of phallogocentrism. Cixous provides critical lens to read the only male character who is also given a voice, the culminating voice in the series, Vipin, in the women's informal collective is signified the "unthinkable, unthought of" and precipitates the form of collective seen in the climax.

Based on the example of another village that succeeded in keeping girls in school and Smita's own love of all that is green, they begin their work literally in a garden. Rock hard, dry, they make it arable with the guidance of old women who know the land. What was barren yields fruit; the girls who labored at home begin to attend school. Aseema realizes her mother's dreams, teaches the young, and finds solidarity with thousands. Smita, even then unable to make a wood-rose grow like the one of her childhood, grows dozens of other types of trees and sustains new dreams of *azadi*. In opposition to patriarchal normativity, the narrative continues despite the "barrenness" of land and women.

Maternal Melancholia in Child's Life

The sadness of mothers is the preponderant impetus toward community formation. In effect, the sadness of mothers brings the saddened together like communities in mourning. The novel opens on Smita's memory-driven voice. Upon encountering her house two decades later, her every memory is immediately countered by her sister, Nameeta's more pragmatic and correct version. Smita remembers a wood-rose plant whose seeds, black and hard as rocks, she buried in her mother's garden, out of which sprung a bushy plant which gave huge buds that refused to blossom. Smita remembers her jubilant dance of joy when the rose finally blooms. Nameeta refutes this and insists their mother only planted more useful plants. The wood-rose symbolizes Smita's imaginary. To Smita, whose mother's memories are always slipping beyond reach, the mother becomes a site of power and regeneration. Every tree in full blossom stands as the bosom of the mother she misses and every experiment in the collective, action to mobilize women from below becomes an effort at rekindling the earliest sisterhood lost to her, that of the one between mother and daughter.

Aseema, partnered with her mother, rejects the father, and in turn, his name, law, and wealth. In renaming herself "limitless," she enshrines her rejection of father-right and phallogocentrism in general. The mother's joie de vivre descends to her daughter as a life force. She is fulfilled because as she says, "माँ की ढेरों स्मृतियाँ हैं मेरे पास।"[33] (I have a heap of my mother's memories), and these memories, along with her new found patience, give Aseema vigor.

Julia Kristeva's maternal semiotic provides essential frame to understanding the melancholic identifiers and very reason that Vipin and Neeraja come together. Kristeva writes, "a mother is a continuous separation, a division of the very flesh. And consequently a division of language,"[34] and in Vipin's case, the mother who never stopped mourning her husband, manages to instill in Vipin a dread of the all-consuming nature of love. Julia Kristeva places mother language as exceeding the father's symbolic language, a maternal symbolic that has to be a constant referent in the seeming heart of all things:

> No language can sing unless it confronts the Phallic Mother. For all that is must not leave her untouched, outside, opposite, against the law, the absolute esoteric code. Rather it must swallow her, eat her, dissolve her, set her up like a boundary of the process where "I" with "she"—"the other" "the mother"—becomes lost. Who is capable of this? "I alone am nourished by the great mother," writes Lao Tzu.[35]

Neeraja, in her rage against her mother, Nameeta's melancholy, suffering, and savagery at the father who lay dying, operates on a differing plane. She chooses a man closer to her father's age, conscious and mocking of Freud all the while, with the pragmatic assignation of giving him the child he desires. While Neeraja sets the Phallic Mother as a boundary of binaries she does not seek to reproduce, she enters the masculine symbolic each time as a womb functionary. To Vipin, she promises a child. Unable to fulfill her aim, she enters the contract of matrimony with a widowed doctor who needs a mother for his two children. The mother's melancholy, despite Neeraja's grandest rhetoric, becomes the axe upon which she grinds her life. The relationship of characters to their mothers, and their melancholia, dictates their mood and persona even though their lives are long distanced from the actual figures of their mothers. Vipin joins his friends to be fused in community by the common affect of maternal melancholia.

A Dialog of Worlds and Differences

Homi Bhabha unpacks the teleology of colonialist domination by reading the function of signs of hybridity closely, and reads the variations or guises in which resistance becomes apparent. He writes,

> Resistance is not necessarily an oppositional act of political intention, nor is it the simple negation or exclusion of the "content" of another culture, as a difference once perceived. It is the effect of an ambivalence produced within the rules of recognition of dominating discourses as they articulate the signs of cultural difference and reimplicate them within the deferential relations of colonial power—hierarchy, normalization, marginalization and so forth.[36]

Each of the characters in Garg's novel produce the "ambivalence" with their given identity and manners of discourse contrast against the dominating discourse of the state and cultures of the moment. The main characters introduce polyglossic panoply that invert normative hierarchy, question normalization, and contest their own seeming marginalization. In Marianne, the white character who speaks Hindi peppered with English, Garg makes it her *right* to write outside the limitations imposed by the nation-state most obviously associated with Hindi and fashions a character who is clearly not Hindi-speaking but gives her first person narrative in Hindi, a contradiction that is greatly prevalent in the European novel but one that establishes a new moment within the Hindi novel tradition. Also, by doing so, Garg inaugurates a bridge between communities of women that transcend linguistic boundary and commune across radical difference.

As Bhabha writes, "Hybridity represents that ambivalent 'turn' of the discriminated subject into the terrifying, exorbitant object of paranoid classification—a disturbing questioning of the images and presences of authority,"[37] Garg's characters exist in an aporia between the margins and the center, seemingly belonging in neither and both places at once, and profoundly seek to question the systematic ways of incorporating their bodies under the Name of the Father as augured by the state. For them, fulfillment is measured in the distance they find from the objects of their desire. The novel, significantly, ends on themes of melancholic distance. Such is the nature of the hybrid; she transforms in the moments immediately preceding any form of authoritative classification.

Pathology of Kinship Structures

Reading Claude Lévi-Strauss alongside linguistics that follow Ferdinand de Saussure, one might conclude quite legitimately that while poststructural accounts of language do exist, the same is not true for kinship.[38] Poststructural accounts of kinship are scant. In the manner that Lévi-Strauss makes conscious the biology outlined by Freud while explaining the incest taboo, the family is left intact as an institution that is automatic and natural. Oedipalization emerges in the private sphere, a space sequestered from State, but here the father is incorporated corporeally. Oedipalization is conflated with the phallus and the State simultaneously. Judith Butler in *Antigone's Claim*[39] points to the family condition as creating a possibility for the emergence of the state. David Schneider in his text, *A Critique of the Study of Kinship*[40] offers many alternative ways to organizing kinship but eventually returns to biology. David Eng proposes in a discussion on imagining the restructuring of kinship, "We have to tap into the realm of affective possibility, envision another structure, other relationship outside structures which is not necessarily about 'identity' but 'being,' a way to connect to others in structures outside kinship. Affect itself marks a history that demands a symbolic life. Affect works as a trace that points to missing history, a symbolic life."[41] Eng's observation helps to reimagine the affective possibilities in *Kathgulab*, and envision new structures, new ways of being.

Kathgulab presents conditions where the structural taboo against incest is readily overturned for more perverse form of control and pleasure. The novel's repeated refrain is the gender iniquity where a man who occupies or has wrested the patriarchal seat of high authority decides to utilize it to sexualize and capitalize upon the women in the family, even if they are virtually his own sisters. The sexual servitude imposed on Smita, Narmada, and others verify the punitive regime of the domestic.

The order of the day within *Kathgulab* reiterates examples of traditional kinship structures as doomed to failure, fracture, and decay. The women come together under the strangest circumstances; they connect outside the traditional structures of kinship in a state of ontological self-creation in a collective of willed solidarity amidst women. In reading from below then, grassroots mobilization that starts under the banner of RAW and Oxfam augurs more liminal communities not discernible to the state. Grassroots mobilization, a method of reading from below as espoused within the circles of subaltern theories, forms the *pinjar* (skeleton), the bones upon which Garg sculpts the flesh of her characters, managing to offer in tandem poststructural accounts of kinship.

Feminist Identity-making

Garg's novel is populated by women who refuse to reproduce. Although she has been criticized in this novel for concentrating too heavily on issues of women's reproduction and issues of child birth, Garg makes a counter point. The narrative insists on feminist identity making that does not rest fully in her ability to voice her womb, or silence it either but in an aporia in between where the literary word seeps in.

Smita's husband beats the child in her womb to death in one of his chronic fits of abuse and rage. Marianne produces novels after novels as the filial product of her episteme, rather than producing a child in the more corporeal form. Narmada considers herself fortunate not to have born a child out of her incestuous relationship with her Jija whom she eventually leaves. Aseema adamantly refuses to configure herself into the traditional structures of kinship which alone could have led to her chance to reproduce in the stifling conservatism of middle-class normativity. Neeraja tries every method available to the doctor to reproduce but finds herself to be unable to ovulate. Vipin remains alone as the character who wishes to see the patronymic continued in the corporeality of flesh of his flesh. When all the women meet in Aseema's house after Darjin Bibi's death, Narmada's statement that other than Nameeta, all of the women are sterile, it provokes the novel to be read as a movement of the infertile, *banjh striyon ka andolan*. The women's infertility is the novel's productive force.

Elaine Showalter reads Gilbert and Gubar, Alicia Ostriker, and Rachel Blau DuPlessis to make her point about the vulnerability of feminist biocriticism because in centering the place of the womb as a site of creative production, women run the risk of reiterating the hegemonic hierarchy already in play in our gendered history. A difference in sex is the very reason such dominance of one sex over the other exists in the first place. Quoting the editors of *Questions Feministes* and Nancy Miller, Showalter writes, "The difference of woman's literary practice, therefore, must be sought (in Miller's words) in 'the body of her writing and not the writing of her body.'"[42] Garg implies this lacunae of feminist biocriticism and posits within her polemical novel a number of women protagonists, who for a variety of reasons, do not reproduce. The body is not the center of their identity and the difference between the sexes not the justification of their beings. Indeed their epistemic restructuring arises from a vision of feminist world making, an identity that springs out of the affect that relates them to one another so that the loss of the child of the womb remains as a melancholia that enables in world making. Instead of writing of their bodies, the body of their collectives takes precedence, doubly signifying Garg's own vast body of writing as the subliminal text to all the ongoing relief work within the confines of the novel.

Spectrum of Actions: Speech/Body/Collective

Judith Butler writes "on linguistic vulnerability" in her text, *Excitable Speech: Politics of the Performative*, "Language sustains the body not by bringing it into being or feeding it in a literal way: rather, it is by being interpellated within the terms of language that a certain social existence of the body first becomes possible."[43] *Kathgulab* is replete with speech acts that literally bring the body into social existence: Smita tells Nameeta that she can never forgive her sister for keeping silent through the period of the most volatile abuse; Marianne tells her sterile husband that he is a thief and a plagiarist and she is leaving him; Aseema tells a myriad people her opinion on the ills of normativity, particularly defined by patriarchy and state hegemony. When an irate Jija comes to recover Narmada as a lost possession, she charges back at him with bitter invective, a speech act that literally brings her into social existence and gives room for her body to simply be. She leaves the confines of her former home as a prisoner liberated from her confines and rekindles the relationship with Darjin Bibi and her daughter. To her Jija, Narmada orates a speech both political and performative, and sends him shrinking back from a woman he no longer recognizes.

फिर कभी इस घर में आने की हिम्मत की तो दोनों टांगें तोड़ के सड़क पर फेंक दूँगी। भड़ुवे, जा अपनी बीवी के पल्लू में जाके सो । मैं तेरी रखैल ना थी, तू मेरी रखैल था । कमा-कमा के तुझे खि-लाया मुस्टंडे, इसलिए, कि तू और तेरी बीवी मिलके मेरा हक मारो । जा, नामर्द समझ के अपना हिस्सा माफ किया । पर याद रख, एक दिन आके वसूल कर लूँगी । वह मेरी बहन ना दुसमन है, पहले जान लेती तो तुम दोनों की बोटी-बोटी काट के चील-कौवों को खिला देती। हिम्मत हो तो आ मेरे सामने। [44]

[If you ever dare to come to this house then I will break both your legs and throw them on the street. Pimp, go and hide in your wife's sari palloo. I was never your concubine, you were my concubine. I earned and earned and fattened you up, you jerk, so that you and your wife could dominate me. Go, I forgive you because you are impotent. But remember, I will come and take my part one day. She was never my sister but my enemy and if I had known this before, I would have cut you both to pieces and fed you to the hawks and vultures. If you have any courage, come in front of me.]

After this remarkable speech act, Narmada actually stands on the threshold of the house of women with a knife though her words have already performed the labor of self-preservation. In naming him as the pimp, she makes public his private degradations and brings him into the market place. She insists on the primacy of her labor and reminds him that it is her economic autonomy that ensures the health of his household. Additionally her speech serves as the "weapon" much in the manner of Butler; words wound because they emasculate; she calls him *namarad* or "not a man" and invites him to go and hide behind his wife. All of these encode culturally and linguistically specific idioms that despite being lost in translation, present performative rebuttals to classic patriarchy.

Finally, it is a declaration of the collective that forms the most substantial speech act in *Kathgulab*. Darjin Bibi, on her death-bed, teaches the significance of having passed on her gift to the next generation. In the same way that Narmada is autonomous, she will be the one who helps others do the same. Darjin Bibi says:

उन जैसे कितने ढेर बच्चों की माँ बन सकती हैं तू । मुझे देख, बीसियों बच्चे हैं मेरे । तभी इतने विश्वास के साथ कह सकती हूँ, एक बच्ची मेरा काम सँभालेगी, एक मेरी चिता को आग देगी, बाकी सम्मानजनक जीवन जिएँगी। किसी एक की खातिर मुझे कलपने की जरूरत नहीं है । [45]

[You can be a mother to so many kids like those. Look at me, I have dozens of children. That is why I can say with such certainty, one daughter (does not signify biological kinship) will take over my business, one will light my pyre, and the rest will live lives of dignity. I don't have to worry about any one.]

This is the reply to the emptiness experienced by the women, especially Narmada's own declaration that she is a barren women, and Garg's refutation of the societal prescription that defines a fulfilled woman as one who has reproduced. As Narmada fulfills Bibi's declaratives, she continues a radical revision of normative motherhood; her progeny will grow unencumbered unlike the limitations of biological reproductions.

Butler finds in the propositions of Catharine MacKinnon and Rae Langton a Habermasian theory of speech which seeks to make all speech acts permissible of everyone else's consent and rights: "In having a speech act silenced, one cannot effectively use the performative. When the 'no' is taken as 'yes,' the capacity to make use of the speech act is undermined. This seems to be the very project in which Habermas and others are engaged—an effort to devise a communicative speech situation in which speech acts are grounded in consensus where no speech act is permissible that performatively refutes another's ability to consent through speech."[46] Darjin Bibi's speech act, unlike those examples stated by Narmada (oral) and Aseema (physical), fall under this ideal rubric of communication: her speech act neither negates, harms, or silences another human being. Instead it seeks to become the agent of autonomy, self-dignity, and voice for nameless others, a universal configuration to collapse the margins.

In the spectrum of feminine to feminist actions offered within Garg's novel, Darjin Bibi's pivotal death-bed request forms a postcolonial sequel to Mary Wollestonecraft's declarations and Sojourner Truth's truisms. Like the wood-rose that spreads with the wind and blooms in the strangest of places, Darjin Bibi's action is one that contains the possibility of self-willed dissemination so the event of speech is consensual, egalitarian, and implies *sammanjanak* ("respectable" and "dignified") lives for everyone involved. The community hinted at the end of Garg's novel is at once here and elsewhere, an imagined community deeply immersed and aloof from life wherein women find the freedom to utter, uplift, and cohere with one another.

Mahasweta Devi's *Hazaar Chaurasi Ki Maa*

Mahasweta Devi has a literary and activist career that is longer than the life of the modern Indian nation. She has produced a corpus of works dedicated to figures marginalized or misunderstood in history and contemporaneity. She is such a popular and polemical figure in South Asia that her works have been translated into all the major languages in India and have been translated by many different scholars into English. Of all these, one might say that Gayatri Spivak's translation inaugurates her into the American academy. Returning to the paucity of South Asian women novelists in contemporary lists of authors, despite the growing numbers of diasporic writers such as Anita Desai, Bharati Mukherjee, Chitra Banerjee Divakaruni, these catalogues still exclude major writers such as Devi. In most contemporary encyclopaedic guides to women's literatures, Devi is absent, let alone Garg and Durrani. Gayatri Spivak, having translated her stories in *Three Stories by Mahasweta Devi: Imaginary Maps*, instructs on practices of reading, a necessary intervention when sites of reading are so distant from locations of production:

> The possibility of social redistribution in these states, uncertain at best, is disappearing even further.
> In this context, it is important to notice that the stories in this volume are not only linked by the common thread of profound ecological loss, the loss of the forest as foundation of life, but also of the complicity, however apparently remote, of the power lines of local developers with the forces of global capital. This is no secret to the initiative for a global movement for non-Eurocentric ecological justice. But this is certainly a secret to the benevolent study of other cultures in the North. And here a strong connection, indeed a complicity, between the bourgeoisie of the Third World and migrants in the First cannot be ignored. We have to keep this particularly in mind because this is also the traffic line in Cultural Studies. Mahasweta's texts are thus not only of substantial interest to us, but may also be a critique of our academic practice. Is it more or less "Indian" to insist on this open secret?[47]

Devi informs and concludes this project as a critique precisely of "our academic practice" and enriches the subterranean levels of community that has been at work so far. Mahasweta Devi has made it her life's work to record the excesses of the state, particularly as it applies to its native inhabitants, labeled "tribals" in India, and the degradations against the environment. In reading Devi's novel, *Hazaar Chaurasi Ki Maa*, in Hindi, I address a novel that has received less academic attention though it has been noted by the popular media thanks to a fine filmic version of the novel, Govind Nihalani's "Haazar Chaurasi ki Maa" (1998), a success in the world of parallel Indian cinema. I explore community in this less-studied work of Mahashweta Devi's in order to make a case for creative partnerships between feminist scholarship and feminist activism.

In the novel, *Hazaar Chaurasi Ki Maa*,[48] she ventures into the un-familiar terrain of the middle-class to record the familiar, the death of an activist, a college student of around twenty or so years. This novel stands aloof in Devi's oeuvre because in this she tackles the middle-class which has not provoked the passionate ire with which she has gravitated toward advocating for the subalterns of the subcontinent. Within the scope of this project, however, this particular novel of Devi fits within the radical shifts of community-making possible within the domestic sphere.

Told through the eyes of a mother mourning the second anniversary of her son, Vrati's death, Devi tells a day in the life of this mother, Sujata Chatterjee. Sujata's son, Vrati is killed in a spate of extreme state repression of student activism that marked Calcutta of the late 1960s and early 1970s, an episode that only receives passing mention even in the annals of the Communist Party of India (CPI-M, Marxist–Leninist). In this period, thousands of student activists were killed, maimed, and imprisoned by state authorities. Divided into four parts, morning, afternoon, evening and night, it details a day of meeting another mother who meets other people touched by her son and who could fill in the missing narrative of Vrati's life for Sujata. The narrative begins and builds a growing distance felt on Sujata's part toward her remaining family for being culpable in some way of the very damning structures that not only end her son's life, but erase his memory from everyone's minds.

A Time to Grieve, a Time to Grieve Again

Time is a central lever in all the novels herein. Both novels, *Paradise* and *The Farming of Bones* stage community in the good clean darkness of night. Mahasweta Devi leaves us in no mystery as to the significance of time in her narrative of a middle class woman mourning the death of her son; Devi's *Hazaar Chaurasi Ki Maa* is divided into four episodes: morning, afternoon, evening, and night. Time is essential to the women's novel for a number of reasons; in the states of chaos and violence which are markers in this novel, conditions in which these women tell their stories, it is the shade of night that offers refuge from the light that bares many to the scrutiny of state, the male gaze, and other institutions of power which can wreak havoc upon these women. Devi furthers this survivalist specter into a metaphor for the Bengali middle-class. Time is the systemic hand which governs the life and body of women. Each hour is regulated as to duties that must be abided by amidst a number of gendered prescriptions. By evening, she should be home and at night, whether the husband chooses to have other partners or not, she should be in bed waiting to attend to him. Devi ascribes to the authorial decision to tell one day as metonym for the entire life of one who suffers greatly; much like Solzenitsyn's Ivan Denisovich, Devi tells the four parts of one day in the life of a woman in order to suggest the magnitude of the injustices suffered over a lifetime of such accumulating days.

Sujata Chatterjee is trapped in the tyranny of numbers. In the opening pages itself, her narrative is marked by all the various manners in which she is calculating the loss of her son, Vrati, and she makes this apparent from the opening word itself: "बाईस साल पहले"[49] (22 years ago) a morning to which she returns and finds herself packing to go to the hospital to deliver her fourth and last child, Vrati. She is now fifty-three, and the morning before Vrati's birth when she was in labor, it was the sixteenth of January, 1948, a few months into the life of the nation, a fact important since the state is also a prime character in this narrative. The morning when a metallic voice on the phone coldly asks her to come to the mortuary at Kantapukur, she was fifty-one and her husband, Divyanath was fifty-six. Vrati was the last, born when his eldest brother, Jyoti was ten, his sisters, Neepa and Tuli were eight and six respectively. Possibly the novel can be seen as an elaborate exercise in answering the question posed by the faceless agent of the state on 17 January 1970, "व्रती चाटर्जी आपका कौन लगता है?"[50] (Who is Vrati Chatterjee to you/or, how is Vrati Chatterjee related to you?) along with the more obvious homage: Sujata's tortured and silent mourning of her son.

Sujata engages in her world-making based on two new truths—the state is the greatest perpetrator of violence, and she is the maker of her own identity. In mourning for her son, and an absence of such affect in her middle-class household where his name is anathema, his possessions locked, and his memory erased the morning of his murder, she begins to insist on her own voice, and as a consequence, resists the normative values imposed upon women within the patriarchal order. The women seek community despite the chokehold of domesticity and in finding it reconstitute normative notions of femininity. For Sujata, her youngest child, Vrati, from his entry into the world presents her exit-ticket out of the prison of patriarchy. It takes her twenty-two years after his death to exercise this freedom. His birth causes her to first, refuse to bear any more children, and second, refuse to quit her employment at the bank at her husband's behest. Vrati's death leads her to do what he had signified her to do in lesser words: break out of the prison of their home, realize her own strength, and find a voice.

Self, Other, and Mother: Forging Identity

Sujata's journey to self-realization, burgeoning over the years, can be marked at the moments immediately following the deadly phone call informing her about Vrati's corpse, a body marked by the numbers "1084" giving her another layer of newfound identity, "hazar chaurasi ki ma" (the mother of 1084). While this is anonymous and tragic and depicts the cold turnings of state machinery, it is the number itself that pulls in a thousand and more mourning mothers along with their dead sons as figures who populate this text as unwritten and voiced beings always alongside the protagonist, Sujata. Her own immediate family acts in a manner she finds depraved; they celebrate the very same nation that unjustly murders her son. They celebrate without compunction while refusing to celebrate his memory or memorialize the day of his death.

जैसे करोड़ों साल पहले इस आदिम धरती पर विस्फोट हुआ था और उस विस्फोट से पृथ्वी पर के महादेश छिटककर नक्शे के दूर-दूर के छोरों पर बिखर गए थे -- बीच की सपाट दूरी को समुद्र ने पाट दिया था l[51]

[Like millions of years ago an explosion broke the large landmass on this earth into pieces that spread themselves far from one another and the infinite distance between filled by oceans.]

The female protagonist, in her moments of awakening when she begins to deem her husband dead, sees the self as the earth itself, a primordial female archetype and seemingly gains power from this contrary image of dissolution. Consequently when she arises out of her period of self-quarantine, three months after Vrati's end, she laughs at her foolish son, Jyoti who removes the telephone from her room as if to save her from future doom of such eventful calls.[52] She catalogues the positions of her remaining family members. Her husband owns an office of char-tered accountants. Their eldest son is a junior officer in an English firm. Neepa's husband is a high-end customs official and Tuli's suitor owns a textile store in Sweden. Sujata knows that the lives of none of these peo-ple involve the sort of deeds that could pull them in the face of danger and award another fateful telephone call. Vrati, her son of twenty, who addresses his father as the "father" oft-labels himself, "boss" confesses in bold rhetoric that he does not hate his father as an entity in isolation. To his mother in a conversation she recalls, he tries to explain:

दिव्यनाथ चैटर्जी एक व्यक्ति या एक इकाई के रूप में मेरे शत्रु नहीं हैं। उनका जिन चीज़ों, जिन मूल्यों पर विश्वास हैं उन्हीं पर और भी कितने लोगों का विश्वास हैं। इस मूल्य-बोध को जो पाल-पोस रहा है वही वर्ग हमारा शत्रु है। वे उसी वर्ग के हैं।[53]

[Divyanath Chatterjee as a person or in isolation is not my enemy. The things and values in which he believes are also the same things in which so many others hold stake. The class that nurtures this value-system, that class is my enemy. He is of that class.]

Allied with a Marxist consciousness which infects the Bengali youth movement of the early 1970s in India, Vrati seeks to uplift and change the status quo even though he has, as his poor friend, Samu's mother ac-knowledges, "everything." However, Vrati, even though he is perceived by his friends and their families as a young man who has "everything" carries a sense of alienation from his own class. It is as though, in his mother's mourning and resistance, Vrati's class consciousness is resuscitated.

Vrati's affect within home transports him with fluidity to a locus of class deprivation, a basti forgotten to be developed by the Calcutta Metropolitan Development Authority (CMDA). At home, the only person to whom he feels kinship other than his brooding mother is the domestic worker, Hem who speaks of him as "younger brother" and knows of his comings and goings, and even his love interest, the dark-skinned Nandini. When asked to switch the old blue shawl in which he wraps himself at home, he points to Hem and says that she is the one who values the shawl for the heat it gives on really cold days. In a spirit of camaraderie that flows from the dead son to mother, just as a hole-riddled shawl does not stop giving heat, a file once closed does not end the story. Vrati is different and dies for that difference, Sujata comes to understand, due to the difference in her own maternal affection for him. Even though he is called a sissy and a milksop by his father, she nurtures his difference into a sensitivity with which he is able to see the very injustices that eventually annihilate him.

Mothers in Mourning

In the afternoon, she meets Samu's poor mother whom she ritualistically meets each year on the death anniversary of their sons for the comfort and solace that eludes her in her own home. Instead of routing home after picking up the jewelry from the bank for Tuli, who greedily asks for Vrati's share as well now that he is dead and will not be marrying anyone, Sujata meets Samu's mother in her thatched and dilapilated quarters where the public specters of mourning, such as black wagons carrying corpses, curfews, and other forms of state control have disappeared. While Sujata seeks solace in the collective, a comfort she finds only annually in front of Samu's mother, she knows in the glance of the embittered sister who supports the family at this point, that she is no longer welcome. And yet, it is only at this woman's house that Sujata finds all the missing pieces of her son's life, all the things left unspoken between them, all the principles and assignments he kept hidden from his own mother. She found a family that knew her Vrati better than anyone in his own household, another woman who carried the sound of his laughter in her melancholic memories. Despite the difference of class and dialect of language spoken by the two women, there is a kinship that surpasses their many differences, summarized by the sniffling woman at the end of their conversation, "एक दुखिया ही दुखिया का दरद समझत है"[54] (Only a sad/suffering/wretched[55] woman can understand another sad/suffering/wretched woman). Though Sujata is asked to come again since there is a peace of melancholic sharing in their meetings, Sujata knows that this bridge to her son is also lost to her.

Her son, Vrati, who leaves her with a smile and advises her not to worry knowing that he is going to caution his friends about government spies in their midst and that his mission is dangerous, slept on Samu's floor, with his friends, Samu, Parth, Vijit, and Laltu. He used to arrive at this home often, exchanging gossip, chatting and laughing, asking for tea in ways Sujata thought were only reserved for her. And by this, instead of being rankled as her husband would have to know of his son's amity with a class of people he deems beneath him, she feels rejuvenated. In finding Vrati, Sujata forges a newer sense of self, a self unencumbered by *bhadralok* prescriptions and limitations. Though his own family keeps all his possessions hidden in his room and the state burned his writings deemed anti-state, here exists a nest of fresh-found memories amidst people she could never have found on her own. Correcting and revising her own memories, she also reviews that newspaper reading, the goings-on of city affairs, was a propensity which suited only her and Vrati. The others found it burdensome and ugly, intrusive upon their more non-violent and comfortable lives. And even then, before Vrati's end, she had an inkling, "Calcutta is a wrong city."[56] Even before she is told of the details: the mob which threatened and beckoned the young men to come out, the bullets in the night which scattered the mob and brought to the scene a more institutional power, the brutal and particular endings of each of the friends, like Laltu found wrapped in his own innards, and the police van which arrives so slowly that the murderous mob is allowed to disperse into the dark, Sujata knew that Calcutta was a wrong city.

It is only with Samu's mother that she can also piece together the fractured stories and receive glimpses of the grieving mothers, a collective feminine mourning. Vijit's mother has been carted off to Kanpur. Parth's mother is mad with grief, ailing, and still beating her breasts, bed-ridden. Laltu has no one left behind to mourn his horrific ending. Samu's mother, meanwhile, disappears and becomes half of who she was, with each passing year. And with all the details given to Sujata once again in the ritualistic ceremony of mourning she forces herself to undergo with Samu's mother, she is not able to share the burden of silence, the impossibility of bellowing out one's sorrow at home. She wrestles to understand her family's hypocritical silence and how they fit ideally within the *bhadralok* norm of the polite smile and the hollow life, and shoulders the sorrow of not being able to relate her condition to her sister in mourning. It is a culture that rests to her on an earth without roots, a dead culture that is embarrassed to cry out loud. Further, she feels defeated in front of Samu's mother and the thousands of others who knew more than she did; she never knew what Vrati was really doing, not familiar in the way that Samu's mother was so that she was able to give all the sons refuge on their last night, and so, Sujata could never caution him. She cuts away cultural baggage of things like "maternal instinct" because on that fateful evening when Vrati bid her good-bye, she had no premonition of things to come.

In addition to the city of Calcutta, Sujata holds the state, the entire nation accountable for a silencing that is intrinsic to the national process. As she critiques and awakens to the existence of a collective with which she can never form literal bridges, she comments that even though none of the activists, intellectuals, or poets raise their voices against the state, the mothers know. The mothers possess knowledge and are armed in a collectivity of mourning against the ignorance and mass amnesia sponsored as propriety on part of those who claim to have attained some level of economic and material stability. Her grief does not stop at mourning for Vrati alone. It, like the earth she brings up as metaphor earlier, envelops other atrocities perpetrated by the state in other places and times and questions the silence of the citizens who have agency and yet, choose to not exercise it.

व्रती जैसे लोग जेल में सड़ रहे हैं, हिंसक जनता के हाथों मारे जा रहे हैं, लेकिन पूरे राष्ट्र की नीति और विवेक के समान जो लोग हैं वे सब चुप्पी साधे हुए है - यह ही एक विषय है जिस पर बोलते समय सबकी ज़ुबान पर ताला पड़ जाता है । लोगों की यह सहज स्वाभाविकता सुजाता को बहुत डरावनी लगती है । उसे डर लगता हैं जब वह देखती हैं कि ये लोग अपने-आपको सहृदय, विवेकवान और सामान्य समझते हैं । बाहर देखते वक़्त इनकी दृष्टी ही बहुत दूर तक चली जाती हैं, लेकिन अपने घर में वही दृष्टी धुन्धली और अस्पष्ठ हो जाती हैं ।[57]

[People like Vrati are rotting in prison, dying at the hands of enraged mobs, yet the people of the entire nation who stand by the law and wisdom of the state assume a silence—this is the only topic during which tongues remain tied. Sujata found such easy civility of people to be quite frightening. She feels scared when she sees that these people think of themselves as respectful, thoughtful, and average. While looking outside, their eye sight roams really far, but at home, this same sight turns feeble and unclear.]

Sujata understands that people like Vrati, not just her own Vrati, are suffering in prisons, are being murdered by violent people, and yet, those with power and the vote refuse to desist. Unlike the punitive gaze of the patriarch, Sujata's recoded gaze is empowered by the critical roving clear eye of the awakened woman. In many ways, mourning in solidarity gives her the power to see how violence discursively orders the relationship between the punitive regime of the prison and the state.

Awakening

Sujata's aim is to recollect pieces of the dead in a communion with mourners, form a figment of community with the impossible—the living who are distant from her like Samu's mother and Nandini (Vrati's now-blind lover) and the long dead, like Vrati and a thousand others like him. The language of resistance at the heart of this novel motions towards an implicit community of the dead and the living who seek to counter the master narrative expounded by the state, who broach the subject of telling the stifled stories, who transgress state control by remembering what is not the given space on the official record. Against all habit, Sujata places her hands upon Nandini's both to seek and give comfort. Admonished by Divyanath to stay away from windows while she watched storms, here she enters a literal maelstrom of society and joins rank with those who stand looking at it in the eye. Here, Sujata marks the separation of the two spheres of her life: the exterior sphere which is her domestic and regulated realm of space shared with her husband and children, and then, an interior sphere, what she calls "अन्दर की दुनिया"[58] (inside world) populated by Vrati, Samu's mother, Nandini, a world that she knows also exists inside Nandini and all the other mourners with whom Sujata is linked. This inside world is also her "कालकोठरी" or prison, a place she occupies alongside the innocent others, a place in which she communes, punishes, and remembers what the rest of her immediate kin forget so readily. At the same time, the "inside world" also promises a freedom she guards from the immediate imprisonment of domesticity. It is her own wild zone in which she can travel, commune, and form connections as she wills. It is a space in which she can continually write her own narrative of mourning and write an anti-narrative to the official one upheld by her family and the state.

Simultaneously, mourning urges Sujata to question every object, person, relationship in her life, the meaning of things. Things, like time, are critical in the dwindling light of evening. Sujata notices the dusty and useless books of law lying in the room in which the two sit facing one another, "Law" a signifier emptied of meaning or metaphor, tomes that have lost all utility. Nandini educates Sujata, a younger woman teaching an older woman the essential of belief removed from material culture, commodification and normative values.

By nightfall, "Raat," the fourth and final section of the novel, Sujata returns from her day of imagining community to her real house, muttering "nahi, nahi" under her breath. The home, set for Tuli's engagement party, a debauched affair in Sujata's eyes, with wine bottles and flower vases and plates full and white table clothes decking the house, and not a sign of Vrati anywhere, Sujata enters with protest and exits with a scream. Now that towards the end of the day she finds her identity, *astitva*, she rekindles this community she finds in herself with Vrati's memory so that her "inner world" is the site of an imagined community with not only all those who mourn their dead sons, but also her dead son, Vrati himself.

Having denied herself warm water because of an overworked Hem who is not able to attend to her in the midst of the gala, she sits naked on the cold floor under the icy water—an awakening, a birth, a cleansing. The entire novel enters and exits, all its player and themes in this solitary moment of Sujata cleansing her tired body alone.

बर्फ की तरह ठंडा पानी। बर्फ की सिल्ली पर तुरन्त मरा हुआ, खून से लथपथ शरीर डालकर रखो तो खून बंद हो जाता हैं। ठंडा पानी! शीतल - व्रती की उँगलियों की तरह, व्रती के माथे की तरह, हाथों की तरह ठंडा और कुछ नहीं हो सकता। आज सारे दिन व्रती के साथ रही थी। व्रती की उँगलियाँ कितनी ठंडी, कितनी बर्फ-सी ठण्डी उसकी पलकें, बंद काली बरौनियाँ, तांबाई गोरा रंग, बाल ठंडे पानी से भीगे ठंडे-ठंडे हिमशीतल! आज सारा दिन व्रती के साथ थी। श्मशान में अंधेरी रात। पुलीस के पहरे में व्रती। श्मशान में रोशनी की बाढ़। दीवार पर इबारत। एक के बाद एक नाम। नाम, नाम, अलुमिनियम का दरवाज़ा धड़ से गिरा - व्रती! बिजली की आग के अंदर व्रती को सेंका जा रहा हैं। दिन भर व्रती के साथ थी। राख लीजिए, अस्थियाँ लीजिए, मिट्टी से निकालिये, गया में फेंकनी होंगी। व्रती के साथ थी वह सारा दिन।[59]

[Water cold as ice. A sheet of ice. If one places a recently dead body, bloodied and bruised on a sheet of ice, then the blood stops. Cold water! Soft—like Vrati's fingers, like Vrati's forehead, cold like his hands and like nothing else. Today she was with Vrati all day. A dark night at the cemetery. Vrati lying in police custody. A spot of light in the cemetery. Writing on the wall. Names one after the other. Names, names, and the steel door claps shut—Vrati! An electric fire is broiling Vrati. Today she was with Vrati all day. "Take the ashes; take the bones; Sift them from the mud; You might need to toss them in the river." Today she was with Vrati all day.]

The ice leads her to bodies lying on ice, bodies that stop bleeding because of the ice, Vrati's cold fingers, and how she spent an entire day with her Vrati. The police crematorium and handing over of ashes through metal doors. Sujata communes with her dead son since she rejects the sequestration of her domesticity and finds comfort in her "inner world" wherein an imagined community with the dead is allowed to be. She repeats she has spent the day with her son, rejecting the immediacy of the company of merry-makers who are all gathered in her house. To Sujata, the imagined community with the dead is far more reasonable and significant than the rational event of the betrothal over which she presides. Communing with the disembodied helps disassociate from the embodied.

Sujata breaks her silence. To her husband, she confesses boldly that she knows. She knows about his philandering and never thought to ask him where he spent all the evenings and holidays away from home. To her daughter, Tuli, who spends all her years serving her father and helps him preserve his relationship with his mistress, she refuses to give Vrati's share of jewelry. To none of them, she explains her absence or the necessity of time spent away from home on their big day. To all of them, she asks to shut up and leave her alone.

The pain, rising and ebbing all through the day, finally erupts. The novel ends on Divyanath's anti-climactic cry that her appendix has finally broken, giving us the rational excuse for Sujata's blood-curdling scream. Echoing Nandini's earlier scream that ends the evening, Sujata screams and stops all narrative. The novel's meaning, questions that threaten institutional sanction and structural oppression on many levels, indicts readers, scholars and characters alike. The scream, a sound beyond coherent and grammatical meaning, consumes the lacunae present throughout, the pauses and shudders, the images that never leave, the memory that collides with daily living. This scream, as Devi situates, is not uttered in empty time or space, and left unheard. The patriarch is the one who helplessly records the explosive sound while the narrator shows its descent into every house in Calcutta, it becomes a sound of history that does not go unheeded.

एक विस्फोट की तरह यह प्रश्न फूटकर बिखर गया-कलकत्ता के हर घर में, शहर के नींवों में धंस गया, आकाश के शून्य में मिल गया, हवा के साथ प्रदेश के कोने-कोने में फैल गया । इतिहास के साक्षी खंडहरों के अँधेरे, इतिहास के परे पुराणों के विश्वास की नींवें काँप गईं। भूला हुआ, न भूला हुआ अतीत वर्तमान, आगामी काल-सबकुछ जैसे यह क्रंदन सुनकर काँप गए। हर सुखी-सुखी दिखनेवाले अस्तित्व के सच तार-तार हो गए।[60]

[Like an explosion, this question tore apart to pieces—in every house in Calcutta, it was embedded in the gullies of the city, the top of the sky, along with the wind, it spread to every corner of the land. Those witness to the darkness of history, those who believed in history trembled. Forgotten past, the unforgotten past, the present, what is to be—all trembled from hearing this bloodcurdling sound. All who emody happiness are torn to shreds.]

Harkening back to the explosion on the day of Vrati's murder when Sujata understands the edifice of her life to be made of sand, this one causes itself to be heard in every house in the nation, and finds its way into the lost caverns of history. It is a scream which carries in it, "the scent of blood, the promise of protest, the impatience of melancholy."[61] The scream breaks Sujata out of the cycles of connection to the state which murdered her son, and the family structure that binds her to maintain a rigid silence about the matter. It is not relevant here, as in the case of many archetypal women's narratives of the nineteenth and twentieth centuries whether the protagonist lives or dies past the novel; suffice it to say that her manner of exit dignifies the text with meaning, and presents rupture from the structures of normalcy that have heretofore imprisoned and kept her voiceless. Having found voice, she exits with a sound that transcends language. Within the interior sphere, she cries out to Vrati to stop running and return to her, a maternal voice, her more public voice seeks to know who will be the next one wounded in the line of resistance? Who will the next bullet kill? Whose son or daughter?

Once again, the woman returns through the symbol of the explosion to a primordial earth, and her dismemberment, as of archetypal goddesses from preclassical antiquity, is of consequence. Out of her emerges a new world; her melancholy and the sound of her explosion are never forgotten, as recorded in the epic and here, Devi signifies is a function completed by the very state and history that leaves out the woman and her losses. The unintelligibility of the final utterance hints at the spatial realm of an imagined community beyond what is deducible and evident within disciplinary regimes of surveillance and punishment. At the novel's exit, Sujata enters her "real" on her own terms.

Conclusion

These novels, while strikingly different in mood, historical moment, style of writing, and the subjects of their imaginative landscapes, also present a unity of utterance. In each text, the author, and narrator of any voice, first or third, remains deeply aware of the scarcity of their very women-centered epistemologies. The voices, while teeming with a polyphony of differences, also strike at a common denominator which attends consciously to its very own existence: each word of the writer is an homage to the space it provides for the woman to come into the world of writing, and thereby, the world itself.

While *Kufr* charts the singular voice of a woman, Heer, cloistered in extreme isolation within the prescriptions of patriarchy, the novel manages to implicitly make the point that all of patriarchy legitimizes itself through the violence of power, perversity, and sadism. Though the narrative highlights the excesses of Pir's authority, Durrani's catalogue of other marital relationships also show a deficit of consideration, mutual love, and most importantly, female autonomy. All three novelists indict patriarchy—Garg adopts a multiple-voiced narrative to add plurality and power to her critique and Devi urges a multi-valent critique that arrives at an imagined community beyond language and intelligibility, a space unregulated by the father of the family or the father of the state. Garg's novel, narrated in the many voices of its disparate characters, hints at community-building in the novelistic discourse itself because the women are never alone and their stories stand in regard to one another. Community is always already on Garg's agenda and it goes from the formal (RAW) to the grassroots (women's center at Godhra) to the provisional and indiscernible (the women who come together in the wake of Darjin Bibi's death). Devi's community is counter-intuitive; it exists apart from and beyond the flesh of bodies. Sujata's scream upon her exit from the narrative suggests the beginning of an imagined community of the dead. Much like the novels by Morrison and Danticat, Devi's novel develops more elusive concepts of an imagined community that is beyond measure and regulation and affords the women characters an exercise of power despite being positioned as powerless.

Community, the rootless and moving sort hinted in the introduction as *jangama*, arrives at the cost of the women characters' long stay in patriarchal strongholds, i.e., the domestic space, and often times, their complicity with the systems in place. Heer seeks out the vulnerable girls who come to rest under her awning—the orphaned, the disabled, the poor and brings them to Pir to do as he wills. While Heer's suffering is hinges around complications of class and community, in Devi's novel, class hints at a failure of the earthly and material community of mourning mothers because no matter how much Sujata wishes, she is not welcome in the world of poverty and depredations of her son's friends. Nandini accuses her in so many words about complicity with the oppressors in her life lived as the wife of Divyanath and mother of her other children, children who are known by their proper names to the state and not a number. Similarly, in Garg's novel, sisters and mothers are complicit often in how patriarchy plays out on the bodies of women. Narmada's sister, Smita's sister and mother all participate in prolonging the suffering and in retrospect, silencing or altering the narratives of oppression. In this context then, community making is not simply the gathering of women. It is really the communing of consciousness, women in flight who have finally come into their own. The release is found in this alternative space of an imagined community wherein former alliances are shaken off and culpabilities give way to amity and enfranchisement.

Community, the static and claustrophobic traditionalism found within domesticity, such as Pir's household, or the myriad domestic spaces in Garg's and Devi's novel wherein domesticity assures the rampant perpetration of sexual and physical abuse, is shunned. The women characters search out an alternate community, much like Bataille suggests by characterizing the more ideal community as one that is headless, or Mani suggests can be found when women's subjectivities are regarded seriously. The rootless, ephemeral quality that characterizes the imagined community is found towards the conclusion of all three novels. Here it is the women's speech acts, a singular act of profanity as Aseema or Narmada utter, or Sujata's scream, or the entire corpus of their passion with which they record their narratives, that brings them into self-actualization beyond the cloisters of domesticity. Blasphemy—an irreverence to the patriarch, the state, and stately notions of community—brings them into the statelessness and evanescence that promises the possibility of an alternate and less stifling cohabitation in an imagined community of women, both living and dead.

5

The Cracking of India in Amrita Pritam's *Pinjar* and Mohandas Nemishrai's *Aaj Bazaar Band Hai*

Cracking Open the Cage: Amrita Pritam's *Pinjar*

Often times, print media is quite easily overpowered by the goliath, the visual media, especially in the South Asian context dominated by Hollywood's powerful and much more prolific twin, Bollywood. In the case of authors lucky enough to compete in the contemporary marketing blitz of stories that appeal but are no longer read, Amrita Pritam is one such significant voice in the canon of twentieth century Indian literature. Pritam (1919–2005) was a prima donna of Punjabi literature, her works of such popular and mass appeal that they were translated into scores of other Indian languages as well as in English for an even larger global audience. Her poetry and fiction often concerns itself with the voice and condition of women, and ways in which the feminist and modern author can empower her ambiguous position within patriarchy into something meaningful and autonomous. Pritam's work is most obviously a Punjabi-Hindi-Indian *écriture féminine* as much as a body of writing by a woman writer in India comes to be; her work concerns itself with a woman's way of thinking about history and contemporaneity. Her language in the original, Punjabi, is infused with a passionate rhetoricity particular to the feminine. One such novel, *Pinjar* (1982) which can be translated as skeleton and a cage both, achieved name in its glamorous mutation onto the large screen in 2003, in a film under the same name directed by Dr. Chandraprakash Dwivedi, a film that achieves notable popular success.

Pritam's novel is the very fragment that finds its narrative[1] in a time of the great friction known in South Asia as "batwara" or partition of Second British Empire into the nations of India, Pakistan, and at the time, East Pakistan, or what is known today as Bangladesh. She tells the story of one woman, Pooro, whose story begins a decade or so before the events of the partition and then, through the ensuing years, her story becomes woven into the story of all the women who live, experience, and suffer the trials of partition. Through Pooro and her experiences, we connect to multiple levels of injustices committed upon women and find ways, albeit small against the vast machinery of the newly-formed states, yet significant as she becomes the prism of condensing the vast array of indignities suffered and recorded by women.

Urvashi Butalia's *The Other Side of Silence: Voices from the Partition of India* (2000) provides the most urgent scholarship to fill the historical gap on this exodus of violence. In it, Butalia finally gives what scholars were unable to provide in decades of research, the effects of partition on women, and articulates how the cost of writing the narrative of the fledgling nation-state is done in blood on the bodies of its own women. In order to enter the story of Pooro, it becomes necessary then to understand how Butalia explains the intimate nature of dialectic between modernity, the young nation, and loss and restoration of women who suffered violence in various forms: rapes, abductions, mutilations, and murders. Butalia writes:

> National honor: the honor that was staked on the body of Mother India, and therefore, by extension, on the bodies of all Hindu and Sikh women, mothers and would-be mothers. The loss of these women, to men of "other" religion, was also a loss to their "original" families. These, and not the new families which the women may now be in, were the legitimate families, and it was to these that the women needed to be restored. If this meant disrupting the relationships that they may now be in, that they had "accepted" for whatever reason, this had to be done. The assumption was that even if asked for their opinion, women would not be able to voice an independent one because they were in situations of oppression. And there was some truth in this. But the obverse was also true: that even in their "own" families women are seldom in situations where they can freely voice their opinions or make a choice. Nonetheless, these were the families that were held up as legitimate; women therefore had to be removed from those "other" non-acceptable families and relocated into the "real" ones. This, for the State, was the honorable thing to do.[2]

The same state, whose own agents had felt free during the orgy of violence of 1947 to damage women deemed as "other" within their own communities, saw fit to engage in acts of redemption by rescuing what they saw as their own, and in the case of secular India, this proved to be Hindu women on the other side of the border. In case of Amrita Pritam's protagonist, this is a direct trajectory of examination: Pooro's abduction ten years prior to the systemic violence that overtakes the Punjab during the events leading up to 1947 and her role during the events in assisting women at every turn, in direct odds with the state and its way of rescuing its blighted daughters.

Pooro, a fifteen-year-old Hindu girl, the eldest of a family of Shahs in Gujarat, is kidnapped by a young Muslim man, Rashid around 1935 and then forced to undergo a life of legitimate matrimony with him: a marriage, name change to Hamida and a son born of this union. As the story progresses, Pooro grows to live with her bitterness, develops fondness for a husband and a son she felt were attached to her like a worm or a disease, and then, becomes a source of strength for girls and women alike who are vulnerable due to the general conditions of patriarchal cultural norm, and facts of partition. By the end, Pooro rises as gloriously as any warrior princess, and valiantly rescues Ramchand's sister, the Hindu fiancé once promised to her, and transports her safely to the border from where she returns to her Rashid, rather than cross lines and take her place in the long line of "rescued women" in the newly formed Indian state. In effect, Pooro becomes more interested in forming alternative forms of community with the vulnerable, mostly women, and is not interested at any point in accepting her gendered condition of passivity. The communities she forms are beyond borders in that the women she rescues are from all sides of the shifting paradigm of new nations. Finally she is never interested in the nation she rightly belongs, a nation wherein she would be welcomed as a disenfranchised secondary citizen who is in need of institutional rescue and societal pity.

Both the state and the patriarchal institution are directly indicted in this text, as in Devi's text, because both institutions are seen as enforcing their violent will on the bodies of women. Rashid falls in love and abducts Pooro on a vengeful family promise recited and inculcated into him by family elders who want him to avenge the honor of their "Sheikh" name: a generation before, one of Pooro's grand-uncles kidnapped, raped, and cast away one of Rashid's grand-aunts in a statement of victory against the Muslim family. One after the other, Pritam offers us instances of patriarchal violence that is seemingly resolved upon the woman's body, and later, when the state involves itself in even more violent atrocities on women considered to be of the "other state," it simply seems like a continuation of the language of patriarchy as it exercises its will upon the personal to the language of the state which exercises its will upon the political. For the woman, it is no wonder then that the personal becomes political and vice versa at the dawn of nationalist-inspired modernity.

The narrative opens on a scene of domestic labor specific to women's work, Pooro shelling peas. However the ordinariness and familiarity of the task turns on itself and invites us to a psychological layer not present in the pure act of labor; the gray day reveals a further grayness of spirit as Pooro recoils from a white worm recovered from the peas. Pooro flings it away while the narrator reveals how Pooro feels like the string of peas, carrying a repugnant worm inside and it takes little to work out the metaphor: a pregnant Pooro reminisces on the past to introduce us to her torturous present.

The past is an elaboration of patriarchal history, losses, and gains where the woman is trained and found primarily in the locus of the private: the domestic realm, doing work within the house with her body, such as kitchen work, or within her body, such as pregnancy and childbirth. Pooro, the eldest in a family of six children with the mother pregnant again, praying and hoping for a boy after the long spate of girl children, is the ideal daughter: she is aesthetically appealing and trained to the height in domestic chores, making her a friend and helper to the mother and ideal for a groom. At fourteen, when the family returns to recover their indebted home from Siyam to Chattoaani, her father begins to look for a groom for her and finds a good match. Of Pooro's match, they speak of it in terms of a "burden" that has to be relieved, "इस बार वह पक्की तरह सोच कर आई थी कि इस भार को उतारकर ही लौटेंगे,"[3] so that it is part and parcel of daily colloquia that the woman can be metonymically referred from the more familiar patriarchal angle, a "bhaar" or "burden," "weight" or "heaviness." For the immediate audience of Pritam, whether it is in Punjabi or the multiple other Indian languages in which she is read, the translation is common and does not presage any contextualization for most of the commonly spoken languages in India contain the same replacement or words of such homonymic tone, "bhāram" in the Dravidian languages of the south also referring often to women or daughters as burdens who need to be dispatched away from the familial.

As for Pooro's mother, having given birth to three daughters in a row, Pritam writes of her, "पूरो की मा का मन शुब्ध-सा हो गया था।"[4] Her mother could only recover from her dejection and shock of bearing three daughters by praying and landing a boy this time around. The layers of mythic narrative are also rich for deconstruction: "Vidhi Mata" or the "Fate mother" or "Mother of our destinies" is beseeched in song and dance by a collective of women, who sing these lines in Punjabi, "*Bidhmaata russi aavi te manni jaavi*,"[5] Bidhmaata supposedly is also a wife, and if she quarrels with her husband, she will come to your house and be in hurry to return. With all the time at hand, she will create what is god's most superior creation, a boy who takes more deliberate care to make. If Bidhmaata comes in a merry mood, that means she will return sooner to her cohort and thus do a shabby job at your residence, leaving you with a girl. It is the strings of the patriarch upon which even the most powerful female deity dances, and she creates in a hurry what is you, the woman. The woman's imagination, curtailed with the feminine subculture of patriarchy, is doubly consigned to its oppressive domination; even in thought, there is no escape from the secondariness imposed upon women as a sex. Even the mythic sub-structures point to her gender as shabby and secondary.

Pooro's girlish fantasy about her fiancé is intruded by the repeated appearance of a dark, stalking local Muslim youngster, Rashid who fancies Pooro. In a short description of what seems like inconsequential flirtation turns life-altering for the dreamy-eyed young girl when lost in dreams of broken red bangles and hobbling in her new shoes, she is abducted while picking okra for the night's dinner with one of her younger sisters. Rashid breaks all reveries; what began as an evening when Pooro's mother sings a lament for her daughter who will soon be leaving for her in-laws turns ominous since Pooro leaves sooner than expected, and not for the legitimate and prescribed residence of her arranged suitor. Instead she is whisked away on horseback by a man unknown to even have stalked her by her family, since on her friends' mocking counsel, such matters are ordinary in the lives of young girls and not to be shared with family. Pooro's mother's song, rich in subtext like Pritam's signature choices of folklore, distinguishes and bemoans how sons receive high palaces while the daughters are fated to go to strange and faraway lands. Literally also, the speed of the narrative reflects the short respite for the reader in which one can bury themselves in the calm before great violence and unrest; Pooro is hardly a girl and in the time of a few pages, she is in a dark and locked room, unconscious of the number of days lost, refusing food and in a state of shock from which the rest of the novel never fully recovers. It is not surprising then that feminist discursivity is spawned at the heels of women locked in dark rooms, veritable symbols of patriarchy that trail across the literary imaginary of Durrani, Garg, Sidhwa, and Pritam.

Pooro's relationship with Rashid is the most fraught and hardest to read in this novel. There are no easy ways out. Pooro begins in shock, repugnance, and depression. Within fifteen days of her abduction, she is married to Rashid, and soon after, her new name, "Hamida" is tattooed onto her arm. Rashid never rapes her before tying the matrimonial knot. He sits by her side gently putting "ghee and gud," a rich combination of clarified butter and brown sugar, into her mouth to induce her back to health. He buys her a set in red for their wedding and continues to address her as "Pooro" even when he moves away to a new place far away to begin again, Sakkadaali. He is gentle, caring, and urges her to smile and begin to enjoy life for the sake of their son, Javed. When sick for ten long days, he begs for her mercy in his fatigued delirium. Pooro, for her part, swaying in the doldrums of self-pity, thoughts of the phantasmagoric Ramchand, and the severing of her kin, turns into a serious woman who begins to eye the most vulnerable girls and women with sagacity, ready to lend a helping hand wherever and whenever she can. She pours her blood and sweat into healing Rashid back to life and at the end of the novel, when offered a chance by kith and kin to forsake this man for a new life across the newly-sketched border, she relinquishes it to stay in the home she has found with Rashid. Either this can be read as the South Asian obsession with preserving the sanctity of matrimony, no matter the terms under which the knot was negotiated, or further, a deference to masculine hegemony, but in many ways, I think that the relationship of Pooro with Rashid cannot be easily codified for a number of reasons. Her relationship is a materialization of her own wishes, her autonomy which runs counter to the national and religious narratives of the time. While women are urged, forced, or choose the correct nation and religion, she makes her own choice.

Femininity and Sexuality as Transgression

In the recent text, *The Anthropology of Sex*, Donnan and Magowan observe, "Borderland sex lives also play a major role in the narrative elaboration of the self and the nation, whereby these are imagined in contrast to the sexual representations of others beyond. In many cases national understandings about the reproduction of the nation are closely tied to ideas about the contaminating potential of sex across borders, whether this is in the form of disease or moral corruption."[6] These prescient insights, mostly limited to contact zones between the European and the global south nations such as US and Mexico or Dominican Republic, stand true on the newly-erected border between the twin nations of India and Pakistan in 1947–1948 when both nations quickly scramble together repatriation laws explicitly written to bring women to the right side of the newly-minted nations. Pooro's rejection of the national edict proves to be her rejection of these totemic masculinist notions of borderland sex lives and the ways in which they govern women's bodies and lives; further, it is the most legible exercise of her agency in a narrative that seems to unfailingly catalogue women's losses.

Despite Pooro's origins in the most ordinary of routes, a young girl waiting with bated breath to be married within all the rules and norms she has learned from her mother, the abduction serves as a rupture for her from the so-called normalcy that keeps most women in a state of amnesiac obedience. Pritam calls attention repeatedly to Pooro's overheated thoughts which can never find expression in language, her radical ways of thinking that constantly keep her occupied and make her question the most facile of situations, such as the ribaldry of "Baisakhi Mela" or the harvest festival when young men and women carouse with each other. She wonders what if suddenly all the men were to kidnap all the women, if situations would turn and women would realize the mass injustice of their historical plight? I argue that it is not the abduction alone that proves as the rupture, but the rejection from her parents, particularly her father.

When Pooro rushes out of her prison before her wedding to Rashid, and finds her parents' home in the dark, it is only her mother who embraces Pooro like the prodigal daughter. The father never bats an eyelash, worries about consequences, and clearly tells her that his home no longer has any place for her. The woman, within patriarchal confines, once stigmatized even against her volition, is defiled for the common use of matrimonial barter and thus, no longer can be carried along even as the "bhaar" she was before. The mother reads the father well and realizes that in order to avert violent repercussions upon the remaining family, Pooro has to be sacrificed. It is she who says to Pooro, "बेटा! जनमते ही मर गई होती! अब यहाँ से चली जा।"[7] (Son! Alas, if only you had died at birth! Now go from here.) It is quite common in the North Indian languages, especially Punjabi, that a daughter when addressed by the greatest affection by one's parent, is addressed as a "son," another rich moment of erasure, because it is authentically the son who deserves such a bridge of love. Never have I heard a mother address a son affectionately as a daughter in spoken Punjabi or Hindi. In this apocalyptic moment of rejection, Pooro, lovingly called "beta" is asked to leave, find shelter or death and not cause any more "bhaar" to the family, because at this point, she has turned from "bhaar" to its anima, "sharam" or "shame." The final rejection carries in it the doubly-encoded mother's lament masked as bile, a curse to Pooro's life and disappointment that she dared to live for this long. Pooro, dead or alive is no longer of any interest to her family. Stumbling out in the early morning dark, Pooro is enlightened a second time in her short life. When Rashid shields her back to his home, she walks willingly and soon after, they are married. She bears him a son, begins to arise as a woman out of the ashes of her girlhood, and slowly recovers from the shards of her broken dreams the images of women who surround her and the role she has to play in resisting the general plight of femininity. It is when Pooro finally realizes the disposability of the female in patriarchal circles of kinship that she accepts her fragile connection to it, and looks toward making her own community of females within it.

To return to the complex web of discourse alive in Pooro's relationship with Rashid, it is necessary to engage with how she begins to revise her own history. When looking back to her younger days at home, she remembers that a particular sweetmeat she desired to have cooked in a certain way was Muslim, and now, ironically enough, it is what she makes for her husband. She resists Rashid, then her parents's dogmatic ways. She accepts Rashid at his darkest hour, when he is ready to give up his life sorrowing for his greatest misdeed. To Pooro, there is a nobility of spirit and uniqueness of mind. Her way of reading the world and the woman's perspective alters even as the love for Rashid builds. She is a complicated woman who is able to love despite the taboo against it for women, in the most accepted situations. At the end of the novel, when she accepts Rashid over the new nation-state of India to which she supposedly belongs, she rejects the patriarchal dictum in favor of feminine agency. Even Rashid is surprised, not desiring to impose his will upon her a second time in life. Pritam creates in Pooro a prototype of feminist resilience and self-generated voice that resists an easy reading under the western gaze.

The Reconstituted Feminine Self

Awakened to a resilience that forms the new matter of Pooro, she emerges as a good Samaritan and a listener. To the young and abused orphan child, Kammo, overworked by her family, Pooro shares some of her "bhaar" by carrying her "batloi," and over time, giving her a pair of new shoes, warm clothes, and companionship. Early in her transition, Pooro sees this aspect of her own self as an effort at being a good mother to Kammo since she feels that she failed at being a daughter. When Kammo tells her about her family, their distaste for the Muslim Pooro's company and the fact that she is known as a woman who ran away from her own home, Pooro is profoundly wounded, feels broken. And yet, when she sees a yellowed woman in the neighborhood who looks more sickly after each visit with her husband's family, Pooro is empathetic enough to not dismiss Taro like the rest of the community and finds out the cause of her despair; married to a man who lives with his lover, Taro feels like a "veshya" and in her gloom, becomes a beacon of light for Pooro. Pooro has never heard such open castigation of patriarchy or such seen such angry protest at the inhumanity practiced in its name. Having found the space to nurture and the ear to listen, Pooro expands her universe to such a degree that by the time the mad woman arrives in their midst, Pooro walks the fine line between the heretic and the saint. And this line leads directly to the community of women she forms through a real and imagined kinship with the berieved.

The mad woman appears right in the center of the novel, a metonymic emplacement significant to Pritam's larger project of woman's voice within patriarchy. Nameless, homeless, and ambiguously connected to any legitimate structure of masculinity or hegemony, she wanders as she pleases, eats whatever she wants whenever she wants and comes and goes at will. Her movements are not dictated by the masculine regulation of female movement, curtailed within the domestic sphere. She appears first as an ill omen on the open street, so that the proper women in their appropriate locations, their homes, quickly pull their children in and shut their doors. The order of the day dictates that not only women have to dress appropriately and cover their torsos with the loose garment known as a "chaddar" or a "chunni" regardless of religion since propriety looms large as a cultural norm, women also are not generally to be seen alone wandering on the village streets or outlying farms unless accompanied by a man, and certainly are not to look at anyone, especially a man directly in the face. The novel opens on one such stipulation gone wrong when a naive Pooro stares into a stranger's face who decides in the spate of some days to abduct and marry her. The mad woman, clearly beyond such regulations, walks in torn garments, generally the loose pants known as a "salwaar" without the "kameez" or blouse on top. Bare-chested, dreadlocked, and sun-burnt, she brings with her a vision of terror and doom so that the commoner avoids any close contact with her. And yet, she is allowed to be, exist in their midst without the surveillance ordered upon the rest of her sex. The mad woman, I believe, is also a metonym for the wild zone of female community, the uncontrollable and powerful aspects of female collectivity Pooro finds in the rest of the text.

The response to her presence can be read as gendered dichotomy: while it is the women who leave out food for her in their porches and clothes according to the condition of her tatters, staying away from her but still enabling her to survive in their midst like a lost sister, the men try repeatedly in bands and as suggested, alone, to erase her. The men cart her away to a faraway location from where she returns once again to resume her familiar wanderings in their midst. The threat of the mad woman also resembles the threat the women at the convent pose to the 8-Rocks in *Paradise*.[8] One man, or more, must have raped her since Pooro, along with all the shocked women of her village, note the protruding pregnant belly on the mad woman. In a methodology that echoes what Foucault charts in his research on quarantining the mad since medieval times in Europe, here the mad are allowed to wander, as in pre-medieval times, and yet, the regulation is active and ominous. The male gaze purveys the female flesh and seizes it at its most vulnerable stage, infancy, or old age, or madness, all depicted in this novel when geography is tormented by the seismic violence of partition later. The mad woman, outside ordinary patriarchal governance, nonetheless pays the price for her sex, and suffers through a series of rapes that leave her in a state of tragic obliviousness to her pregnancy.

At the outset of her presence in Sakkadaali, Pooro thinks of her with empathy though she herself never found an escape from torment in a state of delirium, like Taro or this new character, "Pagli" [mad woman]. Pooro's epistemological framework emerges from an organic ontology of the digestion of daily experience through the gendered lens of each phase of her life, so that Pagli's pregnancy fills her with despair only possible in sisterhood, not a state of judgment or enmity. Pooro thinks,

जिसके पास न सुन्दरता थी, न जवानी थी, माँस का एक शरीर, जिसे अपनी सुध न थी, जो केवल हड्डियों का एक जीवित पिंजर...एक पागल पिंजर था...चीलों ने उसे भी नोच-नोचकर खा लिया... सोच-सोचकर पूरो थक जाती थी।[9]

The masculine consumption of the female body is reduced to a theoretical consistency; Pooro no longer sees the male quest to possess a woman as having to do with sex or beauty, but a pure act of control as iterated in contemporary feminist theories. The man is seen as a scavenger, ready to consume even a carcass that whiffs of woman, so long as his power can be signed upon her body in the form of rape and any of its consequences, such as death or pregnancy, both of which befall Pagli. Patriarchal discourse reduces the woman to her material sign alone, the gendered being as flesh.

Happenstance, Pooro alights upon the dead body of Pagli next to her newborn infant sucking his thumb contentedly by her side. Pooro, seized by maternal affection for the hapless babe, carries him home and begins to nurse him to life. She is able to induce her breasts to produce milk again for the child and nurses the baby like her own, along with her two year old son, Javed. The dead woman's absolute lack of agency in this context translates into Pooro's clear act of will, a feminist inscription of acceptance into societal community despite the patriarchal impulse to cast away. Laura Sjoberg and Caron Gentry's central thesis around women who act outside the norms of culture through acts of violence also applies to the compassion Pooro exhibits. To her compassion also we need to attribute the agency that Sjoberg and Gentry extend to women outside the pale of social contract. They note, "The mother, monster and whore narratives imply that when women choose, they choose within a specified spectrum of socially acceptable choices. When women behave outside of the realm of these choices, they have not chosen to do so."[10] Pooro *chooses* to adopt the newborn. Pooro's adoption of this child that is otherwise sure to die, its body inscribed by patriarchal rejection, is an act of radical compassion.

Not thinking of community or differences or any sort of disdain for a child born to a mother not in the right mind, Pooro simply steps out of her life to bring a vulnerable being into it, envelopes the being in her fold and continues the circle of sisterly and motherly love that are central tenets in this novel. The implacability of patriarchy insists on inscribing the patriarchal law upon this act of human compassion. Pooro lifts and cares for the child outside any sanction or process of deferment to the masculine authorities. Soon enough, these authorities insist on being heard. Authority, communal differences, and the power of a people searching for a new state, all converge in the decision of the Hindu elders in the neighboring village to force Rashid to give up this child to be raised as an orphan or "other" in the Hindu community since the origin of Pagli was putatively Hindu. Pooro, a true humanitarian at this point, comes to an understanding that surpasses all these meaningless divisions since from her vantage point, she is the living emblem of a dissolution of these differences.

Shari Daya's powerful reading of a feminist claustrophobia in contemporary literature is powerfully rebutted by Pritam's text. Daya notes three trends in writings about the new Indian women: "the narrative rendering of women as passive, silent, and implicitly acquiescent; the objectification of the woman as symbol in a denial of an autonomous identity in her own right; and the narrative positioning of the reader as complicit in the act of abuse rather than able to identify with the woman as an independent agent."[11] Pritam's text identifies Pooro as an independent agent. From a pinjar without any autonomy, she begins to act as an agent of change and progress via compassion. This rankles the institutions of masculine power that seeks to carve its signature on all that occurs within its umbra, and bristles under the idea that the child could have found its right home despite a shocking conception and delivery. They seize the child from a distraught Pooro and take it to be raised by women in their own community, women who are even more prescriptively bound by taboo of caste and differences.

The child, yanked from the only mother he has known, and forced to drink buffalo's milk, refuses. In a couple of weeks when the child lies at death's door, the band of men brings the child and tosses it back to Rashid and Pooro saying they do not want sin upon themselves and to do what they can with it. Rashid, in a fit of manliness, seeks to retaliate but holds himself back for Pooro's sake, who heals the child back in a week's time.

Patriarchal power attempts in this situation to assert its hegemony over this infant and fails where Pooro succeeds. Her plan to exercise compassion, love the child as her own, and give the babe a home, is the alternative offered to the twisted mechanics of masculine law. Pooro, as she is being questioned, knows too well the "stone-like ears" of religion which listens to no one, a radical realization from a woman who is forced to convert from the folds of one to another, because she knows that god is the poorest listener in the scheme of things. Pooro fills the lack left by patriarchal supremacy and god-taken rights by exercising compassion, a woman rising to sign in the gaps left between spaces of law. Like the mad woman, Pooro also cannot be fully explained within the purview of patriarchy. Her love, wild and against traditional rules, blossoms without sanction, as for her feelings for Rashid, and then Kammo, Taro and now a nameless Pagli who leaves behind a child Pooro feels ready to give her own milk. Pooro draws together new lines of kinship. While she is an outcast from her own community, she chooses to extend community to those exiled from it.

Confronting Her Past, Writing Her Future

It is inevitable that Pooro's narrative pulls her to Rattovaal, the village she would have called her home had she married Ramchand as designed. To accompany Rahim's old mother for some eye cure, she travels with her younger son to Rattovaal and dreams the whole route of a marriage procession which would have taken her to Ramchand's home. Even the most peripheral event of the text is inscribed with feminist subtext; the curative is not a doctor or a wise man but a mad woman whose water can heal the sick and wounded. Earlier, Pooro continues the legacy of a mad woman by engaging in a mad love for the infant, and here, Pooro stands in the shadows of a woman, again outside patriarchal epistemology, who can heal by nurturing. It is not surprising then that the rest of the novel evolves into the cementing of Pooro as a savior, heroine, and healer.

In Rattovaal, Pooro makes it a point to find Ramchand's farms and when she meets him, she is tongue-tied, calculating a lifetime of losses that can never be appeased again. In the dead of night, she returns to the spot under the Peepul tree where she met Ramchand and there he is, waiting to know if it is Pooro as he suspected. The only statement she utters is a confirmation and negation at the same time, "पूरो तो कबकी मर चुकी है ।"[12] (Pooro has been dead for a long time.) The final sections of the novel return us to the unfinished story of Pooro's life in a way that gives her the autonomy to meet, reveal herself, and cause the positive changes that people desire. Pritam skips over a long period of time, a decade or more to bring us closer to the year of nation making, when Pooro's sons are older and Rashid's farms are burned in Chattoaani. From the rumors, it is clear that Pooro's younger brother, now a man, lit the fires to Rashid's harvest. Realizing the gravity of the matter, Pooro is allowed by the author to be torn for now her love extends back and forward; Rashid is as much her family as the brother lost to her. Pooro's heart extends to both—the man who suffered the loss of his harvest, and the man who lit the fire. Unlike patriarchal authority which seeks to destroy what it does not understand, such as the brother's coming-of-age assertion, Pooro, who stands outside its prescriptions, loves in all directions. Instead of the head that directs a community's function, Pooro is all limbs reaching out to connect and love.

The mayhem of 1947 is written upon the bodies of women, their stories accumulating at a rate faster than all the relocations and desertions that mark this time. Pritam accounts for the mass-scale kidnappings, rapes, and murders of women on both sides of newly-forming borders and underlines the "pinjar" (skeleton) left from burnt bodies. In the midst of the carnage and orgy that mark 1947, Pooro feels as though someone threw pieces of glass in her eyes. She finds a procession of nine or ten young men parading in front of them a naked and bruised woman. She does not know from which village they come or where they will go. "पूरो को लगता मानो कि संसार में जीना दुर्भर हो गया हो, मानो इस युग में लड़की का जन्म लेना ही पाप हो ।"[13] (Pooro was feeling that it is no longer possible to live in this world, that it is a sin in this age to be born a girl.) Not surprisingly, Pritam's lucid prose is packed tightly with aphoristic colloquialisms, and this one, about the sin of being born a woman, is one that is given much room in common parlance. For the women who suffer en masse what Pooro suffers alone in 1935, Pooro has empathy and the power now to aid and rescue. When she discovers a cowering young woman who has been raped in different Muslim households[14] for nine nights, she takes her home, hides her in her own granary and with Rashid's willing help, she transports the lost woman to one of those long processions of people heading to India. On this good will mission, knowing that the caravan comes from Rattovaal, Pooro finds Ramchand and has a full and proper conversation with him. Silent when she meets him on his farm years before and careful now because of the soldiers hovering about, the two exchange information like old conspirators, a spirit of affection beyond any sort of legitimacy thickening their discourse. To each, the other was unfulfilled desire. Without breaching any codes of conduct, but yet overturning the norm of patriarchal heroism, Pooro promises to find his lost sister, Lajjo who is now married to Pooro's brother just as Ramchand is married to her younger sister. It is no small feat that Pooro, a woman from whom the beginning of her adult life snatched all agency, is the prime navigator for her own life and an orchestrator and rescue worker in the lives of all whom she meets.

The climax, consequentially, to this story of layered binaries, is Pooro's rescue mission that works in concordance with her husband, Rashid, who finds Lajjo, shelters; her in their home, and finally takes her to Lahore safely to her waiting brother and husband. These final scenes show a development of both characters, Pooro and Rashid. Rashid finds redemption in helping Pooro by carrying Lajjo on horseback to their home. Pooro is able to inhabit a number of guises with ease as she negotiates her way to finding and securing Lajjo. When a soldier questions her about her interaction with Ramchand, she shows him diamonds she attained in return for food she gave, though he remains mystified since Hindus are known to favor gold, not diamonds. At the old woman and her son, Allahditta's place, or Ramchand's home they occupy, she finds Lajjo, a broken-faced woman with no hope for a return to the familiar, and here, she adopts the guise of a saleswoman. She carts blankets and other homespun products for days in Rattovaal so as not to cause suspicion, enters homes till she finds in Ramchand's old home the occupiers and kidnappers of the daughter of the house, her name carved on her arms. Dressed as a barterer or an exchanger of commodities, Pooro comes full circle from once having been traded against her wishes for the sake of restoring family pride.   .

The patriarchal edict of identifying women by branding their names upon their bodies turns to function in a subversive form of empowerment; for Pooro, it took a quick seizing of the wrist and lifting away the clothing to confirm her suspicions. When questioned by Allahditta about her religion and who exactly she was, it was life-saving to calmly hold her arm as proof of her identity, Hamida carved in blood on her body. To the male gaze, male inscriptions become the highest form of truth, a writing of the Name of the Father on the woman's body. For the women caught in its broils, it serves then as a form of subversive self-recognition and feminine subterfuge. But even before reading the Name of the Father upon Lajjo, Pooro recognizes Lajjo as a fellow *pinjar*, with a face that resembles the skeleton of a bird caught as prey, "पूरो को लाजो का उतरा हुआ चेहरा याद आया, और उसे लगा कि मानो लाजो का मुंह उस चिड़िया के पिंजर की भाँति हो जो इस गलीज चील के पंजों में कई दिन तक फँसी रही हो ।"[15] This is an interesting performance of *écriture-féminine*, a woman's way of recognizing another's identity based on a reading of the language of pain.

On her final exit from the village she romanticizes and fictionalizes for the last decade, Rattovaal, she realizes that it is her new name, Hamida that saves her from the skeleton her supposed home had become. Her arrival is marked by irony to her in multiple ways. When she first arrives to Rattovaal with the old woman, no one announces her or comes to welcome her as the new daughter of the town. When she meets Ramchand, she is too shocked to utter her name and for her, there will always be a confusion of the exact location of this label. What Pooro understands with the greatest clarity is the phenomenon of the *pinjar*: the way she felt after being doubly wounded in the abduction and rejection from her family, and then a similar language of skeletonhood written upon the faces and bodies of women across temporal and spatial locations. Interestingly enough, the word that had only signified the sufferings of women in patriarchy shifts in meaning to a physical location, such as Ramchand and Lajjo's home in Rattovaal, reduced in meaning after its legitimate residents are thrust aside for new occupants in the vagaries of nation-making. Women are not locked into a state of disempowerment and dislocation; structures of male stability and identity also come to be associated with *pinjar* leading to a difference, an ultimate impossibility in locating the exact location of Pritam's meaning with the word. In essence, any institution or being affected by the patriarchal ways of understanding the world, even men themselves, such as the burnt bodies that spill out of the Hindu mansion, suffer the wrath of this ideology that seeks to destroy in order to construct itself.

In Sakkadaali, the two women, Pooro and Lajjo spend days and months in secrecy, exchanging stories, giving and seeking comfort, and commiserating with each other's woes. Pooro does not hesitate to point to the complexity of her own reality; the man she once considered her nemesis has finally come to mean companionship, support, and family. Lajjo feels she cannot have, i.e., return to her family and husband because Pooro was not given a similar second chance. Here nation-making comes to rescue when Pooro informs Lajjo of the Inter-dominion Treaty. This treaty makes it law that women who have been kidnapped have to be returned to their rightful homes, which of course, lie across new borders. Butalia writes about the complications to the good intentions of this law, which should have aided the victims, and instead, at times, furthered their agony:

> Interestingly, neither government denied that abductions had taken place—presumably they knew their men well—and both agreed to set up machinery to rescue abducted women from each other's territories. They agreed too that women living with men of the other religion had to be brought back, if necessary by force, to their "own" homes—in other words, the place of their religion. It was a curious paradox—at least for the Indian state. India's reluctance (although recent history has questioned this) to accept Partition was based on its self-perception as a secular, rational nation, not one whose identity was defined by religion. Yet women, theoretically equal citizens of this nation, could only be defined in terms of their religious identity. Thus, the "proper" home for Hindu and Sikh women who were presumed to have been abducted was India, home of the Hindu and Sikh religion, not the home that these women might actually have chosen to be in. Theoretically, at Partition, every citizen had a choice in the nation he/she wished to belong to. If a woman had had the misfortune of being abducted, however, she did not have such a choice.[16]

While the law at this time favors the very choice Lajjo would like to make, i.e., return to her brother and husband across the border in India, Pooro's is a different case. Had she chosen to reveal her condition as an abducted bride in a Muslim household, the authorities would have necessitated it upon her to leave Rashid, her sons, and

take her place in the lorry with the countless other women heading to
shelters where they remained, many till the end of their lives. Pooro,
familiar with the hegemony and inflexibility of law, is careful not to
reveal herself as Pooro and stands back, alongside her Muslim family, not wishing to do what she would have wanted a decade ago, to
be rescued and returned to her blood kin. She takes Lajjo and bids
her farewell like she would have for a sister being married off, with a
packet of homemade *laddus* and red silk salwaar set. She settles for the
dust after the lorry takes off. While this episode can be written as the
dire choice for a woman oscillating between the Name and Law of the
Father, it is critical to note here that Pooro makes the choice all on her
own, and does it with certitude based on love, not law. Regarding this
moment of repatriation in South Asian history, Debali Mookerjea-
Leonard writes:

> Nationalist anxiety about colonialism manifested iteslf in, and intensi-
> fied, gender pathologies, and the discursive developments around chas-
> tity in the colonial and nationalist era clearly had concrete consequences
> for women, because their bodies were not simply sites for discourse but
> were also sites of patriarchal constraint and violence.[17]

While these nationalist anxieties bring forth the laws that produce
these reunions, Pooro resists the patriarchal inscriptions upon her own
body. She chooses her home and it is contrary to the governing wisdom
which dictates to her where she belongs. The reunion of Pooro with
Ramchand and her brother is filled with affect and melancholy. The
men, Ramchand and Rashid embrace, an awkward embrace of regret
and redemption. The brother is shame-faced and overwhelmed at finding his wife and long-lost sister. Pooro utilizes the moment to deliver a
speech act, "कभी भूल से भी लाज्जो का निरादर ना करना।"[18] (Even by mistake,
don't ever disrespect Lajjo.) An order and a command at once, Pooro
exceeds her role as a kidnapped and lost sister. She is the one with full
autonomy at this moment of exchange and articulation between the
newly-formed nation-states and she utilizes it to dictate the owners of
patriarchy, men like Ramchand and her brother that they ought to and
should respect women, even one who they imagine as blemished. This
speech act continues itself into the conclusion as Pooro thinks to herself,
a continuous exercise that causes significant action in the novel's plot
movement:

चाहे कोई लड़की हिन्दू हो या मुसलमान, जो भी लड़की लौटकर अपने ठिकाने पहुँचती है, समझो कि उसी के साथ पूरो की आत्माँ भी ठिकाने पहुँच गई । [19]

[Whether a girl is Hindu or Muslim, whoever returns and reaches her domicile, understand that pooro's soul also has reached its domicile.]

Pooro, always exceeding her metonymic locus within the novel, becomes the archetypal voice of all women, and finds respite in easing feminine suffering, suffering that is a direct result of patriarchal practices and edicts. Endowed with powers beyond the limitations expressly placed upon her due to cultural norms, Pooro expresses the affect of some historical agent of change, much like Walter Benjamin's angel who looks back and forward, to history and doom all at the same time. Thereby Pritam's text, which is a critique of the ills of patriarchy as perpetuated in its more virulent forms of nation-making and its concomitant communal fervor, makes room for the oppressed to rise, resist, and form their own imagined woman's community of solace and self-identification.

Pooro forms community with battered and troubled women of her time. Her labors heal the women she encounters. At the same time, Pooro fantasizes and works out an alternate community of womanhood in which her being traverses across lands seeking greater and greater communion and refusing to abide by the law of the father as marked by modern national boundaries.

Women, Things, Markets: Mohandas Nemishrai's *Aaj Bazaar Band Hai*

The myth of the mysterious prostitute abounds in literature. More than popular media or the visual medium, literature perseveres to add layer upon layer to the veiled and marginalized figure of the prostitute who is present in the most ancient of texts. From Tamar in the Genesis to Dante's punitive location for her in the recesses of his inferno, she is gallivanting about with Chaucer's pilgrims and succulently reemerges in the renaissance of European literatures. It is only in the non-western traditions of antiquity, from the temple priestesses of Inanna in Mesopotamia to the devadāsi tradition in Indian temples where the prostitute is valorized rather than demonized.[20] Repressed within puritannical literatures as the figure who incurs wrath and ought to be excluded from the tea rooms of high discourse and propriety of the Victorian living room, she reemerges in the twentieth century, especially masculine literature as the figure who begins to represent more than herself, the vanishing charm, allure, and mystery of an earlier era. The writer begins to distinguish between the low-class street whore who has to do business in a populist sense with every man and the woman on the higher end who chooses an exclusive clientele, is skilled in classical arts, dance or poetry, can provide company to the most cerebral poet with equal wit, and seems to preserve a sense of autonomy.

Needless to say, the body of the woman itself is the charged locus of sexuality that includes in its variations the body of children and literature reflects this meditation on the woman's body, a preying upon the most vulnerable in any community, the woman who has to utilize her body as site of labor. From the prostitutes who parade all over Joyce's Dublin to Nabokov's Lolita, the image of the sexualized woman's body on the transgressive edge of legitimacy abounds in twentieth century literature. As early as 1905, one of the great Urdu novelists of British India at the time wrote his masterpiece, *Umrao Jaan Ada* about the peregrinations and life of a courtesan, Umrao Jaan.[21] Made into a film in 1981 by Muzaffar Ali, the character of Umrao and her weaker imitations become archetypal fixtures within South Asian literature, film and popular imagination. This is the figure of the prostitute at the high end, the courtesan of the eighteenth and nineteenth centuries who was trained in *Shayiri*, writing of ghazals, singing and dancing *Kathak* and performed for a large ring of admirers amidst whom she chose a smaller group of men who could enter her private quarters. While the figure of the courtesan, or geisha, or *tawayaf* is given a certain autonomy and the sympathetic author infuses in her melancholy the sadness of a generation that is no more, and a time that cannot be captured, the figure of the prostitute in itself is erased in all these literary projects. This touches upon Lata Mani's contention that in all the historical accounts of the events of Sati, the women's subjectivity was erased in nearly all the accounts. The pure ontological trauma of being a prostitute is washed out to make greater room for the tribulations of the author. His concern with the state of the arts and history, and the woman's body as a site of economic exchange, albeit highly aesthetized one, is indubitably wiped out in one of the most powerful exercises of arch-écriture of our times.

Andrea Dworkin writes with passion, rage, and precision about this issue in all her writings, especially the essay, "Prostitution and Male Supremacy," which was given as a lecture initially at University of Michigan Law School in 1992, where she talks about prostitution from experience and as an activist. She is careful not to veer away from the actual acts of penetration and their repetition that define the condition essential to prostitution and is very careful to not move away from this central act into the "world of ideas" because it becomes much more palatable and easier to digest. She attests to the basic element that unifies all types and facets of prostitution which is that it is "an abuse of the woman's body" and can be said to be analogous to gang-rape. She explains how a system of male dominance that functions to fulfill male desire requires the creation of a class of people, women who serve as prostitutes. Once paid whatever amount it is, the prostitute is said to be beyond a condition of being wounded, damaged, or human even. She is a sexualized commodity to be used and discarded, her name and face and body forgotten in the generic satsifaction of the "woman" qualifier as having fulfilled the necessary service. Dworkin points to homelessness as the metaphor that induces the conditions inimical to the creation of a class of people who are at the bottom in every society, in every national culture, the prostitutes. The woman, already considered to be dirty once she has had intercourse as a cultural norm, is multiply so as a prostitute and she is considered to be nothing more than "vaginal slime" upon whom the actual man can perform any form of violence and it is sanctioned. Prostitutes exist at such a social bottom, according to Dworkin, "a social bottom beneath which there is no bottom" and her dehumanization is severe. Her solution is a political upheaval, a radical change in the system which operates on male dominance and patriarchal hegemony, which would shift the social dominance in favor of women. What appears and is explained as lust or desire in masculine language, Dworkin unmasks it as misogyny. She writes, "When men use women in prostitution, they are expressing a pure hatred for the female body. It is as pure as anything on this earth ever is or ever has been. It is a contempt so deep, so deep, that a whole human life is reduced to a few sexual orifices, and he can do anything he wants."[22]

Nemishrai's politics address Andrea Dworkin's politics and speak across the divide to the western feminist. A Marxist Dalit activist based in Delhi, India, he has written numerous novels, plays, collections of poems amidst a host of other literary productions like biographies, television serial scripts, and received myriad awards, like 'Dr Ambedkar Award'—1993, 'Journalist's Award/People's Victory'—1993 to name only a few of the prestigious national awards. Nemishrai is a contemporary Hindi writer who echoes Dworkin's rage and call to action in his life works and the introduction to the novel, *Aaj Bazaar Band Hai* (Market is Closed Today) begins on the need to write in a new way about prostitutes because of the misrepresentation and continuing condition of patriarchal oppression. Donnan and Magowan sum up what Marx noted, a figure important to Nemishrai's own intellectual allegiance, "sex in prostitution is alienated from the conditions of its production, allowing the degradation of prostitutes and their intellect as they become just one element within a much larger system."[23]

Nemishrai's narrative reckons with such alienation built into the structures of economic and bodily exploitation that is embodied by the prostitute. The figure of the prostitute, generally presented as a *tawayaf* or courtesan in some high-end salon in the more accessible and disseminated media of film through Bollywood, takes the bite of realism to bring the juice of titillation, voyeurism, and entertainment to its generally conservative audience of middle-class Indians at home and abroad. Nemishrai, rightfully indignant at the abundance of misrepresentations that do much to erase the reality of torture, trepidation, and deprivation that mark the lives of prostitutes, tells in his introduction of his own encounter with this labor force as impetus for the writing of this novel. Twice, he enters the market with friends who utilize these services, and each time, the humanity and largesse of the women in these houses of business strikes him as aloof, and demanding of a more accurate narrative than the ones inundating the literary and cinematic stalls. Nemishrai finds fault with even the left-leaning organizations and NGOs that have given this labor force a new title, "sex worker" with the sole aim of reducing AIDs and HIV proliferation, perversely assisting in the spread and continuation of structures of exploitation the author finds perverse and unjust.

Dworkin concludes her lecture at Ann Arbor with a cry for action on part of each and every person in her audience and she encourages the would-be lawyers to use their knowledge of the system to thwart one of its oldest institutions. She says,

> You, a well-trained person, can stand with the abuser or with the rebel, the resister, the revolutionary. You can stand with the sister he is doing it

to; and if you are very brave you can try to stand between them so that he has to get through you to get to her. That, by the way, is the meaning of the often misused word choice. These are choices. I am asking you to make a choice.[24]

Nemishrai's text is the exercise of such a choice. He, wielding his words, attempts to stand between the prostitute and her customer and bring the economic transaction of sex to a close. Written in the vein of activist Dalit literature, and this aspect will become clearer upon a closer look at the character, Sumeet, Nemishrai writes a polemical text on all the structural reasons this institution perseveres, and a resistance from within that has already been ignited before the narrative begins. Nemishrai's text, built around the awakening brought about by a male figure who rescues and awakens the women in this narrative, reflects what Madhu Kishwar, the founder of Manushi and much heralded figure of women's rights in India, observes:

It is noteworthy that a majority of women's rights struggles and movements in modern India have often been initiated, led and sustained by men. On the one hand, the traditional culture trains men to accept the multi-dimensional power and manifestations of the feminine principle. Men are taught and conditioned to be reverential towards women, at least towards women in motherly roles. On the other hand, traditional literature, including the great epics, makes them aware of, and guilty about, the many ways in which they have wronged women; the numerous Puranic tales of women's strength, loyalty and dharmic steadfastness are constant reminders that men need to make amends.[25]

While Kishwar goes on to elaborate on this point through nineteenth century figures like Vidyasagar and twentieth century exemplar like Gandhi who advocated for a change in women's conditions, Kishwar's thematic of male feminists is to be taken seriously in order to read Nemishrai's text with some seriousness. Otherwise it becomes easy to dismiss his text as a masculine attempt at appropriation and advocacy on women's behalf while participating in some form of gender sovereignty. Sumeet's ascendant role need not erase the awakening experienced by the women because this is a text, imagined along a Marxist ethic, on solidarity and alliances across class and gender boundaries.

Masculine Imaginary, Feminist Awakening

In this novel, a number of prostitutes stage a protest by surrounding the local police station and demanding justice. The novel opens in its wake as the police force opens itself up in the democratic staging of a press conference to a group of reporters. After a debate in which neither side really gives in, with the police refusing to accept any culpability, the reporters go directly to the red-light district and interview prostitutes. Here we meet the house that is at the heart of the novel, a "kotha" (bungalow) occupied by the aging Shabnam under whom work Haseena, Mumtaz, Phool, and Parvathi.

Here, we see the uncomfortable encouter between middle-class reporters who couch their rhetoric of curiosity and embarrassment in objective assessment, all of which dissolve under the acerbic truth tossed by the women in the kotha. More scenes unfold about the rumble in the nation due to the newspaper story that is released about the prostitutes and we are given an interior and exterior view: while the politicians fight amidst themselves about who is most responsible for the resurgence of this underground economy, the prostitutes fight their customers for a shred of dignity. Shabnam, meanwhile, is the elder who has left the life of the flesh for the more spiritual realms of a temple and bitter questioning of a life that feels utterly wasted. The novel shifts into the more direct face of resistance once the neophyte, a journalist named Sumeet in search of a job in the big city, enters the kotha by mistake seeking shelter from the sudden riots in the city. Once in the house of women, Sumeet becomes a permanent member of a family that becomes more organic and sustaining with his appearance.

Resistance is spelt out more clearly with his politics, connections to the Dalit newspaper in which he attains a job, and his desire to see all the women sustain themselves in a form of labor that does not devalue their bodies. Sumeet is arrested when he goes out in search of food for everyone in the house during the riots. This becomes the initial act of sacrifice which earns him an authentic place of trust and solidarity with the prostitutes in his own kotha and the others in the district. Soon enough, Sumeet encourages and succeeds in persuading Parvathi, the prostitute with whom he has an affective connection from the outset, to give up her profession. She follows him into his activist resistance as well, and he, in turn, proposes to marry her and gives her the legitimacy denied to her within patriarchal normativity. By the time the novel concludes, Shabnam is on her deathbed, blessing the couple who is in prison for their collective resistance, supported by innumerable prostitutes who are all in one way or the other negotiating their way out of their subhuman[26] existence. First, I present how Nemishrai writes the Name of the Father into a national allegory within his novel. Second, I read the symbology that is rife within his text. Finally, I will point to the lacunae within the novel.

Nemishrai wields an Andersonian and Lacanian lens, by interpellating upon the nation-state the Name of the Father, the authority of law which effectively casts its mercenary shadow upon the prostitutes in its more hidden economic and spatial realms. While Nemishrai stages his opening by inscribing the Name of the Father in its many realms, such as a functioning police force, journalists, cabinet, religious freedom, he also writes into it the paradox: the patriarchal name of the nation does not really function fully in all its democratic ideals in many ways. Thus, while Nemishrai is interested in portraying the many facets of the modern nation at various levels of functioning, he shows the dissolution and hollow presence of these functions as well. What remains as the most solid act of nation-building remains the shaking from within, a resistance presented by the collective of educated and subaltern people against the ills of the system at large. The police show the physical arm of the law, the politicians the legal framework, and the journalists the privilege of confronting either.

However with the police, the journalists succeed in only hitting the brick wall of canned answers rather than any revelation about the corruption within its structures. While the journalists accuse the police of forcing from the prostitutes a percentage of their earnings, and assisting to keep the underground economy functioning, the police simply parrot that they are doing their job and need the support of the public in executing their onerous task. Disappointed, the journalists in their interview of the prostitutes, learn of their differences from this subset of people who unmask the prejudice within the rank of the journalists towards these women. Within the cabinet, the politicians scream at one another about the breaking news story and who can be squarely blamed for the publicity, rather than the injustices portrayed within the reports. The police, presented as scavengers and customers, are the vilest; they curse the women while expecting them to clean up the vomit they may leave behind. Nemishrai's omniscient narrator reveals the creases in the Name of the Father in its most ineffective and grotesque performance:

the persecution of its most vulnerable population, the women and girls who are putatively given rights and protected as citizens of the new republic, liberty, equality, and fraternity for all. Somehow the prostitutes are fraternized in ways far more incestuous than deemed appropriate within the traditional family structure. Placing upon them the specter of lifelong brides stripped of any rights, the narrator writes:

वे अधिकार रहित वधुएं थीं...सच कहा जाए तो वे राष्ट्र वधुएं थीं।पुरुष सत्तात्मक समाज में वे ऐसी संपत्ति थीं, जिसे कहीं भी ले जाया राकता था। उनके टूटने या ख़राब होने का डर भी न था। हर मौसम में उनका एक जैसा ही मिजाज़ रहता था...वहाँ सब कुछ था, पर फिर भी वे अपने घरों को घर नहीं कह सकती थीं। लोग उनके घरों को चकला कहकर पुकारते थे।वे भड़कती-तड़कती औरतें थीं।माँ, बहन, तथा बेटियाँ नहीं थीं, सिर्फ रंडियाँ थीं. उन्हें यह सब मंज़ूर था।[27]

[They were brides without rights … truth be told, they were brides of the nation. Within the patriarchal system, they were the sort of property that could be transported anywhere. One need not worry about them breaking or spoiling … even though their houses had everything, they could still not call these their homes. Other people labelled their houses as places of exchange. These were women who angered and trembled. They were not mothers, sisters and daughters, just sluts. They accepted these conditions.]

The narrator provides the heartfelt and honest assessment of how the Name of the Father inscribed upon the most vulnerable bodies is an inhuman practice and a decadent affair. By connecting the prostitutes directly to the nation, Nemishrai leaves little room for doubt as to the relationship between the nation-state and its marginalized population of prostitutes. By calling them brides of the nation, he brings to life Freud's dead patriarch and gives authority within language, making a direct and illegitimate matrimonial link between the Law and its illegitimate heiresses. Soon after, he puts imaginary words in the mouths of the prostitutes who welcome the clients into their kothas caustically remarking that instead of the Hinduism more familiar to the masses, the Sanatana Dharma of these women is to service, be punished, beaten, and spit upon in any way chosen by the man who meagerly pays for their bodies. Caged and homeless at once, Nemishrai lets his narrator write out the polemics of the novel in occasional bursts of idealistic fervor. While he notes that these women who cannot be daughters and sisters do not have any brothers or fathers to speak for them, or protect them, it is actually the Name of the Father that forces upon them the servitude of the ultimate barter with the body.

Symbols are a key function in this novel, so bare and Spartan in many ways. The author refuses to indulge in the artifice of stage setting or background or foreground. Characters speak and they represent organizations, such as newspapers or police force or the political office, and there is nothing more given about their being or location. Conversation and verbal discourse are central, and scant images hold the narrative together in a semblance of novelistic momentum. In this milieu, symbols take on the added affect of all the unsaid. Shabnam visits a temple for some relief from the troubles of life at her "kotha" in which she no longer has any interest. The temple here, though clearly Hindu, is stripped of its religious affiliation and becomes a symbol of a shrine, or a sanctuary. Shabnam could well have visited a mosque or a church to have a similar conversation with the priest and reveal her anxiety but this being a major city in the north of India, temples are abundant and that is where Nemishrai takes Shabnam for respite. Actually, Shabnam, a prostitute of Muslim descent visits a Hindu holy place, and this is also not lost to the native readership. Long in practice amidst many communities where people of Hindu and Muslim faith intermingle and frequent one another's shrines due to long practice and belief, this hybridity underlines the complicated and polymorphous nature of spiritual discourse of a nation teeming with multiple others. It is necessary to understand that Shabnam visiting a temple is radical and at once, ordinary, so commonplace in fact that we can strip the temple of its religiosity and read it as pure symbol, a place of sanctuary distinguished from all the other locations seen in the novel, such as the police station, the parliament, and the red light district. Similarly, we can take the practice of "Yoni Puja" (worship of the vagina) prominent amidst the prostitutes apart from its Hindu lineage, and read it as an affirming and feminist action practiced by the disempowered. It is precisely after the Yoni Puja that Shabnam Bai lets go of the young girl who is brought to her by a local pimp. She listens to the girl plead, gives her money, and asks her to run away. She asks her name, and tells her the secret route to liberation.

The Visible Hand of Man, the Invisible Hand of the Market

Fifteenth August, the day of Indian Independence from British rule, comes to mark the halfway point and is deeply layered with meaning.

The prostitutes turn away customers because they take it upon themselves to give themselves the day off too. While customers leave cursing, the ladies explain to the little boy, Phool's son that it is a national holiday for them at home just like it is for him at school. In the conversation amidst the ladies the little boy, Babu, the boy asks them if he can meet the president of the country because after all, "Aren't we also citizens of this state?"[28] To this, the ladies are silent and then, they are interrupted by another knock. They seek to free themselves from the oppressor as an ode to the nation they call home; in seeking liberation from the visible hands of men who commodify them, they seek to escape the invisible hand of the market.

The day of national independence also becomes symbolically the day that most directly a person within this community questions, albeit innocently, their place within it, and their rights. Subalterns within the city, these are women without voice in the national debate on their very own condition. Others argue for them, such as the police, ministers, and journalists and when they attempt to insert their voice into the polemic, they are generally punished with a prison sentence for defiance and disrespect of authority. On this same day, riots break out in the city of an unnamed nature and cause. On this same day, the narrative introduces the heroic figure of Sumeet, the roaming reporter who arrives in the city in the storm of riots to seek a job. All in all, the day of independence, a day of all days to mark the creation of the nation out of the ashes of empire and fight for freedom, symbolically transforms into a day of questioning the very same freedom, a day of the dissolution of freedom and the day a new type of freedom fighter emerges. What are the freedoms written into the constitution of this free republic for its own oppressed, marginalized, and commodified? Sumeet, born long into the postcolonial era for India, prefigures as the freedom fighter who continues the fight for all the populations and people caught in the shackles of bondage long into the freedom of the larger nation.

Sumeet's affective connection to Parvathi begins the first night he spends at their kotha in her room where he is alone and comes upon her diary. Reading her words which tell the naked truth about the duress of servitude, and her own yearning for freedom, Sumeet sees a face beyond the face of Parvathi, and a truth not admissible in verbal or the more common physical exchange that the women practice on a regular basis. The diary is symbol of a freedom already won, a resistance in process long before Sumeet's arrival and awakening to the conditions of these women. The diary is a testimonial and a rebel's cry, a revolution from within, writing in the spaces between speech. A transcription of souls, it brings Sumeet and Parvathi together in a partnership for the rest of the text because theirs is a relationship forged in the fire of a woman writing. The gendered binary of man/woman dissolves in this *ardhanarishwara*[29] figure which emerges as the partnership of these two souls, and thus, Sumeet–Parvathi come to resemble the fighting duo in one body, Shiva–Parvathi.

The dying prostitute, Sunhari Begum, who awaits to see Sumeet once before expiring, prefigures the death of Shabnam Bai. The end of the novel, Shabnam Bai's death augurs a new beginning. Shabnam, the woman for whom all the others worked, acknowledges her own culpability in a way that none of the other people who speak the Law do, frees the others and symbolizes the dawn of a new era for her "kotha" of bonded laborers. The mad woman is a prostitute who attempted freedom all on her own and harassed by her entombment in patriarchal institutions goes mad and roams the streets of the red light district symbolizing the condition of the solitary rebel. Action happens in collectivity, and by the end of this novel, what the mad woman desires alone is attempted together by a larger number of women together. While Shabnam requests to be cremated so nothing remains of her but ashes for the winds, the president of the country visits the renowned freedom fighters, Sumeet and Parvathi in prison. The subalterns are being heard, and being included in the national polity. Nemishrai ends his novel on a note of hope and possibility.

Nemishrai's narrative, despite his most acute efforts to thematically and stylistically account for the feminine voice and patriarchal oppression, is not feminist. Caught within the existing framework of masculine novelistic discourse and Dalit resistance literature, it fails in subtle ways, in similar ways to how Spivak, amidst a school of subaltern scholars asserts that the western educated elite intellectual cannot speak for the subaltern or make the subaltern speak, to speak for the woman. Deeply indebted intellectually and creatively to the activist genius of his forefather, Dr. Ambedkar, Nemishrai casts an Ambedkar figure in the novel in the guise of Sumeet. Sumeet is the savior and hero of this novel, a male savior in the narrative of female subjugation, the voice of reason that lifts the prostitutes from their doom and torpor in continuing to accept their oppression. Again, women's lives are negotiated in the lofty discussions amidst men in which they are not allowed to exercise their voices.

Sumeet's rhetoric echoes verbatim the speeches Dr. Ambedkar makes to colonies of prostitutes when asking them to join the Dalit resistance movement where they would be whole-heartedly welcomed if and only if they renounce their life style as labor in the sex industry. Instead of allowing the feminine voice of the prostitute to emerge, the novel repeatedly takes the stance of the outsider peaking in, the outsider being a middle-class Indian citizen who finds, much to his or her surprise, that the prostitute is not just a pound of sexualized flesh but a person with feelings, intellect, and rationale. The outside gaze informs the interior life of the prostitute in Nemishrai's text in the examples offered of the police men, journalists, cabinet ministers, religious figures like priests, and finally and most importantly, Sumeet. They come to find out that these are women who resemble their own mothers, sisters, and wives, the familiar status accorded and the only way women are legitimized within patriarchy, more than some demonic other that was born and ontologically meant to inhabit their station in the red-light district.

Nemishrai remains deeply aware of structural and societal institutions that encourage, establish, and continue the underground economy of sex, yet the exterior gaze that informs his novel is fundamentally interested in asking the prostitute, "Why do you do what you do—this selling of the body? Why don't you just stop it?"[30] Even the conversations generated by the prostitutes themselves never reach the clarity of pointing to the conservative forces in mainstream culture that pivot these economies; instead the prostitutes themselves equate their labor with the pleasures of sex thereby convoluting the argument only further. The novel attempts haphazardly to point fingers at all the criminal intent of conservative societal powers but finally, succeeds only in seeking the solution with the prostitutes themselves who could overturn the hegemony of sex economy if they just stopped. Economy is divested from the sexual act, and the prostitutes remind the journalist that even she does the same at home. Later, one prostitute remarks that while they only sell their bodies, others sell their philosophy and their countries. Yet, neither the prostitutes or any of the highly-educated and well-meaning or left-leaning reporters make an attempt at understanding the larger circumstances that bring such a large number of women into this trade, and why they decide to eventually stay until they turn bitter, resigned, mad, or die like the examples offered of older prostitutes throughout the text. Too much of the text still rests on moral discourse of "bad work" rather than question the structural machinery of exploitative systems. The prostitutes, by questioning the hesitation and deference on part of the journalists, especially the female journalist, regarding matters of sex, put their fingers on the hypocritical prudery of bourgeoisie but are not able to bring the duly needed attention upon the basic matters of law, economics, politics, and history that keeps them shackled in their subaltern positions within Indian society. The form of the book in some ways, though critical of classic patriarchy, never fully escapes it. The novel here occupies the alternate site of masculine schizophrenia by mirroring statist criminalization of the prostitute's body while simultaneously capitalizing upon it.

Sumeet is the man who awakens in the prostitutes a sense of dignity and freedom struggle. It is only after his arrival that someone like Parvathi who has repeatedly tried to free herself, and writes a diary which shows a deep-rooted consciousness about her condition, feels closer to her dream of freedom. When she asks him a question about the historicity of the practice of prostitution, he is the one who detects in her an acumen and perspicacity which will assist in her freedom from the bondage of her sexual labors. When she says, inspired by him, she will wait for the day of her freedom, he incites her, "You will have to fight, not wait." To this, Parvathi's reply is a familiar echo of the house-bound wife who follows her husband's every principle as her religion, "If you are with me, I will do everything."[31] There is little difference in the politics of pre-women's movement Ambedkar statement to prostitutes where he asks them to renounce their "apamanit" or "without dignity or humanity, meaning humiliating" lifestyle, and Nemishrai's constructed Sumeet who asks Parvathi and her consorts to do the same, without offering them any pragmatic alternative recourse. In Parvathi's case, their relationship evolves into a romantic one because the affect generated between the two kindles this spark at the outset. Soon enough, Sumeet asks her to marry him and he makes of her a "respectable lady" as Ambedkar had once urged the prostitutes to do, leave their humiliating lifestyle and live like other women in proper matrimony instead of choosing to remain mired in circumstances that bring them deeper into the sex trade.[32]

While the inspector later demands Parvathi's services and is irate when he learns that she no longer is free for service, the novel does not push the culpability of powerful interests in keeping alive this "shameful"[33] tradition. Parvathi pledges to stop and stops with the hope that Sumeet will be her partner, and he, in turn, encourages her to write and become an author. Along with Parvathi, the women of Shabnam's house all quit their trade one by one but it is never made clear how they subsist in the absence of any form of income at all. During the days of the riots, a few days without customers while Sumeet stays with them turns to absolute starvation. They do not even have milk to make tea. Nemishrai gives such minutiae to depict the duress of riots and curfew on a household but he does not pay the same attention to the condition of the women once they stop earning their income in the sex trade. Where and how do they earn an income? What do they eat? How does the mother, Phool look after her little boy, Babu and afford to send him to school? In the absence of any legitimate profession, there is the great chance that once Sumeet completes this phase of his resistance, is released from prison, continues his job at *Pratatantra* newspaper and begins life with his wife, Parvathi, the other women might easily slip back into the familiar oppression of their former trade. There is the greater chance that Phool's innocent school boy son might cave into the numerous pressures put upon the young, uneducated and unemployed, such as membership and participation in the local mafia, or right-wing religious organizations that condone much more systemic forms of violence against populations deemed the other. None of these concerns are addressed within the scope of the novel. Such positions reify rather than resist the heteronormative.

The archetypal masculine savior steps into the morass of feminine ineptitude as Sumeet and saves them all. An entire resistance is sparked off by his mere presence. Nemishrai writes:

सुमीत ने उन्हें गुलामी की नींद से जगाया था। वेश्याओं के बीच अच्छी सुगबुगाहट हुई। अच्छा बनने और मुक्ति की राह पर चलने के लिए। अपने अपने पिंजरे में कैद उन सबको मुक्त होना था। चारों ओर मुक्ति के गीत गूँजने लगे थे। पहल हुई शबनम बाई के कोठे से। सुमीत की संगत का रंग अपना असर दिखाने लगा था। पार्वती के भीतर के पंख फड़फड़ाने लगे थे। शबनम बाई अपने अंतिम दिनों में अच्छी माँ बनना चाहती थी।[34]

[Sumeet had awakened them from the sleep of slavery. In the midst of the prostitutes, there was a great restlessness. To be good and walk on the path of freedom. Caged alone, they wanted to be free. Everywhere songs of freedom were being sung. The humming began from Shabnam Bai's *kotha*. The effect of Sumeet's company was beginning to show. Parvathi's wings began to flutter. Shabnam Bai wanted to be a good mother in her last days.]

To add to Kishwar's point made earlier, here the masculine savior figure appropriately reassigns upon the female protagonists roles of legitimacy within patriarchy. Shabnam, a woman who never had any children, and considered herself sterile until today, thinks of him as her son. She wishes to be a good mother in her last days, a last act to redeem herself. Parvathi will be made into a wife. The other women who follow this Piperesque figures are left in limbo. When the women express concern about Parvathi's assurance and support, Shabnam reads it as jealousy and the central issue of self-reliance is sidelined. Appropriate roles are not assigned for the other women within patriarchy except as better women for having abdicated a life of sin. In novels by women, women play the heroic roles, such as Sujata in *Hazaar Chauraasvi ki Maa*, Pooro in *Pinjar*, Heer in *Kufr*, Smita in *Kathgulab*, and women do the work of self-realization such as Aseema in the final Hindi novel; in *Aaj Bajaar Band Hai*, the rational and epistemic awakening is masculine.

The women merely follow never subverting their gendered secondariness. Within Nemishrai's text, one character escapes his own masculinist discourse, the mad mother of Parvathi. Since Parvathi was inculcated into the profession as part of the Dalit community in her village who historically have to service the temple as "devdasis"[35] along with her mother, now aged and mad, the mother runs around the village spitting at the stone idols. Since she is old and closer to death, the villagers leave her alone and do not institutionalize her, or bring her back into the appropriate cells of patriarchy for such bad behavior. She remains free, spitting on the most sacred symbols of patriarchy, roaming the streets and expressing her scorn for the institutions that had once subjugated her. A passing reference in the text, this character along with the prostitute who turns into a beggar as a change of professions, a mad beggar who articulates her ire at the hegemons, constitutes a slippage on the author's part, an aporia that leaves room for an alternative and ethical feminist discourse to emerge.

In the same vein that Sumeet saves the women, Nemishrai establishes a relationship with his readers. He leaves little to the imagination of the readers generating a very rigid novelistic discourse that leaves little room for any emotional or imaginative elasticity. Since the author's interpretations, politics, and axis of meaning are made apparent in the novel, it reads more like polemics disguised thinly as a novel, rather than a novel that articulates politics in the polyphony of themes.

The final scene is a conflagration of clashing institutions, the resistance in full fire where the police actually clubs the aged Shabnam to death and an acceptance. The husband of the nation, Rashtrapati, or president, releases the imprisoned Parvathi and Sumeet so that they are at Shabnam's side during her last moments. Overdone and melodramatic, the scene shows the symbolic return to the patriarchal fold for the marginal figures. The nation accepts the struggle of the marginalized and the marginalized, like Parvathi, become legitimate in their association with a patriarchal figure of power. Though the end stages a scene of resistance, it doubles back upon itself as walking the fine line into the Althusserian ideological state apparatus of patriarchal hegemony. Within this cartography, the faintest of community, that of the suffering women and those in solidarity with them, briefly emerges only to be snuffed out by the state. Community emerges as the phantom muse of a nation at war with its own people. Community remains an ideology, a cause célèbre, but in lockdown. Nearly half a century after independence, community remains a much scarcer commodity than the bodies of women who are ritually commodified.

Conclusion

Notes from the Trenches of Patriarchy

Multiple forms of violence persist in South Asia, each event marking a watershed moment in furthering intransigence and intranational discord—the carnage at Godhra, the three day siege of Mumbai, governor and journalist assassinations in Pakistan, to name a few. The root of these mass industrialized *spectacular* events of violence remains patriarchal vis-à-vis Deniz Kandiyoti's catalogue of the unity across South Asian spaces as one form of classic patriarchy.[1] Writing in the differing national (*desh*) and diasporic (*videsh*) spaces, a widening community of women novelists resist the law of the father by escaping from its symbolic order. To quote Cixous,[2] they steal language; however, they do so not only to produce *écriture féminine* but to unwrite patriarchal inscriptions on the woman's body. This final chapter engages in a form of deterritorialization inspired by Edouard Glissant's future of community where poetics is a form of desire and relations is novelistic expression. Further, I draw from Deleuze's rhizomatic multiplicity of the "book," a place of discursive liberation, healing, and bridge-building apart from Hegelianism, hierarchy, and manicheanism. Thus, this chapter moves beyond the tired representations of "borders" as landscapes teeming with armed soldiers to a reframing, through women's writing, of the nations as metonyms where India, Pakistan, and Bangladesh can be reimagined through modalities of past antiquity, present struggle, and future dream. Such agglutination, then, is the novelistic step away from the politics of partition, national identities formed of trauma and thus, a step forward into the poetics of reconciliation.

I

It is important to establish the salient fact that resonates through all the novels seen thus far—the woman is always already reduced to the subaltern citizen–subject for whom the state, at best, offers ambiguous rights. On one hand, it is the agent promising protection, rights, and some privileges as seen most evocatively in the Justice of the Peace agent who arrives amidst the suffering Haitian people in Danticat's *The Farming of Bones* to collect stories of witness in order to compensate them once their suffering has been weighed by the state.[3] Neither do all the waiting people ever tell their stories, nor do they receive the said compensation. Earlier, it is the hand of the state that slays its laboring people through the orders of Trujillo in Dominican Republic. In Devi's *Hazaar Chaurasi Ki Maa*[4], the state coldly asks a mother if she knows "Vrati Chatterjee" and if so, can she come to the morgue to identify his body. Later the son, killed by excesses of the state, is given a nameless cremation.

In Taisha Abraham's probing analysis of the rape of Sathin Bhanwari's case, Abraham notes, "Patriarchy both creates contradictions and represses them."[5] Sathin Bhanwari, a grass-roots women's rights organizer in Rajasthan, is raped by irate men in town who equate police intervention against a child marriage with Sathin's grass-roots mobilization. In retaliation, they rape her but when she approaches state officials such as police officers and later, district officers, she is repeatedly misled, mistreated, and maligned. Abraham points, "… violence has been validated by a linguistic misogyny which creates a rupture between the word and its meaning for the corporeal act of violence itself to slip through."[6] Margaret Abraham refers to the South Asian woman's condition in United States as atomized and isolated in terms of being unable to find support from those who bear witness to her abuse as she seeks routes to state-sponsored support.[7] It is in these violent slippages that the feminist imaginary performs the productive labor of anti-imperial contestations and forging community because as Charlotte Bunch observes, "male dominance and female subjugation *are* often defended in the name of venerable tradition."[8] For the woman then, the word already is differentially a rupture and a wound. In the interstices of the world and its order, the feminist imaginary finds succor.

To move from the world to the word, let us attend to Glissant's meditations on the violence encoded in the episteme of the myth and the epic. In the discourse of the myth and the epic, there are no relations to the other. Violence becomes the hidden means with which to challenge the very ontological possibility of the other. And here, it is useful to attend to how Glissant explicates the heart of his vision, the poetics of relations, which he does through an elaboration of his moniker, "Chaos-monde" which is not a simple term of contrast to the order of the world. He writes:

> The ambition of poetics, rather, is to safeguard the energy of this order. The aesthetics of *chaos-monde* is the impassioned illustration and refutation of these. Chaos is not devoid of norms, but these neither constitute a goal nor govern a method there.
>
> *Chaos-monde* is neither fusion nor confusion: it acknowledges neither the uniform blend—a ravenous integration—nor muddled nothingness. Chaos is not "chaotic."
>
> But its hidden order does not presuppose hierarchies or pre-cellencies neither of chosen languages nor of prince-nations. The *chaos-monde* is not a mechanism; it has no keys ... totality's imagination is inexhaustible and always, in every form, wholly legitimate that is, free of all legitimacy.[9]

Glissant updates Bataille's figuration of community as the headless body politic. Glissant's poetics offers the antidote to the sort of western linear stratifications that make it impossible to speak of Morrison and Danticat next to Mridula Garg and Amrita Pritam. Each novelist, especially the female novelist who is caught in some prismatic subservience to the dominant order, needs justification in order to belong, a license for community. The Law of the Father needs to name and give legitimacy for such belonging. Glissant's chaos-monde moves away from legitimizing hierarchies and normalizing chokeholds, cultural sanctions, national circumscriptions. Thus, such belonging becomes "wholly legitimate—that is, free of all legitimacy" because it is only upon becoming free of the various categories that are null identifiers such as nation, race, ethnic, and geographic identity—masculinist notions of knowing that the engendered space of the novel is truly born. Glissant's poetics is a form of desire and relations are novelistic expression. Imagining through this lens allows for an optic which can translate from Glissant's capacity to endure to the modes of survival and resistance that are key functions in the engendered women's novels.

In thinking through the relations between Europe and its Other, Glissant unpacks the impassability of Kant's schema and Todorov's successes. Kant speaks of unity in time and cannot conceive of the plurality Glissant recovers in his poetics, a claim that bridges over to Gilles Deleuze and Felix Guattari's conceptions of the rhizomatic instead of the arboreal in their text, *Thousand Plateaus: Capitalism and Schizophrenia*.[10] Through the gendering of Glissant's *chaos-monde* and Deleuze and Guattari's rhizome, I come to the political mapping of world where Morrison and Danticat speak to Garg and Pritam without the need for introductions, justifications, or prevarications. It is not the simple gathering of subalterns or a meeting of the margins. It is a new alignment without the orthodox recourse to the genealogy of continental theory and philosophy.

Deleuze and Guattari posit the book as a flight, deterritorialization, destratification, an assemblage, acceleration, a rupture. The book scatters the linear unity of the word. It is not the root, trunk, branches unitary but rather a plurality, multiplicity, a branching outward and downward in all directions. The flowering tree at the root of a universal mythos is reconceived as the rhizome in the middle of everything, replacing the linear and ontological "to be" with "and" in the center of things. In the historical schema where psychoanalysis centers around Freud, the unconscious remains rhizomatic, uncentered, and perhaps even, unrestrained. Thus, Deleuze and Guattari engage in a remapping where India is no longer the other but North America becomes the new East which leads to the image of the plateau which is always in the middle. It leads them to position nomadology as the opposite of history. These modalities open up the way that I approach a project that encompasses a conversation between novels across global divisions, nationalistic walls, demilitarized zones, decades of fratricide, détente, and deaths as if it is the conversation between a coterie of women talking at the common kitchen, laundry, or well, earlier spots of cross-cultural communication that happens across borders but under the radar of patriarchal surveillance. Rhizomatic poetics of relations have always already existed; it is the modern engendered novel where they are conceptualized to a degree of literary authority and collective acumen. Thus, I argue for a rhizomatic poesis that forms the *nepantla*, a middle zone as Gloria Anzaldua inspires us to borrow from the Nahua,[11] the middle of the middle where the women novelists bridge into conversation that is legitimate precisely because it lacks all legitimacy in the strictly historical, literary, or philosophical sense of the word.

II

Instead of questions of nation, race, ethnicity, and other particular podiums that essentialize and further isolate women's intellectual and public spheres, I argue for a radical politicization of woman's word, i.e., the woman's novel as political and cross-cultural so that the political is always already a radical politics that bleeds across masculinist notions of self and other, nation and foreign. Ilina Sen points how the modern Indian women's movement offers useful arbitrage when one constellates the material reality of laboring women in the different public and private spheres of Indian body politic.[12] Returning to literary studies, Nancy Armstrong's theory of the novel sheds critical light in a project that moves from the Novel to the multiple novels that strike back from peripheries of empire.

> ...domestic fiction unfolded the operations of human desire as if they were independent of political history. And this helped to create the illusion that desire was entirely subjective and therefore essentially different from the politically encodable forms of behavior to which desire gave rise.
>
> In effect, I am arguing political events cannot be understood apart from women's history, from the history of women's literature, or from changing representations of the household. Nor can a history of the novel be historical if it fails to take into account the history of sexuality. For such a history remains, by definition, locked into categories replicating the semiotic behavior that empowered the middle class in the first place.[13]

Armstrong's points need to be carefully elaborated as we move across the multiple novels of the genre. Sexual history is not entirely subjective and not easily distanced from political history. For those who grapple with literature, the concomitant study of history is necessary. Following Foucault, she asks us to pay heed to the history of sexuality. And she asks for charge to be taken by the woman novelist; the middle-class woman's novelist is not writing exactly from a position of powerlessness but a locus of complicity replicating and cementing class power. The novel is thus in the doubled and doubling position of marking gendered subjectivity while also perpetuating class-based hegemony of the female pen. In this Marxist–Foucauldian feminist critique, it is key to point to how Armstrong seeks to unveil the ways in which liberal feminist traditions of writing are also ways of locking in modes of more radical resistance.

Raka Ray's research points to such misreading when she unpacks the contexts of understanding feminist struggles across the major metropolitan centers and arrives at the binary of Bombay–Calcutta wherein the former resonates with global feminist activists whereas the latter stays mired in a more Marxist-activism around issues of food, labor, and economics that do not center the "female subject" as such.[14] In rescuing Calcutta as an authentic site of feminist activism, Ray locates the unconscious mechanisms in which struggles are often subjected to similar strategies of ossification as are the subjects themselves. The feminist humanist, conscious of such entombments, needs to articulate a viable politics of radical liberalism as found in the literary imaginary of an academic, author, and thinker like Toni Morrison.

Toni Morrison's words, as recapitulated by Salman Rushdie in his interview in 1992 after the publication of *Jazz*[15], are apt, "America has, so to speak, an ideology of freedom and a mechanism of oppression."[16] When discussing the novel, especially the novel as generated by the author/intellectual who is deeply in tune with institutions of oppression, it is fundamental to assess ideologies alongside mechanisms, the text alongside its context, literature concomitant with history. For authors like Morrison and Garg, the complicity of the middle-class itself is the subject of history, the object of literature. Unlike the English novel where we attend to what ensures within the parlor, and we need scholars of the ilk of Edward Said to tell us of the history of the sugar that goes into the tea that the perpetual inhabitants of the parlor drink, the novelistic text generated by female novelists like Morrison or Garg, always already poised on the periphery, is interested in the fabric of marginalization, alienation, subjugation, and subjective ontology. Morrison's *Paradise* dwells in the vagaries of history which does not give shelter to a wandering caravan of African American farmers from stationed and established African American communities over the coastal plains and into the inlands of Oklahoma.[17] Her narrative interrogates the construction of middle-class, the costs, sacrifices, and betrayals that are inherent to the process of community-building and begins where the middle-class often stops imagining. Her novel lingers on alterity, the community that emerges in the interstices of normative belonging, community that is not regulated, does not appear in any city or state ledgers, and is vulnerable to complete erasure. Such is the material of Morrison's novel and it disrupts the very novelistic complicity Armstrong critiques.

III

The South Asian novels taken up here, be it Bapsi Sidhwa's *Cracking India*[18] and Amrita Pritam's *Pinjar*[19] that hover at the interstices of nation and community, or Mahasweta Devi's *Hazaar Chaurasi Ki Maa* or Mridula Garg's *Kathgulab*[20] that construct middle-classedness as a pathology or a cloister that needs to stage its own demise and exit—the novels stage middle-class as the difficult zone, class boundaries as categories that are fraught with anxieties generated alongside other hierarchies produced from a multiplicity of indigenous patriarchies. The novel's impetus is to resist the statist logic at its center.

It is useful to attend to activist logic that arises out of the NGO sector in Bangladesh, and counters statist patriarchal systems while enfranchising women and the poor. Shireen Huq articulates the aims and ambitions of Naripokhho, an organization that was deemed "*Bhalo lagey kintu bhoyo lagey*" (attractive but dangerous) and Naila Kabeer's own reflections on the work of Nijera Kori, an organization that does not seek to provide services but rather strategizes how to arm the poor with the discourse of rights, both bring material evidence to the table about how statist logic is resisted even through normative means to shift gender politics of the everyday.[21] Elora Halim Chowdhury, in her assiduous work on women organizing against acid burn violence amidst other forms of gendered oppression, also reflects on Bangladeshi media, especially a telefilm, "Ayna" wherein Chowdhury points to how the film script imagines a slight reconfiguring of traditional patriarchal arrangements due to capital bought in by laboring women in slum communities. According to Chowdhury, "while patriarchal divisions of labor are not entirely subverted, new kinds of kin arrangements and newer gendering patterns of urban space are forged."[22] Female agency, across the spectrum, allows for paradigm shift in traditional kinship arrangements and the forging of new sorts of communities.

Sally Merry's inferences around indigenization and vernacularization of feminist activist struggles is quite pertinent here, especially in light of the sort of friendships that align across nation, class, and region in Garg's novel.[23] Thus, the novelistic project extends across the north–south

border through refracted lens that attend to gender injustices as interpellated through the form of the modern novel. Chandra Talpade Mohanty's lifework lays inspiring groundwork for the cross-cultural conversations of this project.

Categories such as gender, race/class are profoundly and visibly unsta-
ble at such times of crisis. These categories must thus be analyzed in
relation to contemporary reconstructions of womanhood and manhood
in a global arena increasingly dominated by religious fundamentalist
movements, the IMF, the World Bank, and the relentless economic and
ideological colonization of much of the world by multinationals based in
the United States, Japan, and Europe. In all these global economic and
cultural/ideological processes, women occupy a crucial position.[24]

Gender violence and gendered resistance are the literary vestiges that
I excavate through a study of novelistic projects from the global south.
Mohanty, along with a host of feminist scholars such as Minnie Bruce
Pratt, Andrea Smith, Patricia Hill Collins, and Kumkum Sangari, just to
name a few, attend to the difficult circumstances of gendered presence
in the interstices of the new global mappings of power, capital, nation,
and information. Lois Weis's anthropological insights[25] are very acute in
pointing to the frictions within the American binary where the gender
line cuts across race in critical ways. Weis finds honesty when analyzing
the presence of violence in both black and white women, but structural
analysis about the decay of neighborhoods is more prevalent in black
women's networks rather than white women who speak about neighborhood decay in racial terms of white flight and brown and black invasion.
Morrison's choice in configuring community across the historical praxis
of discursive honesty and temerity amidst women of color then finds
valence in material reality.

The modern novel is part of the project of functioning as realigning the
poetics of relations in rhizomatic ways that oppose traditional discourses
and normative mappings, and also, as a way of resisting older extant
narratives that dictate gender norms and discourses. As has been evident
with the scholarly labors of Purnima Mankekar, Lata Mani, Rajeshwari
Sunder Rajan, Christophe Jaffrelot, Arvind Rajgopal, and many others,
the epic from Sanskritic antiquity, *The Ramayana*[26], has had its effects
on gender relations and keeping intact a heternormative patriarchal domestic ideal within contemporary Hindu India, especially in a present

that has had to pay its price to the rise of Hindu fundamentalism and its proliferation on the global stage. Tamsin Bradley's work attends to the need for disciplines across the Social Sciences to pay attention to the place of religion in the Indian public sphere, especially the effects of the epic on private lives. In a book that anthologizes the scholarship around the issue of dowry, a practice that is premised on the secondary status of women, Bradley notes, "Although the Ramayana does not specifically talk about or prescribe dowry it does promote the dominance of men within heterosexual marriage and for many women represents the first link in the chain that leads to dowry and then to dowry-related violence and other forms of violence against women."[27] The authors herein find ways to resist the capitalistic underpinnings of violence against women while accounting for the chokehold it has, increasingly so under the entombing rhetoric of timeless tradition and religious habit.

Dowry practices, that have been enhanced, excessive and exorbitant in the globalized world of commodity fetishism, hyper-connectedness, technology, cross-national migrations, and other massive shifts to increase the accumulation of capital are now declared in popular idiom as rituals and markers of collective identity, a way to continue what is particularly "ours" and not "theirs," a systemic exclusion of sorts that marks the oppressive regimes of control and domination as noted by Edouard Glissant. Interestingly enough, feminist scholarship is dynamic for its ability to truly become interdisciplinary and the work of a feminist literary scholar such as Nancy Armstrong is echoed later in the projects of political science/international relations scholars like Laura Sjoberg and Caron E. Gentry who insist on the inscription of international politics on women's lives: "…international politics is inscribed on women's lives, and women's lives are international politics."[28] This project of comparative literature then attends to the ontological realism of a gendered condition—women's lives are intellectually being staged as always already international, global, necessary, and in conversation.

Women's bodies can at once be the object of sexual desire while also being the site for an uncompromising, clinical approach to the production of male heirs. The inherent underlying contradictions of the expressions of sexual desire and of the calculated misogyny of son preference beg for such attention. Such a line of questioning might push the limits of hetero-normative underpinnings of the biological reproduction of sons and daughters so often taken for granted within policy and public discourses on son preference. Why is it, for instance, that despite it being scientifically proven that it is men's chromosomes which determine the sex of the child, it is women's bodies which continue to bear the burden of sex determination?[29]

Navtej Purewal's research into son-preference syndrome is a very urgent text that points to the growing tragic gap in numbers which is coming to haunt India and China, two nations that have systematically reduced the number of female babies so that the next few decades will witness the consequences of the absence of a generation of missing girls.[30] In a Derridean sense, the woman's body signifies a site of absent presence, absent from the cultural episteme of value and legitimacy but present as the vessel of producers of male heirs. These heteronormative ideologies that continue to enact gender surveillance, form gendered social traditions and enact consequences in a materialist sense upon women's bodies through a spectrum of reproductive technologies—amniocentesis, abortions, surrogacy, adoptions, etc., yield a corpus of literatures that wrestle with the many incarnations of gender violence and injustices that occur across the global south. In a way then, this project chooses to relate the materiality of gender injustices performed on the woman's bodies[31] to the corpus of literary texts that arise in the aftermath of this violence and attempt to recode the narratives of patriarchal violence and feminist resistance. In linking the corpus of the woman's body to the corpus of text generated through the literary imaginary, the project here attends to the anti-corporeal facet that is only possible within the genre of the novel, an illumination that causes Morrison's "sightings" or Danticat's visitors from across the river or the many different ghosts and specters that haunt the landscapes of Durrani, Garg, Pritam, and Devi.

IV

Morrison has a canonic place in North American, world and institutionally—sanctioned literatures at this point; having been the recipient of the Nobel, elevated from a position of power at a powerhouse publishing company to the most prestigious universities of the global north, Morrison cannot be mistaken for a voice from the margins. I have had the eerie experience of speaking of her as one such voice in the early 1990s as I sat and interviewed the feminist memoirist and radical activist, Kamala Das. I argued with Das that the world stage has yet to acknowledge Morrison appropriately and would not a Nobel be the corrective toward legitimacy, so many of us sought for her through her novelistic enterprise, Das moored solidly in Kerala, India spoke of the distance between North American gender politics with those familiar to her at home. However pivotal Morrison's 1993 honor becomes, it does not subsume the radical critique of her ideological position; nor does it eviscerate her theories from being grounded in the material reality of an African American historiography wherein a person was not wholly a person because of her race; a people were not fully deserving of human rights because they were not deemed a worthy people and a history not deserving of honest accounting in the master archives of American chronicles. Thus, despite the distance that becomes explicit in the discursive domain of first world-third world feminists when gathering at world forums, Morrison's mappings offer urgent markers in thinking across the global south to arrive at new alliances and friendships, at new figurations of community. Most significantly, as her literary and theoretical landscapes allows for *nepantla*,[32] a middle zone borrowed from Gloria Anzaldua, Morrison helps in creative figurations of subjecthood and subjectivations.

In Foucault's discursive order, resistance is denied to the body. The soul remains an instrument at best, sublimated within the body, and the two are simultaneously subjected to the authority of the state. The state disciplines and punishes the soul and the body, so the soul becomes an instrument and extension of the body. As Butler summarizes, resistance is also part of the narrative of power and thus, Foucault charts a constitutive loss or self-subversion. In Foucault, subjection is repeatedly produced and staged. However, Butler raises key questions:

> Where does resistance to or in disciplinary subject formation take place? Does the reduction of the psychoanalytically rich notion of the psyche to that of the imprisoning soul eliminate the possibility of resistance to normalization and to subject formation, a resistance that emerges precisely from the incommensurability between psyche and subject?[33]

Butler's compares Foucault's confining sense of interiority with her own elaborations of the unconscious. Butler maps an interiority of the body that exists apart from the narrative of power and its vagaries. Butler is interested in the possibilities, methods, and manifestations of such resistance as emerging from the unconscious of the soul. Morrison puts forth the historical shape to Butler's question on possibilities; in her conversations with Rushdie on her novel, *Jazz*, that I quote earlier, she speaks about sexual, predatory, and fatal violence as being the "menu" for black women, and she says, "Black women took it upon themselves, and therefore not be easy, easy prey." Morrison insists on black women's psychic need for resistance to normative notions of victimhood and self-fortifications in order to survive against hegemonies of historical violence and trauma that have thus arranged "the archaeology of the history of black people in the U.S." While the strict Foucauldian might find the landscape of resistance too impossible, Butler's question is answered evocatively in Morrison's summations about the ability, need, desire, and language of North American black women who refuse to be easy prey though power writes otherwise on their bodies.

Isabel Hoving, a scholar who attends to the works of Caribbean migrant women writers, speaks of the dialectic of violence and liberation as parts of the two epistemic poles and notes, "Caribbean women's writing is irreducibly different."[34] While writing against prescriptive notions of the postcolonial and how it remains impoverished when speaking to the struggles of the Caribbean women writers, Hoving notes the centrality of staging writing that occurs in the perennial contact zone, that is, the Caribbean. What she learns is against the tradition of European enlightenment and its insistence of genealogies of time in contrast to the feminization of space, for the writers of her milieu, Hoving notes that "space and time cannot be separated." Hoving's particular notions of a Caribbean feminist/womanist practice informs the imagination across borders that fuels my book.

Morrison's oeuvre, her suggestive motifs more and more appear as the bridge upon which I see a gathering of kindred scholars and writers of the global south, women who resist beyond the surveillance of the state, and step outside traditional regulations of women's bodies that are the mainstay of patriarchal vigilance and subjugations. Hoving's "place, voice, silence"—the tripartite ode to alterity and resistance is present in the arc that connects the African American and Caribbean women's "difference" to South Asian writers who seek to break out of spells of classic patriarchies that have been cemented in their own particular spheres of intimacy. This project then engages in cross-cultural comparisons that are deeply knowing of the complicity between fields of comparative literature and fields of empire (Said).[35] Natalie Melas' project on comparative literature and postcoloniality offers sound basis on which to find historical alternatives to this disciplinary project of empire that has been in vogue for the last century. Her points about the incommensurability between comparison and equivalence does reckon with the five hundred year of colonial structures and apparatus that brings the world into an empirical totality. In charting the historical forces that cohere around a discipline as it comes to its contemporary form in the twentieth century, a product of East Coast elitism and privilege, Melas observes, "Comparison is indistinguishable from imperial progress."[36] Thus, for this project's basis, aware of the discipline's complicity with hegemonies of empire and excesses of power, it is critical to resituate the project's logical momentum around a signifier of established alterity—a literary genealogy inspired by the novelist of lacunae, Toni Morrison, rather than the repositories of continental theories.

Morrison's point about the paradox at the heart of the American narrative—ideology of freedom with a mechanism of imprisonment is noted centrally in the work of feminist activist and scholar of Native American ancestry, Andrea Smith, who notes in her text, *Conquest*, "The 'freedom guaranteed to some individuals in society has always been premised upon the radical unfreedom of others. Very specifically, the U.S. could not exist without the genocide of indigenous peoples. Otherwise visitors to this continent would be living under indigenous forms of governance rather than the U.S. empire."[37] Sexual violence forms the structures of imperial control that engineer the multiple nations into nation-state apparatus, and Smith's scathing critique brings us back to the feminist indictment of nation-state. The nation as the first half of this appellate is rife with possibilities of autonomy, indigeneity, identity, and gendered presence whereas the nation conjoined with state connotes cemented structures of hierarchy, bureaucracy, authority, and power sutured under the ideologies of patriarchy and paternalism. For the woman then, stepping out of confinement forecasts a migration to borderlands—home, family, community, nation, and state. For the woman who is further, an author, a novelist then, the text is the radical landscape wherein alternative communities that refuse to comply by the ideologies of the Law of the Father exist. It is in these novel elisions that the imagined community with the dead allows for the porous diaphanous borderland apart from the opacity of patriarchal injunctions, nationalist entombments, and masculinist imperialisms.

For the engendered voice, the nation is a space of confinement, inscription, law. Partha Chatterjee's recovery of how the binary of home and world are scripted upon the woman's body finds echoes in the feminist scholarship of Meyda Yeğenoğlu who notes how the presumptions of the state in Algeria (Islamists and imperialists) and Turkey (nationalists and Islamists) translate into law with consequence on the woman's body. Unpacking Chatterjee, Yeğenoğlu writes, "... when home, and by extension woman, are regarded as the principal site for expressing the nation's culture, controversies about woman's dress, manners, food, education, her role at home and outside become intensified. The outcome of this controversy was the emergence of a new definition of woman which was not only contrasted with modern Western society, but also distinguished from the indigenous patriarchal tradition."[38] The contestations only further isolate, marginalize, and erase the figure of the woman, asserts Yeğenoğlu, thus leaving the woman's figure as the elliptical question between embattled political forces in Turkey and Algeria.

Amina Jamal's sociological analysis offered from Pakistan reflects on feminisms of the global south as she too builds on Chatterjee's figurations around the woman's body in the home and the world. Through the case study and legal orations around the controversial Samia case of mid-1990s, Jamal argues that the "domestication of the 'pure Muslim girl' enabled the pathologizing of women's autonomy as deviance."[39] In thinking through modern contestations around national identity in Pakistan, patriarchal and religious self-identifications have been worked out as cultural prescriptions upon the woman's body. Along with Amina Jamal, Shahnaz Khan's projects make it evident from a whole host of cases starting in the early-80s that the impact of the Zina laws as orchestrated in the aftermath of Zia's Hudood ordinance was resisted in formidable ways by Women's Action Forum, a feminist activist group that resists the punitive surveillance of the Pakistani state.[40] In some ways, Morrison's generalized sentiment of the social injustice that stitches together the fabric of the American state is the continuous thread bringing together the multiplicity of Smith, Yeğenoğlu, and Jamal. The trajectory of the gendered subaltern figure is that liberation is comprised of narratives of surveillance, inscriptions, punishment, and imprisonment.

V

Morrison concludes her novel, *Paradise*, with the spectral figures of women laboring from below. *Paradise* is the work of women bettering the structural iniquities of violence across the many borders—nation, ethnicity, race, gender, and sexuality. Maythee Rojas pulls together the many strands of feminist endeavors and provides urgent inspiration in this comparative worlding that occurs at the heart of this book. Countering the problematic of comparisons as inherently imperial as noted by Natalie Melas, my comparisons are an effort to resist the normative borders and seek a coalition across what Caren Kaplan and Inderpal Grewal point is a "homogenized figure of racialized and sexualized difference."[41] Rojas urges love as the arch-necessity compelling feminist worlding. The love that we direct in our intimate lives needs to take on larger incarnations and energetic dimensions in the labors of community-building and paradise-making as signified by Morrison in her fictive landscapes. Rojas writes, "Loving, empathetic traveling becomes especially salient when we consider the acceleration with which U.S. women of color and women in third world nations become subject to the same systems of economic and gender exploitation as countries grow more globally intertwined."[42] Rojas' suggestion of cross-cultural cross-national love is premised on sidelining normative boundaries and masculinist paradigms in order to bridge across borders, to speak to one other despite the prevalence of barbed wires, demilitarized zones, warfare, and other violent impasses that make such conversations impossible.

In research coming from opposing sites, South Asian conflict zones, Anuradha Chenoy notes, "… the situation of most women as combatants has been one of subservience to men. Some women do achieve positions of leadership in situations of conflict, but since laws and social practices do not change … women as a whole do not improve their position or receive new rights."[43] Chenoy's research also points us to the problematic of valorizing women with guns as heroic harbingers of change. Armed women in conflict zones only further perpetrate patriarchal systems of domination except in the special circumstances where women step into male territories and learn severe compliance of the patriarchal state. It is in fact, at the other end of the conflict zone, where women step out in the public sphere as peace makers that they do bring change, not only against the violence they decry but patriarchal regimes of order.

In fact, feminist processes need to reckon with not only institutional and ideological apparatuses but also, psychic ones. Within South Asian trajectories, there exists the passive gendered positionality that women are the forbearers of new generations and old traditions, and thus, they are celebrated for their endurance, in particular, endurance to pain and suffering. Lauren Leve's anthropological field work in women's support of the Maoist insurrection in Nepal states the binary of *sukha* (happiness) and *dukha* (sorrow) wherein social structures rely on psychic underpinnings that "it is through certain types of suffering that the adult feminine subjectivity is produced."[44] Countering the feminine materiality of suffering, what I propose instead is that the female subject comes into full subjectivity through an embrace of *sukha*. Learning to inhabit spheres of happiness in itself is an act of radical feminist self-assertion; loving across borders and communing with feminine subjectivity is a negation of female subjection. Within the body of the novel then, the female comes into subjectivity through new transnational belongings.

VI

The sheer quantity of Mahasweta's production, her preoccupation with the gendered subaltern subject, and the range of her experimental prose—moving from the tribal to the Sanskritic register by way of easy obscenity and political analysis—will not permit her to be an isolated voice.[45]

This book thinks through the various definitions and conceptualizations of community that are in literary circuit. In borrowing from Bataille to Giorgio Agamben, Lata Mani, and Rajeswari Sunder Rajan, it extrapolates the tensions between normative notions of community and heterodox positions on community-formation. Ramanujan's medieval Kannada poem, a devotional poem that hinges on the radical and comes out of the poet's umbrage at normative manners of reaching God, provides the ballast for this project. In the binary between "things standing" (*sthavara*) and "moving ever" (*jangama*), my project rests. Interested in the South Asian literatures that are at the heart of this project, I attempt new connectivities for reading and theorizing South Asian contemporary women's literature.

While the normative notions of community arise out of a sense of rootedness, stability, and fixed identity, the heterodox notions point to a mobility, invisibility, and dynamism leading to alternative forms of community which arise as a resistance to hegemonic structures such as statism, masculinity, religious and/or racial supremacy. In a brilliant articulation of the differences between community and coalition, Nick Mansfield neatly summarizes the critique of community that speaks to my own larger project of disembodied or alternate communities.

It includes and excludes, and always on terms that are imagined pre-set, pre-determined by an identity also already determined or incipient, yet always legitimate, receiving the credit, the credibility it deserves. ... Normalizing judgment is the genre of signifying practice which most clearly defines community. Community is not unrelated to family, one of its isotopes ... The impetus of community is to *naturalise*. It cites an identity, imagined to be pre-given, and then renders it incontestable by making it the lodestone of a local policy, one that can be used to make you an offender.[46]

Such are the heterodox notions that account in my work for Bataille's headless torso, Mani's emphasis on female subjectivity, Sunder Rajan's charges of the state, Agamben's states of exception, Glissant's poetics, and Deleuze and Guattari's rhizomatic cross-pollinations collectively point to the contestations I find in the novels included in this study. What I propose is that the static and normative community is always already in a state of disintegration so that the community that possibly contains the elements of communion—openness, inclusion, non-violence, friendship regardless of status is the alternative form found within particular contemporary novels written by women wherein such communities are present. Margaret Chatterjee's poem, "From the Abyss" which appears in an anthology of contemporary Indian women poets, *In Their Own Voice* (1993), speaks to the melancholic force of collective loss:

We who have known destruction
And who were destroyed
Speak ...
When people talk of a bomb
Like children of a new toything,
Remember us, you who never knew our names or saw our faces.
When rich men make poverty a virtue
Tell them we died of hunger.
When people talk of toleration

Tell them our synagogues were smashed,
Our temples and churches desecrated.
When they talk of democracy
Tell them that some of us died in Spain
Because we cared too much.
You world-makers, lovers of towers and mountains,
Who fashion the time of day with visions,
Who are not put off with fine phrases-
We also loved the world and died in exile.
We have no voice left but yours ...[47]

Chatterjee's poem speaks from the dead as do the communities that emerge within this project. Chatterjee signifies a global solidarity that dives back in history to the holocaust and the Spanish Civil War and ties Bengal to Buchenwald in a kinship of the dead who seek justice across the globe. Her "large company" certainly involves the collective labor addressed in these pages. In opening with "we ...who were destroyed/ Speak," Chatterjee invokes the power of the absent. However when she includes the refrain, "We have no voice left but yours," her poem ends on a plea to the powerful which is in stark contrast to the way the imagined communities herein negotiate with the powerful.

While Chatterjee's dead speak, they still seem to leave the actual speaking to others with whom they must plead and demand sympathy. In locating these alternate communities of the dead, this project reads them as polyphonous, diachronic, and anarchic. They populate their own unique world which crosses over and discourses with the living, and forms a dynamic bond of dialogue, and yet, they are content in their aloof labor without addressing the powerful: an example of this unique world can be seen in the itinerant community that congregates in the convent and recedes further "inside" instead of traveling "outside" in Haven.

In the caution Spivak gives us during her meditation on Mahasweta Devi, that Devi is never an isolated voice, I gather together the force of this project. All the novelistic voices gathered together in this project, albeit alone in the hermetic exercise of novel making, are a collective. The worlds of the women portrayed within present a pluralistic struggle waged by multiple and starkly different characters. While I do believe and see the labor of resistance being carried out in other literary genres, especially poetry as exampled by Margaret Chatterjee, it is the sheer expanse of the literary stage that makes the novel unique in the room it allows such work to inhabit. In the novel's unhinging of the epic form and accessing the polyglossic linguistic forms of the various people it references, its use of parody, chronotope, linguistic free play, it is a form that allows for the dimensions of radicalism that allows for the spatialization of this imagined community at the heart of this project. The various novels of this study stem from contexts of marginalization where the women writers negotiate their narrative out of the historical and literary amnesia about their particular conditions.

This project posits that the language of liberation is beyond decipherability. In the scream that disrupts and ends Sujata's day and Devi's novel, or Santha's eyes that haunt the latter pages of *Cracking India*, liberation does not arrive packaged in the clarity of novelistic prose. Its illumination exceeds the limits of the novel. The book, in essence, constructs a south–south bridge between contexts of marginalization in the Americas and South Asia. Instead of privileging European theorists and literature, I sought to read the South Asian works alongside western texts that do not prescribe or sit easily in their respective locations, i.e., western texts that are non-western. While Morrison and Danticat arise from North America and the Caribbean, their politics, literary lineage, and historical context places them in the literary "south." By reaching toward the South Asian works via Morrison's novelistic conduit, I begin a south–south dialectic that deprivileges the west, is non-hierarchical, and recharges the simple and anxious binary of western vs. third-world feminists.

Spivak's "gendered subaltern subject" roams the pages of these novels, seeking community so that she will ontologically finally gain her own selfhood. For the women characters of each of these novels, the overseeing hegemonic apparatus, whether it is the state, a smaller body such as a town, or the immediate patriarch within the domestic realm, they are wary of any community which asks questions to admit them, and then, casts the pall of control, surveillance, and punishment. In all these novels, the characters resist the institutional machinery by finding an alternative community, which I call an imagined community with the dead.

Since my definition of community demands a variability, the imagined community with the dead shifts in appearance, meaning, and locus in each of these novels. This concept is less a direct aspect of the literary novel and more a place holder for a pluralistic form of resistance to hegemonic bodies such as the state, culture, history, patriarchal tradition, etc., so that in many of the novels, it manifests itself as the ways in which the women characters reject the conscriptions imposed upon them by the conditions of modernity, secularism, and economic necessity and find more collective methods of mourning, exercising their right to exist and be enfranchised. Since twentieth century can be considered the century of massacres of scales unimaginable before the advent of the technical innovations that aided campaigns of horror, I was interested from the outset in the condition of those who are slaughtered and those who are left behind, mourning and surviving. Since the dead and the diasporic, those who are killed and those who flee to survive are apprehended into nationalistic narratives against their will, I was interested in the thematic of agency. In what way do those who are erased from formal records, those who matter so little that their lives are expendable to the national story, matter? In what ways do these souls exert power and wherein do we locate their agency? I determine that it is in women's novel, those writing from the margins about marginal contexts, that we located a spatialized "paradise down below" pointing to many imagined communities of the dead, fleeting, evanescent, and prolific.

Morrison's *Paradise* composes the paradigmatic heart of this book. The women who are shot in the first sentence of the novel rise again and travel back to the sites of their original wounds, and in effect, heal themselves back to life in death. Traveling with one another and gathered around the goddess Piedade, they are the most apparent imagined community with and of the dead. In Danticat's *The Farming of Bones*, Amabelle imagines community with the dead in order to live the rest of her material life. For the Haitian to survive the massacre instituted by the Dominican President at the time meant the necessary skill to commune with those who were removed in death and exile. Remembering also involved communing with the absent, and death does not signify the end of narrative. In mining Morrison as the theoretical apparatus for this project, new epistemologies have sprung up linking these disparate literary worlds and have augured the plenitude of power and melancholy not only in the American works, but the South Asian ones as well. It would be a misreading to accord Morrison an elevated status in comparison with the South Asian works because her novel, an understudied one, is the compass in discussing novels that speak of the margins. Thus, her novel does not displace the "disposable." Instead this epistemological scheme lobbies for a discourse of communing with abandon, without surveillance or shadow, an actual communing of communities of the dead. Lata Mani, in charting female subjectivity in actual accounts of Sati in nineteenth century British India, sums it up best:

> The issue, returning to Spivak's question, may not be whether the subaltern can speak so much as whether she can be *heard* to be speaking in a given set of materials and what, indeed, has been made of her voice by colonial and postcolonial historiography. Rephrasing Spivak thus enables us to remain vigilant about the positioning of woman in colonial discourse without conceding to colonial discourse what it did not, in fact, achieve—the erasure of women.[48]

Bapsi Sidhwa's *Cracking India* exposes the dichotomous trajectory in which I read "community" by beginning on the note of an idealized community of egalitarian bliss where men of different religious backgrounds gather in peace around a desirable young woman and then, disband into contentious sections broken up by the stagnant identifications along religious, linguistic, nationalistic, and ethnic lines as the new nation-states are born. Here, Santha finds an alternative community of women in motion, women who were severed from their homes and pasts and thrown into the historical turmoil of nation-making. At the same time, her absence from the text signifies a communion between Santha and all the dead, disappeared, and dispossessed of this period in time called the partition. Each text emboldens an altered imagined community. Yet what we see happen in all of them is that the women characters wrestle against the oppressive systems in place to find new ways to resist, wield agency, and speak to one another.

The Hindi novels discussed in the second half of the book give urgency to the discussion at hand because of the intimacy of the hegemonic assault. In the three novels, starting with Durrani's *Kufr*[49], women characters find themselves in confrontations with the manifestation of the state and religious authority in their spouses or fathers. The aggressor is the immediate patriarch who polices the women's sexuality through repressive tactics of physical, psychic, and sexual abuse. Basically silence belies acceptance of patriarchal surveillance. Instead it veils alternate forms of resistance which requires a less obvious form of dialogue; the women commune with ghosts, the spirit of their own dead selves as in *Kufr*, or a coalition of women laboring at the grassroots level as in *Kathgulab*, or informal conversation that might appear to be seemingly incoherent as in *Hazaar Chaurasi Ki Maa*. The sum total impact of the novel yields a counter plot to statist notions of family and community; the women form their alternate circles of kinship which allows them to turn their grief outward into the imagined community with the dead.

An imagined community of the dead reveals multiple facets of the labor of resistance. In the novel, it provides new epistemic ways of suturing a sense of loss with agency, power, and female voice. One has to be wary of the instinct to label those who lose as "victims" with little recourse or access to exert their presence in the larger narratives that contextualize their losses. Instead the novel provides the space in which the most disparate female voices negotiate toward imaginative forms of resistance. The dead exert presence, speak, commune, and write themselves back into the very narratives that excised them. Future projects along these lines can address the numerous questions that arise at the end of such a study: What does it mean to have such a large corpus of souls negotiating power at the edges of states? What are the ways in which the novel contributes to the melancholy of not belonging? In what ways can we resituate the margins if it asserts itself in profound ways upon the literary imagination?

Notes to the Chapters

Introduction

1. Toni Morrison, "Recitatif," in *Confirmation: An Anthology of African American Women*, ed. Amiri Baraka and Amina Baraka (New York: William Morrow and Company, Inc., 1983), 261.
2. Toni Morrison, *Playing in the Dark: Whiteness and the Literary Imagination* (Cambridge, Massachusetts: Harvard University Press, 1992), XI.
3. See Elizabeth Abel, "Black Writing, White Reading: Race and the Politics of Feminist Interpretation," *Critical Inquiry* 19 (1993): 470–498 on critical race and feminist theories, and Juda Bennett, "Toni Morrison and the Burden of the Passing Narrative," *African American Review* 35, no. 2 (Summer, 2001): 205–217 on reader-response theory. For a particularly plangent psychoanalytical reading, see Kalpana Seshadri-Crooks, *Desiring Whiteness: A Lacanian Analysis of Race* (New York: Routledge, 2000).
4. Morrison, "Recitatif," 245.
5. Abena P. A. Busia, "The Artistic Impulse of Toni Morrison's Shorter Works," in *The Cambridge Companion to Toni Morrison*, ed. Justine Tally (London: Cambridge University Press, 2007).
6. A. K. Ramanujan, *Speaking of Siva* (New York: Penguin Books, 1973), Basavanna 820.
7. Georges Bataille, "I Throw Myself among the Dead," in *The Impossible*, trans. Robert Hurley (San Francisco: City Lights, 1991), 147–164, read in Fred Botting and Scott Wilson, ed., *The Bataille Reader* (Malden, Massachusetts: Blackwell Publishers, 1997), 105.
8. Botting and Wilson, *The Bataille Reader*, 4.
9. Botting and Wilson, *The Bataille Reader*, 93.
10. Morrison, "Recitatif," 252.
11. Toni Morrison, *Paradise* (New York: Knopf, 1998), 221. Morrison describes Connie Sosa's cellar as such a place where she lies in her alcohol-drenched melancholy and is also the site where she brings the woman in her circle into autonomy, a place literally beneath the radar of patriarchal surveillance. A recent novel, Daniel Black's *A Sacred Place* (New York: St. Martin's Press, 2007) in its title and the novel's narrative crux, points to such a site in the wilderness which is beyond the white gaze and if observed with the requisite vision and wisdom, allows one to see into the community of spirits who linger on. "A good clean darkness" then frames the geography beyond the Law of the Father in which radical communities converge.

12. Children's literature documents this alternative epistemology by telling the story of slaves who could fly or walk on water back to Africa. It is not easy to categorize this literature as fairy tale or folktale or legend because its manner of telling is in the vein of history. It literally seeks to present history in the form of story to children, the famous example being Virginia Hamilton's *The People Could Fly*.

13. Abena P. A. Busia, "Those Ibos! Jus' Upped and Walked Away: The Story of the Slaves at Ibo Landing as Transcendental Ritual," in *Proceedings of Conference on Repurcussions of the Atlantic Slave Trade: The Interior of the Bight of Benin and the African Diaspora*, eds Carolyn Brown and Paul Lovejoy (Trenton, New Jersey: Africa World Press, forthcoming), 12.

14. David Bradley, *The Chaneysville Incident* (New York: Harper & Row, 1981), 428.

15. E. Patrick Johnson's *Sweet Tea: Black Gay Men of the South, An Oral History* (Chapel Hill: University of North Carolina Press, 2008) fills in the important gap by recording the very lives left unrecorded and unmapped and becomes through Johnson's creative, performative, and brilliant narration, an important text to fill the gaps in histories of the present.

16. I borrow from Busia's title where she signifies a "transcendental ritual" in the stories of Ibos who fly or walk on water and end up being far trickier than their oppressors.

17. Maurice Blanchot, *Friendship*, trans. Elizabeth Rottenberg (Stanford, California: Stanford University Press, 1997), 291.

18. Jean-Luc Nancy, *The Inoperative Community*, ed. Peter Connor, trans. Peter Connor, Lisa Garbus, Michael Holland, and Simona Sawhney (Minneapolis, Minnesota: University of Minnesota Press, 1991), 22.

19. Botting and Wilson, *The Bataille Reader*, 228.

20. Jean-Luc Nancy, *The Birth to Presence*, trans. Brian Holmes et al. (Stanford, California: Stanford University Press, 1993), 339.

21. Jean-Luc Nancy, *The Experience of Freedom*, trans. Bridget McDonald (Stanford, California: Stanford University Press, 1993), 95.

22. Giorgio Agamben, *The Coming Community*, trans. Michael Hardt (Minneapolis, Minnesota: University of Minnesota Press, 1993), 85.

23. Morrison, *Paradise*, 3.

24. Christophe Jaffrelot, *The Hindu Nationalist Movement and Indian Politics 1925 to the 1990s: Strategies of Identity-Building, Implantation and Mobilisation (with special reference to Central India)* (New Delhi, India: Penguin Books, 1993), 18.

25. M. M. Bakhtin, " Discourse in the Novel," in *The Dialogic Imagination: Four Essays*, trans. Caryl Emerson and Michael Holquist (Austin: University of Texas Press, 1981), 337.

26. Bakhtin, *The Dialogic Imagination*, 356.

27. Chantal Mouffe, *On the Political: Thinking in Action* (New York: Routledge, 2005), 101.

28. Mary Dietz, "Context is All: Feminism and Theories of Citizenship," in *Dimensions of Radical Democracy: Pluralism, Citizenship, Community*, ed. Chantal Mouffe (New York: Verso, 1992), 76.

29. Read Chandra Talpade Mohanty, *Feminism without Borders: Decolonizing Theory, Practicing Solidarity* (Durham: Duke University Press, 2003).

30. Gayatri Chakravorty Spivak, *A Critique of Postcolonial Reason: Toward a History of the Vanishing Present* (Cambridge, Massachusetts: Harvard University Press, 1999), 151–152.
31. Samir Amin, *Eurocentrism*, trans. Russell Moore (New York: Monthly Review Press, 1989), 111.
32. Lata Mani, *Contentious Traditions: The Debate on Sati in Colonial India* (Berkeley, California: University of California Press, 1998), 162.
33. Rajeswari Sunder Rajan, *The Scandal of the State: Women, Law, and Citizenship in Postcolonial India* (Durham, North Carolina: Duke University Press, 2003), 145.
34. Paul A. Anderson, "My Lord! What a morning: The 'Sorrow Songs' in Harlem Renaissance Thought," in *Symbolic Loss: The Ambiguity of Mourning and Memory at Century's End*, ed. Peter Homans (Charlottesville, Virginia Area: University Press of Virginia, 2000), 98.
35. William Watkin, *On Mourning: Theories of Loss in Modern Literature* (Edinburgh: Edinburgh University Press Ltd., 2004), 191.
36. Shoshana Felman, "Camus' *The Plague*, or a Monument to Witnessing," in *Testimony: Crises of Witnessing in Literature, Psychoanalysis, and History*, eds. Shoshana Felman and Dori Laub, M.D. (New York: Routledge, 1992), 117.
37. Cathy Caruth, *Unclaimed Experience: Trauma, Narrative, and History* (Baltimore, Maryland: Johns Hopkins University Press, 1996), 18.
38. Edward W. Said, *Representations of the Intellectual: The 1993 Reith Lectures* (New York: Vintage Books, 1994), 23.
39. Isabel Allende, "Writing as an Act of Hope," in *Paths of Resistance: The Art and Craft of the Political Novel*, ed. William Zinsser (Boston: Houghton Mifflin C, 1989), 50.

Chapter 1

1. Jean-Luc Nancy, *The Inoperative Community* (Minneapolis, MN: University of Minnesota Press, 1991), 143. Nancy's thesis no. 40 in his essay, "Of Divine Places," explains this distance: "We should therefore rather lead community toward this disappearance of the gods, which founds it and divides it from itself. Over divided community, selfsame with its expanse, like a sort of ground plan, the traces of the paths along which the gods withdrew mark out the partition of community. With these traces community inscribes the absence of its communion, which is the absence of the representation of a divine presence at the heart of community and as community itself. Communion is thus the representation of what the gods have never been, but instead what we imagine to ourselves when we know they are no longer present. In place of communion, in fact, there is the absence of the gods, and the exposure of each of us to the other: We are exposed to each other in the same way as we could, together, be exposed to the gods. It is the same mode of presence, without the presence of the gods."
2. Morrison narrates the history of Haven, a thriving black town in Oklahoma, through the magical memory of Deek Morgan, one of the twins who remembers

every detail of his collective ancestry as if they were personal incidents that occurred in his own life. "Having been refused by the world in 1890 on their journey to Oklahoma, Haven residents refused each other nothing, were vigilant to any need or shortage." Toni Morrison, *Paradise* (New York: Alfred A. Knopf, 1998), 109.

3. Cathy Caruth, *Unclaimed Experience: Trauma, Narrative, and History* (Baltimore, MD: Johns Hopkins University Press, 1996), 18.

4. Caruth reads Freud's *Moses and Monotheism* to adduce the condition of trauma. Once Freud points to Moses as the outsider, an Egyptian who leaves to preserve monotheism, the Jewish return to Canaan becomes a "departure" and the original act, the murder of Moses, a historical event that cannot be grasped. Caruth's remarks of Hebrews being the chosen people is relevant, not simply because Morrison's landscape is profoundly biblical, but also because both collectives find their paths on originary acts of violence. She writes, "The history of chosenness, as the history of survival, thus takes the form of an unending confrontation with the returning violence of the past" (69).

5. Charlotte Perkins Gilman, *Herland: A Lost Feminist Utopian Novel* (New York: Pantheon, 1979).

6. Sojourner Truth, "Look at Me! Ain't I a Woman?" *The Crisis*, 01/1999, 106:1, 31.

7. Rokeya Shakawat Hossain, "Sultana's Dream," in *Sultana's Dream: A Feminist Utopia and Selections from The Secluded Ones,* ed. and trans. Roushan Jahan (New York: The Feminist Press at CUNY, 1988).

8. Edwin Ardener, "Belief and the Problem of Women," in *Perceiving Women*, ed. Shirley Ardener (New York: Halsted Press, 1978), 3.

9. Toni Morrison, *Beloved* (New York: Alfred A. Knopf, 1987).

10. Toni Morrison, *Jazz* (New York: Alfred A. Knopf, 1992).

11. Juliet Mitchell, "Femininity, Narrative and Psychoanalysis," in *Modern Criticism and Theory*, eds. David Lodge and Nigel Wood (New York: Pearson Education, 2000), 392.

12. Morrison, *Paradise*, 307.

13. Chela Sandoval, *Methodology of the Oppressed* (Minneapolis: University of Minnesota Press, 2000), writes, "Indeed, the location of the middle voice is similar to the place exacted of those 'oppressed' citizens who, as Fanon points out, reflexively act to self-consciously effect themselves in acting, always remaining inside the action—and outside the action as well—in the transitive, mobile, middle location of 'doubled consciousness.' The technology of the middle voice thus politicized represents a mechanism for survival, as well as for generating and performing a higher moral and political mode of oppositional and coalitional social movement" (156). Sandoval, in proposing a hermeneutic that sounds against the decolonization she finds inherent to all Western canonic thought, populates différance with such a capacious effect of reinvention and resistance that her lens really help to "see" Morrison's "sightings."

14. I would like to weave in ideas of community beyond the content, layered in multiple ways throughout the text, and according to Peter Kearly who writes on the popular reception to this novel seen as difficult to read, he presents a notion of community concurrent with reader-response theories. His ideas become useful in complicating the levels of community that exist upon the immediacy of reading

the first enigmatic line of this novel. Peter R. Kearly, "Toni Morrison's *Paradise* and the Politics of Community," *Journal of American and Comparative Cultures* 23, no. 2, (Summer 2000): 9–16, writes, "The act of reading *Paradise*, therefore, is performing an alternative way of making community, where individuals derive a sense of belonging and identity, a sense of having a place in the world not just by following a predetermined order, but by accepting the diversity of living in the moment. Communities are created by individuals through their interactions with one another, based upon common history. A history of the community is the collective memory individuals bring to that community. Stored in this collective memory are experiences and perspectives of interpersonal relationships and social values that are transmitted from generation to generation through the language and objects of culture."

15. Marc C. Conner, "From the Sublime to the Beautiful: The Aesthetic Progression of Toni Morrison," in *The Aesthetics of Toni Morrison: Speaking the Unspeakable*, ed. Marc C. Conner (Jackson: University Press of Mississippi, 2000), 73–74, writes on the novel, *Paradise*, "Though its depiction of a community that preys upon its own young, its own women, and those outside of its narrow confines seems in some respects to return to the war between self and society depicted in Morrison's earlier work—indeed, War was Morrison's working title for the book ('This Side of Paradise')—nevertheless the novel reveals a continuation of the direction announced with *Beloved* and continued in *Jazz*. In her depiction of a community that is isolated, fearful and hating of all that is outside of its narrow confines, Morrison reveals the devastation that hatred and isolation wreak upon their perpetrators. If *Beloved* examines the glories and excesses of mother-love, and *Jazz* the glories and excesses of human love, Paradise shows the glories and excesses of love of God."

16. Andrea Dimino, "Toni Morrison and William Faulkner: Remapping Culture," in *Unflinching Gaze: Morrison and Faulkner Re-Envisioned*, eds., Carol A. Kolmerten, Stephen M. Ross, and Judith Bryant Wittenberg (Jackson: University Press of Mississippi, 1997), 40, writes, "Like literary and cultural critic Edward Said, whose work she admires, Morrison seeks to reveal cultural links between 'canon building' and 'Empire building.'"

17. Racial erasure is an act of racism, and this translates into the act of barbarity that marks the great flaw of American civilization. Toni Morrison, *Playing in the Dark: Whiteness and the Literary Imagination* (Cambridge, Massachusetts: Harvard University Press, 1992), 45, writes, "Why is it seen as raw and savage? Because it is peopled by a nonwhite indigenous population? Perhaps. But certainly because there is ready to hand a bound and unfree, rebellious but serviceable, black population against which Dunbar and all white men are enabled to measure these privileging and privileged differences.

Eventually individualism fuses with the prototype of Americans as solitary, alienated, and malcontent. What, one wants to ask, are Americans alienated from? What are Americans always so insistently innocent of? Different from? As for absolute power, over whom is this power held, from whom withheld, to whom distributed?

Answers to these questions lie in the potent and ego-reinforcing presence of an Africanist population. This population is convenient in every way, not the least of which is self-definition. This new white male can now persuade himself that

214 Women Writing Violence

savagery is 'out there'. The lashes ordered (500 applied five times is 2500) are not one's own savagery; repeated and dangerous breaks for freedom are 'puzzling' confirmations of black irrationality; the combination of Dean Swift's beatitudes and a life of regularized violence is civilized; and if the sensibilities are dulled enough, the rawness remains external." These rubrics of violence, its secret mission of self-definition, and "out there" are inverted in ironic and self-critical ways in this novel.

18. Elizabeth Ann Beaulieu, *The Toni Morrison Encyclopedia* (Westport, Connecticut: Greenwood Press, 2003) provides a coherent and precise summary of the entire novel, summed by popular assessment as a difficult read. She identifies one of the "primary struggles in the novel results from the efforts of Ruby's youth to resist the repressive and isolationist policies of their parents' generation" (261) and draws conclusions a little too neat from a novel too tangled to be dissected so precisely. Beaulieu's declaratives that Pallas is the white girl, that the three women running are shot edit into the Morrison narrative a certitude that simplifies the original text. Though such a summary is essential within the stage of reader-response theory, it undercuts the very project undertaken by Morrison in this definitive and phenomenal imaginative landscape that is purposefully unyielding, resistant, and slippery.

19. Missy Dehn Kubitschek, *Toni Morrison: A Critical Companion* (Westport, Connecticut: Greenwood Press, 1998), 163.

20. Jeanette King, *Women and the Word: Contemporary Women Novelists and the Bible* (New York: St. Martin's Press, LLC, 2000), 158, provides the etymological chart of 8-Rock as a mining term that is a label for the coal found deep within the earth's womb, a color significantly interpreted as pure and necessary to be authentic within the genealogic and biblical map of Ruby. Echoes of the Pentateuch, the chosen people, and the prophet Zechariah who warns against the excess of disobedience and a scattering of his people are present within the rhetoric of 8-Rock.

21. Kristin Hunt mentions the haunting Indian figure marking this novel. She locates in Anna one of the few people who is able to sense what is lost, as is Deacon later who is tracing the path of the lost, and the great failure of Ruby lies in having lost touch with both native and African ways completely.

22. Kristin Hunt, "Paradise Lost: The Destructive Forces of Double Consciousness and Boundaries in Toni Morrison's Paradise," in *Reading Under the Sign of Nature: New Essays in Ecocriticism*, eds. John Tallmadge and Henry Harrington (Salt Lake City: The University of Utah Press, 2000), 120.

23. Theodor W. Adorno, *Prisms*, trans. from German by Samuel and Sherry Weber (Cambridge, Massachusetts: The MIT Press, 1986), 99. The world of the novel materializes Huxley's worst fears about modernity, a reading that Adorno superimposes upon the American nation, a community of communities fashioned after the multiple "conditionings" formulated in Huxley's ordered new world, void of ennui and disenchantment. "Conditioning" is a key concept making its way across Morrison's landscape also, which can be said to take place in "past anterior"—imagining the historical past simultaneous to modernity in another way. However Adorno opposes the schematic present in the novel as empty and bereft of meaning since it contains a hollow cry against a future prognostication of absolute satiation; it does little to contend with the malefactors of today. While Huxley does away with the possibility of paradise, Adorno's adamant opposition to such a perspective yields

room for the sort of paradise "down here" that Morrison hints by the end of her novel.

24. Walter Benjamin, *Illuminations*, ed. Hannah Arendt, trans. Harry Zohn (New York: Schocken Books, 1969), 254–255.

25. Morrison, *Paradise*, 307.

26. In acknowledgment of the work done by South Asian Subaltern Studies Collective, Gayatri Spivak, and Latin Subaltern Studies Collective, and the anthology assembled by Ileana Rodriguez, I have culled meaning for the subaltern as a figure outside the state, severed from agency who operates in shadow economy and is not present in the historical archive or master narratives of any sort.

27. Katrine Dalsgard, "The One All-Black Town Worth the Pain: (African) American Exceptionalism, Historical Narration, and the Critique of Nationhood in Toni Morrison's Paradise," *African American Review* 35, no. 2 (Summer 2001): 233–248, adduces the differences in Morrison's notions of history from the generation of scholars who believe in black nationalism provided it is filtered through the lens of feminism and other politics more coherent with inclusion of the oppressed, positions espoused by scholars like E. Frances White. Morrison, more deconstructive in her focus, and in tune with Foucauldian scholar like Catherine Belsey, she attests to the image of history never being outside itself, never able to articulate one truth, constantly refracted within itself. The novel, according to Dalsgard, rests in this unease with master narratives, like Barthes's "tissue of quotations" and moving from Anderson's insistence on needing to understand nationhood, Bhabha's theory of nationhood becomes central. Dalsgard writes, "Within her narrative framework, Morrison's deconstruction of exceptionalism as an (African) American national narrative may be further understood in relation to Homi Bhabha's preface to his anthology of scholarly articles on the cultural significations of the nation's foundation, *Nation and Narration* (1990). In this book Bhabha suggests that the concept of 'the nation' is haunted by an ambivalent tension between 'the certainty with which historians speak of the "origins" of nation as a sign of the "modernity" of society,'" on one hand, and the 'transitional social reality' inscribed by the nation's 'cultural temporality,' on the other."

28. Morrison, *Paradise*, 18.

29. Kubitschek, *Toni Morrison: A Critical Companion*, 181. She also observes that it is this artificial and absolute binary established between good and evil that causes the pivotal action in the novel to occur, the violence against the women in the convent. She catalogues a number of examples of Rubians who follow this dichotomy to its insane consequence, of disallowing a part of their own selves much like the Black town in Fairly rejects the ancestors of Haven on their trek westward. She mentions Zechariah who rejects his own twin because he dances for the white man, Patricia who rejects her own daughter to gain favor in the eyes of her righteous neighbors, and Sweetie who rejects the runaway, Seneca who aids her like a pathfinder in a moment of darkness rather than see her for the savior she was, all because of this immutable line that divides those who are good from those who are putatively evil.

30. On this same theme of control and order faced by the outcaste from the powers-that-be, Jill C. Jones, "The Eye of a Needle: Morrison's *Paradise*, Faulkner's

Absalom, Absalom! and *American Jeremiad!*," *Faulkner Journal* 17, no. 2 (March 2002): 3–23, writes, "Paradise stands in a long tradition of American jeremiads, asking us to consider the nature and the language of exclusion, or as Morrison said in her Nobel lecture, the 'lethal discourses of exclusion'. From the opening revelation that the New Fathers are on a mission to 'target ... detritus: throwaway people', to the interpretation of the words on the Oven, language and exclusion, history and myth, are intertwined. When phrases like 'racial purity' and 'blood rules' become part of our vocabulary, ethnic cleansing cannot be far behind. Language well-used, Morrison indicates in her Nobel speech, is the best of things. But words, stories, language carry the potential as well 'to sanction ignorance and preserve privilege'. While Faulkner's novel seems to record the tragic end of a world, a culture, a system, Morrison's novel, like all American jeremiads, holds out the hope for redemption as well as the possibility of damnation."

31. Morrison, *Paradise*, 87.
32. Morrison, *Paradise*, 205.
33. Morrison, *Paradise*, 222.
34. Morrison, *Paradise*, 304.
35. Caruth, *Unclaimed Experience: Trauma, Narrative, and History*, 18.
36. Beaulieu point this out in the passages on violence in her encyclopedia on Morrison.
37. Nancy J. Peterson, *Against Amnesia: Contemporary Women Writers and the Crisis of Historical Memory* (Philadelphia: University of Pennsylvania Press, 2001), 91, emphasizes Morrison's personal interests in this era of black migration westward. A small aside in such an article talked about two caravans of black people being turned away by a black town. On this, she writes, "Provoked by this incident of black settlers refusing to help or even to welcome a prospective group of poor black migrants, Morrison crafts a novel that explores the repercussions of this troubling moment in African American history. The result is that Ruby, which might have been a paradise, a haven from white racism and lynching, which might have provided black people with unprecedented economic, political and cultural opportunities based not on the color of their skin, but on their own self-worth, turns out to be a failure."
38. Morrison, *Paradise*, 16.
39. Morrison, *Paradise*, 155.
40. Kubitschek, *Toni Morrison: A Critical Companion*, 179, expresses this difference between the twins based on the shape of the story each imbibes, and the genders transcribed upon it. She writes, "Deacon's greater capacity for growth may result from his spiritual wellspring. His image of the sacred differs significantly from Steward's veneration of Zechariah and Rector Morgan. First, it comes directly from his own boyhood experience, rather than from stories of historical experience. Second, it focuses on women rather than men—the group of nineteen elegant women that he and Steward see during their tour of all-black towns in 1932."
41. Jeanette King, *Women and the Word: Contemporary Women Novelists and the Bible* (New York: St. Martin's Press, 2000), 169, also observes the feminine nature of the oven, its womb-like shape serving as a round center of nourishment, a symbol of community and identity at once. As the nature of Ruby becomes more material

and individual, Soane wonders why her husband Deek cares more about his bank and profit, marking a shift from the utility of the once-operational oven which represents only a figurehead of power at this point.

42. Partha Chatterjee, "The Nation and Its Women," in *A Subaltern Studies Reader 1986–1995*, ed. Ranajit Guha (Minneapolis: University of Minnesota Press, 1997), 244–246.

43. Morrison, *Paradise*, 85.

44. Peter Widdowson, "The American Dream Refashioned: History, Politics and Gender in Toni Morrison's *Paradise*," *Journal of American Studies* 35, no. 2 (2001): 325.

45. Jeanette King, *Women and the Word: Contemporary Women Novelists and the Bible*, 158, returns to the early Jewish tribes and their similarities to the tribe in Ruby as configured under the aegis of the Law of the Father. She notes that there is no crime in Ruby, or transgression of a public nature, because this law has been internalized by the populace.

46. Rob Davidson, "Racial Stock and 8-Rocks: Communal Historiography in Toni Morrison's *Paradise*," *Twentieth Century Literature: A Scholarly and Critical Journal* 47, no. 3 (Fall 2001): 355–373.

47. Morrison, *Paradise*, 306.

48. Justine Tally, *Paradise Reconsidered: Toni Morrison's (Hi)stories and Truths* (Hamburg: Lit Verlag, 1999), 48, writes, "Anna and Richard, both agents for the future of a Ruby connected to the world, 'see' or rather 'sense' a signal while making a last visit to the Convent. Holding five warm eggs, symbol of fertility and rebirth, Anna sees a door (to another realm of consciousness?), while Misner, who holds pepper pods of green, red and plum black (an integrated mix of colors and peoples), sees an open window, a sign of possibility or alternative knowledge."

49. Morrison, *Paradise*, 16.

50. Roberta Rubenstein, *Home Matters: Longing and Belonging, Nostalgia and Mourning in Women's Fiction* (New York: Palgrave, 2001), 143, writes, "Linking home with nurturance, food is a recurring image and central symbol in the narrative. In addition to the obvious symbolism of the Oven itself, a significant number of events occur within the context of nourishment being prepared, served, shared, or received, as Morrison emphasizes the centrality of hunger and the gratification or denial of appetites both physical and spiritual. Virtually all of the women in the narrative, both those who live in the Convent and those who reside in the community of Ruby, are associated with literal food or symbolic nurturance or both."

51. Roberta Rubenstein, *Home Matters: Longing and Belonging, Nostalgia and Mourning in Women's Fiction* (New York: Palgrave, 2001), 144, remarks about the "maternal ambience" of the Convent, emphasized by the number of children born there or present in the laughing voices of Merle and Perle, and underlined by the form of the novel which is divided into nine sections of literary gestation.

52. Nada Elia, *Trances, Dances, and Vociferations: Agency and Resistance in Africana Women's Narratives* (New York: Garland Publishing, Inc., 2001), 115.

53. Tally, *Toni Morrison's (Hi)stories and Truths*, 42.

54. Patricia McKee, "Geographies of Paradise," *CR: The New Centennial Review* 3, no. 1 (Spring 2003): 198, points out the importance of this space in Morrison's

landscape. She writes, "The liberating potential of her 'borderlessness', of both conceptual and practical kinds, lies within as well as outside of places. Morrison's spatializations of freedom reinforce revisions of modernity proposed by numerous theorists of African American cultures, who argue concepts and experiences of home cannot be separated from discourses of freedom."

55. Morrison, *Paradise*, 41.
56. Morrison, *Paradise*, 64.
57. Kubitschek, *Toni Morrison: A Critical Companion*, 174. Other critics also wonder about the exact nature of Pallas's violation following the severe wound of seeing her mother and lover, Carlos, becoming lovers themselves. Some conclude that there is a horrifying episode of being gang-raped by a lake during her dangerous and lonely journey on the roads and then being rescued by a truck full of Indians who deposit her to Billie Delia's clinic.
58. Morrison, *Paradise*, 173.
59. McKay Jenkins, "Metaphors of Race and Psychological Damage in the 1940s American South: The Writings of Lillian Smith," in *Racing & (E)Racing Language: Living With the Color of Our Words*, eds. Ellen J. Goldner and Safiya Henderson-Holmes (New York: Syracuse University Press, 2001), 112–113. McKay Jenkins quotes Morrison from *Playing in the Dark*: "If we follow through on the self-reflexive nature of these encounters with Africanism, it falls clear: images of blackness can be evil and protective, rebellious and forgiving, fearful and desirable—all of the self-contradictory features of the self. Whiteness, alone, is mute, meaningless, unfathomable, pointless, frozen, veiled, curtained, dreaded, senseless, implacable. Or so our writers seem to say" (1990, 59). Then, Jenkins adds his own analysis, "Morrison's comment, mirroring the thoughts of Lacan and Rose, makes clear the double-edged blade that cuts both races to the quick: not only do metaphors of virility and desire and danger demonize blacks, the other, they eviscerate the souls of whites, who are ironically denied access to the very life forces they have demonized blacks for embodying. For Smith, this system of inquiry found effective enunciation throughout her work, but it is to one particular field of vision, her treatment of women and children, that I will now turn. Her writing brims with descriptions of children who are spiritually damaged before they can even define what race is and with white women who have become utterly detached from their own physical and spiritual presences. They float through her work like disembodies ghosts, pale, shriveled, human voids. The southern offer of a detached, ambient, pervasive 'glory' in exchange for sexual and spiritual neglect, it becomes clear, Smith saw as a direct outgrowth of race. Just as embodiment and specifically sexuality become troped as black, estrangement and repression are inevitably written as white."
60. Morrison, *Paradise*, 231.
61. Bell Hooks, "Women Who Write Too Much," in *Word: On Being a (Woman) Writer*, ed. Jocelyn Burrell (New York: The Feminist Press at The City University of New York, 2004), 17. In *The Dancing Mind*, Toni Morrison suggests that the therapeutic ways in which writing can function are at odds with, or at least inferior to, a commitment to writing that is purely about the desire to engage language imaginatively. She contends: "I have always doubted and disliked the therapeutic claims made on behalf of writing and writers.... I know now, more than I ever did

(and I always on some level knew it), that I need that intimate, sustained surrender to the company of my own mind while it touches another.... "Morrison's description of the urge that leads to writing resonates with me. Still, I believe that one can have a complete imaginative engagement with writing as a craft and still experience it in a manner that is therapeutic; one urge does not diminish the other.

62. Richard L. Schur, "Locating Paradise in the Post-Civil Rights Era: Toni Morrison and Critical Race Theory," in *Contemporary Literature*, 45(2), Summer 2004, 290–291.
63. Morrison, *Paradise*, 241.
64. Morrison, *Paradise*, 242.
65. Cheryl Lester, "Meditations on a Bird in the Hand: Ethics and Aesthetics in a Parable by Toni Morrison," in *The Aesthetics of Toni Morrison: Speaking the Unspeakable*, ed. Marc C. Conner (Jackson: University Press of Mississippi, 2000), 128, describes in an extremely moving piece framed as a call and response to Morrison's famous words in Stockholm. I quote from Lester's account Morrison's telling of the tale which is valuable to include in its entirety as does Lester. In the version I know the woman is the daughter of slaves, black, American, and lives alone in a small house outside of town. Her reputation for wisdom is without peer and without question. Among her people she is both the law and the transgression. The honor she is paid and the awe in which she is held reach beyond her neighborhood to places far away; to the city where the intelligence of rural prophets is the source of much amusement.

One day the woman is visited by some young people who seem to be bent on disproving her clairvoyance and showing her up for the fraud they believe she is. Their plan is simple: they enter her house and ask the one question the answer to which rides solely on her difference from them, a difference they regard as a profound disability: her blindness. They stand before her, and one of them says,

"Old woman, I hold in my hand a bird. Tell me whether it is living or dead." She does not answer, and the question is repeated. "Is the bird I am holding living or dead?"

Still she does not answer. She is blind and cannot see her visitors, let alone what is in their hands. She does not know their color, gender or homeland. She only knows their motive.

The old woman's silence is so long, the young people have trouble holding their laughter.

Finally she speaks, and her voice is soft but stern. "I don't know," she says, "I don't know whether the bird you are holding is dead or alive, but what I do know is that it is in your hands. It is in your hands."

66. Linda J. Krumholz, "Reading and Insight in Toni Morrison's *Paradise*," *African American Review* 36, no. 1 (Spring 2002): 33, writes, "The women gain insights through painting; readers can find insight in Morrison's novel. When reading a novel a reader, like Consolata, 'steps in' or 'sees in' to another and thus may discover new thoughts, new possibilities of knowledge or action, and new ways of understanding what is within oneself. Readers 'raise the dead' insofar as the dead

characters on the page come alive within the reader. Misner preaches that 'what is sown is not alive until it dies'; like the five women who live on after their deaths at the end of the novel, the characters must be reborn in the reader's life and imagination to effect the world."

67. Morrison, *Paradise*, 262.

68. These are the same questions that inspire dread, outrage, and irritation in a good many readers from all circles, from Oprah's Reading Club to other public forums and inspired irate and conservative reviewers, like Geoffrey Bent, to rail against all the thematics of the novel as hyperbolic, heavy-handed, or ludicrous. Except for occasional glimpses of brilliance in her writing abilities, when recording a character's observations or Seneca's abandonment in the apartment as a child, Bent finds little that is salvageable in Morrison's novel. Geoffrey Bent, "Less than Divine: Toni Morrison's Paradise," *Southern Review* 35, no. 1 (Winter 1999): 145–149, writes, "One of paradise's shortcomings as a concept is that it's too schematic, a place that's all of this and none of that. Morrison's new novel falls prey to this same exclusivity. Virtue and vice seem to have been rigorously sorted along the convenient divide of gender; all the women are good, all the men bad. Even if we employ the euphemisms of anthropology and say that Morrison is exploring the patriarchal in conflict with the matriarchal—certainly a rich subject, and one of great significance in the history of African Americans—the theme is still too broad and emotionally unengaging to propel an affecting novel." Rife with errors and thick-skinned in its readings, Bent does not see the goodness in Misner, a male character, or the redemption of Deacon, another male character, or the negativity portrayed by female characters like Sweety, Arnette, etc. By missing the metaphors embedded deep in the novel that move beyond a simple critique of patriarchy but eschew ideas of elitism, nationhood, biblical apotheosis, exclusion of the other, transcendence, Bent centers his argument around not being moved by the novel. He finds it "not affecting" and says the cruelty of the men towards the women to be not believable. To a reader who might understand "horsewhipping the women" over having them shot, a gradation of violence devoid of any sense of context or perspective, it becomes implicit in the critique the color of the sentiments being expressed. I include the popular perspective to ground the text in the difficulty of forming community when even the imaginary proves to be impossible for readers steeped in hierarchies of the evident. By including the opposition, I mean to point to the direction of pragmatic exclusion faced by the blind criers of wisdom, as faced by Consolata within the story, the old blind woman in Morrison's own parable delivered in Stockholm, and finally, all of them standing as metonyms for the author herself as she composes a narrative that is, to the anxious, disingenuous.

69. David Bradley, *The Chaneysville Incident: A Novel* (New York: Harper & Row, 1981), 428.

70. Bradley, *The Chaneysville Incident*, 208.

71. Justine Tally, "Reality and Discourse in Toni Morrison's Trilogy: Testing the Limits," in *Literature and Ethnicity in the Cultural Borderlands*, eds. Jesús Benito and Ana María Manzanas (New York: Rodopi, 2002), 40, attests that Connie's "seeing in" and revenants populating the last sections of the novel symbolize the African tradition present in this narrative. I veer from this perspective in that I see in the

Morrison imaginary not only an amalgamation of African, Caribbean, and Latin tradition of familiarity with the supernatural, but also in her play with magical realism a possibility of events not imagined or ritualized before, a condition that results when the subaltern, or suffering dead, instead of ceasing to be begins to exist in the collective in tangible and unforgettable ways.

72. Philip Page, "Furrowing All the Brows: Interpretation and the Transcendent in Toni Morrison's *Paradise*," *African American Review* 35, no. 4 (Winter 2001): 637–664, writes, "In *Paradise*, and especially its last four chapters, Morrison constructs an elaborate model of reading and interpreting. She creates a fictional world in which many answers are not given or are hidden so well that readers are forced to look for answers. Like Patricia, they want to fill in the missing gaps, the apparent holes and spaces in the very surface of the text. But such attempts, like Patricia's, are bound to fail, focused as they are on narrow pursuits of facts and deductions. Instead, Morrison suggests that readers use their whole selves, pass beyond the merely rational, and truly become co-creators rather than merely passive respondents by emulating Lone's and Connie's stepping in, the Convent women's loud dreaming, and Richard and Anna's sensing of mystical portals to the unknown. Readers are urged to step into the fictional world, to share in the author's breathing of life into it, to join the characters and each other in voicing their co-creation of the novel's stories and of their own stories, and to sense and perhaps even pass through the open windows of transcendent worlds." Page's deduction about "passing beyond the merely rational" is useful in my further elaborations about the women who appear and reappear toward the end of the narrative.

73. Morrison, *Paradise*, 310.

74. Morrison, *Paradise*, 311.

75. Morrison, *Paradise*, 312.

76. Morrison, *Paradise*, 313.

77. Morrison, *Paradise*, 314.

78. Morrison, *Paradise*, 317.

79. Morrison, *Paradise*, 318.

80. Ana Fraile Marcos, "The Religious Overtones of Ethnic Identity-Building in Toni Morrison's *Paradise*," *Atlantis XXIV*.2 (2002): 109, writes, "Rejecting both Manicheism and immovability, the Convent exists as a liminal land, a border area where the acknowledgment of difference and cultural hybridity are made possible. Transformed into a purgatory, the space where Catholics believe a soul tainted by sin can purify itself before joining God in Heaven, the Convent disrupts the dualistic theology of Ruby men by introducing an axis that brings the poles of Hell and Heaven together. Furthermore, the Convent shuns immovability by not remaining a purgatory but by turning itself into a paradise for the women living there, demonstrating that improvement relies on the viability of the change and fluidity that the men in Ruby eschew. The rejection of Manichean polarities is also perceived in the blurring of racial boundaries that takes place in the Convent. Race is actually deconstructed by its changing, chameleaonic quality when applied to the Convent women."

81. Ana Maria Fraile-Marcos, "Hybridizing the 'City Upon a Hill' in Toni Morrison's *Paradise*," *MELUS* 28, no. 4 (Winter 2003): 4.

82. Connie, not having been tried but convicted by a jury of vigilantes, the patriarchs of Ruby, suffers the punishment, shot in the forehead in a room of her own home. Here Morrison echoes an earlier period of American history, not long after the period which Walter Johnson focuses in his treatise on the auction block, the post slavery period when a good number of African Americans, tried or often not tried, were deemed to be guilty of whatever crime had been committed in their vicinity and paid with their lives for mostly, crimes that had little to do with them. Suzanne Lebsock writes about the trial of four African Americans at the turn of the century, three woman and a man, the man convicted and hung, all three women released on the unusual recognition on part of the court of their innocence. Out of these three, two were eloquent interlocutors on their behalf, arguing and speaking clearly about their lives, circumstances, and actions at the time a wealthy white woman was murdered, so articulately that Lebsock imagines if born a hundred years later, they could have been emissaries of the law themselves. One of the convicted, a young woman, Pokey Barnes, speaks so convincingly that she commands a large following of people who flock to see her just to hear her talk, for it is deemed that she talks her way out of a sure road to perdition. Susan Lebsock, *A Murder in Virginia: Southern Justice on Trial* (New York: W. W. Norton & Company, 2003), 255, writes, "Pokey was perfect. SHE WAS A VERY EFFECTIVE WITNESS IN HER OWN BEHALF, declared the *Times* headline. IF AN ACTRESS, A CONSUMMATE ONE." "Many who believed her guilty," the article went on to say, "now proclaim that she is innocent."
83. Morrison, *Paradise*, 263–264.
84. Ron David, *Toni Morrison Explained: A Reader's Road Map to the Novels* (New York: Random House, 2000), 174–187, writes with verve and lack of literary adornment on the hidden meanings and projects within the last of her trilogy, *Paradise*. He sums up the thematics of the novel with his two points: the presence of something absent, and doubling or twinning. He also arrives at a valuable observation while moving rationally through the logos here: by excess of God-love, it is not being insinuated that Ruby is the ideology of killing those who do not believe in God, but killing Goddess herself if the love is too profound, as expressed in David's summation, "I love God so much that under certain circumstances I would kill Her" (180), and that the novel is not about men's mythology, but women's mythology. David cheers himself as he links Morrison's intellectual projects with that of Elaine Pagels who wrote the *Gnostic Gospels* and spends a good amount of time examining female centers of divinity. David's conclusions are honest and bare, in that he reveals with alacrity the scholarly process and exuberance at finding meaning, though I have reservations about such scientific expeditions into the literary heart of darkness to which I wish to leave some aura of mysticism and indecipherability.
85. Morrison, *Paradise*, 318.

Chapter 2

1. Edwidge Danticat, *The Farming of Bones* (New York: Soho Press, 1998), 310.
2. Mallay Charters, "Edwidge Danticat: A Bitter Legacy Revisited," *Publisher's Weekly* 245, no. 33 (August 1998): 43.

3. Lois Parkinson-Zamora, *The Usable Past: The Imagination of History in Recent Fiction of the Americas* (Cambridge: Cambridge University Press, 1997), 174.

4. Ranjana Khanna, lecture, "Asylum and Its Indignities," Collective for Asian American Scholarship, Rutgers U, Plangere Writing Center, New Brunswick, NJ, 12 Apr. 2007.

5. Carolyn Forché, *Against Forgetting: Twentieth Century Poetry of Witness* (New York: W. W. Norton & Co., 1993), 37.

6. Joan Dayan, "Haiti, History, and the Gods," in *After Colonialism: Imperial Histories and Postcolonial Displacements*, ed. Gyan Prakash (Princeton: Princeton University Press, 1995), 66–97, opens by referring to the anxiety caused by the liberation and formation of the second republic and first black nation-state in the western hemisphere in 1804 when Dessalines named his land, Haiti.

7. Susan Buck-Morss, "Hegel and Haiti," *Critical Inquiry* 26, no. 4 (Summer 2000): 821–865. Buck-Morss indicts the great European philosophers of the Enlightenment who, she charges were deeply aware of the problematic of slavery within their dialectic of liberation. She reads the silences of philosophical ruminations, especially that of Hegel in order to read into it a profound cognizance of the despair and anxiety caused by the liberation and statehood of the first black nation in the western hemisphere. She ultimately concludes that it is upon the enslavement of the darker races that the white nations wrote their treatises of human rights and freedom, in both the Americas and Europe. In the act of Hegel being a habitual reader of the papers, especially Minerva, Buck-Morss proposes that he imagines the dialectic of master–slave narrative from his knowledge of the Haitian condition. And still, western historiography and enlightenment scholarship remains silent as if Haiti, either does not exist, or does not matter. Buck-Morss wishes for a rupture from these disciplined and limited ways of thinking, imagining an alternate set of undisciplined stories. I am interested in resuscitating these stories that have been refused entry in the master narratives of historical archives, philosophical pontification, and the literary landscape.

8. Bernard Diederich, *Trujillo: The Death of the Dictator* (Princeton: Markus Wiener Publishers, 1978), 12.

9. Ernesto Sagás, *Race and Politics in the Dominican Republic* (Boca Raton: University Press of Florida, 2000), 4–5.

10. Michel-Rolph Trouillot, *Silencing the Past: Power and the Production of History* (Boston: Beacon Press, 1995) provides a seminal text in comprehending the historical silence over the genesis of Haiti. Trouillot delves into the lack of access to means of historical production as a prime reason for large silences, and silencing of the Haitian revolution is a prime example of this deficit as instituted by practitioners of western historiography.

11. Deborah Cohn's synthesis of Faulkner, Fuentes, and Ortiz states the historical iniquity—even within the living communities then called sugar economies, blacks gained little from their labors. She writes:

> Sugar, cotton, tobacco, and slaves. White and black, white for black. A chromatic exchange that is financial and political as well: the import and export of goods, labor, people, and power. Silver for flesh and blood and pain.... Blacks have sown, but they have reaped little benefit for themselves from a

nature which cannot balance the social equations governing their lives and their homelands' economies.

Thus, while the economy rests on the labors of its black peoples, it gives little back in terms of wages, compensation, and dignity. In such contexts, the dead are an excess from a lifetime of labor and exploitative practices. In all geographies of depredation, the dead become as vital as the living. Read Deborah N. Cohn, *History and Memory in the Two Souths: Recent Southern and Spanish American Fiction* (Nashville: Vanderbilt University Press, 1999), 184.

12. Deleuze and Guattari's proposed relations between desire, capitalism, the social machine, and universal history are useful here. As they chart the slow disjuncture from savage barbarian to the civilized man, they find the erasing tendency to be an essential part of the project of universal history, especially the writing of it. There is neither innocence nor surreptitiousness in this effort to code the flows of desire and making "ruptures and limits" an integral part of universal history. Exploitation, the violent instances of great cruelty are necessary for inscribing this historical writing upon the human body and for privatizing the various parts of the human body. These seismic spates of violence lead to the conditions of enlightenment and birth of a "nation of thinkers." Thus history is broken as are bodies; stories are kept secret as is desire; memory is "fashioned" as is the various forms of exploitation of man. The social machine, intent on marking and inscribing, places a collective investment in the totalizing tendency to destroy man, his narrative, his being and the mask, his ghost. Even the Nietzschean creation of man is an act forged in forgetfulness. Deleuze and Guattari make explicit the culpability involved in material projects of desire production, historiography, and nation making.

Cruelty has nothing to do with some ill-defined or natural violence that might be commissioned to explain the history of mankind; cruelty is the movement of culture that is realized in bodies and inscribed on them, belaboring them. That is what cruelty means ... For even death, punishment, and torture are desired, and are instances of production. It makes men or their organs into the parts and wheels of the social machine.

Read Gilles Deleuze and Felix Guattari, *Anti-Oedipus: Capitalism and Schizophrenia* (Minneapolis: University of Minnesota Press, 1983), 145.

13. M. M. Bakhtin, *The Dialogic Imagination*, ed. Michael Holquist and trans., Caryl Emerson and Michael Holquist (Austin: University of Texas Press, 1981), 278, writes, "...the prose writer witnesses as well the unfolding of social heteroglossia surrounding the object; the dialectics of the object are interwoven with the social dialogue surrounding it. For the prose writer, the object is a focal point for heteroglot voices among which his own voice must also sound; these voices create the background necessary for his own voice, outside of which his artistic prose nuances cannot be perceived, and without which they 'do not sound.'" Danticat's word is born in this Bakhtinian dialogic because as a Haitian living in Brooklyn and writing about a French Caribbean nation and imagining it in a language, Kréyol, already distanced doubly from French and English, the dialogic is born in the mixing and distancing of at least three languages at once. Empire and subject, power and powerless, the state and subaltern are all thematics engaged within this dialogic.

14. Michael Burkard, *Entire Dilemma* (Louisville, Kentucky: Sarabande Books, 1998), 37–38.
15. Azade Seyhan, *Writing Outside the Nation* (Princeton: Princeton University Press, 2001), 39, echoes Geoffrey Hartman who quotes Walter Benjamin, when she writes, "Hartman sees official history as the greatest danger to public memory: 'Even the dead, as Walter Benjamin declared, are not safe from the victors, who consider public memory part of the spoils and do not hesitate to rewrite history.'"
16. *The Farming of Bones* places this observation in Sebastien Onius's mouth as he makes love to Amabelle praising the midnight blue of her skin.
17. Danticat, *The Farming of Bones*, 2.
18. Zamora, *The Usable Past: The Imagination of History in Recent Fiction of the Americas*, 77.
19. Ileana Rodriguez, "Apprenticeship as Citizenship and Governability," in *The Latin Subaltern Studies Reader*, eds Ileana Rodriguez and María Milagros López (Durham: Duke University Press, 2001), 362–363.
20. Danticat, *The Farming of Bones*, 1.
21. Jacques Lacan, "The Insistence of the Letter in the Unconscious," in *Modern Criticism and Theory: A Reader*, eds. David Lodge and Nigel Wood (England: Longman, 2000), 72, says, "...the metaphor occurs at the precise point at which sense comes out of non-sense, that is, at that frontier which, as Freud discovered, when crossed the other way produces what we generally call 'wit' (Witz); it is at this frontier that we can glimpse the fact that man tempts his very destiny when he derides the signifier.... By pushing to its limits the sort of connaturality which links that art to that condition, he lets us glimpse a certain something which in this matter imposes its form, in the effect of the truth on desire." While Lacan negotiates his own dream of conflation between Saussure and Freud in order to chart the unconscious not in terms of biology but linguistics, he offers the map of desire as "unachievable, public, contagious." Once the child enters the realm of language and articulates his desire within a semiotic cartography, the object of his desire, absolute union with the mother, becomes impossible. Thus, desire becomes an eternal lack, as shown with Amabelle, estranged even in the beginning from her taciturn parents, then from her lover, and later even from herself. However Amabelle steps out of the Lacanian world in that she turns the "lack" into a presence, a positive force. It is this very lack that propels a new world of communings and community, a world where she can be soothed by the visitations from the dead and in turn, join the dead as a final act of will. In this project, we trace the path of desire to see that it yields to an imagined community with the dead which travels on a different wave length than a Lacanian journey.
22. By "end of desire," I refer to a popular strain of Eastern philosophy stemming from Hinduism, Buddhism, Taoism, etc. referred in popular discourse as "vitrushna" or "lack of desire," equating enlightenment with having reached a state where one is left with no desires.
23. Hélène Cixous, "Sorties," in *Modern Criticism and Theory: A Reader*, eds. David Lodge and Nigel Wood (England: Longman, 2000), 268, writes, "No, it is at the level of sexual pleasure (jouissance) in my opinion that the difference makes itself most clearly apparent in as far as woman's libidinal economy is neither identifiable by a man nor referable to the masculine economy. For me, the question 'What

does she want?' that they ask of woman, a question that in fact woman asks herself because they ask it of her, because precisely there is so little place in society for her desire that she ends up by dint of not knowing what to do with it, no longer knowing where to put it, of if she has any, conceals the most immediate and the most urgent question: 'How do I experience sexual pleasure? What is feminine sexual pleasure, where does it take place, how is it inscribed at the level of the body, of her unconscious? And then how is it put into writing?' Cixous's fundamental questions marking an era of French feminism raises its feminized response to Freud's earlier troubling anatomical divide in female sexuality as one between early masculinity, clitoridal, aggressive against the feminine, vaginal, passive adult sexuality. Cixous places woman's ownership of pleasure in the center of the discourse on desire and the masculine economy with *jouissance* as prefiguring her own hypothetical prehistory about matriarchal originary era and altogether other forms of passion. Cixous's binary oppositions loom large in Danticat's text in Amabelle's relationship to the masculine in various forms: Sebastien, her father, the doctor, Señor Pico, the state.

24. Jacques Derrida, *Dissemination*, trans., Barbara Johnson (Chicago: The University of Chicago Press, 1981), 220–221.

25. Danticat, *The Farming of Bones*, 52.

26. Michael Hardt and Antonio Negri, *Empire* (Cambridge: Harvard University Press, 2000), 61, write, "Just as Empire in the spectacle of its force continually determines systemic recompositions, so too new figures of resistance are composed through the sequences of the events of struggle. This is another fundamental characteristic of the existence of the multitude today, within Empire and against Empire. New figures of struggle and new subjectivities are produced in the conjuncture of events, in the universal nomadism, in the general mixture and miscegenation of individuals and populations, and in the technological metamorphoses of the imperial biopolitical machine. These new figures and subjectivities are produced because, although the struggles are indeed antisystemic, they are not posed merely against the imperial system—they are not simply negative forces. They also express, nourish, and develop positively their own constituent projects; they work toward the liberation of living labor, creating constellations of powerful singularities. This constituent aspect of the movement of the multitude, in its myriad faces, is really the positive terrain of the historical construction of Empire. This is not a historicist positivity but, on the contrary, a positivity of the *res gestae* of the multitude, an antagonistic and creative positivity. The deterritorializing power of the multitude is the productive force that sustains Empire and at the same time the force that calls for and makes necessary its destruction." In further tracking the life of the multitude and Empire, they refer to Marx's postulate of the Empire as being "a vampire regime of accumulated dead labor that survives only by sucking off the blood of the living" and later Althusser's rubric of comparing Machiavelli's *The Prince* to Marx-Hegel's *The Communist Manifesto* in order to trace the similarities in structures between the two. As they weave a "relationship of immanence" in a process of self-production, a materialist teleology that eventually works its way back into Spinoza's "prophetic desire" connected to the multitude. This is the place where I think the power of the subaltern dead of Danticat's landscape begin to have a powerful/prophetic place in the world of the living. The suddenly dead are not completely so, and they, in fact, carry this power and production within themselves.

27. Danticat's Kongo is reminiscent of others in a long line within the French–Caribbean literary tradition: Chamoiseau's Kongo who defenestrates as resistance to the brutality of the state, symbolic mourning taking flight after Solibo's death, like the African flight back over the seas. Kongo, like Maryse Conde's Xantippe in *Crossing the Mangrove*, Josef Zobel's Medouze in *Black Shack Alley*, Jacques Romain's Bienaime in *Masters of the Dew*.
28. Danticat, *The Farming of Bones*, 208.
29. Danticat, *The Farming of Bones*, 310.
30. Edouard Glissant, *Caribbean Discourse, Selected Essays*, trans., J. Michael Dash (Charlottesville: University Press of Virginia, 1981), 120–121.
31. Walter Benjamin, *Illuminations*, ed. Hannah Arendt, trans., Harry Zohn (New York: Schocken Books, 1969), 254.
32. George B. Handley, *Postslavery Literatures in the Americas: Family Portraits in Black and White* (Charlottesville: University Press of Virginia, 2000), 3.
33. Sigmund Freud, "Mourning and Melancholia," in *The Complete Psychological Works of Sigmund Freud*, XIV (London: Hogarth, 1957), 243–246.
34. Ranjana Khanna, *Dark Continents: Psychoanalysis and Colonialism.* (Durham, NC: Duke University Press, 2003), 23. Khanna's work questions, "…what does it mean to foreground individuated memory when writing of social contexts? And what political use could be made from writing of ghosts?" (17). Khanna's project, in bringing to light the "ongoing worldification" of the project of psychoanalysis, frames the importance of the differing world presented in Danticat's novel. Amabelle's invitation of the ghosts brings the counter-narratives at play within the novelistic discourse.
35. George B. Handley, *Postslavery Literatures in the Americas: Family Portraits in Black and White* (Charlottesville: University Press of Virginia, 2000), 14.
36. Sagás, *Race and Politics in the Dominican Republic*, 18.
37. Danticat, *The Farming of Bones*, 136.
38. Frantz Fanon, *The Wretched of the Earth*, trans., Constance Farrington (New York: Grove Press, 1968), 237.
39. Danticat, *The Farming of Bones*, 56, "Sometimes the people in the fields, when they're tired and angry, they say we're an orphaned people. They say we are the burnt crud at the bottom of the pot. They say some people don't belong anywhere and that's us. I say we are a group of vwayajè, wayfarers. This is why you had to travel this far to meet me, because that is what we are."
40. Walter Benjamin, *Illuminations*, 255.
41. Danticat, *The Farming of Bones*, 277–278.
42. Danticat, *The Farming of Bones*, 243.
43. Walter Benjamin, *Illuminations*, 257.
44. April Shemak, "Re-Membering Hispaniola: Edwidge Danticat's *The Farming of Bones*," *MFS: Modern Fiction Studies* 48, no. 1 (Spring 2002): 83–112, notes in her final section in her essay about "the ambiguous nature of the border's history." Shemak also makes a powerful connection between Amabelle's early prowess as a midwife, its connection to labor and now, as midwife to the border in the ending. She underlines the importance of the protagonist's refusal to return home to Haiti and instead, "situate herself in the border between the two nations."
45. Danticat, *The Farming of Bones*, 378.

46. Susan Strehle, "History and the End of Romance: Danticat's *The Farming of Bones*," in *Doubled Plots: Romance and History*, eds. Susan Strehle and Mary Paniccia Carden (Jackson: University Press of Mississippi, 2003), 24–44. I find Strehle's reading of romance as an "absent presence" in the text to be very important, though I disagree the degree to which she reads romance into this text and absolute insanity upon the professor at the river.

47. Strehle, *Doubled Plots: Romance and History*, 41.

48. Danticat, *The Farming of Bones*, 272.

49. Danticat, *The Farming of Bones*, 285.

50. Danticat, *The Farming of Bones*, 285.

51. I wish to include here references to papers published within the disciplines of anthropology, religion, or history that make apparent the Haitian belief system in the afterlife, and a cultural ideological system that engenders the possibility of characters who walk between worlds and help facilitate the communication between communities of the living and the dead.

52. Danticat, *The Farming of Bones*, 300.

53. Sagás, *Race and Politics in the Dominican Republic*, 47.

54. Benedict Anderson, *Imagined Communities: Reflections on the Origin and Spread of Nationalism* (London: Verso, 1983), 9–10.

55. Kelli Lyon Johnson, "Both Sides of the Massacre: Collective Memory and Narrative on Hispaniola," *Mosaic: A Journal for the Interdisciplinary Study of Literature* 36, no. 2 (2003 June): 75–91, writes, "These Haitian survivors understand the traditions of history: if an event is written, documented, contained in a book, it is real. As part of the written record, their testimonies somehow will become the truth" (88), when explaining the event of Amabelle gathered with Man Denise and the villagers who wish to tell the government official, the justice of the peace, their harrowing personal encounter with the massacre. I wish to point that the Haitians perform a careful orchestration between the need for record keeping with the living and the dead.

56. Yanick Lahens, "Exile: Between Writing and Place," *Callaloo* 15, no. 3 (1992): 735–746.

57. Danticat, *The Farming of Bones*, 25.

58. Danticat, *The Farming of Bones*, 310.

59. Danticat, *The Farming of Bones*, 266.

60. Shemak, *Modern Fiction Studies*, 103, points to Amabelle's body as an archive of alternative memory.

61. Zamora, *The Usable Past: The Imagination of History in Recent Fiction of the Americas*, 39.

62. Edwidge Danticat, "Nineteen Thirty-Seven," in *Krik? Krak!* (New York: Vintage Books, 1996), 31–49.

63. Gayatri Chakravorty Spivak, "Diasporas Old and New: Women in the Transnational World," *Textual Practice* 10, no. 2 (1996): 245–269.

64. Homi K. Bhabha, *The Location of Culture* (New York: Routledge, 1994), 18. Bhabha raises the questions that are integral to my own study as the foundation for his text, "How are subjects formed 'in-between,' or in excess of, the sum of the 'parts' of difference (usually intoned as race/class/gender, etc.)? How do strategies of representation

or empowerment come to be formulated in the competing claims of communities where, despite shared histories of deprivation and discrimination, the exchange of values, meanings, and priorities may not always be collaborative and dialogical, but may be profoundly antagonistic, conflictual and even incommensurable?" (2).

65. Joan Dayan, "Haiti, History, and the Gods," in *After Colonialism: Imperial Histories and Postcolonial Displacements*, ed. Gyan Prakash (Princeton: Princeton University Press, 1995), 82–82, writes, "With independence, the underground opposition to the now defeated white oppressor did not disappear, for the spirits, and the people's need for them, was not contingent on being suppressed. On the contrary, vodou came, to some extent, out into the open to thrive. But haltingly so, as though the people were keeping some of the old secrets hidden, ready to serve in other repressive situations that did not fail to occur."

Chapter 3

1. The notions Bakhtin puts forward in *The Dialogic Imagination* are fundamentals at work in Sidhwa's novelistic discourse. He proposes that the novel is the sole genre that continues to develop but as of yet, is incomplete. A parody of other genres, it exists in a state of constant self-deprecation and criticism which makes it the most intractable of all genres—ready to criticize other genres and do the same to itself. Encoded in its three main principles—stylistic three-dimensionality, chronotype, and maximal contact with the present, Sidhwa's novel fulfills these principles as if keeping the Bakhtinian rubrics at the forefront. In the way that Bakthin proposes that laughter destroys epic by eliminating distance and refusing to record the distant and sacred past, Sidhwa institutes Lenny's and Ayah's and their friends' laughter to not valorize the sacred history of the nation's genesis. The child's perspective eliminates any possible hagiographical tonality, and veers strictly away from elevating the fractious history of 1947 formation of India and Pakistan. Bakhtin summarizes his grand theory in five simple points: 1. Since he estimates that the novel forms its roots in folklore, the "folklore" is ever present in *Cracking India*. Whether it is in the mythic arrival of Parsis in India, or the stories spun by the national leaders to orchestrate new narratives of political autonomy, or Santha, who tells Lenny about the star-crossed lovers, Sohni and Mahiwal, the folklore flows as main arteries throughout the novel. 2. Bakhtin stresses the particularity of certain historic periods as ripe for the novel. Partition is an episode of South Asian history that gave rise to a large number of novels on both sides of the border, some of the famous ones being Bhisham Sahni's *Tamas*, Yashpal's *Jhoota Sach*, Amrita Pritam's *Train to Pakistan*, etc. In a period when the historical archives are being gradually suddenly shifted from the repositories in the empire to its now self-determined colonies, many narratives are lost and the novelistic forms steps in to fill the gaping hole in memory formed from such sudden seismic movements in time. 3. Epic distance disintegrates. Lenny is as close to the flesh and blood of 1947 as we can possibly be when we reach back in time to look at the losses accrued at that time—a child who enters the hearts of the people around her and manages to centralize the

notion of an imagined community with the living and the dead. 4. Other genres such as the epic, the poem, the lyric, and the play are threatened since they cannot convey the details given in the novel, and they are incorporated and consumed by the novel. Examples of all the other genres, such as Ghalib's ghazals and refrains from songs dot Sidhwa's narrative, a sign of the successful gluttony of the novelistic form. 5. By nature, such a genre is not canonic and this can be seen in the popular appeal of Sidhwa's novel, which circles around marginal people—children, women, lower classes, battered, and beaten people. Turned into a film in 1998 by Canadian director, Deepa Mehta, "Earth," it functioned in mainstream media as a film for everyone, breaking out of the confining and narrow art circle.

2. Ian Watt, *The Rise of the Novel* (University of California Press, 2001[1957]). Watt contrasts the realism apparent in painting and philosophy of the eighteenth century with what he sees in the novels of Fielding, Richardson, and Defoe—realism in the novel does not rest in "the kind of life it presents, but in the way it presents it." First, the novel rejects traditional plots borrowed from mythology or its predecessors and spins its plot around the individual, thus losing formal conventions in order to gain a sense of realism. Second, the individual is not an unbelievable or fantastic archetype used in previous narratives but extremely specific and unique. Third, these individuals are given names, most often first and last names in order to show that they are particular individuals in particular environments. Fourth, the novel pays attention to time, chronology, memory, and specific moment in history in which events and individual arises. Fifth, the same attention is paid to places so that an authentic portrait of the individual arises. The novel is thus the most translatable of all genres. Finally Watt astutely connects the novel and the Law. In both fields, the reader and jury respectively need all the facts and the novel provide this rich detail unlike its literary counterparts. Watt also points that this genre gives the closest correspondence between life and art, a correspondence so severe that it can read like proceedings in a courthouse. In conclusion, Watt declares that what brings the novel into its current and aloof existence is the lowest common denominator, this "formal realism." Sidhwa's narrative is not strictly of the school of formal realism, since the child's voice leaves aspects of the logical momentum unexplained, mysterious and possibly magical. Still, most of Watt's structures are apparent in the novel—the characters are specific, named, and located, and rooted in a particularly well-known episode of history, an episode deeply connected to its specific time and places. Like the annals of the law, this novel with all its details makes the case for culpability to be distributed to not one individual, or one community, or even one nation, but evenly across a pluralistic canopy of culprits.

3. Frederick Cooper, *Colonialism in Question: Theory, Knowledge, History* (Berkeley: University of California Press, 2005), 53. History, and more particularly, historiography is constantly in question when a feminist modern voice addresses its silent spots, such as Sidhwa in this particular novel. Thus, it is salient to attend to the voice of a crucial historian and attend to the teleological ruptures at hand, and out of some such blank space arises the character of Ayah.

4. "To have a body is, finally, to permit oneself to be described," writes Gayatri Spivak, "Can the Subaltern Speak?" in *Marxism and the Interpretation of Culture*, eds. Cary Nelson and Lawrence Grossberg (Chicago: University of Illinois Press, 1988), 216.

The question of permission is the most wrestled and complex issues in this ground-breaking piece on representation of the subaltern figure, the woman who remains outside the purview of state and history. Though the self of the woman might feel or say otherwise, simply in the act of assuming and having a body is equal to giving permission to others to describe this self. Thus, the act of agency could be involved in suicide, which mask under the political economy of patriotism or nationalism such as the Jauhar female suicides or Bhubaneswari Devi's 1926 suicide on the very day she was menstruating a rupture from main stream discourse and patriarchal representations of women. Spivak takes on the onerous task of questioning the intentions and voice of the intellectual—and though devout Foucauldians or Deleuze-Guattarians might disagree, she extends the Saidian collusion between the text and empire. She establishes a direct relationship between western capitalistic exploitation and intellectual production. She brings to the table the violent aporia present between the subject and object status. In the great historical slippage between the sixteenth century legalist misreading of a Rig Vedic document on mourning, in which the powerful position of married women celebrating the dead turns into the burning of living widows, she bring to light the power of the yoni (vagina) and the underlying point of her whole study: "there is no space from which the sexed subaltern subject can speak." While the subaltern female can be heard, once translated and rendered mute in patriarchally familiar and acceptable forms, she, as herself, has no voice. So, Spivak famously concludes: "Subaltern rewriting of the social text of sati-suicide as much as the hegemonic account of the blazing, fighting, familial Durga. The emergent dissenting possibilities of that hegemonic account of the fighting mother are well documented and popularly well remembered through the discourse of the male leaders and participants in the independence movement. The subaltern as female cannot be heard or read" (308). Ayah is the subaltern figure in Sidhwa's text, and despite the fact that the novel is devoted to telling her story, it is clear that she does not speak and cannot be heard in the course of the novelistic discourse. Her stage motif is an act of constantly receding until the final disappearance across the border, a place of aporias and ambiguity from which she never is allowed to speak again. Lenny's memory and guilt thus inform the reader above the great subaltern silence; her alternate voice forms another type of alterity which is the subject of this chapter.

5. Robert J. C. Young, *Postcolonialism: A Very Short Introduction* (New York: Oxford University Press, 2003), 64. Young positions postcolonial theory within a political sphere of representation for those without access to it on their own; by shaking it from the elite positioning within the academy and bringing attention to its originary purposes, he reminds readers of the urgency of such ideology in a world further shattered on a daily basis by the accumulating differences between the have's and have-not's. This certainly is the rubric oft-repeated by scholars of the Subaltern Studies Collective, such as Ranajit Guha in his work with peasant farmers, or Gayatri Spivak in her literacy teaching in Bengal that all of their works involve reading from below. Young defines postcolonialism as deeply syncretic and radical. He writes:

> Postcolonialism, with its fundamental sympathies for the subaltern, for the peasantry, for the poor, for outcasts of all kinds, eschews the high culture of

the elite and espouses subaltern cultures and knowledges which have historically been considered to be of little value but which it regards as rich repositories of culture and counter-knowledge. The sympathies and interests of postcolonialism are thus focused on those at the margins of society, those whose
cultural identity has been dislocated or left uncertain by the forces of global
capitalism—refugees, migrants who have moved from the countryside to the
impoverished edges of the city, migrants who struggle in the first world for
a better life while working at the lowest levels of those societies. At all times,
postcolonialism stands for a transformational politics, for a politics dedicated
to the removal of inequality—from the different degrees of wealth of the
different states in the world system, to the class, ethnic, and other social
hierarchies that operate at every level of social and cultural relations. Postcolonialism combines and draws on elements from radical socialism, feminism,
and environmentalism. Its difference from any of these as generally defined
is that it begins from a fundamentally tricontinental, third-world, subaltern
perspective and its priorities always remain there. For people in the west,
postcolonialism amounts to nothing less than a world turned upside-down.
It looks at and experiences the world from below rather than from above.
Its eyes, ears, and mouth are those of the Ethiopian woman farmer, not the
diplomat or the CEO. (114)

And he provides a further example removed from the academy as a postcolonial
practice:

In many ways, the MST (*Movimento Sem Terra* in Brazil) figures as a model
for a postcolonial politics: a grassroots movement formed to fight a system
of injustice and gross material inequality that is sustained by powerful local
interests and international power structures of banks, businesses, and investment funds that want to maintain the status quo of the global economic
market. (48)

6. Abdirahman A. Hussein, *Edward Said: Criticism and Society* (New York: Verso,
2002), 132. Hussein reads in Said's work a "technique of trouble" and presents
the portrait of Said as laboring to articulate the role of the intellectual in modernity. The intellectual ought to raise uncomfortable questions and attempt to jar
the status quo away from passivity and sameness. The intellectual is the voice of
those without one, those who are not represented. Hussein concludes by comparing Said to significant twentieth century thinkers like Sartre, Williams, Foucault,
and Chomsky. Such a "technique of trouble" resonates with Sidhwa's stance in attempting to represent the condition of the Ayah as a boundary figure.

7. Elaine Scarry, *The Body in Pain: The Making and Unmaking of the World* (New
York: Oxford University Press, 1985), 41. She writes, "Beside the overwhelming
fact that a human being is severely hurt, the exact nature of the weapon or the mim-
ing of the deconstruction of civilization is at most secondary. But it is also crucial
to see the two are here forced into being expressions and amplifications of one
another: the de-objectifying of the objects, the unmaking of the made, is a process
of externalizing the way in which the person's pain causes his world to disintegrate;

and, at the same time, the disintegration of the world is here, in the most literal way possible, made painful, made the direct cause of the pain." In this sense, Ice-candyman is the weapon that causes Ayah pain, and then, he amplifies and furthers the pain by forcing her continued existence in a space of exploitation, where the torture continues habitually. Her disintegrating world also is the cause of her exacerbating her pain in direct and daily method of torture.

8. Gayatri Chakravorty Spivak, *A Critique of Postcolonial Reason: Toward a History of the Vanishing Present* (Cambridge, Massachusetts: Harvard University Press, 1999). "I will simply develop the suggestion that nineteenth-century feminist individualism could conceive of a 'greater' project than access to the closed circle of the nuclear family. This is the project of soul making beyond 'mere' sexual reproduction. Here the native 'subject' is not almost an animal but rather the object of what might be termed violation, in the name of the categorical imperative" (122–123). And later, she writes, "I have suggested that Bertha's function in Jane Eyre is to render indeterminate the boundary between human and animal and thereby to weaken her entitlement under the spirit if not the letter of the Law" (125). Spivak attends to the transformation in Bertha as a beastly figure in Jane Eyre to a humanity given to her in Rhys's 1965 experiment of "writing her a life." By doing so, Rhys brings to attention the cruelty of the law and imperialistic endeavors as the axiomatics impelling Bertha's violence, not bestiality as given by Brönte. Kant's "categorical imperative" to endow the figure of alterity with humanity is "catachretized" in similar ways in the figure of Lenny, privileged yet outside the circle of power like Rhys's Antoinette, a.k.a. Bertha. A slight slippage where Lenny could just as easily be both Jane, and Bertha and their pasts as well, while Santha is beyond the trajectory of these proto-western feminists tracts.

9. Graham Huggan, *The Postcolonial Exotic: Marketing the Margins* (New York: Routledge, 2001), 87. Huggan explains the logical development of his rubric of "staged marginality" from the socialist, Dean MacCannell's earlier term, "staged authenticity." He writes:

> Yet there is more in common between Naipaul's and Rushdie's novels than might at first sight be supposed. Like Rushdie, Naipaul advocates the cause of flexibility: the need to adapt to changing circumstances, to reinvent oneself if necessary. And like Naipaul, Rushdie finds a place in his novel for the rituals of mourning—his characters reconcile themselves to a past that they can change but never abandon. My initial focus here, however, will be on the novels' theatricality and on their staging, more particularly, of disparate experiences of social and cultural marginalization. My term "staged marginality" comes initially by way of the sociologist Dean MacCannell, who in his influential 1976 study of modern tourism analyses the trope of "staged authenticity."

For MacCannell, staged authenticity refers to the ways in which tourists are given access to "real-life" settings or, alternatively, to touristic objects that are made to display their "authenticity." As MacCannell wryly notes, tourist settings are designed so as to "promise real and convincing shows of local life and culture. Even the infamously clean Istanbul Hilton has not excluded all aspects of Turkish culture (the cocktail waitresses wear harem pants, or did in 1968). The 'reality-effect' (to adapt Barthes' term) that is produced by such obviously manufactured settings is carefully orchestrated so as to cater to tourists" expectations of exotic peoples and/ or cultures. Staged marginality refers to a similar phenomenon, but in a domestic setting: it denotes the process by which marginalized individuals or social groups are moved to dramatize their "subordinate" status for the benefit of a majority or mainstream audience. Staged marginality is not necessarily an exercise in self-abasement; it may, and often does, have a critical or even a subversive function.

10. Bapsi Sidhwa, *Cracking India* (Minnesota: Milkweed Editions, 1991), 12. From here on, I will refer to this novel as *Cracking India*.
11. Bapsi Sidhwa, *Cracking India*, 101.
12. Bapsi Sidhwa, *Cracking India*, 29.
13. Bapsi Sidhwa, *Cracking India*, 134.
14. Bapsi Sidhwa, *Cracking India*, 141.
15. John Thieme, *Postcolonial Con-texts: Writing Back to the Canon* (New York: Continuum, 2001), 8. Thieme investigates the trope of "writing back" to the empire by entering texts that posit a beginning in canonic western texts and then, regurgitate it after a circuitous amble through the colonies. He works through ur-texts of English canon—Defoe's *Robinson Crusoe*, Conrad's *Heart of Darkness*, novels of Brontes and mixes them with Rushdie and Walcott to look at its dissemination and reception and then, produce this highly charged dialectic contained in the fundamentals of "writing back"—how differently R. K. Narayan and Naipaul read Dickens. He destabilizes filial and fictional authority in these "writing back" narratives. Using Said's trope of "filiative relationships being replaced by affiliative ones" (so that families and genealogies wrestle for control with the name of the father), Thieme points to the importance of this context in decoding postcolonial literatures. In the case of Ice-candy-man and his obscure origins in the Kotha, this is important in that the Kotha is a hybrid place, a market where not only the classes mingle to barter the woman's body, but the colonialist and the native. His blurred parentage makes him oddly resonant with the more famous Tagorian character, Gora.
16. Bapsi Sidhwa, *Cracking India*, 168.
17. Bapsi Sidhwa, *Cracking India*, 170.
18. Bapsi Sidhwa, *Cracking India*, 179.
19. Bapsi Sidhwa, *Cracking India*, 179.
20. Bapsi Sidhwa, Lecture, "In Ink: South Asian and Diasporic Writers," University of Pennsylvania, Philadelphia, PA, October 23, 2003.
21. Bapsi Sidhwa, *Cracking India*, 195.
22. Bapsi Sidhwa, *Cracking India*, 272.
23. Ambreen Hai, "Border Work, Border Trouble: Postcolonial Feminism and the Ayah in Bapsi Sidhwa's *Cracking India*," *MFS* 46, no. 2 (Summer 2000): 379–426. She writes, "But unlike Lalun, Ayah becomes altogether the marginalized victim, not a border inhabited with any agency. The ability to deploy one's in-between status is reserved for her savior; the storyteller and her family" (406). Also, she later writes, "The young Lenny's participant observer's complicity in betraying quite literally then is no minor detail in her story. Tricked by Ice-Candy-Man, she gives away Ayah's hiding place to the waiting crowd of men, for her guilt mirrors the

text's repressed complicity in the traitorous use it makes of Ayah" (414). Finally, she writes, "As such, this contradictory text reveals both its good intentions and its myopias, its aspirations and its insufficiencies: as a border worker, it depends upon the use of a figure that finally becomes its own site of limitations and occasions its greatest troubles" (416).

24. Jill Didur, "Cracking the Nation: Gender, Minorities, and Agency in Bapsi Sidhwa's *Cracking India*," *ARIEL: A Review of International English Literature* 29, no. 3 (July 1998): 43–64. Didur observes how patriarchy and the state are resisted through the figure of Ayah.

25. Harveen Sachdeva Mann, "*Cracking India*: Minority Women Writers and the Contentious Margins of Indian Nationalist Discourse," *The Journal of Commonwealth Literature* 24, no. 2 (1994): 71–94.

26. Bapsi Sidhwa, *Cracking India*, 168.

27. Bapsi Sidhwa, *Cracking India*, 168.

28. Bapsi Sidhwa, *Cracking India*, 288.

29. Bapsi Sidhwa, *Cracking India*, 31.

30. Bapsi Sidhwa, *Cracking India*, 252.

31. Bapsi Sidhwa, *Cracking India*, 253.

32. For more, read Christophe Jaffrelot, *Dr. Amdedkar and Untouchability: Fighting the Indian Caste System* (New York: Columbia University Press, 2005).

33. Bapsi Sidhwa, *Cracking India*, 125.

34. Bapsi Sidhwa, *Cracking India*, 126.

35. Alamgir Hashmi, "Prolegomena to the Study of Pakistani English and Pakistani Literature in English," in *English Postcoloniality: Literatures from Around the World*, eds. Radhika Mohanram and Gita Rajan (Connecticut: Greenwood Press, 1996), 114. Lenny's descriptions of her relationship with her younger brother, Adi, the Cousin, the constant teasing between Godmother-Slavesister and Dr. Modi and the banter between the men in the garden are all infected with this mockery of sacred facts and subtle reification of the very same facts.

36. NCDHR. *National Campaign on Dalit Human Rights*. July 29, 2005. http://www.dalits.org/default.htm (accessed on November 5, 2011).

37. Deepa S. Reddy, "The Ethnicity of Caste," *Anthropological Quarterly* 78, no. 3 (2005): 543–584.

38. Patrick Colm Hogan, *Colonialism and Cultural Identity: Crisis of Tradition in the Anglophone Literatures of India, Africa, and the Caribbean* (New York: State University of New York Press, Albany, 2000), 221.

39. Kelly Oliver, *The Colonization of Psychic Space: A Psychoanalytic Social Theory of Oppression* (Minneapolis: University of Minnesota Press, 2004), 90.

40. Bapsi Sidhwa, *Cracking India*, 227.

41. Bapsi Sidhwa, *Cracking India*, 254.

42. Bapsi Sidhwa, *Cracking India*, 273.

43. Elaine Scarry, *The Body in Pain: The Making and Unmaking of the World* (New York: Oxford University Press, 1985), 40.

44. Bapsi Sidhwa, *Cracking India*, 276.

45. Bapsi Sidhwa, *Cracking India*, 289.

46. Bapsi Sidhwa, *Cracking India*, 159.

47. Bapsi Sidhwa, *Cracking India*, 40.
48. Bapsi Sidhwa, *Cracking India*, 31.
49. Bapsi Sidhwa, *Cracking India*, 142.
50. Bapsi Sidhwa, *Cracking India*, 21.
51. Bapsi Sidhwa, *Cracking India*, 103.
52. Bapsi Sidhwa, *Cracking India*, 213.
53. Bapsi Sidhwa, *Cracking India*, 66.
54. Bapsi Sidhwa, *Cracking India*, 124.
55. Bapsi Sidhwa, *Cracking India*, 141.
56. Bapsi Sidhwa, *Cracking India*, 129.
57. Bapsi Sidhwa, *Cracking India*, 168.
58. Bapsi Sidhwa, *Cracking India*, 189.
59. Bapsi Sidhwa, *Cracking India*, 186.
60. Bapsi Sidhwa, *Cracking India*, 188.
61. Bapsi Sidhwa, *Cracking India*, 195.
62. Bart Moore-Gilbert, *Postcolonial Theory: Contexts, Practices, Politics* (New York: Verso, 1997), 94–95. For example, the construction of the "degraded" native woman as a subject to be "redeemed" creates a role for the benevolent Western woman (as missionary, for instance), which provides a new public space or role in citizenship into which she can emerge. Spivak elaborates her argument principally through analysis of the function of Bertha Mason within *Jane Eyre* (to which Said had already alluded suggestively, albeit in a very compressed fashion, in *The World, the Text, and the Critic*). While recognizing that Bertha is in fact a white Creole and a member of the plantocracy which built its wealth on slavery, Spivak reads her "catachrestically" as occupying the position of the colonized subject ("the woman from the colonies") within the text, a reading particularly invited by the insistence in Brönte's novel not only on Bertha's origins in the West Indies, but on her dark features and "animal" qualities. For Spivak, it is only through the effacement of this resistant colonial female subject "that Jane Eyre can become the feminist individualist heroine of British fiction (and subsequent Anglo-American criticism)."
63. Bapsi Sidhwa, *Cracking India*, 204.
64. Bapsi Sidhwa, *Cracking India*, 224.
65. Bapsi Sidhwa, *Cracking India*, 88.
66. Husain Haddaway, *Arabian Nights: The Thousand and One Nights* (New York: W. W. Norton & Co., 1990).
67. Giovanni Boccaccio, *The Decameron*, trans. G. H. McWilliam (New York: Penguin, 2003).
68. Bapsi Sidhwa, *Cracking India*, 94.
69. Bapsi Sidhwa, *Cracking India*, 149.
70. Bapsi Sidhwa, *Cracking India*, 195.
71. David Punter, *Postcolonial Imaginings: Fictions of a New World Order* (New York: Rowman & Littlefield Publishers Inc., 2000), 33. Punter attempts to marry geography of postcolonialism to theory. In his opening, he relates maps to ideologies of world subjugation.
72. Bapsi Sidhwa, *Cracking India*, 194.

Chapter 4

1. Meenakshi Mukherjee, *Realism and Reality: The Novel and Society in India* (New York: Oxford University Press, 1985).

2. Bibhutibhushan Bandopadhyay, *Pather Panchali* (Bengali novel) (New York: Oxford University Press, 1929), immortalized through Satyajit Ray's trilogy of films, first of which was *Pather Panchali* (1955).

3. U. R. Anantha Murthy, *Samskara: A Rite for a Dead Man* (Kannada novel), trans. A. K. Ramanujan (New York: Oxford University Press, 1979).

4. Munshi Premchand, *Godan* (Hindi novel), trans. Anurag Yadav (Delhi: Pustak Mahal, 2010).

5. Mirza Muhammad Hadi Rusva, *Umrao Jaan Ada* (Urdu novel), trans. David Matthews (Delhi: Rupa & Co., 1996).

6. David Rubin, Review of "Meenakshi Mukherjee's text, *Realism and Reality: The Novel and Society in India*," *The Journal of Asian Studies* 45, no. 5 (November 1986): 1101.

7. Malcolm Bradbury and James McFarlane, *Modernism*, 1976. All their points lead to a sense of crisis in art, all of which resonate with the works at hand.

8. Marshall Berman, *All that is Solid Melts into Air: The Experience of Modernity* (London: Penguin Books, 1988), 36. What Berman borrows from Marx, suggesting the always already nature of change, the disappearance of all things familiar, provides valuable lens to look at these novels.

9. Toni Morrison, *Paradise* (New York: Knopf, 1998).

10. Elaine Showalter, *A Literature of their Own: British Women Novelists from Brontë to Lessing* (Princeton: Princeton University Press, 1998), 3–36.

11. Samuel P. Huntington, "A Universal Civilization? Modernization and Westernization," in *The Clash of Civilizations and the Remaking of World Order* (New York: Simon & Schuster, 1998), 78, concludes by noting the gap between the two movements, "Modernization, in short, does not necessarily mean Westernization. Non-Western societies can modernize and have modernized without abandoning their own cultures and adopting wholesale Western values, institutions, and practices. The latter, indeed, may be almost impossible: whatever obstacles non-Western cultures pose to modernization pale before they pose to Westernization. It would, as Braudel observes, almost 'be childish' to think that modernization or the 'triumph of *civilization* in the singular' would lead to the end of the plurality of historic cultures embodied for centuries in the world's great civilizations. Modernization, instead, strengthens those cultures and reduces the relative power of the West. In fundamental ways, the world is becoming more modern and less Western."

12. Partha Chatterjee, "The Nation and its Women," in *A Subaltern Studies Reader 1986–1995,* ed. Ranajit Guha (Minneapolis: University of Minnesota Press, 1997), 245.

13. Oliver Mendelsohn and Upendra Baxi, Introduction, *The Rights of Subordinated Peoples* (Delhi: Oxford University Press, 1994), 5, "We would argue that the value of approaching particular issues through the idea of 'subordination' is that it cuts

across conceptual divisions of race, class, and gender, without denying the importance of these perspectives. Our effort has been to move towards a more inclusive conception of oppression or subordination than is possible under any one of these rubrics. Thus it is possible to see subordination arising from a number of sources: colonialism/imperialism, including a considerable diversity of examples such as European colonization of the New World and the 'internal' colonialism of India (relative to the 'tribals') and of the USSR; patriarchy; religion; developmentalism, with its devastating ecological and human consequences; and something as broad as statism. All these forces have in common an ideological and cultural drive to subordinate social formations that stand in their way."

14. Janet Wolff, "The Invisible Flâneuse: Women and the Literature of Modernity," *Theory, Culture, and Society* 2, no. 3 (1985): 141–148, also notes that the very same modernity which allows the men a greater freedom in the public sphere keeps the women confined within the private. This point is critical to understanding the melancholic subtext of the narrator's voice in Durrani's novel, *Kufr.*

15. Aimé Césaire, *Discourse on Colonialism*, trans. Joan Pinkham (New York: Monthly Review Press, 2001), 13.

16. Arun Kumar, "Mere Aaka Aur Tahmina Durrani," in *Stree: Mukti ka Sapna*, eds. Arvind Jain, Leeladhar Mandloi along with helping editors, Kamla Prasad and Rajendra Sharma (New Delhi: Vani Prakashan, 2004), 510–515. The information in this paragraph is borrowed directly from this critical essay written by Kumar on Durrani in Hindi.

17. What was known as "Hindustani" until the mid-twentieth century was partitioned (by the sole criterion of script) quite abruptly with the territorial partition of British India. My intention is not to conflate Hindi with Urdu but to point to a fluid boundary that exists between them. Thus "Urdu," when written in Nagri script, is comprehensible to a large extent by virtue of shared vocabulary to those categorized strictly as "Hindi speakers." As late as 1947, Gandhi insisted on Hindustani as a national language for India, "To confine oneself exclusively to Hindi or Urdu would be a crime against intelligence and the spirit of patriotism." Granville Austin, *The Indian Constitution: Cornerstone of a Nation* (Oxford: Clarendon Press, 1966), 272.

18. Tahmina Durrani, *Kufr,* trans., Vineeta Gupta (New Delhi: Vani Prakashan, 2004), 13. The translations are all mine.

19. The novel opens on the scene of Heer returning from college. She is accosted by Chandi who confesses that her brother is sweet on Heer and would like to talk to her. Durrani really takes the reader for a spin by portraying a false start and giving the illusion of a love story. Heer–Ranjha are the mythic star-crossed lovers whose stories of love circulate on the plains of Punjab. Ranjha, the lover and partner meant to be, disappears for nearly the entire narrative space.

20. Tahmina Durrani, *Kufr,* 17.

21. Tahmina Durrani, *Kufr*, 26.

22. Chandra Talpade Mohanty, "Under Western Eyes Revisited: Feminist Solidarity through Anticapitalist Struggles," in *Feminist Theory Reader: Local and Global Perspectives*, eds. Carol R. McCann and Seung-kyung Kim (New York: Routledge, 2010), 459.

23. Jean Baudrillard, *The Mirror of Production*, trans. Mark Poster (St. Louis: Telos, 1975).
24. Tahmina Durrani, *Kufr*, 143.
25. Tahmina Durrani, *Kufr*, 129.
26. Tahmina Durrani, *Kufr*, 177. Later Heer goes on to say: In my eyes, what should have happened here according to the prescriptions of Islam, that would happen now. The only truth in the name of Allah was Pir Sai's death.
27. "I read the Qur'an as a 'believing woman,' to borrow a term from the Qur'an itself. This means that I do not question its ontological status as Divine Speech or the claim that God speaks, both of which Mustlims hold to be true. I do, however, question the legitimacy of its patriarchal readings, and I do this on the basis of a distinction in Muslim theology between what God says and what we understand God to be saying. In the latter context, I am especially interested in querying the claim, implicit in confusing the Qur'an with its patriarchal exegesis, that only males, and conservative males at that, know what God *really* means. It is this claim that I believe underwrites sexual oppression in Muslim societies and therefore needs to be contested." Asma Barlas, "Believing Women," in *Islam: Unreading Patriarchal Interpretations of the Qur'an* (Austin: University of Texas Press, 2002), 19. For another great reference in furthering feminist interpretations (*tafsir*) by women of faith, read Amina Wadud, *Qur'an and Woman: Rereading the Sacred Text from a Woman's Perspective* (New York: Oxford University Press, 1999).
28. Fawzia Afzal-Khan and Bina Sharif, "Jihad Against Violence: A One-Act Play," in *TDR: The Drama Review* 54, no. 2 (Summer 2010): 60–69.
29. Tahmina Durrani, *Kufr*, 219.
30. Walter Benjamin, *Illuminations*, ed. Hannah Arendt, trans. Harry Zohn (New York: Schocken Books, 1969).
31. Gurleen Grewal, *Circles of Sorrow, Lines of Struggle: The Novels of Toni Morrison* (Baton Rouge: Louisiana State University Press, 1998), 10–11. Deleuze and Guattari is quoted from their text, *Toward a Minority Literature*, 16–19.
32. Hélène Cixous, "Sorties," in *Modern Criticism and Theory: A Reader*, 2nd Edition, eds. David Lodge and Nigel Woods (New York: Longman, 2000), 265.
33. Mridula Garg, *Kathgulab* (New Delhi: Vani Prakashan, 2004), 190.
34. Julia Kristeva, "Stabat Mater," in *The Kristeva Reader*, ed. Toril Moi (New York: Columbia University Press 1986), 178.
35. Julia Kristeva, *Desire in Language: A Semiotic Approach to Literature and Art*, ed. Leon S. Roudiez, trans., Thomas Goza, Alice Jardinie, and Leon Roudiez (New York: Columbia University Press, 1980), 19.
36. Homi K. Bhabha, *The Location of Culture* (New York: Routledge, 1994), 110–111.
37. Bhabha, *The Location of Culture*, 113.
38. Claude Lévi-Strauss, *The Elementary Structures of Kinship* (Boston: Beacon Press, 1969).
39. Judith Butler, *Antigone's Claim* (New York: Columbia University Press, 2002).
40. David Schneider, *A Critique of the Study of Kinship* (Ann Arbor: University of Michigan Press, 1984).

41. David Eng makes this comment as an introduction to the discussion session we had on March 4, 2002 in his class on "Psychoanalysis, Reimagining kinship and Asian Literature and Film," while we discussed the texts of David Schneider and Judith Butler.

42. Elaine Showalter, "Feminist Criticism in the Wilderness," in *Modern Criticism and Theory: A Reader*, 2nd Edition, eds. David Lodge and Nigel Woods (New York: Longman, 2000), 315 quotes Nancy K. Miller, "Women's Autobiography in France: For a Dialectics of Identification," in *Women and Language in Literature and Society*, eds. Sally McConnell-Ginet, Ruth Borker, and Nelly Furnam (New York: Praeger, 1980), 271.

43. Judith Butler, *Excitable Speech: A Politics of the Performative* (New York: Routledge, 1997), 5.

44. Mridula Garg, *Kathgulab*, 178.

45. Mridula Garg, *Kathgulab*, 186.

46. Butler, *Excitable Speech: A Politics of the Performative*, 86.

47. Mahasweta Devi, *Three Stories by Mahasweta Devi: Imaginary Maps,* trans., Gayatri Chakravorty Spivak (New York: Routledge, 1995), 198–199.

48. I chose to read Devi's Bengali novel in its Hindi translation (given by Santvana Nigam) for the simple reason that I cannot read Bengali. A South Indian who speaks one of the Dravidian languages as removed from Indo-Sanskritic tongues of the north, Malayalam, I grew up in the capital, Delhi learning to speak and write English, Hindi, and Punjabi. My fluency in both Hindi and English aligns me to fact that in the linguistic arc of kinship, Hindi is much closer to Bengali than is English, and Bengali translated into English, other than some successes like Tagore, is generally lost in translation. Hindi is closer, its affect is familiar and it is what I have for now. I am glad to have read Devi in the Nagri prose as given to me by Nigam.

49. Mahasweta Devi's novel, *Hazaar Chaurasi Ki Maa*, trans., Santvana Nigam (Delhi: Radhakrishna, 1979), 11.

50. Devi, *Hazaar Chaurasi Ki Maa*, 15.

51. Devi, *Hazaar Chaurasi Ki Maa*, 17.

52. Evidence of a humorous berating is noted in thinking of her eldest son as "bevakuf" or "idiot."

53. Devi, *Hazaar Chaurasi Ki Maa*, 26.

54. Devi, *Hazaar Chaurasi Ki Maa*, 81.

55. There is no adequate translation for the word "dukhiya" since no English word encapsulates the meaning and nuance of this commonly-utilized word of Hindi. Literally it denotes the image of the long-suffering woman, a victim of circumstances at the mercy of fate, a woman without control of her life. However translated, it has really no pertinent place or locale within which it conveys the same affect as it does in Hindi.

56. Devi, *Hazaar Chaurasi Ki Maa*, 61.

57. Devi, *Hazaar Chaurasi Ki Maa*, 72.

58. Devi, *Hazaar Chaurasi Ki Maa*, 93.

59. Devi, *Hazaar Chaurasi Ki Maa*, 119.

60. Devi, *Hazaar Chaurasi Ki Maa*, 143.

61. Devi, *Hazaar Chaurasi Ki Maa*, 143, translated by self.

Chapter 5

1. I play here with the title and thesis of Gyanendra Pandey's article as part of the Subaltern Studies Collective, "In Defense of the Fragment: Writing about Hindu–Muslim Riots in India Today," *Representations* no. 37, Special Issue: Imperial Fantasies and Postcolonial Histories (Winter, 1992), 27–55.

2. Urvashi Butalia, *The Other Side of Silence: Voices from the Partition of India* (Durham: Duke University Press, 2000), 152–153. Butalia goes on to further explain how this bloody formulae calculated on the backs of women evolves into the more contemporary ill of communalism connecting the partition of 1947 to more recent spates of violence that took place in 1992–1993 in Ayodhya, Bombay or in 2000 in Godhra, Gujarat, and other neighboring cities. Such identity-formation places great stake on self-idolization and constructing a fictive and demonic "other" which is less civilized, pure, and worthy of humanity, thereby causing the rift between the fractured communities of Hindus and Muslims to grow over the decades.

3. Amrita Pritam's *Pinjar* from *Chune Hue Upanyas*, (Delhi: Bharatiya Jnanpith, 2004). The statement means, "This time they had decided resolutely that they will only return after relieving themselves of this burden."

4. Pritam, *Pinjar*, 12, meaning, Pooro's mother's mind had turned into a state of stunned shock.

5. Pritam, *Pinjar*, 12, meaning, "if Vidhi Maata comes sulking, then she will listen to your pleas."

6. Hastings Donnan and Fiona Magowan, *The Anthropology of Sex* (New York: Berg, 2010), 112.

7. Pritam, *Pinjar*, 24.

8. Toni Morrison, *Paradise* (New York: Alfred A. Knopf, 1998).

9. Pritam, *Pinjar*, 45, meaning, "Someone who possesses neither youth nor beauty, just a body of flesh, who is not aware of herself, who is only a number of bones in a living skeleton … was a mad skeleton … the eagles/scavengers even clawed her apart and ate her … Pooro was tired of thinking.

10. Laura Sjoberg and Caron E. Gentry, *Mothers, Monsters, Whores: Women's Violence in Global Politics* (New York: Zed Books, 2007), 190.

11. Shari Daya, "Embodying Modernity: Reading Narratives of Indian Women's Sexual Autonomy and Violation," in *Gender, Place, and Culture* 16, no. 1 (February 2009), 105.

12. Pritam, *Pinjar*, 60.

13. Pritam, *Pinjar*, 66.

14. Amrita Pritam is clear about not ascribing more blame to the Muslims even though the novel might show more instances of Muslim violence upon Hindus. Upon annotating the year 1947, the narrator explains that the Muslims victimize Hindus in the same way that the Hindus victimize Muslims, depending on which side of the border you are on. Since Pooro is now a Muslim woman staying in a Muslim community in modern-day Pakistan, the minorities who are victimized in 1947 happen to be Hindu.

15. Pritam, *Pinjar*, 81, meaning, "Pooro remembers Lajjo's downcast face, and she felt that Lajjo's face was like the skeleton of a little bird caught in the paws of a mercenary eagle for days on end."

16. Urvashi Butalia, *The Other Side of Silence: Voices from the Partition of India* (Durham: Duke University Press, 2000), 110–111.
17. Debali Mookerjea-Leonard, "Quarantined: Women and the Partition," in *Comparative Studies of South Asia, Africa and the Middle East* 24, no. 1 (2004), 35.
18. Pritam, *Pinjar*, 89.
19. Pritam, *Pinjar*, 91, meaning, "Whether a girl is Hindu or Muslim, whoever returns and reaches her domicile, understand that pooro's soul also has reached its domicile."
20. Donnan and Magowan, *The Anthropology of Sex*, 60–62.
21. Mirza Muhuammad Hadi Ruswa, *Umrao Jan Ada*, trans., M. A. Husaini & Khushwant Singh (Delhi: Disha, 2006).
22. Andrea Dworkin, "Prostitution and Male Supremacy," in *Life and Death: Unapologetic Writings on the Continuing War Against Women* (New York: Virago Press, 1997), 145.
23. Donnan and Magowan, *The Anthropology of Sex*, 75.
24. Dworkin, *Life and Death: Unapologetic Writings on the Continuing War Against Women*, 151.
25. Madhu Purnima Kishwar, *Zealous Reformers, Deadly Laws: Battling Stereotypes* (Delhi: Sage Publications, 2008), 131.
26. Here I combine Dworkin's charge that people who utilize prostitutes really hate women, and treat the prositute as the bottom, as less than human, with Nemishrai's politics that do much of the same and attempt to seek a humanity denied to the prostitute in her status quo.
27. Mohandas Nemishrai, *Aaj Bajaar Band Hai* (New Delhi: Vani Prakashan, 2004)
28. Nemishrai, *Aaj Bajaar Band Hai*, 71.
29. One of the Hindu gods of trinity, Shiva is often seen in a harmonious union with his wife, Parvathi or Shakti (energy/power, also that which makes the universe before the trinity) in one figure, a form which is half-man, half-woman.
30. Nemishrai, *Aaj Bajaar Band Hai*, 29–30, refers mainly to the female journalist, Rashim's questioning that finally is clearly articulated when she asks the group of prostitutes why they don't just stop what they are doing. This leads them to lose their tempers and warrants the reply, "You tell me this—didn't your mother do all this? If she did not take it inside, then bitch, how would you have come outside?"
31. Nemishrai, *Aaj Bajaar Band Hai*, 88–89. Sumeet uses the multi-valent word "sangarsh" which wraps in its layers actions of fighting, resistance, and struggle.
32. Nemishrai, *Aaj Bajaar Band Hai*, 6–7, Ambedkar's statements as quoted by the author in the introduction.
33. I use "shameful" referring to Sumeet, and in turn, the author and Ambedkar's stance on the profession as a shameful act on part of the women themselves.
34. Nemishrai, *Aaj Bajaar Band Hai*, 114–115.
35. Devdasis can be summarily translated as "temple prostitutes" but they have a long and tortured presence in South Asian history. Generally chosen through caste or priestly edict, the women and girl children born to them are forced to devote their lives to the temple and its surrounding community. Often this meant they entertained, danced, recited poetry, and sexually serviced the men of the court, clergy, and high caste with little or no remuneration even, serving a sort of sexual bondage through generations.

Conclusion

1. Deniz Kandiyoti, "Bargaining with Patriarchy," *Gender and Society* 2, no. 3 (1988): 274–290.

2. Hélène Cixous, "The Laugh of the Medusa," trans., Keith and Paula Cohen, *Signs* 1 (1976): 875–893.

3. Edwidge Danticat, *The Farming of Bones* (New York: Soho Press, 1998).

4. Mahasweta Devi's novel *Hazaar Chaurasi Ki Maa* translated by Santvana Nigam to *Mother of 1084* (Delhi: Radhakrishna, 1979).

5. Taisha Abraham, "The Politics of Patriarchy and Sathin Bhanwari's Rape," in *Women and the Politics of Violence*, ed. Taisha Abraham (New Delhi: Har Anand Publications, 2002), 281.

6. Abraham, *Women and the Politics of Violence*, 283.

7. Margaret Abraham, *Speaking the Unspeakable: Marital Violence among South Asian Immigrants in the United States* (New Brunswick: Rutgers University Press, 2000), 153.

8. Charlotte Bunch, "Patriarchal Customs cause Violence against Women," in *Violence Against Women: Current Controversies*, eds. James D. Torr and Karin L. Swisher (San Diego: Greenhaven Press, 1999), 99. I substituted the word, "are" instead of the dash as was present in Bunch's much longer sentence for the sake of clarity.

9. Edouard Glissant, *Poetics of Relations*, trans., Betsy Wing (Ann Arbor: University of Michigan Press, 1997), 94–95.

10. Gilles Deleuze and Félix Guattari, *A Thousand Plateaus: Capitalism and Schizophrenia*, trans., Brian Massumi (Minneapolis: University of Minnesota Press, 1987).

11. Gloria Anzaldua, *Borderlands/La Frontera: The New Mestiza* (San Francisco: Aunt Lute Books, 2007).

12. Ilina Sen, "A Space within the Struggle," in *Writing the Women's Movement: A Reader*, ed. Mala Khullar (New Delhi: Zubaan: An Imprint of Kali for Women, 2005), 80–97. For more, read Ratna Kapur who thinks across wide-ranging feminist contestations as configured through issues of complicity and resistance to patriarchy when it comes to legal reform aimed at uplifting women's condition. Also, Maxine Molyneux's chapter offers critical insights on the negotiations between the female subject and citizenship in Latin American and Caribbean regions. See Ratna Kapur, "Challenging the Liberal Subject: Law and Gender Justice in South Asia," in *Gender Justice, Citizenship, and Development*, eds. Maitrayee Mukhopadhyay and Navsharan Singh (New Delhi: Zubaan: An Imprint of Kali for Women, 2007), 116–171, and Maxine Molyneux, "Refiguring Citizenship Research Perspectives on Gender Justice in the Latin American and Caribbean Region," in *Gender Justice, Citizenship, and Development*, eds. Maitrayee Mukhopadhyay and Navsharan Singh (New Delhi: Zubaan: An Imprint of Kali for Women, 2007), 58–116.

13. Nancy Armstrong, *Desire and Domestic Fiction: A Political History of the Novel* (New York: Oxford University Press, 1987), 9–10.

14. Raka Ray, *Fields of Protest: Women's Movements in India* (New Delhi: Kali for Women, 2000).

15. Toni Morrison, *Jazz* (New York: Alfred A. Knopf, 1992).
16. *Toni Morrison: Conversations*, ed. Carolyn C. Denard (Jackson: University Press of Mississippi, 2008), 55.
17. Toni Morrison, *Paradise* (New York: Alfred A. Knopf, 1998).
18. Bapsi Sidhwa, *Cracking India* (Minnesota: Milkweed Editions, 1991).
19. Amrita Pritam's *Pinjar* from *Chune Hue Upanyas* (Delhi: Bharatiya Jnanpith, 2004).
20. Mridula Garg, *Kathgulab* (New Delhi: Vani Prakashan, 2004).
21. Shireen P. Huq, "Bodies as Sites of Struggle: Naripokkho and the Movement for Women's Rights in Bangladesh," in *Inclusive Citizenship: Meanings and Expressions*, ed. Naila Kabeer (London: Zed, 2005), 164–180, and Naila Kabeer, "Growing Citizenship from the Grassroots: Nijera Kori and Social Mobilization in Bangladesh," in *Inclusive Citizenship: Meanings and Expressions*, ed. Naila Kabeer (London: Zed, 2005), 181–198.
22. Elora Halim Chowdhury, *Transnationalism Reversed: Women Organizing against Gendered Violence in Bangladesh* (New York: State University of New York Press, 2011), 139.
23. Merry works out the politics and logistics of a coalescing of local/global feminisms most cogently through her analysis of "nari adalats," a body of women who address the issues that pertain to women to shift traditional structures of power in Indian villages across Uttar Pradesh and Gujarat in the mid-1990s. For more, Sally Engle Merry, "Transnational Human Rights and Local Activism: Mapping the Middle," *American Anthropologist New Series* 108, no. 1 (2006): 38–51.
24. Chandra Talpade Mohanty, *Feminism without Borders: Decolonizing Theory: Practicing Solidarity* (Durham: Duke University Press, 2003), 133.
25. Lois Weis, "Race, Gender, and Critique: African American Women, White Women, and Domestic Violence Issues in the 1980s and 1990s," *Signs* 27, no. 1 (2001): 139–169.
26. A long list of important translations in English exist for this epic of Sanskritic antiquity of which, the following references are listed:
C. Rajagopalachari, *Ramayana* (Bombay: Bharatiya Vidya Bhavan, 1990); R. K. Narayan, *The Ramayana* (New York: Penguin, 1972); William Buck, *Ramayana* (Berkeley: University of California Press, 1976); and Ramesh Menon, *Ramayana: A Modern Retelling of the Great Epic* (New York: North Point Press, 2001).
27. Tamsin Bradley, "The Interfaces between Gender, Religion, and Dowry," in *Dowry: Bridging the Gap between Theory and Practice*, eds. Tamsin Bradley, Emma Tomalin, and Mangala Subramaniam (London: Zed, 2009), 103.
28. Laura Sjoberg and Caron E. Gentry, *Mothers, Monsters, Whores: Women's Violence in Global Politics* (London: Zed, 2007), 200.
29. Navtej K. Purewal, *Son Preference: Sex Selection, Gender and Culture in South Asia*, (New York: Berg, 2010), 51.
30. Indu Grewal and J. Kishore, "Female Foeticide in India," *Internatioanal Humanist and Ethical Union*, May 2004, http://www.iheu.org/female-foeticide-in-india (accessed October 28, 2011)
31. I am thinking here of various forms in which patriarchal ideologies of surveillance are inscribed upon the woman's body, from statist violence to much more subtle

forms of institutional sanction, such as cultural productions like music. Kirk Hutson points to nineteenth century American musical traditions and how the refrains and lyrics of southern music affirms and in fact, encourages violent punishment for women for various transgressions such as adultery, betrayal or just simply, to keep them in their place. For more, read C. Kirk Hutson, "Whackey Whack: Don't Talk Back: The Glorification of Violence against Females and the Subjugation of Women in Nineteenth-Century Southern Folk Music," *Journal of Women's History* 8, no. 3 (1996): 114–142.

32. Also see Gloria Anzaldua, *This Bridge Called My Back: Writings by Radical Women of Color*, eds. Gloria Anzaldua and Cherríe Moraga (New York: Kitchen Table Press, 1984).

33. Judith Butler, *The Psychic Life of Power: Theories in Subjection* (Stanford: Stanford University Press, 1997), 87.

34. Isabel Hoving, *In Praise of New Travelers: Reading Caribbean Migrant Women Writers* (Stanford: Stanford University Press, 2001), 2.

35. Edward Said, *Orientalism* (New York: Vintage, 1979); *Representations of the Intellectual: The 1993 Reith Lectures* (New York: Vintage, 1994); and *Culture and Imperialism* (New York: Vintage, 1994).

36. Natalie Melas, *All the Difference in the World: Postcoloniality and the Ends of Comparison* (Stanford: Standford University Press, 2007), 21.

37. Andrea Smith, *Conquest: Sexual Violence and American Indian Genocide* (Cambridge: South End Press, 2005), 184.

38. Meyda Yeğenoğlu, *Colonial Fantasies: Towards a Feminist Reading of Orientalism* (Cambridge: Cambridge University Press, 1998), 125.

39. Amina Jamal, "Gender, Citizenship, and the Nation-State in Pakistan: Willful Daughters or Free Citizens?" *Signs* 31, no. 2 (Winter 2006): 286.

40. Khan, Shahnaz. "Locating the Feminist Voice: The Debate on the Zina Ordinance," *Feminist Studies* 30, no. 3 (2004): 660–685.

41. I had the special privilege of attending a Feminist Pedagogies workshop at University of Houston on April 15, 2011 with Robyn Wiegman, Minoo Moallem, Caren Kaplan and Inderpal Grewal. Their new feminism offers transnational ways of tracing and bringing together a constellation of global voices without sublimating, displacing or effacing differences and local concerns. Caren Kaplan and Inderpal Grewal, "Transnational Practices and Interdisciplinary Feminist Scholarship: Reconfiguring Women's and Gender Studies," in *Women's Studies on Its Own*, eds. Robyn Wiegman (Durham: Duke University Press, 2002), 66–81.

42. Maythee Rojas, *Women of Color and Feminism* (Berkeley: Seal, 2009), 147.

43. Anuradha M. Chenoy, "Women in the South Asian Conflict Zones," *South Asian Survey: Sage Journals Online* 11, no.1 (2004): 41.

44. Lauren Leve, "Failed Development" and Rural Revolution in Nepal: Rethinking Subaltern Consciousness and Women's Empowerment," *Anthropological Quarterly* 80, no. 1 (2007): 153.

45. Gayatri Spivak, *Outside in the Teaching Machine* (New York: Routledge, 1993), 77.

46. Nick Mansfield, "Coalition: The Politics of Decision," *M/C Journal* 13, no. 6 (2010), http://journal.media-culture.org.au/index.php/mcjournal/article/viewArticle/319 (accessed January 16, 2011).

47. Margaret Chatterjee, "From the Abyss," in *In their Own Voice: The Penguin Anthology of Contemporary Indian Women Poets*, ed. Arlene R. K. Zide (New Delhi: Penguin Books India, 1993), 29–30.

48. Mani, *Contentious Traditions*, 190.

49. Tahmina Durrani, *Kufr*, trans. Vineeta Gupta (New Delhi: Vani Prakashan, 2004).

Bibliography

Abel, Elizabeth. "Black Writing, White Reading: Race and the Politics of Feminist Inter-
pretation." *Critical Inquiry* 19 (1993): 470–498.
Abraham, Margaret. *Speaking the Unspeakable: Marital Violence among South Asian Im-
migrants in the United States.* New Brunswick: Rutgers University Press, 2000.
Abraham, Taisha. "The Politics of Patriarchy and Sathin Bhanwari's Rape." In *Women
and the Politics of Violence,* edited by Taisha Abraham, 277–291. New Delhi: Har
Anand Publications, 2002.
Adorno, Theodor W. *Prisms: Essays on Veblen, Huxley, Benjamin, Bach, Proust, Schoenberg,
Jazz, Kafka.* Translated by Samuel and Sherry Weber. Cambridge, Massachusetts:
MIT Press, 1986.
Afzal-Khan, Fawzia, and Bina Sharif. "Jihad Against Violence: A One-Act Play." In *TDR:
The Drama Review* 54, no. 2 (Summer 2010): 60–69.
Agamben, Giorgio. *The Coming Community.* Translated by Michael Hardt. Minneapolis:
University of Minnesota Press, 1993.
Allende, Isabel. "Writing as an Act of Hope." In *Paths of Resistance: The Art and Craft of the
Political Novel,* edited by William Zinsser, 39–63. Boston: Houghton Mifflin, 1989.
Amin, Samir. *Eurocentrism.* Translated by Russell Moore. New York: Monthly Review
Press, 1989.
Anamika. *Kahti Hai Aurtein.* Delhi: Itihaas Bodh, 2003.
Anantha Murthy, U. R. *Samskara: A Rite for a Dead Man* (Kannada novel). Translated by
A. K. Ramanujan. New York: Oxford University Press, 1979.
Anderson, Benedict. *Imagined Communities: Reflections on the Origin and Spread of
Nationalism.* London: Verso, 1983.
Anderson, Paul A. "My Lord! What a Mourning: The 'Sorrow Songs' in Harlem Re-
naissance Thought." In *Symbolic Loss: The Ambiguity of Mourning and Memory at
Century's End,* edited by Peter Homans, 83–102. Charlottesville: University Press
of Virginia, 2000.
Anzaldua, Gloria. *This Bridge Called My Back: Writings by Radical Women of Color.* Edited
by Gloria Anzaldau and Cherrie Moraga. New York: Kitchen Table Press, 1984.
——. *Borderlands/La Frontera: The New Mestiza.* San Francisco: Aunt Lute Books,
2007.
Ardener, Edwin. "Belief and the Problem of Women." In *Perceiving Women,* edited by
Shirley Ardener, 3–14. New York: Halsted Press, 1978.
Ardener, Shirley. *Defining Females: The Nature of Women in Society.* Oxford: Berg Press,
1993.

Armstrong, Nancy. *Desire and Domestic Fiction: A Political History of the Novel.* New York: Oxford University Press, 1987.

Austin, Granville. *The Indian Constitution: Cornerstone of a Nation.* Oxford: Clarendon Press, 1966.

Bakhtin, Mikhail. *The Dialogic Imagination: Four Essays.* Translated by Caryl Emerson and Michael Holquist. Austin: University of Texas Press, 1981.

Bali, Indu. *Mai Kharghosh Hona Chahti Hoon.* Delhi: Suyogya, 1994.

Bandopadhyay, Bibhutibhushan. *Pather Panchali* (Bengali novel). New York: Oxford University Press, 1929.

Barlas, Asma. *"Believing Woman" in Islam: Unreading Patriarchal Interpretations of the Qur'an.* Austin: University of Texas Press, 2002.

Bataille, Georges. "I throw myself among the dead." In *The Impossible,* Translated by Robert Hurley. San Francisco: City Lights, 1991, 147–164

Baudrillard, Jean. *The Mirror of Production.* Translated by Mark Poster. St. Louis: Telos, 1975.

Beaulieu, Elizabeth Ann, ed. *The Toni Morrison Encyclopedia.* Westport: Greenwood Press, 2003.

Benito, Jesus and Ana Maria Manzanas. *Literature and Ethnicity in the Cultural Borderlands.* New York: Rodopi, 2002.

Benjamin, Walter. *Illuminations.* Edited by Hannah Arendt, Translated by Harry Zohn. NewYork: Schocken Books, 1969.

Bennett, Juda. "Toni Morrison and the Burden of the Passing Narrative." *African American Review* 35, no. 2 (2001): 205–217.

Bent, Geoffrey. "Less than Divine: Toni Morrison's Paradise." *Southern Review* 35, no. 1 (1999): 145–149.

Berman, Marshall. *All that is Solid Melts into Air: The Experience of Modernity.* London: Penguin Books, 1988.

Bery, Ashok and Patricia Murray, eds. *Comparing Postcolonial Literatures: Dislocations.* New York: St. Martin's Press, 2000.

Bhabha, Homi K. *The Location of Culture.* New York: Routledge, 1994.

Blanchot, Maurice. *Friendship.* Translated by Elizabeth Rottenberg. Stanford: Stanford University Press, 1997.

Bharti, Dharamvir. *Gunahon ka Devta.* Delhi: Bhartiya Jnanpith, 2005.

Bhatiya, Sarala. *Behad Paraye.* Delhi: Aatma Ram & Sons, 1994.

Black, Daniel. *The Sacred Place.* New York: St. Martin's Press, 2007.

Boccaccio, Giovanni. *The Decameron.* Translated by G. H. McWilliam. New York: Penguin, 2003.

Bose, Brinda, ed. *Translating Desire: The Politics of Gender and Culture in India.* Delhi: Katha, 2002.

Botting, Fred, and Scott Wilson, eds. *The Bataille Reader.* Malden: Blackwell, 1997.

Bradbury, Malcolm, and James McFarlane. *Modernism: A Guide to European Literature, 1890–1930.* London: Penguin Books, 1991.

Bradley, David. *The Chaneysville Incident: A Novel.* New York: Harper & Row, 1981.

Bradley, Tamsin. "The Interfaces between Gender, Religion, and Dowry." In *Dowry: Bridging the Gap between Theory and Practice,* edited by Tamsin Bradley, Emma Tomalin and Mangala Subramaniam, 87–114. London: Zed Books, 2009.

Buck, Claire, ed. *The Bloombsbury Guide to Women's Literature.* New York: Prentice Hall General Reference, 1992.

Buck-Morss, Susan. "Hegel and Haiti." *Critical Inquiry* 26, no. 4 (2000): 821–865.

Buck, William. *Ramayana.* Berkeley: University of California Press, 1976.

Bunch, Charlotte. "Patriarchal Customs cause Violence against Women." In *Violence Against Women: Current Controversies,* edited by James D. Torr and Karin L. Swisher, 96–100. San Diego: Greenhaven Press, 1979.

Burkard, Michael. *Entire Dilemma.* Louisville: Sarabande Books, 1998.

Burrell, Jocelyn, ed. *Word: On Being a (Woman) Writer.* New York: The Feminist Press at the City University of New York, 2004.

Busia, Abena P. A. "The Artistic Impulse of Toni Morrison's Shorter Works." In *Cambridge Companion to Toni Morrison,* edited by Justine Tally, 101–111. New York: Cambridge University Press, 2007.

———. "Those Ibos! Jus' Upped and Walked Away: The Story of the Slaves at Ibo Landing as Transcendental Ritual." In *Proceedings of Conference on Repercussions of the Atlantic Slave Trade: The Interior of the Bight of Benin and the African Diaspora,* edited by Carolyn Brown and Paul Lovejoy. Nike Lake Resort, Enugu, Nigeria. Trenton: Africa World Press, 2000.

———. "What is Africa to Me? Knowledge Possession, Knowledge Production, and the Health of Our Bodies Politic in Africa and the African Diaspora." *African Studies Review* 49, no. 1 (2006): 15–30.

Butalia, Urvashi. *The Other Side of Silence: Voices from the Partition of India.* Durham: Duke University Press, 2000.

Butler, Judith. *Antigone's Claim.* New York: Columbia University Press, 2002.

———. *Excitable Speech: A Politics of the Performative.* New York: Routledge, 1997.

———. *The Psychic Life of Power: Theories of Subjection.* Stanford: Stanford University Press, 1997.

Caruth, Cathy. *Unclaimed Experience: Trauma, Narrative, and History.* Baltimore: Johns Hopkins University Press, 1996.

Césaire, Aimé. *Discourse on Colonialism.* Translated by Joan Pinkham. New York: Monthly Review Press, 2001.

Chamoiseau, Patrick. *Texaco.* New York: Vintage, 1998.

Charters, Mallay. "Edwidge Danticat: A Bitter Legacy Revisited." *Publisher's Weekly* 245, no. 33 (1998): 42–43.

Chatterjee, Margaret. "From the Abyss." *In their Own Voice: The Penguin Anthology of Contemporary Indian Women Poets,* edited by Arlene R. K. Zide. New Delhi: Penguin Books India, 1993, 29–30.

Chatterjee, Partha. "The Nation and its Women." In *A Subaltern Studies Reader, 1986–1995,* edited by Ranajit Guha, 240–262. Minneapolis: University of Minnesota Press, 1997.

Chenoy, Anuradha M. "Women in the South Asian Conflict Zones." *South Asian Survey* 11, no. 1(2004): 41.

Chowdhury, Elora Halim. *Transnationalism Reversed: Women Organizing against Gendered Violence in Bangladesh.* Albany: State University of New York Press, 2011.

Cixous, Hélène. "The Laugh of the Medusa." Translated by Keith and Paula Cohen. *Signs* 1 (1976): 875–893.

Cixous, Hélène. "Sorties." In *Modern Criticism and Theory*, edited by David Lodge and Nigel Woods, 263–270. New York: Pearson Education, 2000.

Cixous, Hélène and Jacques Derrida. *Veils*. Translated by Geoffrey Bennington. Stanford: Stanford University Press, 1998.

Cohn, Deborah N. *History and Memory in the Two Souths: Recent Southern and Spanish American Fiction*. Nashville: Vanderbilt University Press, 1999.

Condé, Maryse. *Crossing the Mangrove*. Translated by Richard Philcox. New York: Anchor, 1995.

Conner, Marc C. "From the Sublime to the Beautiful: The Aesthetic Progression of Toni Morrison." In *The Aesthetics of Toni Morrison: Speaking the Unspeakable*, edited by Marc C. Conner, 49–76. Jackson: University Press of Mississippi, 2000.

Cooper, Frederick. *Colonialism in Question: Theory, Knowledge, History*. Berkeley: University of California Press, 2005.

Dalsgard, Katrine. "The One All-Black Town Worth the Pain: (African) American Exceptionalism, Historical Narration, and the Critique of Nationhood in Toni Morrison's *Paradise*." *African American Review* 35, no. 2 (2001): 233–248.

Danticat, Edwidge. *The Farming of Bones*. Maine: Thorndike Press, 1998.

Danticat, Edwidge. "Nineteen Thirty-Seven." *Krik? Krak!* New York: Vintage Books, 1996.

Danticat, Edwidge. "We are Ugly, but We are Here." *The Caribbean Writer* 10 (1996), n.p. http://www.webster.edu/~corbetre/haiti/literature/danticat-ugly.htm

Das, Veena. "Cultural Rights and the Definition of Community." In *The Rights of Subordinated Peoples*, edited by Oliver Mendelson and Upendra Baxi, 117–158. Delhi: Oxford University Press, 1996.

David, Ron. *Toni Morrison Explained: A Reader's Road Map to the Novels*. New York: Random House, 2000.

Davidson, Rob. "Racial Stock and 8-Rocks: Communal Historiography in Toni Morrison's *Paradise*." *Twentieth Century Literature: A Scholarly and Critical Journal* 47, no. 3 (2001): 355–373.

Daya, Shari. "Embodying Modernity: Reading Narratives of Indian Women's Sexual Autonomy and Violation." *Gender, Place, Culture* 16, no. 1 (2009): 105.

Dayan, Joan. "Haiti, History, and the Gods." In *After Colonialism: Imperial Histories and Postcolonial Displacements*, edited by Gyan Prakash, 66–97. Princeton: Princeton University Press, 1995.

Deleuze, Gilles, and Felix Guattari. *Anti-Oedipus: Capitalism and Schizophrenia*. Minneapolis: University of Minnesota Press, 1983.

———. *A Thousand Plateaus: Capitalism and Schizophrenia*. Translated by Brian Massumi. Minneapolis: University of Minnesota Press, 1987.

Delgado, Richard, and Jean Stefancic, ed. *Critical Race Theory: The Cutting Edge* 2nd Edition. Philadelphia: Temple University Press, 2000.

Denard, Carolyn C, ed. *Toni Morrison: Conversations*. Jackson: University Press of Mississippi, 2008.

Derrida, Jacques. *Dissemination*. Translated by Barbara Johnson. Chicago: The University of Chicago Press, 1981.

Devi, Mahasveta. *Hazaar Chauresvein Ki Maa*. Translated to Hindi by Santvana Nigam. Delhi: Radhakrishna Pvt. Ltd, 1979.

Didur, Jill. "Cracking the Nation: Gender, Minorities, and Agency in Bapsi Sidhwa's *Cracking India.*" *ARIEL: A Review of International English Literature* 29, no. 3 (July 1998): 43–64.

Diederich, Bernard. *Trujillo: The Death of the Dictator.* Princeton: Markus Wiener, 1978.

Dietz, Mary. "Context is All: Feminism and Theories of Citizenship." In *Dimensions of Radical Democracy: Pluralism, Citizenship, Community,* edited by Chantal Mouffe, 1–24. New York: Verso, 1992.

Dimino, Andrea. "Toni Morrison and William Faulkner: Remapping Culture." In *Unflinching Gaze: Morrison and Faulkner Re-Envisioned,* edited by Carol A. Kolmerten, Stephen M. Ross, and Judith Bryant Wittenberg, 31–47. Jackson: University Press of Mississippi, 1997.

Durrani, Tahmina. *Kufr.* Translated from Urdu to Hindi by Vinita Gupta. New Delhi: Vani Prakashan, 2004.

Dworkin, Andrea. *Life and Death: Unapologetic Writings on the Continuing War Against Women.* New York: Virago Press, 1997.

Dwyer, Rachel. *All You Want Is Money, All You Need is Love: Sexuality and Romance in Modern India.* London: Cassell, 2000.

Elia, Nada. *Trances, Dances, and Vociferations: Agency and Resistance in Africana Women's Narratives.* New York: Garland Publishing Inc, 2001.

Eng, David. "Psychoanalysis, Kinship, Asian Literature and Film." (Graduate English Seminar, Bishop House, Rutgers University, New Brunswick, NJ, March 4, 2002).

Fanon, Frantz. *The Wretched of the Earth.* Translated by Constance Farrington. New York: Grove, 1968.

Felman, Shoshana, and Dori Laub, M. D., ed. *Testimony: Crises of Witnessing in Literature.* New York: Routledge, 1992.

Fisher, Sue, and Kathy Davis, ed. *Negotiating at the Margins: The Gendered Discourses of Power and Resistance.* New Brunswick: Rutgers University Press, 1993.

Forché, Carolyn. *Against Forgetting: Twentieth Century Poetry of Witness.* New York: W. W. Norton & Co, 1993.

Freud, Sigmund. "Mourning and Melancholia." In *The Complete Psychological Works of Sigmund Freud,* XIV. London: Hogarth, 1957.

Fultz, Lucille P. *Toni Morrison: Playing with Difference.* Chicago: University of Illinois Press, 2003.

Garg, Mridula. *Kathgulab.* New Delhi: Bhartiya Gyanpeeth, 2004.

Gilman, Charlotte Perkins. *Herland: A Lost Feminist Utopian Novel.* NY: Pantheon, 1979.

Glissant, Edouard. *Caribbean Discourse: Selected Essays.* Translated by J. Michael Dash. Charlottesville: University Press of Virginia, 1981.

Glissant, Edouard. *Poetics of Relations.* Translated by Betsy Wing. Ann Arbor: University of Michigan Press, 1997.

Grewal, Gurleen. *Circles of Sorrow: Lines of Struggle: The Novels of Toni Morrison.* Baton Rouge: Louisiana State University Press, 1998.

Grewal, Indu and J. Kishore. "Female Foeticide in India," International Humanist and Ethical Union, http://www.iheu.org/female-foeticide-in-india

Gupta, Kusum. *Agni Pariksha*. Delhi: Vidhya Vihar, 1990.

Haddaway, Husain. *Arabian Nights: The Thousand and One Nights*. New York: W. W. Norton & Co., 1990.

Hai, Ambreen. "Border Work, Border Trouble: Postcolonial Feminism and the Ayah in Bapsi Sidhwa's *Cracking India*." *MFS* 46, no. 2 (2000): 379–426.

Hamilton, Virginia. *The People Could Fly: The Picture Book*. New York: Alfred A. Knopf, 1985.

Handley, George B. *Postslavery Literatures in the Americas: Family Portraits in Black and White*. Charlottesville: University Press of Virginia, 2000.

Hardt, Michael, and Antonio Negri. *Empire*. Cambridge: Harvard University Press, 2000.

Harris, Trudier. *Fiction and Folklore: The Novels of Toni Morrison*. Knoxville: The University of Tennessee Press, 1991.

Hashmi, Alamgir. "Prolegomena to the Study of Pakistani English and Pakistani Literature in English." In *English Postcoloniality: Literatures from Around the World*, edited by Radhika Mohanram and Gita Rajan, 107–117. Connecticut: Greenwood, 1996.

Hawthorn, Jeremy. *A Glossary of Contemporary Literary Theory*. New York: Arnold, 1998.

Hitchcock, Peter. *Dialogics of the Oppressed*. Minneapolis: University of Minnesota Press, 1993.

Hogan, Patrick Colm. *Colonialism and Cultural Identity: Crises of Tradition in the Anglophone Literatures of India, Africa, and the Caribbean*. New York: State University of New York Press, 2000.

Hooks, Bell. "Women Who Write Too Much." In *Word. On Being a (Woman) Writer*, edited by Jocelyn Burrell, 16–23. New York: The Feminist Press at the City University of New York, 2004.

Hoving, Isabel. *In Praise of New Travelers: Reading Caribbean Migrant Women Writers*. Stanford: Stanford University Press, 2001.

Huggan, Graham. *The Postcolonial Exotic: Marketing the Margins*. New York: Routledge, 2001.

Hunt, Kristin. "Paradise Lost: The Destructive Forces of Double Consciousness and Boundaries in Toni Morrison's Paradise." In *Reading Under the Sign of Nature: New Essays in Ecocriticism*, edited by John Tallmadge and Henry Harrington, 117–127. Salt Lake City: The University of Utah, 2000.

Huntington, Samuel P. *The Clash of Civilizations and the Remaking of World Order*. New York: Simon & Schuster, 1998.

Huq, Shireen P. "Bodies as Sites of Struggle: Naripokkho and the Movement for Women's Rights in Bangladesh." In *Inclusive Citizenship: Meanings and Expressions*, edited by Naila Kabeer, 164–180. London: Zed Books, 2005.

Hussein, Abdirahman A. *Edward Said: Criticism and Society*. New York: Verso, 2002.

Hutson, C. Kirk. "Whackey Whack: Don't Talk Back: The Glorification of Violence against Females and the Subjugation of Women in Nineteenth-Century Southern Folk Music." *Journal of Women's History* 8, no. 3 (1996): 114–142.

Jaffrelot, Christophe. *Dr. Amdedkar and Untouchability: Fighting the Indian Caste System*. New York: Columbia University Press, 2005.

Jaffrelot, Christophe. *The Hindu Nationalist Movement and Indian Politics 1925 to the 1990s: Strategies of Identity-Building, Implantation and Mobilisation (with special reference to Central India)*. New Delhi: Penguin, 1993.

Jahan, Roushan and Hanna Papnanek, Trans. *Sultana's Dream: A Feminist Utopia and Selections from The Secluded Ones*. NY: The Feminist Press at CUNY, 1988.

Jamal, Amina. "Gender, Citizenship, and the Nation-State in Pakistan: Willful Daughters or Free Citizens?" *Signs* 31, no. 2 (2006): 283–304.

Jenkins, McKay. "Metaphors of Race and Psychological Damage in the 1940s American South: The Writings of Lillian Smith." In *Racing & (E)Racing Language: Living with the Color of Our Words*, edited by Ellen J. Gouldner and Safiya Henderson-Holmes, 99–123. New York: Syracuse University Press, 2001.

John, Mary E., and Janaki Nair, ed. *A Question of Silence? The Sexual Economies of Modern India*. New Delhi: Kali for Women, 1998.

———. *Discrepant Dislocations: Feminism, Theory, and Postcolonial Histories*. Berkeley: University of California Press, 1996.

Johnson, E. Patrick. *Sweet Tea: Black Gay Men of the South, An Oral History*. Chapel Hill: University of North Carolina Press, 2008.

Johnson, Kelli Lyon. "Both Sides of the Massacre: Collective Memory and Narrative on Hispaniola." *Mosaic: A Journal for the Interdisciplinary Study of Literature* 36, no. 2 (2003): 75–91.

Johnson, Walter. *Soul by Soul: Life Inside the Antebellum Slave Market*. MA: Harvard University Press, 1999.

Jones, Jill C. "The Eye of a Needle: Morrison's *Paradise*, Faulkner's *Absalom, Absalom!* and *American Jeremiad*." *Faulkner Journal* 17, no. 2 (2002): 3–23.

Joshi, Malati. *Antim Sanksep*. Delhi: Vikas, 2001.

Joshi, Manohar Shyam. *Hamzaad*. Delhi: Kitabghar, 1998.

Kabeer, Naila. "Growing Citizenship from the Grassroots: Nijera Kori and Social Mobilization in Bangladesh." In *Inclusive Citizenship: Meanings and Expressions*, edited by Naila Kabeer, 181–198. London: Zed Books, 2005.

Kamleshwar. *Kitne Pakistan*. Delhi: Rajpaal, 2002.

Kandiyoti, Deniz. "Bargaining with Patriarchy." *Gender and Society* 2, no. 3 (1998): 274–290.

Kaplan, Caren and Inderpal Grewal. "Transnational Practices and Interdisciplinary Feminist Scholarship: Reconfiguring Women's and Gender Studies." In *Women's Studies on Its Own*, edited by Robyn Wiegman, 66–81. Durham: Duke University Press, 2002.

Kapur, Ratna. "Challenging the Liberal Subject: Law and Gender Justice in South Asia." In *Gender Justice, Citizenship, and Development*, edited by Maitrayee Mukhopadhyay and Navsharan Singh, 116–171. New Delhi: Zubaan, An Imprint of Kali for Women, 2007.

Kearly, Peter R. "Toni Morrison's *Paradise* and the Politics of Community." *Journal of American and Comparative Cultures* 23, no. 2 (2000): 9–16.

Kembadoo, Kamala. *Global Sex Workers: Rights, Resistance, and Redefinition*. New York: Routledge, 1998.

Khan, Shahnaz. "Locating the Feminist Voice: The Debate on the Zina Ordinance." *Feminist Studies* 30, no. 3 (2004): 660–685.

Khanna, Ranjana. "Asylum and Its Indignities." (Lecture at Collective for Asian American Scholarship, Plangere Writing Center, New Brunswick, NJ, April 12, 2007).

———. *Dark Continents: Psychoanalysis and Colonialism*. Durham: Duke University Press, 2003.

King, Jeanette. *Women and the Word: Contemporary Women Novelists and the Bible*. New York: St. Martin's Press, LLC, 2000.

Kishwar, Madhu Purnima. *Zealous Reformers, Deadly Laws: Battling Stereotypes* 131. Delhi: Sage Publications, 2008.

Kishwar, Madhu, and Ruth Vanita, ed. *In Search of Answers: Indian Women's Voices from Manushi*. London: Zed, 1984.

Kolmerten, Carol A, Stephen Ross, and Judith Bryant Wittenberg, ed. *Unflinching Gaze: Morrison and Faulkner Re-Envisioned*. Jackson: University Press of Mississippi, 1997.

Kristeva, Julia, and Leon S. Roudiez, ed. *Desire in Language: A Semiotic Approach to Literature and Art*. Translated by Thomas Gora. New York: Columbia University Press, 1980.

———. *The Kristeva Reader*. Edited by Toril Moi. New York: Columbia University Press, 1986.

Krumholz, Linda J. "Reading and Insight in Toni Morrison's *Paradise*," *African American Review* 36, no. 1(2002): 21–34.

Kubitschek, Missy Dehn. *Toni Morrison: A Critical Companion*. Westport: Greenwood, 1998.

Kumar, Arun. "Mere Aaka Aur Tahmina Durrani." In *Stree: Mukti ka Sapna*, edited by Arvind Jain, Liladhar Mandloi, Kamla Prasad, and Rajendra Sharma, 510–515. New Delhi: Vani Prakashan, 2004.

Lacan, Jacques. "The Insistence of the Letter in the Unconscious." In *Modern Criticism and Theory*, edited by David Lodge and Nigel Wood, 62–87. New York: Pearson Education, 2000.

Lahens, Yanick. "Exile: Between Writing and Place," *Callaloo* 15, no. 3 (1992): 735–746.

Lebsock, Suzanne. *A Murder in Virginia: Southern Justice on Trial*. New York: W. W. Norton, 2003.

Lester, Cheryl. "Meditations on A Bird in the Hand: Ethics and Aesthetics in a Parable by Toni Morrison." In *The Aesthetics of Toni Morrison: Speaking the Unspeakable*, edited by Marc C. Conner, 125–138. Jackson: University Press of Mississippi, 2000.

Leve, Lauren. "Failed Development and Rural Revolution in Nepal: Rethinking Subaltern Consciousness and Women's Empowerment." *Anthropological Quarterly* 80, no. 1 (2007): 127–172.

Lévi-Strauss, Claude. *The Elementary Structures of Kinship*. Boston: Beacon Press, 1969.

Mani, Lata. *Contentious Traditions: The Debate on Sati in Colonial India*. Berkeley: University of California Press, 1998.

Mann, Harveen Sachdeva. "*Cracking India*: Minority Women Writers and the Contentious Margins of Indian Nationalist Discourse." *The Journal of Commonwealth Literature* 29, no. 2 (1994): 71–94.

Mansfield, Nick. "Coalition: The Politics of Decision." *M/C Journal* 13, no. 6 (2010), http://journal.media-culture.org.au/index.php/mcjournal/article/viewArticle/319

Manto, Saadat Hasan. *Mottled Dawn: Fifty Sketches and Stories of Partition.* Translated by Khalid Hasan. Delhi: Penguin, 1997.

Marcos, Ana Maria Fraile. "Religious Overtones of Ethnic Identity-Building in Toni Morrison's *Paradise.*" *Atlantis* XXIV 2 (2002): 95–116.

Marcos, Ana Maria Fraile. "Hybridizing the 'City Upon a Hill' in Toni Morrison's *Paradise.*" *MELUS* 28, no. 4 (2003): 3–33.

McKee, Patricia. "Geographies of Paradise." *CR: The New Centennial Review* 3, no. 1 (2003): 197–223.

Mehrotra, Arvind Krishna. *A History of Indian Literature in English.* New York: Columbia University Press, 2003.

Melas, Natalie. *All the Difference in the World: Postcoloniality and the Ends of Comparison.* Stanford: Stanford University Press, 2007.

Mendelsohn, Oliver, and Upendra Baxi. *The Rights of Subordinated Peoples.* Delhi: Oxford University Press.

Menon, Ramesh. *Ramayana: A Modern Retelling of the Great Epic.* New York: North Point Press, 2001.

Merry, Sally Engle. "Transnational Human Rights and Local Activism: Mapping the Middle." *American Anthropologist New Series* 108, no. 1: 38–51.

Michael, Magali Cornier. "Re-Imagining Agency: Toni Morrison's *Paradise.*" *African American Review* 36, no. 4 (2002): 643–661.

Miller, Nancy K. "Women's Autobiography in France: For a Dialectics of Identification." In *Women and Language in Literature and Society,* edited by Sally McConnell-Ginet, Ruth Borker, and Nelly Furnam, 271. New York: Praeger, 1980.

Mills, Sara. *Gender and Colonial Space.* Manchester: Manchester University Press, 2005.

Minh-ha, Trinh T. *Woman, Native, Other: Writing Postcoloniality and Feminism.* Bloomington: Indiana University Press.

Mitchell, Juliet. "Femininity, Narrative and Psychoanalysis." In *Modern Criticism and Theory,* edited by David Lodge and Nigel Wood, 388–392. New York: Pearson Education, 2000.

Mohanram, Radhika, and Gita Rajan, ed. *English Postcoloniality: Literatures from Around the World.* Connecticut: Greenwood, 1996.

Mohanty, Chandra Talpade. *Feminism without Borders: Decolonizing Theory, Practicing Solidarity.* Durham: Duke University Press, 2003.

———. "Under Western Eyes Revisited: Feminist Solidarity through Anticapitalist Struggles." In *Feminist Theory Reader: Local and Global Perspectives,* edited by Carol R. McGann and Seung-kyung Kim, 499–535. New York: Routledge, 2003.

Mohanty, Chandra Talpade, Anna Russo, and Lourdes Torres, ed. *Third World Women and the Politics of Feminism.* Bloomington: Indiana University Press, 1991.

Molyneux, Maxine. "Refiguring Citizenship Research Perspectives on Gender Justice in the Latin American and Caribbean Region." In *Gender Justice, Citizenship, and Development,* edited by Maitrayee Mukhopadhyay and Navsharan Singh, 58–116. New Delhi: Zubaan, An Imprint of Kali for Women, 2007.

Mookerjea-Leonard, Debali. "Quarantined: Women and the Partition." In *Comparative Studies of South Asia, Africa and the Middle East* 24, no. 1 (2004): 35.

Moore-Gilbert, Bart. *Postcolonial Theory: Contexts, Practices, Politics.* New York: Verso, 1997.

Moraga, Cherríe, and Gloria Anzaldúa. ed. *This Bridge Called my Back: Writings by Radical Women of Color*. New York: Kitchen Table, Women of Color Press.

Morrison, Toni. *Beloved*. New York: Alfred A. Knopf, 1998.

———. *Jazz*. New York: Alfred A. Knopf, 1992.

———, Toni. *Paradise*. New York: Alfred A. Knopf, 1998.

———. *Playing in the Dark: Whiteness and the Literary Imagination*. Cambridge: Harvard University Press, 1992.

———. "Recitatif." In *Confirmation: An Anthology of African American Women*, edited by Amiri and Amina Baraka, 243–261. New York: William Morrow, 1983.

Mouffe, Chantal. *On the Political: Thinking in Action*. New York: Routledge, 2005.

Mukherjee, Meenakshi. *Realism and Reality: The Novel and Society in India*. New York: Oxford University Press, 1985.

Nancy, Jean-Luc. *The Birth to Presence*. Translated by Brian Holmes and others. Stanford: Stanford University Press, 1993.

———. *The Experience of Freedom*. Translated by Bridget McDonald. Stanford: Stanford University Press, 1993.

———. *The Inoperative Community*. Edited by Peter Connor, Translated by Peter Connor, Lisa Garbus, Michael Holland, and Simona Sawhney. Minneapolis: University of Minnesota Press, 1991.

NCDHR. National Campaign on Dalit Human Rights. July 29, 2005, http://www.dalits.org/default.htm (accessed November 5, 2011).

Narayan, R. K. *The Ramayana*. New York: Penguin, 1972.

Nemishrai, Mohandass. *Aaj Bazar Band Hai*. New Delhi: Vani Prakashan, 2004.

Oliver, Kelly. *The Colonization of Psychic Space: A Psychoanalytic Social Theory of Oppression*. Minneapolis: University of Minnesota Press.

———. *Witnessing: Beyond Recognition*. Minneapolis: University of Minnesota Press, 2001.

Omi, Michael, and Howard Winant. *Racial Formation in the United States: From the 1960s to the 1980s*. New York: Routledge, 1986.

Page, Philip. "Furrowing all the Brows: Interpretation and the Transcendent in Toni Morrison's *Paradise*." *African American Review* 35, no. 4 (2001): 637–664.

Pandey, Gyanendra. "In Defense of the Fragment: Writing about Hindu–Muslim Riots in India Today." *Subaltern Studies Collective*. Special Issue: *Imperial Fanstasies and Postcolonial Histories* 37 (1992): 27–55.

Peterson, Nancy J. *Against Amnesia: Contemporary Women Writers and the Crisis of Historical Memory*. Philadelphia: University of Pennsylvania Press, 2001.

Prakash, Uday. *Paul Gomra ka Scooter*. Delhi: Vani Prakashan, 2004.

Premchand, Munshi. *Mansarovar—Part One: Short Stories*. Translated by. Surajit Mahalanobis. Delhi: Diamond Pocket Books, 1999.

———. *Godaan* (Hindi novel). Translated by Anurag Yadav. Delhi: Pustak Mahal, 2010.

Pritam, Amrita. *Chune Hue Upanyas* (Eight Novels). New Delhi: Bharatiya Jnanpith, 2004.

Punter, David. *Postcolonial Imaginings: Fictions of a New World Order*. New York: Rowman & Littlefield, 2000.

Purewal, Navtej K. *Son Preference: Sex Selection, Gender and Culture in South Asia*. New York: Berg Books.

Pushpa, Maitreyi. *Chalk.* Delhi: Rajkamal, 2004.

Rajagopalachari, C. *Ramayana.* Bombay: Bharatiya Vidya Bhavan, 1990.

Rajan, Rajeswari Sunder. *The Scandal of the State: Women, Law, and Citizenship in Postcolonial India.* Durham: Duke University Press, 2003.

Rakesh, Mohan. *Mohan Rakesh ki Sampurna Kahaniyan.* Delhi: Rajpal, 2001.

Ramanujan, A. K. *Speaking of Siva.* New York: Penguin Books, 1973.

Ray, Raka. *Fields of Protest: Women's Movements in India.* New Delhi: Kali for Women, 2000.

Reddy, Deepa S. "The Ethnicity of Caste." *Anthropological Quarterly* 78, no. 3 (2005): 543–584.

Rodriguez, Ileana. "Apprenticeship as Citizenship and Governability." In *The Latin American Subaltern Studies Reader,* edited by Ileana Rodriguez and María Milagros López. Durham: Duke University Press, 2001.

Rojas, Maythee. *Women of Color and Feminism.* Berkeley: Seal Press, 2009.

Roumain, Jacques. *Masters of the Dew.* Translated by Langston Hughes and Mercer Cook. Oxford: Heinemann, 1944.

Rubenstein, Roberta. *Home Matters: Longing and Belonging, Nostalgia and Mourning in Women's Fiction.* New York: Palgrave, 2001.

Rubin, David. Rev. of "Meenakshi Mukherjee's text, *Realism and Reality: The Novel and Society in India.*" *Journal of Asian Studies* 45, no. 5 (1986): 1101–1102.

Rushdie, Salman. *Midnight's Children.* New York: Penguin, 1980.

Ruswa, Mirza Muhammad Hadi. *Umrao Jan Ada.* Translated by M. A. Husaini and Khushwant Singh. Delhi: Disha, 2006.

Ryan, Kate. "Revolutionary Suicide in Toni Morrison's Fiction." *African American Review* 34, no. 3 (2000): 389–412.

Sagás, Ernesto. *Race and Politics in the Dominican Republic.* Boca Raton: University Press of Florida, 2000.

Sahni, Bhisham. *Tamas.* Delhi: Rajkamal, 2002.

Said, Edward. *Orientalism.* New York: Vintage, 1979.

———. "Traveling Theory." In *The World, the Text, and the Critic.* Cambridge: Harvard University Press, 1983.

———. *Representations of the Intellectual: The 1993 Reith Lectures.* New York: Vintage, 1994.

———. *Culture and Imperialism.* New York: Vintage, 1994.

Sandoval, Chela. *Methodology of the Oppressed.* Minneapolis: University of Minnesota Press, 2000.

Sangari, Kumkum. *Politics of the Possible: Essays on Gender, History, Narratives, Colonial English.* New Delhi: Tulika, 1999.

Sangari, Kumkum, and Sudesh Vaid, ed. *Recasting Women: Essays in Colonial Indian History.* New Brunswick: Rutgers University Press, 1990.

Sarkar, Tanika, and Urvashi Butalia, ed. *Women and Right-Wing Movements: Indian Experiences.* London: Zed Books, 1995.

Scarry, Elaine. *The Body in Pain: The Making and Unmaking of the World.* New York: Oxford University Press, 1985.

Schneider, David. *A Critique of the Study of Kinship.* Ann Arbor: University of Michigan Press, 1984.

Schur, Richard L. "Locating Paradise in the Post-Civil Rights Era: Toni Morrison and Critical Race Theory." *Contemporary Literature* 45, no. 2 (2004): 276–300.

Sen, Ilina. "A Space within the Struggle." In *Writing the Women's Movement: A Reader*, edited by Mala Khullar, 80–97. New Delhi: Zubaan, An Imprint of Kali for Women, 2005.

Seshadari-Crooks, Kalpana. *Desiring Whiteness: A Lacanian Analysis of Race*. New York: Routledge, 2000.

Seyhan, Azade. *Writing Outside the Nation*. Princeton: Princeton University Press, 2001.

Shemak, April. "Re-Membering Hispaniola: Edwidge Danticat's *The Farming of Bones*." *MFS: Modern Fiction Studies* 48, no. 1(2002): 83–112.

Showalter, Elaine. "Feminist Criticism in the Wilderness." In *Modern Criticism and Theory*, edited by David Lodge and Nigel Woods, 308–330. New York: Pearson Education, 2000.

———. *A Literature of their Own: British Women Novelists from Brontë to Lessing*. Princeton: Princeton University Press, 1998.

Shukla, Srilal. *Rag Darbari*. Delhi: Rajkamal, 2005.

Sidhwa, Bapsi. *Cracking India: A Novel*. Minnesota: Milkweed Editions, 1991.

———. "In Ink: South Asian and Diasporic Writers." Lecture, University of Pennsylvania, Philadelphia, PA, October 23, 2003.

Sjoberg, Laura, and Caron E. Gentry. *Mothers, Monsters, Whores: Women's Violence in Global Politics*. New York: Zed Books, 2007.

Smith, Andrea. *Conquest: Sexual Violence and American Indian Genocide*. Cambridge: South End Press, 2005.

Solomon, Barbara H. *Critical Essays on Toni Morrison's Beloved*. New York: G. K. Hall, 1998.

Spender, Dale. *Feminist Theorists: Three Centuries of Women's Intellectual Traditions*. London: The Women's Press, 1983.

Spivak, Gayatri Chakravorty. "Can the Subaltern Speak?" In *Marxism and the Interpretation of Culture*, edited by Cary Nelson and Lawrence Grossberg, 271–313. Chicago: University of Illinois Press, 1988.

———. *A Critique of Postcolonial Reason: Toward a History of the Vanishing Present*. Cambridge: Harvard University Press, 1999.

———. *In Other Worlds: Essays in Cultural Politics*. New York: Routledge, 1988.

———. *Outside in the Teaching Machine*. New York: Routledge, 1993.

———, Trans. *Three Stories by Mahasweta Devi: Imaginary Maps*. New York: Routledge, 1995.

———. "Diasporas Old and New: Women in the Transnational World." *Textual Practice* 10, no. 2(1996): 245–269.

Stave, Shirley A. *Gloria Naylor: Strategy and Technique, Magic and Myth*. Newark: University of Delaware Press, 2001.

Strehle, Susan. "History and the End of Romance: Danticat's *The Farming of Bones*." In *Doubled Plots: Romance and History*, edited by Susan Strehle and Mary Paniccia Carden, 24–44. Jackson: University Press of Mississippi, 2003.

Suleri, Sara. *The Rhetoric of English India*. Chicago: University of Chicago Press, 1992.

Tagore, Rabindranath. *The Home and the World*. Translated by Surendranath Tagore. New York: Penguin, 1985.

Tally, Justine. *Paradise Reconsidered: Toni Morrison's (Hi)stories and Truths*. Hamburg: Lit Verlag, 1999.

———. "Reality and Discourse in Toni Morrison's Trilogy: Testing the Limits." In *Literature and Ethnicity in the Cultural Borderlands*, edited by Jesús Benito and Ana María Manzanas, 35–49. New York: Rodopi, 2002.

Thieme, John. *Postcolonial Con-texts: Writing back to the Canon*. New York: Continuum, 2001.

Trouillot, Michel-Rolph. *Silencing the Past: Power and the Production of History*. Boston: Beacon, 1995.

Truth, Sojourner. "Look at Me! Ain't I a Woman?" *The Crisis* 1 no. 106(1999): 1–31.

Vanita, Ruth, ed. *Queering India: Same-Sex Love and Eroticism in Indian Culture and Society*. New York: Routledge, 2002.

Vanita, Ruth, and S. Kidwai, ed. *Same-Sex Love in India: Readings from Literature and History*. Boston: St. Martin's, 2000.

Varma, Gayatri. *Ankahi-Ansuni*. Delhi: Suyogya, 1993.

———. *Tasvir ke Tukde*. Delhi: Suyogya, 1994.

Wadud, Amina. *Qur'an and Woman: Rereading the Sacred Text from a Woman's Perspective*. New York: Oxford University Press, 1999.

Watkin, William. *On Mourning: Theories of Loss in Modern Literature*. Edinburgh: Edinburgh University Press, 2004.

Watt, Ian. *The Rise of the Novel: Studies in Defoe, Richardson and Fielding*. University of California Press, 2001[1957].

Weis, Lois. "Race, Gender, and Critique: African American Women, White Women, and Domestic Violence Issues in the 1980s and 1990s." *Signs* 27, no. 1(2001): 139–169.

Widdowson, Peter. "The American Dream Refashioned: History, Politics, and Gender in Toni Morrison's *Paradise*." *Journal of American Studies* 35, no. 2 (2001): 313–335.

Wolff, Janet. "The Invisible Flâneuse: Women and Literature of Modernity." *Theory, Culture and Society* 2, no. 3: 37–46.

Yashpal. *Jhoota Sach*. Allahabad, Uttar Pradesh: Lokbharati, 2002.

Yeğenoğlu, Meyda. *Colonial Fantasies: Towards a Feminist Reading of Orientalism*. Cambridge: Cambridge University Press, 1998.

Young, Robert J. C. *Postcolonialism: A Very Short Introduction*. New York: Oxford University Press, 2003.

Zamora, Lois Parkinson. *The Usable Past: The Imagination of History in Recent Fiction of the Americas*. Cambridge: Cambridge University Press, 1997.

Zide, Arlene R. K, ed. *In Their Own Voice: The Penguin Anthology of Contemporary Indian Women Poets*. New Delhi: Penguin Books India, 1993.

Zobel, Joseph. *Black Shack Alley*. Translated by Keith Q. Warner. New York: Three Continents, 1980.

Index

About the Author

Shreerekha Subramanian is an Assistant Professor of Humanities at the University of Houston-Clear Lake. She teaches courses in humanities, literature, women's studies and cross-cultural studies. She is the first recipient of Marilyn Miezskuc Professorship in Women's Studies in 2008. She finished her doctoral work in Comparative Literature at Rutgers University where she received awards for distinguished contribution to undergraduate education and teaching.

She co-edited *Home and the World: South Asia in Transition* (2007) and has published chapters in several anthologies such as *The Masters and the Slaves: Plantation Relations and Mestizaje in American Imaginaries* and *New Essays on the African American Novel,* and also articles in academic journals.